Lived Religion

Meditation in a garden labyrinth. Bon Secours Spiritual Center in Marriottsville, Maryland. Photo courtesy of Bon Secours Spiritual Center (http://bonsecours spiritualcenter.org) and the TKF Foundation (http://www.tkffdn.org).

Lived Religion

Faith and Practice in Everyday Life

MEREDITH B. McGUIRE

OXFORD
UNIVERSITY PRESS

2008

OXFORD
UNIVERSITY PRESS

Oxford University Press, Inc., publishes works that further
Oxford University's objective of excellence
in research, scholarship, and education.

Oxford   New York
Auckland   Cape Town   Dar es Salaam   Hong Kong   Karachi
Kuala Lumpur   Madrid   Melbourne   Mexico City   Nairobi
New Delhi   Shanghai   Taipei   Toronto

With offices in
Argentina   Austria   Brazil   Chile   Czech Republic   France   Greece
Guatemala   Hungary   Italy   Japan   Poland   Portugal   Singapore
South Korea   Switzerland   Thailand   Turkey   Ukraine   Vietnam

Published by Oxford University Press, Inc.
198 Madison Avenue, New York, New York 10016

www.oup.com

Oxford is a registered trademark of Oxford University Press

Library of Congress Cataloging-in-Publication Data
McGuire, Meredith B.
Lived religion : faith and practice in everyday life / Meredith B. McGuire.
  p. cm.
Includes bibliographical references and index.
ISBN 978-0-19-517262-1; 978-0-19-536833-8 (pbk.)
  1. Christian life—United States.   2. United States—Religious life and customs.   I. Title.
BV4501.3.M337 2008
306.60973—dc22   2007040466

9 8 7 6 5 4 3 2 1

Printed in the United States of America
on acid-free paper

For Jim

Acknowledgments

My debts of gratitude for all the help I received in writing this book are extensive, in part because this book was more than ten years in the making and encompasses research and experiences of a lifetime. I greatly appreciate the contributions of my teachers and mentors who challenged my assumptions about sociology, religion, and culture. Particular thanks to Thomas Luckmann, one of my professors at the New School for Social Research, for his ongoing encouragement and collegial exchanges, long after he returned to Europe.

I appreciate the thoughtful suggestions of colleagues, especially those of the International Society for the Sociology of Religion (SISR), the Society for the Scientific Study of Religion (SSSR), and the Program for the Analysis of Religion Among Latinos (PARAL), whose panel discussions with me and responses to papers I presented at those meetings have been invaluable in honing my interpretations. Colleagues from around the world who have been particularly helpful in refining ideas for this book include Nancy Ammerman, James Beckford, Gustavo Benavides, Doug Burton-Christie, John Coleman, Larry Greil, Phil Hammond, Otto Maduro, Mary Jo Neitz, Robert Orsi, Cristián Parker, Ole Riis, Susan Sered, and Jim Spickard. Trinity University and other San Antonio colleagues who have been very helpful include: Paula Cooey, John Donahue, John Martin, Alida Metcalf, Luis Murillo, Elizabeth de la Portilla, Jim Spickard, Amy Stone, and Sheryl Tynes.

In addition to the scholarly help I have received, I am very grateful to several friends for sharing their relevant experiences and insights: Lenore Aman, Mikki Blackman, Kitty Coffey, Ray Forsyth, Becky Kane, Evelyn Savage, and Barbara and Don Zurstadt. In keeping with *promesas* made after the Toulouse meetings of the SISR, I gratefully acknowledge the genial company and thought-provoking conversations, over many years, of "the Perfect"—Jim Beckford, Eileen Barker, Peter Barker, Jim Richardson, Cynthia Richardson, and Jim Spickard. Thanks also to the many interviewees, students, friends, and acquaintances whose openness and thoughtful expressions of their faiths and practices are part of the subject of this book.

I am particularly grateful to those who helped me to obtain good photographs for illustrating Lived Religion—Pedro Rios, Rudi Harst, Lyn Black, Adele Brewer, and especially Jim Spickard. The cover design uses a photo from the website of TKF Foundation, to which I am grateful both for the use of the photo and for the Foundation's support for the creation of the labyrinth and other beautiful spaces for people's everyday opportunities for contemplation and deeper connection with nature. (For further information about the relevant work of TKF Foundation, see its website: http://www.tkffdn.org/what/location/bssc.php, and the Foundation's forthcoming book, tentatively entitled *Open Spaces, Sacred Places: Opportunities for a Few Moments of Peace*.) Thanks, too, for the permission of Bon Secours Spiritual Center, 1525 Marriottsville Road, Marriotttsville, MD 21104, to use the cover photograph of their labyrinth; for more information about the programs and facilities of the Center, see its website at http://www.bonsecoursspiritualcenter.org.

The book was greatly improved by the careful reading of the manuscript and helpful suggestions of Nancy Ammerman and my editor, Theo Calderara, as well as intellectually engaged copyeditor Martha Ramsey. Thanks also to John Donahue, Becky Kane, Luis Murillo, and Jim Spickard, who gave me helpful feedback on drafts of several chapters. Special thanks, also, to Jim Spickard, without whose help with computer software, for management of the citation database, manuscript preparation, and photograph preparation, the manuscript literally would not have existed.

The historical research and the writing were supported, in part, by two Academic Leaves from Trinity University. Some of the prior research was made possible, in part, by a Basic Research grant from the National Institute for Mental Health. The SSSR and Montclair State University provided additional funding assistance. Debra Kantor and Linda Podhurst (as well as Pat Brown, Kathy Lee, and Matt Krautheim) in New Jersey and Tanya Kaplan in Texas provided research assistance. Special thanks to Debra Kantor and Linda

Podhurst, who continued to work on the project, without pay, long after NIMH funding ended.

Chapter 5 is adapted from my lecture by the same title presented as part of the Cassassa Lecture Series at Loyola Marymount University, Los Angeles, October 8, 2002, later published in *Spiritus*, and reprinted in *Minding the Spirit: The Study of Christian Spirituality*, edited by E. A. Dreyer and M. S. Burrows (Baltimore: Johns Hopkins University Press, 2005). That article, adapted and expanded here, is used by permission of Johns Hopkins University Press.

Parts of chapter 6 are from Meredith B. McGuire with Debra Kantor, *Ritual Healing in Suburban America* (New Brunswick, N.J.: Rutgers University Press), copyright © 1988 by Rutgers, The State University, and are used here with permission of Rutgers University Press.

Chapter 7 is based on my earlier article "Gendered Spirituality," in *Challenging Religion: Essays in Honour of Eileen Barker*, edited by J. A. Beckford and J. T. Richardson (London: Routledge, 2003). The adapted version is published here with the permission of Routledge, Taylor and Francis.

I have also drawn on the following previously published material, which I have extensively revised; any parts that remain unchanged here appear by permission as follows: "Health and Spirituality as Contemporary Concerns," *Annals of the American Academy of Political and Social Science* 527 (May 1993): 144–54, by permission of Sage Publications; "Contested Meanings and Definitional Boundaries: Historicizing the Sociology of Religion," in *Defining Religion: Investigating the Boundaries Between Sacred and Secular*, edited by A. L. Greil and D. Bromley, Religion and the Social Order, vol. 10 (Elsevier, 2003), 127–38, by permission of Elsevier; "Religion and Healing the Mind/Body/ Self," *Social Compass* 43 (1) (1996): 101–16, by permission of Sage Publications; "Toward a Sociology of Spirituality: Individual Religion in Social/Historical Context," *Tidskrift for Kirke, Religion og Samfunn* [now published as *Nordic Journal of Religion and Society*] 13 (2000/2002): 99–111, by permission of Tapir Academic Press.

As always, for their encouragement, patience and love, I am very grateful to the members of my family, especially my husband, to whom this book is dedicated.

Contents

Lived Religion

I

Everyday Religion as Lived

This book is about religion as expressed and experienced in the lives of individuals. More than thirty-five years ago, as a graduate student beginning research in sociology of religion, I thought it would be easy to find out what each interviewee's religion was and that individuals' religious activities would be obvious to the careful observer. And, like other sociologists, I assumed that individuals' religious worlds would be linked (sometimes firmly, sometimes loosely) with the beliefs, moral norms, and religious practices promoted by the particular religious organizations of which they were members.

Early in my dissertation research on the "underground church" movement among U.S. Catholics, however, I discovered how complicated my interviewees' religions were. Not only were they dramatically different from other Catholics', but they were even different (in unpredictable ways) from those of other members of the same home worship group. How could I comprehend the religious beliefs and practices of someone who strongly self-identified as Roman Catholic, participated in "underground" Mass twice or more each week, was well-educated about scripture and theology, was highly critical of the bishop and pope, and yet believed that his most important religious practice was his daily activism for peace and social justice? None of my interviewees expressed a pattern of religious belief and practice that fit standard sociological assumptions about individuals' religious worlds. As I and many other researchers have discovered, those standard notions of religion are wholly inadequate.

Scholars of religion, especially sociologists, must reexamine their assumptions about individuals' religious lives. What might we discover if, instead of looking at affiliation or organizational participation, we focused first on individuals, the experiences they consider most important, and the concrete practices that make up their personal religious experience and expression? What if we think of religion, at the individual level, as an ever-changing, multifaceted, often messy—even contradictory—amalgam of beliefs and practices that are not necessarily those religious institutions consider important?

My intent in writing this book is to challenge scholars of religion, especially sociologists, to rethink fundamental conceptualizations of what we study and how we study it. Over the years, the more I learned about real individuals' religious practices and experiences, the less satisfied I became with standard scholarly concepts of religion and religiosity. My earliest research interviews (in the late 1960s, talking with deeply religious Catholic peace and justice activists) confounded my assumptions. My next major research project (in the 1970s) focused on a Catholic religious movement that promoted a distinctly pentecostal style of worship and religious experiences. It was equally complicated by enormous diversity among individuals within the movement, even within the same prayer group.

Looking back, I realize that both of those religious movements encouraged members to blend their "traditional" Catholic practices (which already varied greatly, for instance by ethnic group and education level) with new religious expressions that spoke to their movement's values or to their individual lives.[1] Especially in the early years of the two movements, members consciously experimented with ways to engage in new patterns of spirituality, but to do so as Catholics. For example, the peace and justice activists developed their own liturgies for house Masses that little resembled the liturgy followed at parish churches, yet incorporated all key elements of the Catholic Mass. In songs, readings, gestures, even silence, their liturgies promoted a sense of joyful solidarity with not only each other but indeed all persons of any faith who worked for peace and justice. Martin Luther King (a Baptist) would have been more welcome at Communion than the local bishop, but the core eucharistic practices spoke to members' longtime Catholic sensibilities. Likewise, the pentecostal Catholics (whose movement was later called the Catholic Charismatic Renewal) held prayer meetings that closely resembled Protestant Pentecostal prayer meetings (with speaking in tongues, prophesying, witnessing, and laying on of hands for healing or other "blessings of the Holy Spirit"). Yet my interviewees were adamant that they did not have to become Protestants to bring those "gifts of the Spirit" into their prayer experiences and lives as Catholics.

How would we identify their personal religions? Christian? Yes, if you asked them, many members would have asserted that their religious practices made them better Christians than they were before becoming involved in their respective movements. Yet some individuals had as much in common religiously with Buddhists as with some other Christians. Catholic? Certainly, and many worked hard to stay true to their Catholic identity. Nevertheless, many individuals had more in common with Protestants who marched with them in civil rights or antiwar protests than with other Catholics who supported racial segregation or America's involvement in wars in Vietnam, Central America, or the Middle East. Likewise, individuals who had received "baptism in the Spirit" and shared similar religious experiences with Protestant Pentecostals felt more affinity with those Protestants than with many other Catholics. Clearly, these individuals' religions were not just personal copies of the official package marketed by the American Catholic "firm." Nor were they the result of a taken-for-granted Catholic worldview, set like a gyroscope in members' childhood socialization.

Realizing the complexities of individuals' religious practices, experiences, and expressions, however, has made me extremely doubtful that even mountains of quantitative sociological data (especially data from surveys and other relatively superficial modes of inquiring) can tell us much of any value about individuals' religions.[2] Throughout this book, I raise critical questions about sociologists' core interpretive concepts, such as "religion," "religiosity," "religious traditions," "religious commitment," "conversion," and "religious identity." I agree strongly with anthropologist Talal Asad that we should not view religion as some "transhistorical essence," existing as a timeless and unitary phenomenon.[3] As Asad and many others have demonstrated, not only do religions change over time but also what people understand to be "religion" changes. I intend to explore how some of these historical changes in the very definitions of what is considered to be "religion" or "religious" have become inadvertently embedded in our scholarly conceptual tools, leading to inappropriate, supposedly empirical evidence—some of it pseudodata—about many people's religious beliefs and practices.

Rather than deduce an image of individuals' beliefs and practices from abstractions about religion in general or even about particular religions, I have grappled with how to comprehend individuals' religions-as-practiced, in all their complexity and dynamism. Too often, our concepts for describing and analyzing individuals' religions simply fail to capture how multifaceted, diverse, and malleable are the beliefs, values, and practices that make up many (perhaps most) persons' own religions.

The Diversity and Complexity of Everyday Religion

I use the terms "religiosity" and "spirituality" more or less interchangeably to refer to how individuals attend to matters of the religious or the spiritual, as they understand those matters at a particular time and context, in their own lives. In recent decades, many people have made a distinction between "religious" and "spiritual" in describing their own religious lives or the spiritual attributes of others. We should not accept those distinctions at face value.[4] We need always to be alert to the social meanings behind such distinctions, because making distinctions involves trying to delineate acceptable from unacceptable beliefs and practices, desirable from denigrated identities and statuses, and worthy from unworthy ideals and values. Religious organizations routinely try to shape such boundaries, exerting their authority to distinguish what they approve as proper individual religious practice from all else. When individual members assert their own distinctions, especially when different from the official ones of their religious group, these distinctions may be a form of dissent or, at least, an assertion that persons' individual religion is not a miniature copy of their group's official religion. For instance, many of the Italian Americans Robert Orsi studied made a distinction between "church" and "religion," emphasizing that "religion" was what really mattered to them.[5]

Focusing on individuals' religions, we can observe a great deal of distinction-making today. For example, respondents tell researchers things like "Religious people scare me, but I really admire people who are deeply spiritual," "I don't go to church much any more, but I'm a better Christian than most folks who go all the time, because I practice my religion every day, not just when I'm in prayer meeting," "I'm not a Protestant; I'm a Christian," "You can't be both rich and a true Christian," and so on. Rather than uncritically borrowing the terminology of "religious" *versus* "spiritual," I examine this distinction-making for what it can tell us about religion and society. How can we interpret the complex religious lives of modern individuals? Let's look at a few examples.[6]

Peter

Peter and his wife were members, in 1969, of a group of Christian peace and social justice activists who were living semicommunally in apartment houses in a near-slum neighborhood of an East Coast city. Because my research was about the Catholic underground church movement, I did not then interview Peter, who was one of a few Protestants in this underground church community. He was an ordained Presbyterian minister but worked as a middle school teacher in the community where the group's apartments were located. Ten years later, I reencountered Peter and his wife at a parents' meeting at my children's school. Still strongly engaged in social activism, the couple struggled to make ends meet, relying on Peter's meager income from a nonprofit organization serving homeless families and his wife's income from part-time teaching. They put enormous effort into juggling their emotionally demanding jobs with raising their four children (two of whom were adopted, of mixed race, and fathered by American servicemen in Vietnam).

Later, in the late 1980s, I talked at length with Peter and his wife about their religious lives. Peter described himself as officially "belonging" to a Unitarian church, where they had found a satisfactory religious upbringing for their children. His whole family attended fairly regularly during the school year, but not at all during the summer. He also participated frequently in a contemplative worship service at an Episcopalian church and in a walking meditation at the Quaker meeting house. He had taken this turn to a more contemplative spirituality about four years earlier, and at the time of the interview, he devoted approximately an hour each morning to meditation at home or a nearby park. He joked about meditation and "centering" as being related to his life stage as a parent of teenagers, but it was clear as he described his spiritual practices that his meditation was more than just an escape into quiet.

Despite all his involvement with religious organizations, Peter considered his extensive social activism to be the most important part of his spirituality. He emphasized that activism for peace and social justice is not merely a byproduct of his religion; it is at the core.

Margaret

I interviewed Margaret as part of a large study of nonmedical healing practices in the middle- and upper-middle-class suburbs near where I was teaching in New Jersey. In the more than two hours of our interview, the only question about religion came near the end. By the time I asked about her religious affiliation and involvement, however, I already had learned a lot about Margaret's vital religious life.

Baptized and raised Lutheran in a small town in Ohio, Margaret had not been involved in a church since high school. She was, however, highly engaged in religious practices and experiences not connected with any official religious group. As she talked about her experiences with healing, it became clear that Margaret engaged in deeply meaningful and moving spiritual practices that many would not recognize as "religious." For example, she described gardening as her daily "worship service." She had begun practicing organic gardening years earlier, in order to safeguard her children's diet (because in those years, organically grown food was not commercially available). But as she got "into" gardening, she came to think of it as a valuable spiritual discipline, requiring patience, hope, and "nurturing love." She engages meditatively in even such prosaic practices as preparing the compost, engaging her senses (e.g., being intensely aware of the texture of the compost as she sifts it with her bare hands) yet staying deeply centered.

As her commitment to her spiritual practices grew, Margaret had left her high-powered job as an editor at a major publishing house and had moved to a smaller home in a more rural community. There, her garden evoked a profound tranquility, noticeable even to the first-time visitor. At the time of our interview, she produced far more food than she needed, so she gave her produce to a food bank. Her new job meant a greatly reduced income but allowed her to devote more time and attention to her Buddhist-style meditation, her organic garden, and her involvement in a healing circle. When I asked her about healing for others, Margaret told me stories about the healing circle's weekly meetings. When she described healing for herself, Margaret spoke of the healing effects of working the soil, connecting with nature, and a nearly mystical experience in the rain.

Ron

Ron belonged to a nondenominational evangelical congregation that sponsored several visiting healers in New Jersey, during my research on nonmedical healing. He had been raised Baptist but had stopped attending church as a young teenager and was, in middle age, very negative about all Protestant denominations. He declared emphatically, "I'm a Christian, that's all—not a Baptist or a Methodist or whatever. Nondenominational is the only way to go!" I wish now that I had pursued that comment to comprehend what distinctions and claims he was making.

Ron attended church most weeks with his second wife, Ruth, who was extremely active in their congregation. His first marriage, at the age of nineteen, had been something of a "shotgun wedding," and Ron had "run around a lot," drunk heavily, and gotten into serious debt. Subsequently, he had abandoned his wife and two children in Missouri, moving half a continent away, several years before meeting Ruth. At the time of our meeting, he still had no connection with that first family, but "thank[ed] the Lord for second chances" and for forgiving his previous "hell-raising" ways.

Ron's foremost religious practice was Twelve Step spirituality, learned initially through Alcoholics Anonymous (AA).[7] He had started attending his nondenominational church after a friend at AA told him of their ongoing Twelve Step men's group, which subsequently became his main connection with the church, as well as providing his closest social ties in town. The Twelve Step men's group meetings and the congregation's expectations provided Ron with much-needed structure to support his sobriety, faithfulness to his new wife, steadiness in his work, and eventual financial responsibility. He said that "just knowing" that he would have to confess any backsliding to the Twelve Step group kept him from "even thinking about it." The further structure of having to be mutually accountable to a "Christian buddy" from that group was particularly important in the face of day-to-day temptations.

Joking about the division of labor in his marriage, Ron said that he was not "into" the bible-study, choir-singing, Sunday-school, and prayer-meeting part of their congregation's activities, but that was his wife's "job." His "job" was staying sober and faithful, with the help of his men's group, in order to do well in his business, in order to provide for the family; that way, Ruth would not need to have a paid job and could stay home to attend to their children and her many church activities.

Other than the Twelve Step affirmations in private or group meetings, the main religious practices Ron used were little prayers (only a few words) that he said habitually during the day, either to ward off temptation or to ask for a specific blessing. For instance, if he felt a temptation that might lead to drinking or some other foresworn activity, Ron would say "Get away, in Jesus' name!" or (more often) just "... in Jesus' name." Similarly, if he thought of something (i.e., something not foresworn or forbidden) that he really wanted, for himself or for his family or friends, he would often say aloud softly, but emphatically, "... in Jesus' name," not even voicing the object of request. He believed firmly that many of the objects the family owned and many of the successes he was beginning to have in his upholstering business were due to his god granting these as blessings, because he asked in Jesus' name. To his way of thinking, saying those three words was so important for the success of prayers that sometimes he repeated them later, just in case he forgot to say them when he first thought the prayer request. Ron and Ruth firmly believed that "God wanted" them to be very prosperous and to enjoy an even higher standard of living. For Ron, his material success, as well his successes at staying sober, were signs of divine approval of his new "Christian way of living."

Laura

When my research assistant and I interviewed Laura, during an early 1990s study of middle-class Latinas in Texas, we used a set of questions on religion

and spirituality that was carefully phrased to avoid use of the term "religion."
Our effort was aided by the fact that these interviews were usually in women's
own homes, so early in the conversation we asked if the interviewee kept an
altarcito—a home altar, typically maintained by the mother of the family,
common in Mexican American homes. As Laura showed us her altar and
talked about what she had chosen to place on it, she described a rich inner life,
built on personally selected images and practices, borrowed eclectically from a
wide range of cultural resources.

Laura was in her late thirties, had a master's degree, and was working out
of her home as an author and part-time consultant on reading instruction
for the school district. She was raised Catholic and considered herself to be
Catholic still, although she seldom attended Mass and then just to please her
mother when visiting her several times a year. At the same time, however, she
spoke of nurturing her spiritual life, and she described how she set aside at least
an hour daily for meditation as the first priority for her morning as soon as her
children left for school.

Her home altar held several traditional items, including a family heirloom
cross brought from Mexico three generations ago, pictures of several deceased
or distant loved ones, eighteen candles of all sizes, a small bouquet of wild-
flowers, and an amulet (*milagro*) attached to the frame of one grandmother's
photo (she explained it reminded her to work for the healing of her *abuelita*'s
arthritis). There were numerous and prominent nontraditional items as well:
amethyst crystals used in healing meditations, Asian incense and a Tibetan
prayer bell, a large colorful triptych of Frida Kahlo, and a modern representation of the Virgin of Guadalupe as a young Chicana in running shoes, her blue
cape flowing behind her and athlete's thighs flexed, running vigorously along a
road with a vanquished snake (a motif used in some traditional images of the
Virgin) held confidently in her hand.

Laura described deeply important practices that produced a comfortable
blend of elements of her identity. For example, she explained that she respects
her mother's more traditional Mexican American religious practices, including
popular religious practices such as devotions to *la virgincita* (the dear Virgin),
but she identifies with them in a transmuted form. In response to my query
about other of her mother's popular religious practices she found meaningful,
Laura quickly answered: preparing food. She did not have the time to prepare
the elaborate holiday foods in her own home, but when she joined her mother
in preparing *tamales* for Christmas or special food commemorations for the
Day of the Dead, she experienced it as a valued religious practice.

At the same time, however, Laura's own religion was very different from
her mother's. She described an ongoing struggle, especially during college and

graduate school years, to understand and respect her parents' values and ways while coming to her own position and her own identity. She was an avowed feminist, proud of her Mexican heritage and her bilingual fluency and closely linked with her extended family, and she cared a lot about the well-being and education of children (her own children, her students, and those who read her books). All these commitments and concerns were interwoven into her religious practices, at home, in church, or while going about her everyday activities, including her writing and her frequent interactions with her extended family.

Conceptualizing Individual Religion

It is clear that, if we started with the assumption that individuals commit, or refuse to commit, to an entire, single package of beliefs and practices of an official religion, then we would misinterpret the individual religions of people like Peter, Laura, Margaret, and Ron. For instance, had these four been asked, in a typical social survey, for their religious self-identification, it is likely they would have answered with a simple phrase: "I'm a member of the Unitarian Church," or "I don't belong to any religion," or "I was baptized Catholic," or "I'm Christian." Similarly, using standard indices of religiosity, sociologists would have counted Laura's rich mixture of religious practices merely as "nonpracticing Catholic" or "cultural Catholic." The committed religious social activist, Peter, would have been considered only "Unitarian" and "moderately religious." Margaret, the gardening meditator, would have been described as "unchurched" or having "no religion." And Ron, whose religious practices may have included as much "popular religion" as Laura's, would be categorized as "conservative Protestant" and would appear to have the highest level of religiosity of the four. None of their spiritually or religiously motivated practices, except their church-related activities, would have counted as "religious."

Many scholars of religion have assumed that individuals practice a single religion, exclusive of other religious options; for example, if they take the Presbyterian option, supposedly they cannot also be Catholic and Buddhist. Unfortunately, that concept of individual commitment and belonging has been based, uncritically, on narrow Western (particularly Protestant) norms. I refer to these concepts of "religion" and religious "commitment" as normative, because they take for granted ideas about how adherents *ought* to be committed and about what consonance *ought* to exist between individuals' beliefs and practices and the proclaimed teachings of their chosen religion. The historically Protestant assumptions linked to these norms include voluntarism (i.e., the idea that belonging and commitments *ought to be* freely chosen) and individualism (i.e., the idea that the individuals, rather than family, tribe, or other relation-ships, *ought to be* the relevant unit for making such choices). Because Western scholars' concepts of religion and religious commitment developed out of the European crucible of religious contests, however, our conceptual apparatus has simply failed to question the image of religious membership and individual religious practice built on mutually exclusive, indeed antagonistic, categories. Those assumptions clearly fail to describe adequately how individuals engage in their religions in their everyday lives.

Nor is each individual's biographical narrative simply a microcosm of the grand narrative of some "official" religion. Especially in modern societies, peo-ple change. They may be active in a church at one time in their lives and not another, like Peter, who sought the Unitarian Church to provide a community of shared values for raising his children. They may drop some practices that no longer seem effective but keep and creatively adapt others, like Laura's selective retention of her Mexican American and Catholic traditions. At the level of the individual, religion is not fixed, unitary, or even coherent. We should expect that all persons' religious practices and the stories with which they make sense of their lives are always changing, adapting, and growing.

Lived Religion

The focus throughout this book is on how religion and spirituality are prac-ticed, experienced, and expressed by ordinary people (rather than official spokespersons) in the context of their everyday lives. I am starting with an intentionally broad conception of "religion" in order to encompass individuals' religions, as lived in a particular time and cultural setting. The term "lived religion" is useful for distinguishing the actual experience of religious persons from the prescribed religion of institutionally defined beliefs and practices.[8] This concept of religion is particularly apt for sociological analysis, because it depicts a subjectively grounded and potentially creative place for religious experience and expression.[9] Although lived religion pertains to the individual, it is not merely subjective. Rather, people construct their religious worlds together, often sharing vivid experiences of that intersubjective reality.[10]

A concept of "lived religion" is also more balanced than overly cognitive approaches to individual religion. Individual religiosity is not a mere "mentality" or frame of mind, as too many historians and social scientists have implied. Peter Berger reminds us that religious belief is not just an activity of an indi-vidual's mind, and that maintaining the subjective reality of religion requires concrete social support in the form of what he calls "plausibility structures" (e.g., significant others in one's family or ethnic community).[11] Berger's sociological approach is still too focused on the cognitive, however. Nancy Ammerman correctly argues that these social supports are not so much a shield from doubt and protection of belief, as Berger suggests. Rather, they establish the practices by which religious action is embodied. Both interpretations of the close link between belief and practice, however, remind us that individual religion is, nevertheless, fundamentally social. Its building blocks are shared meanings and experiences, learned practices, borrowed imagery, and imparted insights.[12]

Building on anthropologist Clifford Geertz's[13] definition of religion, Robert Orsi proposes that we think about religion as

> the practice of making the invisible visible, of concretizing the order
> of the universe, the nature of human life and its destiny, and the
> various dimensions and possibilities of human interiority itself, as
> these are understood in various cultures at different times, in order to
> render them visible and tangible, present to the senses in the cir-
> cumstances of everyday life.[14]

Accordingly, the individual is able to experience, rather than simply think or believe in, the reality of her or his religious world. Religious rituals are important contexts for making religious worlds real and present to the senses, but they are occasional and typically removed from the world of everyday life. Orsi argues that for many people, the world of everyday life is mainly affected by embodied practices, by which the sacred is made vividly real and present through the experiencing body.[15]

Embodied Practices

Daily life is filled with routine practices—ways of doing tasks, of walking and sitting, of talking and gesturing, of showing emotions, and so on. Although the tasks, the walking, the conversation, and the like are typically practical ends, the practices themselves can, over time, effect physical, emotional, and spiritual developments for the individuals who engage in them. For example, in his influential collection of talks, *Being Peace*, Vietnamese Buddhist monk Thich Nhat Hanh encourages his (North American) audience to engage in the simple, repetitive practice of breathing and smiling. He asserts that this practice can literally accomplish the kind of inner awareness and mindful being that produces peace—not merely subjective or personal peace, but indeed the kind of objectively effective peace that can end wars and other social violence.[16] In this book, I address how such embodied practices can effectively link the material aspects of people's lives with the spiritual.

FIGURE I.I. Marching in a peace demonstration was a religious practice for many, but not all, of the 35,000 participants in the 2003 annual Palm Sunday procession for peace, held in Melbourne, Australia. Interfaith prayer and song, symbolic banners, palm fronds, and the physical experience of procession with a large throng contributed to a sense of solidarity among the religiously, politically, and socio-economically diverse participants. Courtesy Jim Spickard, used by permission of Toroverde Press.

My foregoing description of Peter's practices included his practice of meditation, using some centuries-old methods for focusing the mind, body, and spirit. I did not mention his many other practices—some of which, on the surface, would not appear to be "religious." For example, early in his work with homeless families, Peter decided to shed his professional distance, and he worked to acquire completely new habits of eye contact, tone of voice, and ways of giving attention to his agency's "clients." He called it "practicing respect," but it took enormous effort at first. These complex practices of relating to the people his agency served were, indeed, part of Peter's religious expression—not only because his social justice activism was so central to his personal religion. They were "religious" also because he was able to "practice respect" by trying to "see God in each" of them—even the mentally ill guy who occasionally shouted abuses at everyone, the snot-nosed kid who had not bathed in weeks, and the overwhelmed teenage mother who neglected that kid. Similarly, Margaret's practices while gardening were often as "religious" as her practices while sitting in Buddhist-style meditation. And Laura's practices at her eclectic altar frequently spilled over into her writing, her mothering, her pace of life, her health, and her sense of well-being.

The "Logic" of Lived Religion

Because religion-as-lived is based more on such religious practices than on religious ideas or beliefs, it is not necessarily logically coherent. Rather, it requires a practical coherence: It needs to make sense in one's everyday life, and it needs to be effective, to "work," in the sense of accomplishing some desired end (such as healing, improving one's relationship with a loved one, or harvesting enough food to last the winter). This practical coherence explains the reasoning underlying much popular religion, which may otherwise appear to be irrational and superstitious.[17]

Orsi tells of how agitated his students became when they considered the apparent irrationality of urban Italian Americans who take home, for healing practices, a bottle of water from the font of a shrine (an imitation of the grotto of Lourdes, built near a neighborhood church), even while knowing full well that water flowing there was piped from the city water system.[18] For the devout, there is no logical inconsistency, because the shrine's water is an effective substitute for the real spring water flowing from a grotto in a distant country. In their experience, it works.

I wonder if, perhaps, we are mistaken in our expectation of cognitive consistency between individuals' religion, as institutionally framed, and a person's actual religion, as lived. It may be only intellectuals who care about rational coherence in religious ways of thinking, perceiving, and acting. After nearly forty years of talking to people about their individual religions, I have the impression that only a small and unrepresentative proportion struggle to achieve tight consistency among their wide-ranging beliefs, perceptions, experiences, values, practices, and actions.

Likewise, it may be mainly intellectuals who care about the apparent inconsistency between religious ways of thinking about the world and scientifically rational ways of thinking. For example, compared to a layperson with relatively little training in scientific approaches to health, a medically educated professional is more likely to be bothered about working for healing using religious practices that seem nonrational according to scientific ways of knowing.[19] One nurse, described in that study, was head of a pediatric unit at the most prestigious hospital in a well-to-do East Coast suburban area, yet she also used several nonmedical healing approaches, particularly in her private healing circle. After working personally with someone needing healing, for instance, she would offer him or her a piece of blessed cloth to use at home when doing healing visualizations in private. While telling me that the cloth had to be cotton or some other natural fiber (and not a polyester blend), she became a little embarrassed about the apparent irrationality of her practice. So she added, "I know, it sounds weird, but it works—it works better with cotton—and that's what matters."

This book aims to understand contemporary patterns of religiosity and spirituality by focusing on people's religions-as-lived. Official religion and what religious organizations promote as "religious" are surely part of the picture, but not necessarily the best part for framing our focus. We must grapple with the complexities, apparent inconsistencies, heterogeneity, and untidiness of the range of religious practices that people in any given culture and period find meaningful and useful. By emphasizing individuals' practices in everyday life, we may avoid some conceptual muddle. More important, by examining lived religion, we may get closer to understanding individual religion in all its complexity and diversity.

Organization of the Book

In this book I draw on my own and others' studies of religion at the level of the individual, in order to rethink sociological interpretations of contemporary religion, religiosity, and religious identity. This focus on individual religion necessitates examining not only people's beliefs, religious ideas, and moral values (i.e., cognitive aspects of individual religion) but also, and more important, their everyday spiritual practices, involving their bodily and emotional, as well as religious, experiences and expressions. As the stories of people like Peter, Laura, Ron, and Margaret suggest, when we consider all these aspects of individual religiosity and spirituality, we discover that they rarely resemble the tidy, consistent, and theologically correct packages official religions promote.

Sociologist Thomas Luckmann noted decades ago that researchers are misguided if they try to describe individuals' religions and religiosity by looking for congruence with a standard package of beliefs and practices that some official religion has authoritatively approved.[20] He argued that the activities and teachings of official religions did not encompass all of the resources individuals today could draw on for their individual religious practices and beliefs. Rather, a vast range of nonofficial resources, most of which would not be recognized as "religious" by standard sociological or theological definitions, informed the religions practiced by modern individuals. Luckmann dubbed these elements "invisible religion."[21]

As long ago as the 1970s, some sociologists like Luckmann were critical of research efforts to tap contemporary individuals' religions, with all their eclectically chosen and often "invisible" elements, by using standard methodologies like survey questionnaires. But it is simply impossible to construct a research instrument that anticipates all the possible elements individuals might choose to weave into their own personal beliefs and practices, much less all the possible permutations and creative intermixing each individual might create from these many diverse elements.[22]

My research includes in its purview the nonofficial, unrecognized, even "invisible" elements of individuals' religions, in all their complexity. This book, likewise, aims to encompass such complex individual amalgams. I wonder, however, whether such eclecticism of belief and practice is all that new. We cannot go back in time to interview or observe individuals in late medieval Europe or the American colonies in early modern times, but we may be wrong in assuming much coherence and homogeneity in individuals' religious beliefs and practices in earlier eras. Several historians suggest that centuries earlier, in both Europe and the Americas, individuals' religious practices may have been far more diverse and complex, eclectic, and malleable than we have realized.[23] Thus, I begin with a fresh look at the historical precursors of today's religious practices.

2

Contested Meanings and Definitional Boundaries

Historicizing the Sociology of Religion

Researchers sometimes discover that assumptions, embedded in their field's basic definitions, get in the way of understanding the phenomenon they are observing. The realization comes as a jolt, because it means that the way we have learned to think about a phenomenon is now hindering our ability to understand what we are observing.[1] Any mature ethnographer of religion has probably had this experience many times, because it is part of the process that makes ethnography such a difficult, albeit rewarding, way of studying religion.[2]

One such jarring research experience happened to me in early 1981, as I was beginning a study of nonmedical healing. I recorded these events in my field notes:

> The healing service took place in an attractive suburban Episcopalian church, the members of which were generally upper-middle class and well-educated. The Sunday evening Eucharistic service each week was designated as a healing service, with scripture readings, prayers, and other elements of the liturgy focused on health and healing. A regular and important part of these services (as I discovered later) occurred after the Eucharist, when the celebrant offered to bless salt and oil for home prayer for healing. With a rustling of brown paper wrappers, the congregation hurriedly opened the spouts of salt boxes and lids of cooking oil bottles so the blessing could "get in."

I was only mildly surprised that these Episcopalians had revived a centuries-old tradition of promoting health and healing with blessed substances. What startled me, however, was the magical image of the blessing that these well-educated suburbanites obviously used: Their practice implied that they had to physically open the containers so that the blessing would reach the contents and thus its power would be effectively contained and transported home, in order for that power to heal at a distant location.

Doing good ethnography required me to examine my own reactions: Why was I startled? If I had observed Ecuadorian *campesinos* engaging in the same practice, I would not have been surprised. Were my reactions in this fieldwork perhaps biased by sociology's assumptions that religion should be "purified" of material concerns and magical thought? What had I assumed about the concepts of "magic" and "religion" that made it difficult for me to understand the ready mingling of magical practices and thinking in these contemporary Episcopalians' religious lives? In these people's lived experience, it was all part of practicing their religion.

At the time, I resolved my conceptual quandary by avoiding the concept of religion and focusing only on a concept that applied well to widely varying (religious and nonreligious) groups in my study: the notion of healing power (e.g., where it was located and how it was tapped, how it got to where it was needed, and what practices promoted its effectiveness). In the subsequent quarter century, however, I have experienced many such problems with the way sociology of religion defines religion and religiosity. Are magic and religion necessarily separate and mutually exclusive or are they integrated in many people's lived religions? Is the realm of the sacred always set apart from the profane, or do people sometimes experience the sacred as part of their work-a-day lives and mundane domestic existence? Is "folk" or "popular" or "non-official" religiosity any less religious than "official" or "church" religiosity? Does "religion" have to pertain to a deity or the supernatural, or could someone be equally religious without worshiping some suprahuman being?

Perhaps sociology, as a discipline, has uncritically adopted a post-Reformation "Protestant"[3] purism that excludes from our purview a large range of practices and beliefs that are, in fact, important parts of the lived religions of many individuals today. Perhaps too, sociology's disciplinary focus on what people believe, affirm, and think, as indicators of their religion and religiosity, is based on Reformation-era theological ideas that privilege belief over practice. If those assessments are correct, then sociology's conceptual apparatus is simply inadequate for understanding people's lived religion. It is thus necessary to examine and reconsider sociology's core definitions, then to refocus our research and methodological strategies accordingly.

I propose that we begin by trying to understand the nature of religion and religiosity in Europe before the Reformation era—before the foundation of a Christian denomination called Episcopalian, and long before anyone would have questioned the appropriateness of a congregation taking blessed substances home in order to carry divine healing power to where and when it was needed. The various "stories"[4] sociologists use to explain the place of religion in modern societies are all based on definitional assumptions. For example, many sociologists and anthropologists assume that in all religions there is a radical dichotomy between the sacred and the profane. Accordingly, religious behavior involves treating sacred places, time, and objects with a sense of profound respect and awe and protecting the sacred from contamination by the profane. If people's actual religious practices in other cultures or other times in history involve melding the sacred and profane, should we conclude that they are not really religious? Or, rather, should we reconsider our assumptions about a sacred-profane dichotomy and what practices count as "religious"?

In this chapter, I will examine how the definitions of what is properly "religion" and "religious" changed during a long period of upheaval in which many people vied, sometimes violently, over precisely those borderlines. Which issues were so critical that people would exert enormous effort and power to control the resulting boundaries? Specifically, I examine four issues that, I believe, are particularly important for understanding that what scholars nowadays think of as definitive of "real" religion and religious action is itself a social construction[5], the result of human struggles over cultural resources and power:

The location of the sacred. Where is the sacred found and how do humans get in touch with it? Is the sacred an integral part of everyday space, time, and social relationships, or is it radically apart from the "profane" world of everyday life? What practices do people engage in to connect with the realm of the sacred?

The nature of divine power. How is divine power exercised in the world? Does it regularly break through in "miracles," changing individuals' situations and affecting the course of events in the world? Is divine power channeled through human actions, and is it responsive to magical rituals?

The focus of individual religious expression. What is really important for each individual to do or to believe in order to be religiously "in good standing"? How does (or should) the individual integrate religious belief and/or practice with other aspects of life?

The purity and authenticity of religious tradition and group identity. Who is authentically "one of us"? Who can authoritatively determine what beliefs and practices are true to a religion's tradition, as opposed to what is misled, alien, or downright heretical? When an individual modifies or selects religious practices to make them more relevant in everyday life, is that person still practicing the group's religion?

Recognizing that these definitional boundaries are social constructions does not mean we must discard the concepts, but does require us to realize that the resulting distinctions are not inherent properties of "religion" or "the sacred." And it requires that we notice how such factors as social class and political or military power shaped the resulting definitions to privilege some groups' religious practices and to marginalize others.'

Certain ways of being religious were once common or even the norm but after a long struggle came to be treated as unacceptable (even sinful or heretical). This chapter sketches the premodern notions that allowed those beliefs and practices to be understood as properly "religious."

Historical Contests and the Creation of Definitional Boundaries

Sociology of religion needs a much deeper appreciation of the historical context of its core definitions. Drawing boundaries is a political and sociohistorical process. Definitional boundaries are the outcomes of *contested meanings;* that is, people have actively exerted their power to affect the outcome and to resist others' efforts to gain control. The resulting boundaries must be understood in the sociohistorical context of that struggle. For Europe and the Americas, dramatic changes in the definitional boundaries of acceptable Christian belief and practice occurred between roughly 1400 and 1700 CE. The intense conflicts within and among religious groups during those centuries illustrate the uses of power in defining religion.

Some historians refer to this period as the Long Reformation because of the sociopolitical prominence of ongoing religious controversies.[6] While Protestant historians and apologists first applied the term "reformation" to their own foundational religiopolitical standpoint vis-à-vis the Catholic Church, most social historians now emphasize that both Catholic and Protestant churches experienced a series of change-promoting movements that aimed to reform Christianity. These reformations were about literally re-forming, re-shaping, and re-defining the core of Christian faith and practice.[7]

The extensive redrawing of religious boundaries during the Long Reformation took place in the context of other massive changes in wider sociopolitical and cultural boundaries. One of the main changes involved the development and elaboration of cultural distinctions between people. Thus, for example, social elites marked and exaggerated the differences between themselves and nonelite social groups, elaborating norms for etiquette, decorum, and demeanor. Some historians examining laypersons' religious practices during this transition period argue that the boundaries around what eventually came to be viewed as proper religious behavior were central to producing and reproducing social elites, as distinguished from common folks. As these boundaries became established norms, aspiring elites and middle classes gradually adopted them as definitive of proper behavior.[8]

Another set of boundaries that were redrawn pertained to people's sense of group identity. Whereas in late medieval times, people's group-identity was grounded in the cultural homogeneity of their local community, that homogeneity was disrupted by struggles over the redefinition of religious, social, and political units. People could no longer assume that others in the same community were like themselves in important areas such as religion, political allegiance, and social class. For example, one might have a stronger sense of identity with others of the same religious "confession" (e.g., Lutheran, Catholic) than with others who shared the same grazing lands or occupation but not "confession." Religious boundaries became especially important in this period of intense demarcation of *cultural identity* in new and complex constellations.

At the same time, religious and civil authorities created and emphasized greater distinction between the social center and the periphery, widening the exercise of their power over politico-religious units (e.g., canton, diocese) and bringing remote rural areas under tighter control.[9] Thus, cultural identity markers were frequently linked with political identity markers, such that decades-long religious wars and recurring violence toward religiopolitical Others eventually reshaped Europe.[10] The contested boundaries between "us" and "them" were, thus, also at stake in the historical processes of defining religion.

Why do sociologists need to pay attention to the historical struggles by which definitive boundaries were established? When we fail to recognize that our conceptual apparatus has been shaped by such battles over boundaries, we risk misapprehending our data and misusing our sociological interpretations. A prime example of such failing is sociologists Rod Stark and Roger Finke's misuses of historical accounts of medieval European religion. They depict medieval Christians as having a very low degree of religiosity, based on such indicators as the paucity and small capacity of parish churches, laypeople's sparse church attendance and infrequent reception of Communion, improper behavior in church, and widespread ignorance of church doctrines and church-prescribed religious practices (such as how to recite the Apostles' Creed).[11]

Their interpretations are limited by an overly institutional conception of religion that is utterly anachronistic.[12] All of those indicators are based on norms for religious behavior that became established, in most of western Europe, only in the modern era.

Our discipline's conceptual tools are, thus, limited by a Eurocentric bias. They do not adequately apply to non-Western religions, especially those religions that are not structured at all like Western religious organizations with "membership" of individuals. Anthropologist Talal Asad has argued that an anthropology (and, I would add, sociology) of religion was made possible by the development, in Western history, of a concept of religion as an objective reality—something that exists universally in the real world, and can be "discovered" and objectively studied.[13] Asad researched the genealogies of "religion" and several related core concepts (e.g., "ritual") to demonstrate how scholarly discourse itself has been shaped by important historical shifts in how power is exercised, how self and society are linked, and how human bodies and emotions are engaged in religion.[14] Unearthing the genealogies of our conceptual tools enables us to understand their limitations. It reminds us that both the social "reality" we study and our ways of thinking about that reality are products of a process of social construction in which human factors of power and privilege play a significant role.[15]

How can we interpret the changes in the social location of religion and the changed place of religion in individual lives if we fail to recognize that our field's core conceptual distinctions are themselves social products? For instance, how can we interpret comparative rates of church membership without acknowledging that the very definition and meaning of membership changed dramatically? How can we compare individual patterns of religiosity over time without admitting that what we researchers count as "religious" is completely different from what, for example, fourteenth-century persons in Languedoc, for example, considered "religious?"[16] Are there not serious biases affecting our interpretations if we privilege, by our fundamental definitions, those expressions of religion that served (intentionally or not) the political purposes of social elites, colonial powers, males, and victors?

To acknowledge that our concepts are the social products of historical contests does not mean we must discard them altogether or must despair of ever having useful conceptual tools. Rather, by historicizing the sociology of religion, we can begin to have a far more critical appreciation of our conceptual tools, as well as a much better understanding of the far-reaching societal changes we seek to interpret.

What were people's religious lives like before these definitional boundaries were drawn? Who were the contesting factions and how did they exert their interests and their meanings over the disputed boundaries? This transition period creates many problems if we are trying to understand ordinary laypeople's as well as elite individuals' religious expressions, because when these various reformation movements "dismantled medieval Christianity, they transformed the definition of religion itself."[17] In recent years, historians have published volumes of careful scholarship on ordinary people's religious practices and meanings in various parts of Europe and the Americas before, during, and after this critical redefining transition.[18] Their findings show that many sociologists' assumptions about religion, magic, the supernatural, and the sacred and the profane are based on faulty, biased readings of history.[19]

Let us examine some of the contested religious meanings around which political and cultural struggles centered in the transitional period of late medieval and early modern times.

Contested Meanings: Where Is the Sacred Located?

Late medieval religion was not, of course, a unified, homogenous entity. Indeed, several historians have argued that one of the hotly contested projects of many Protestant and Catholic reformation movements was to consolidate authority over religious belief and practice in order to make it less heterogeneous.[20] Religious beliefs and practices tied to the location of the sacred help explain this considerable diversity in three ways: (1) localistic practices varied greatly because the sacred was rooted in local geography; (2) individuals could eclectically choose their own devotional options from a large repertoire of locally acceptable practices; and (3) in people's experience, sacred space and time were pervasive and not limited to the church or its rituals. The following sketches serve to give a sense of how the location of the sacred could produce such great diversity of belief, practice, and experience within the same religion.

Some sociologists have treated medieval Europe as monolithically Catholic-Christian. But they have failed to appreciate the enormous diversity that existed within that era's practice of Christianity. Stark and Finke argue that religion of that era epitomizes a religious market monopoly.[21] Their error is due, in large part, to a narrowly Protestant misreading of Catholicism generally, because Catholicism has long encouraged a considerable amount of internal diversity.[22] The market analogy, in particular, does not fit the patterns of medieval Christianity. Although virtually all persons were members of a single church, that membership was a minor part of their religion-as-lived. Individuals' actual lived religions were highly diverse, somewhat eclectic, and much more central to their everyday lives than was the church part alone. When there is only one food market in town, it cannot be said to hold a monopoly if the residents grow most of their own food.

Localism and Heterogeneity

There was enormous difference between one part of Europe and another. Indeed, religion often varied considerably from a community in one valley to the next valley. For instance, the patron saint of one village—around whose patronage many communal religious rituals revolved—might go completely unnoticed in the everyday practices of persons living in nearby villages, which had their own patron saints. Because these practices pertained to a specific geographical place and historical community, they were immensely resistant to the efforts of outsiders to change them. Changes did occur, though, usually gradually and from within.[23] For instance, villagers might increase devotion to a saint whose help appeared to be especially effective in time of an epidemic, or they might lose interest in a practice, such as use of water from a holy well, when it failed to be particularly effective.

Such localism was one of the key characteristics of late medieval religious expression. The modern Westerner is often disturbed by the level of diversity and apparent inconsistency of such highly localistic religion: With that much variation, how can one consider it to be all the *same* religion? But that is precisely the point! So long as they observed a few highly important common translocal practices (*not* common beliefs), people's participation in their immediate community's religious practices made them confident that their religion was "Christian." These localistic ritual practices confirmed community social bonds and ties with the land, which may have been important sources of medieval Christianity's strength. But they also suggest why it simply did not matter to most participants that, in many respects, their regular religious practices differed from those of other Christian villages.

What were the important Christian practices most people held in common and would expect anywhere? Core practices included baptism (for oneself and one's family), attending Sunday Mass whenever practicable, making confession and receiving Communion at least once a year during Easter week, and using some basic prayers (usually the Ave Maria and Pater Noster).[24] We get a clue that ordinary people understood these practices as a central core from the testimony of a character witness for an Inquisition suspect:

> "When he is not tending the herds and is at home in winter or when it rains, or during such times, he always goes to Mass; he always makes the sign of the cross when the Ave Maria tolls, he recites the

Ave Maria, crossing himself first, he rests the oxen from their work at that time; blesses the bread and offers thanks to God after he has eaten; when he goes out to Mass he has a rosary in his hands; in church he is respectful and recites the rosary, and so he performs all the duties of a good Christian."[25]

This peasant from a remote valley in what is now Italy had good reason to expect that the inquisitor—an educated (and dangerous) stranger from a completely different social world—would recognize these religious practices as universally accepted definitive characteristics of a "good Christian." In his experience, lived entirely in the local village context, "good Christians" were, by definition, those who engaged in just such Christian practices.

Cultic Diversity and Devotional Options

Localism was not the only source of widespread heterogeneity. Another important source was individuals' relative freedom to choose (from a large, locally available repertoire), the specific religious practices and cultic devotions they used in their own lives, according to their specific needs. Furthermore, individuals could shape their own understandings of the saints and the meanings of their devotions toward them.[26] For example, one woman's everyday devotional practices might include seeking help from a saint known for protecting and healing children, devotions at a nearby holy well known for promoting fertility, involvement in rituals for the patron saint of her valley, and such routine women's religious responsibilities as the daily blessing of the hearth on rekindling the fire. An older neighbor would have very different everyday religious practices: She might say similar blessings on the hearth and the kitchen, seek a different holy well (perhaps one for the health and fertility of her barnyard animals), pay little or no attention to cults of saints protecting children, but seek the help of those saints who help persons with aches and pains, failing memories, and sore throats.

The men in their households would have different religious practices. One might seek help from the patron saint of farmers; another from the patron of fishermen or smithies. One might choose to tap divine power at an ancient cairn, another at a grotto, and another at a mountaintop shrine. Individual reverence (for example, toward Mary, the mother of Jesus) also varied (by locality, by gender, or by personal preference) as to what image of the holy person was the object of devotional prayers. For example, some people revered the Mary-of-Sorrows, others the Mary-Queen-of-Heaven, or any number of other manifestations of Mary as a holy or powerful religious figure.[27]

Such choice of personal and family religious practices, combined with localistic practices, resulted in a somewhat eclectic pattern of religiosity that differed in many important particulars from that of similar persons elsewhere in the same culture.[28] In order to understand the quality of their religion-as-lived, we need to appreciate how these diverse individual practices made sense in their everyday lives.

Sacred Space and Sacred Time

In premodern Europe, religious meanings pertained to everyday experiences of time and space, such that—without necessarily ever being conscious of it—ordinary people subjectively participated in these religious meanings regularly throughout each day. While people clearly recognized an important distinction between the sacred and the profane, in practice they observed no tidy boundaries between sacred and profane space and time.[29] There appears to have been a casual familiarity with what modern people would consider to be sacred space. This familiarity is in marked contrast with the modern conception of sacred space that is set apart and not used for nonreligious purposes, that is treated with awe and reverence, such that "religious" people respect that space with "proper" behavior, such as attentiveness and decorum. Sociologists who treat such church-defined reverence toward the sacred as a core indicator of religiosity thus fail to notice the many other ways people have of being religious.

The medieval sense of sacred space was that it was nearly ubiquitous and highly accessible to everyone. In both rural and urban settings, the entire local landscape had something of a "sacred overlay."[30] All the people in the community knew numerous spaces where they could readily contact the divine—a votive shrine at a crossroads, a holy well, a home altar, a standing stone or cairn. Often, these places were more important in people's religiosity than the church building and grounds, because they were experienced as more awe-inspiring and imbued with sacred power than the church or its parts.

Most people in a community may have considered their church building itself to be more sacred than most other buildings because of the many ritual exorcisms and blessings on it. However, various parts of the church and churchyard were considered to have different degrees of holiness.[31] The demarcations between these spaces were thus ritually useful and meaningful, because the simple ritual act of moving one's body or an object from one space to a more sacred one would be experienced, by all those acculturated to that sense of space, as a highly meaningful act.[32]

Medieval people certainly considered some space more "sacred" than other space, but they had a very different notion (compared to, say, twentieth-century sensibilities) of what was proper behavior when present in that space. Because people thought of the church space as familiar and communal, they considered it no sacrilege to hold wakes and feast-day celebrations in the nave of the church.[33] They made no tidy boundaries between the religious and nonreligious activities these celebrations entailed. For instance, the wake had obvious religious significance as part of the larger communal ritual response to death, but wake festivities also included lots of eating, drinking, music, flirting and bawdy jokes, games, and jesting.[34]

People's casual familiarity with sacred space applied even during the Mass, the central church-oriented religious event of the routine week. One historian has summarized:

> on the face of it, medieval people would seem to have behaved informally, if not irreverently, at Mass. Apparently, scuffles broke out in parish churches, people sat on the altar steps or squatted on the floor, nipped out at intervals to the wine shop, talked, laughed, scratched, hawked, coughed and spat. They left the service as soon as they decently could, and used the premises for assignations, seductions, flirtations and sales.[35]

In church, some sacred time (like space) was more sacred than others. So, while Mass time generally might have been more holy than work time, within the Mass time, only the period surrounding the consecration of bread and wine was particularly sacred; within that period, the actual elevation of the consecrated host was the solemn moment for most congregants. It was not a breach of community norms to be inattentive in the early parts of the Mass or to leave the service after the elevation had occurred.[36]

The diffuseness of the sacred and its interpenetration with the profane in people's everyday lives were also due, in large part, to how thoroughly a complex series of calendrical rituals structured those lives. In addition to the major liturgical seasons (e.g., Advent, Christmastide, Lent, Easter, and Pentecost) established by the church, there were numerous special holy days to observe by abstention from work, attending Mass, or participating in processions, communal feasts, and private celebrations. Each locality also celebrated the special days associated with its community's own shrines and local patron saints. One historian noted: "To fifteenth-and early sixteenth-century sensibilities the liturgical year was spread over twelve months, . . . and *none of it was secular.*"[37]

Calendrical rituals served to order the experience of time, establishing routines and schedules and creating a sense of *shared temporal regularity*.[38] Not only the liturgical year but also the days of the week and the hours of the day had ritual significance. Just as school bells, "rush hour," and the "six o'clock news" shape some of people's collective temporal regularity nowadays, premodern people experienced time through such calendrical rituals as the daily ringing of Angelus bells, community celebrations of the Sabbath, and numerous seasonal rituals. These calendrical rituals produced a pervasive religiosity that was inherently communal, rather than individual.[39]

Especially solemn feast days were obligatory: Nonobservance (e.g., working a normal workday) was a serious sin. In a typical late medieval German town, for example, solemn feasts included Christmas, Easter, seven major feasts of the Virgin, the feasts of John the Baptist, feasts of the individual apostles, and the feast of the Discovery of the True Cross. Then, local patron saints merited another ten or twelve solemn feast days, and some nonobligatory celebrations as well.[40] Often the local patron saints' feasts were, in practice, more important than those of the officially recognized, higher saints.[41] Feasts were observed with liturgical (i.e., formal church ritual), paraliturgical, and nonliturgical celebrations. For instance, a village celebrating an important holy day might have a religious procession from the parish church's gate through the town and valley to a nearby shrine site, followed by an outdoor celebration of the Mass at the shrine, and later a special meal, with dancing and merriment around a bonfire. Of this day-long celebration, only the Mass was a formal church ritual, but the entire day's activities were part of observing the holy day.

The liturgical cycle shaped the Christian year with rituals for all the important seasons, needs, and emotions. The feast of the Purification of the Virgin (known as Candlemas), on February 2, exemplifies how people used liturgical, paraliturgical, and nonliturgical rituals together to channel divine power to affect their everyday material world. Because the central features of Candlemas itself were generally the same throughout most of Europe, we can draw on historical evidence from diverse countries. Local practices, however, varied in other meanings attached to the beginning of February and the entire ritual cycle of spring. For example, many German-speaking areas also celebrated a weather-predicting saint's day, such that there was religious significance to what Americans now know as "Groundhog Day." The feast of the Purification was also celebrated as St. Bridget's Day[42] in Ireland. In practice, Candlemas was clearly the celebration, simultaneously, of both these Christian saints' themes and the important Feast of Lights of various early European pagan religions. The pagan celebrations also evoked the themes of light, life, and renewal, so the Christian rituals reverberated with powerful cultural meanings.[43]

In church liturgy, the Candlemas feast symbolized the purity of the Virgin and coming of the light of the world (Christ). It was the main feast in a larger cycle of feasts of saints whose celebrations are linked with blessings for new spring life and mating, favorable weather for planting and vine-tending, blessings of animals against sickness, and so on.[44] In popular practice, Candlemas was both a large communal celebration with elaborate processions and, for individuals and families, the source of ritually blessed candles that each household used for protection, healing, and purification throughout the year.

For medieval people, time mattered. Dangerous periods of seasonal transition, such as planting or harvest time, required the ritual protection of the sacred. The ritual calendar also "structured the expression of the deep emotions of grief, love, and hope according to a seasonal and weekly, even hourly pattern."[45] If we consider also the extensive paraliturgical and nonliturgical ritual calendar, we can better appreciate how simply participating in ritual practices structured people's emotional and social experiences, giving them meaning by practice, rather than by ideas or verbal explanations.[46]

Our modern image of a sacred-profane dichotomy does not really apply to the sense of sacred time and space in medieval religion. On the contrary, more often the sacred was experienced as arising *from within* profane space and everyday, mundane activities. Indeed, sacred events/time "could enter the flow of merely human time," and certain religious practices promoted that sense of elision of time.[47]

Rather than diminishing the quality of experience of the sacred, such diffuseness in everyday life made the sacred more useful. Consider, for example, the quotidian usefulness of sacred power infused into blessed substances that one sixteenth-century commentator alluded to approvingly:

> People of old showed great zeal for all kinds of blessings by the
> Church, and everyone wanted to share in them. . . . Each Sunday, the
> old Christians went in crowds to the blessing of holy water and salt,
> and every week each person supplied his house with holy water
> and blessed salt . . . so that everyone had something blessed on his
> table the whole week through.[48]

Both the premodern persons described in this example and the suburban congregation I observed in the 1980s ritually used the blessed substances to carry divine power to where they needed it, for such uses as anointing sick family members or a protective blessing of all before they left the house each morning. Even though they may have viewed the priest's blessing as having greater effectiveness than a layperson's, the act of blessing people, places, or things was an important everyday religious practice. Ordinary laypersons, not ritual specialists, performed much—probably most—ritual practice. Laypersons performed rituals, sometimes precisely, sometimes carelessly, throughout their daily lives, so that divine power might be brought to bear, even if in minute quantities, on their everyday needs and concerns.

This easy familiarity with the realm of the sacred was closely tied to how people used their religious practices as a means of tapping sacred power. People had a relationship with the saints. Veneration of saints was linked to getting concrete help from them to meet family or community needs, but saints who failed to fulfill their role were angrily chided or even abused. For instance, in Germany people called on St. Urban, the patron saint of vintners, to provide good weather for harvesting the grapes. When the weather on St. Urban's feast day was good, people honored him and appreciated his protection of the harvest, but if the weather was bad, his image was thrown in the mud.[49]

One of the effects (if not also one of the goals) of the Protestant and Catholic reformation movements was to limit the realm of the sacred, presumably making it more valuable, set apart, and awesome. A related end was to control the uses ordinary people could make of sacred power. This control was effected by drawing boundaries around the location of the sacred. It had to be differentiated from the everyday, mundane world of the common folk. The new delineations separated sacred space from people's profane space and sacred time from their everyday profane time. According to the logic of popular religion, the sacred pervaded the realm of the profane. Early modern reformation movements contested that sense; they proclaimed that the sacred and profane had to be ritually separated.

Rather than take the notion of a clear sacred-profane dichotomy for granted as a defining feature of religion, what would we understand about individuals' religious lives—now, as well as four centuries ago—if we considered the possibility that some, perhaps many, religious persons experience the sacred as arising *within* the profane world?[50] Many scholars of religion have used a similar dichotomy as definitive: the distinction between magic and religion.[51] Although religious leaders had tried for centuries to control the practice of important rituals, the Long Reformation was a period in which the boundary between religious and magical ritual was theologically and organizationally contested and fortified.[52] In rethinking our conceptual tools, it would be fruitful to examine some cultural understandings of religious, magical, and miraculous powers that were common in the late medieval era, before the definitive boundaries of religion and the religious were redrawn.

Contested Meanings: Miracle, Magic, and Religious Power

As part of their attack on popular uses of sacred power, various agents of reform tried to distinguish religion from magic and to eliminate magical elements from religious practice. For all practical purposes, the definitional boundary between magic and religion did not exist in the late medieval popular imagination. Most people had a magical image of the power of much religious and parareligious ritual. For example, people considered the candles blessed in church at Candlemas to be imbued with sacred power that could be transmitted to where it was needed for protection. Thus, during the dangerous time of childbirth, blessed candles were lit to keep evil spirits from mother and child. Each year, on the ritual calendar's New Year, the head of the household inscribed, in candle wax, a protective mark of blessing on the doors of the house and barn. People also used the blessed candles for healing, burning them at the bedside of the sick, and for purification, burning one to expel evil spirits or ghosts from an afflicted house.[53] Thus, religious uses of these candles seemed entirely consistent with a magical image of their efficacy.

One of the reasons we misinterpret medieval religious practice as merely "superstitious" or "irrational" is that we fail to grasp practitioners' conception of religious power. A mode of action is not irrational if a person perceives it to work. Given their conception of religious power, medieval persons were reasonable to consider ritual actions to be the appropriate and efficacious way to meet certain needs and to accomplish certain tasks. People experienced that power as real. These cultures socialized their members' very senses to perceive divine power.[54] Thus, not only did they *think* about this religious power differently than do most twenty-first-century Europeans but also they had regular experiences in which they *sensed* it.[55] Divine power was not just a matter of belief; it was an awesome and important reality in people's lives.

Historian Edward Muir has argued compellingly that the central contested issue of the Long Reformation was the meaning of ritual action. He observed that the "generalized concept of *ritual* as a distinct kind of activity came into being" during this critical period.[56] That concept was used to distinguish—to mark a boundary—between "true religion" (the religious practices of whoever was making the distinction) and "mere ritual" (the religious practices of the Other).

More important than these rhetorical distinctions, though, was that the Long Reformation resulted in a whole range of new interpretations of ritual *action*—hotly contested debates about the answer to the question "What do rites do?"[57] At one extreme was a dogmatic Catholic answer: Rites were real actions. As such, they had the power to bring something into being (e.g., a marriage), to literally enact something (e.g., the anointment of an emperor or bishop), and to make something present (e.g., Christ's presence in the Mass). At the other extreme was one Protestant (and humanist) position that rites were no more than representations, a form of communication by which meaning is represented symbolically. Accordingly, Communion rituals were reminders of the Last Supper; the rituals of anointment were symbols of an office-holder's change of status, and Christ's presence among gathered believers was metaphorical, not physically real.[58] Other Protestant (and later Catholic) positions were somewhere between these two extremes. This historical process constructing a boundary between "real" religion and "mere" ritual is closely linked with the transition between premodern emphasis on practices by means of which people are religious and the modern emphasis on what and how religious persons believe.

Not only church rites but also everyday ritual practices were considered to have a real physical, as well as spiritual, efficacy. For example, the act of blessing someone, something, or someplace meant literally *doing* something that had the power to change the circumstances of that person, object, or place. People incorporated blessings on a household in their greeting on entering, and other blessings were part of such everyday acts as lighting the fire in the hearth. Parents blessed their children and other members of the household. Workers blessed their tools and often their products-in-process. Blessing was a literal, not merely metaphorical, act of using divine power. Because the power of blessing was considered to be an active power, people used many ritual blessings to channel divine power to where it was needed.[59]

People regularly sought the priest's blessings, especially when the liturgical calendar provided for them. For example, blessings on the feast of St. Blasius, February 3, were considered especially effective for curing illness in humans and cattle. Laypersons, however, could also effectively do the blessing. For example, the head of the household was usually the one to perform the annual blessing of the house and barn on the feast of Epiphany—the religious new year.[60] Similarly, laypersons regularly performed blessings of people, animals, and inanimate objects, by using either a ritual prayer and action or a previously blessed object to pass the blessing on to another person or thing needful of it. Before the Long Reformation, church officials had little control over laypersons' access to or uses of such sacred power.

In late medieval times, many people experienced miracles as real. Medieval religiosity was based on the expectation of miracles, the breakthrough of divine power to affect people's everyday, material lives. "Of course," divine power could save the crops, heal sick people, and protect loved ones from harm! The only question was how to obtain that divine intervention for one's own life. Although sometimes it seemed capricious, this religious power was not utterly without order. People believed that it sometimes accomplished an immanent justice, for example punishing people's sins through plague or crop failure.[61] They thought of the power of the miraculous as reflecting the order of the cosmos; for example, the calendrical ritual order anticipated manifestations of divine power according to the order of nature's seasons.[62]

Divine power was susceptible to something of a contract with a community. In exchange for the community's devotions and faithful practice of necessary rituals, the powers would become that community's protectors and benefactors.[63] The saints personified this relationship.[64] People believed that they could channel divine power directly, without clerical mediation, to where it was needed. Saints' miracles could erupt anywhere.[65] And people could tap the saints' power themselves at home, at wayside shrines, in the fields, on the roads, wherever and whenever needed.[66] Rituals were thus the means by which cosmic order could be brought to bear on everyday life, giving ordinary people access to divine power and thereby a measure of control in the face of the chaos of life.[67] While God might be named as the ultimate source of all this power, in everyday life spiritual powers were treated as more widespread and less remote.

The religious power to help was simultaneously the power to harm.[68] Evil spirits were not the only source of dangerous power; in some instances, the saints were also considered malevolent for using their power to harm humans.[69] Thus, community rituals needed to propitiate these spiritual powers in order to escape their wrath.[70] This notion of religious power also suggests why people often did not care whether the power that accomplished their goal was "good" or "bad" in the eyes of religious authorities. To them, demonic power was merely an alternative means to tap efficacious power. Historians note, for example, instances in which weather bells were blessed in the name of the divinity and, when they did not bring favorable weather, were reblessed in the name of the devil.[71]

The pervasive influence of so many dangerous powers meant that people needed regular ritual practices for protection. There were numerous liturgical and extraliturgical prayers to drive away dangerous spirits and protective symbols one could wear or place on one's house and barn, as well as community works and prayers that might attract helpful spirits.[72] Each candle blessed at Candlemas, for example, was imbued with protective power, because its ritual blessing included the pronouncement that "wherever it shall be lit or set up, the devil may flee away in fear and trembling with all his ministers, out of those dwelling, and never presume again to disquiet your servants."[73] Furthermore, because there was no tidy boundary between the sacred and profane, these ritual actions were integrated in everyday life with other, more purely utilitarian actions, such as the planting of seed, the lighting of the hearth fire, and putting children to bed.

Thus, knowledge of effective ritual actions was valued knowledge. For example, a good mother would know that taking care of a sick child included use of blessed candles and oil, as well as prayers to exorcise the sick room of any bad spirits; she would know how to collect herbs for a healing tea and how to say the correct ritual words while brewing it; she would sponge the fevered child with cool compresses, while addressing prayers to a saint known to be especially effective in curing little ones. Such religious actions were not viewed as apart from purely instrumental ones; ritual prayers were an integral part of how one correctly performed the instrumental tasks. Thus, a mother who did not know these healing practices or who failed to do them properly would be deemed inadequate.[74]

Nevertheless, ritual effectiveness depended on performance, not intention or individual consciousness. Thus, a ritual action performed correctly was believed to be more effective than one performed incorrectly, even if the incorrect actions were done with greater earnestness and fervor. Likewise, actions done with sacrilegious intent or even by accident could effectively tap religious power if they happened to be performed correctly. The tale of the sorcerer's apprentice (even in its trivialized Disney cartoon version) illustrates this conception of performative power. Everyday ritual and magic were intertwined, making the distinction between religious practices and magical practices impossible.[75]

Knowledge of effective ritual actions was thus a potential source of individual power. Priests, as well as midwives, herbalists, bone-setters, healers, diviners, fire(burn)-drawers, and sorcerers, were respected and feared for knowing effective ritual actions the average person in the community did not know. Priest-craft and witch-craft were distinguished not by differences in effectiveness but by presumed benevolent or malevolent intent.[76]

Especially outside the cities, Christian priests were not, in their religious practices, much different from ordinary people. Priests did, however, have a few important ritual roles: They were the only ones who could legitimately perform the Mass, the central and most powerful ritual act. They were the ritual specialists the community sought out to lead processions and pilgrimages and other devotions in honor of local saints. And their ritual efficacy was sought to bless places and objects that were used for channeling divine power to where people needed it. Priests were asked to bless weapons, farm tools, ornaments, fields, and farm animals.[77] In particular, clerical blessings of sacramentals—the many nonliturgical religious objects, such as holy water and candles, that people could use at home in ritual practices and devotions—multiplied ritual opportunities for laypersons to channel divine power.[78]

Delimiting Sacred Power: Magic

The reformation movements—both Protestant and Catholic—attacked the popular idea of sacred power. Reformers tried to distinguish "true" religion from "mere" magic, and by the end of the Long Reformation, most religious organizations severely sanctioned unapproved persons' exercise of sacred power. The sociopolitical effect was the consolidation and control of power. For instance, if a "wise woman" healer successfully healed a sick person, the churches' interpretation was that she did so with the aid of the devil and must be punished severely.[79] Catholic reformation movements did not totally eliminate lay access to magical power. The Catholic Church still allowed some devotions and use of sacramentals to which many members attached magical meanings. Church authorities decried magic, however, and tried to centralize the mediation of divine power in church-approved rituals performed by priests who were under stricter control of the hierarchy.

Various Protestant reformation movements tried to eliminate magic from religion altogether, in part by stripping the churches and worship services of the material and ritual stuff with which magical action is accomplished.[80] Although Protestant religion-as-preached attempted to create a firm dichotomy between religion and magic, historians have shown that popular Protestant religion-as-practiced has not made such tidy distinctions. Because of the importance of the words of scripture in Protestantism, much Protestant magic was based on the magical use of the Bible or scripturally based charms.[81] For example, in the nineteenth and twentieth centuries (as well as today), many Protestants continued to use Bibles for divination or scraps of paper with verses of scripture for charms.[82] Ron (see chapter 1), who made a point of saying ". . . in Jesus' name" with every prayer for protection or petition, was engaged in a similar practice.[83]

Delimiting Sacred Power: Miracle

The Catholic reformation movements kept more of the earlier notion of "miracle," but tried to limit "true" miracles to church-approved mediators of divine power. In particular, they emphasized the miraculous qualities of the Eucharist, in which Christ became fully present in the consecrated Communion host. Only priests were allowed to perform the church-approved rituals through which this miracle occurred, and the Catholic reformation movements increasingly emphasized priests as the proper mediators of divine power in the administration of all church-approved sacraments. The other ordinary channel to divine power was through the saints—persons who had been so holy while alive that they were believed to be closer to the "ear" of God after death. Before the Long Reformation, local convention and popular practice established and recognized the vast majority of saints.[84]

Between the thirteenth and seventeenth centuries, church authorities gradually centralized control of the process of canonization by which saints were officially recognized. The faithful were important in the process of canonization, because evidence of the saint's performance of miracles was a necessary criterion. Without ordinary people's believing in and seeking miracles, saints could not be acclaimed before the Congregation of Rites. By the end of the Long Reformation, however, the process was so formalized that laypeople's testimony was neither sought nor welcomed; thus the church of Rome seldom authorized or recognized popular saints.[85] Nevertheless, popular Catholicism, a vital part of many people's religious practice even today, continued the older notion of miracle and the intervention of the divine through the saints.[86]

Protestant churches, in a long series of reformation movements, tried to limit the possibility of "miracle" to acts of God alone. Many tried to reduce laypeople's use of intermediaries to God's miraculous power. The concept of "disenchantment of the world" developed by classical social theorist Max Weber aptly describes the Protestant churches' attempt to circumscribe the realm of sacred powers.[87] But by focusing on Protestant reformers' theology and Protestant leaders' teachings, Weber and other scholars of religion failed to understand the nature of popular Protestantism. Historian Robert Scribner, concludes: "I do not think that the thesis about the 'disenchantment of the world' will any longer pass muster as a historically accurate description."[88]

The issue for sociological understanding of religion is not how Protestant or Catholic reformation movements changed the church teachings on magic and miracle. The point is that magic and miracle were once completely interwoven with religion; they were integrally part of how people understood religious power. Powerful figures, such as ecclesiastical authorities, leaders of religious movements, and social elites, asserted dramatically different meanings, trying to limit people's access to and uses of religious power. After a long period of cultural and social structural change, certain official meanings delimiting what should be considered "real" religion prevailed, even though many people's religious practice did not fit those official limits. Scholars' definitional boundaries that distinguish magic from religion are themselves social products of that contest and thus culturally and historically bound.

Contested Meanings: Privileging Belief versus Privileging Practice

Sociologists rely very heavily on the assumption that people's religion and religiosity can be identified, measured, and understood by finding out what they believe, but such operational definitions are socially constructed and the results of considerable wrangling (especially during the Long Reformation). Rather than focus on what people believe, by contrast, late medieval religion privileged practice, not only in the ideals for religious virtuosi but also in the expectations for ordinary laypersons. Being a "good" Christian was defined in terms of a few prescribed occasional practices such as properly observing certain holy days, to which people added a myriad of everyday religious practices such as pronouncing blessings on entering a house or crossing themselves when passing a cemetery. A religious person was one who engaged in religious practices, of which only a few were done in church or under clergy auspices. The practice of many quotidian rituals involved people's bodies and emotions in religious experience and expression.

Historian Peter Burke points out that the medieval pattern of calendrical rituals created balance between addressing the needs of the upper body and the lower body—cognitive and spiritual aspects balanced against supposedly baser bodily needs and appetites—such as for food, sex, procreation, health. By contrast, the reform movements of the early modern period recognized only the upper body as proper to religiosity. The rest was treated as sacrilegious and dangerous.[89]

Burke likened the contested boundaries to the images in Brueghel's sixteenth-century painting "The Fight between Carnival and Lent." The painting depicts a busy town square full of people engaged in practices associated with paraliturgical celebrations of these two seasons. In the foreground is a mock jousting match between figures representing Carnival and Lent. Carnival is depicted as a fat man astride a wine barrel, bearing a cooking skewer with remains of a roast pig and propelled by jesters, musicians, and costumed merrymakers. The opposing figure represents Lent, gaunt and pale, with flatbread and fish, and armed with a baker's paddle. His entourage consists of a monk and a dour old lady, with some children eating flatbread. The painting contrasts Lenten somber dress, sobriety, penance, abstinence, and almsgiving with Carnival games, contests, dancing, feasting, sexuality, and mockery. Burke argues that before the sixteenth century, these opposing figures were balanced, emotionally and ritually. The Long Reformation was something of a metaphorical battle between Carnival and Lent, and Lent won.[90]

FIGURE 2.1. Detail from the 1559 painting *Fight between Carnival and Lent* by Pieter Brueghel the Elder, Kunsthistorisches Museum, Vienna, Austria. Courtesy Erich Lessing/Art Resource, New York.

Most reform movements—Protestant and Catholic alike—emphasized bodily control and propriety, especially regarding sexuality. This development had strong religious connotations, but it was also part of the larger "civilizing process" that was linked to the differentiation of social class elites.[91] Thus, the churches became places where the newly marked boundaries between sacred and profane were ritually observed with newly distinguished, class-based norms of propriety and gentility. Religious people were those who showed respect for the sacred in church by controlling their bodies and deporting themselves with proper postures, gestures, and other tightly controlled behaviors. Ordinary people's religious practices, regardless of official religious affiliation, were—by definition—not genteel enough. For example, both Protestant and Catholic clergy in rural Ireland struggled well into the nineteenth century to suppress the popular religious practices surrounding wakes, weddings, and "patterns" (patron saint festivals)—not because of theological concerns but because these practices were viewed as licentious, rowdy, and improper.[92]

At the same time, reform movements tried to eliminate or tightly control the richly sensual aspects of religious practice, opposing the popular emphasis on spectacle and visual imagery. Muir argues that the Long Reformation represented, in essence, a revolution in ritual theory: The old ritual had privileged practice, while the new ritual privileged cognition—such as hearing preaching, assenting to creeds, reading and thinking about passages of the Bible. Protestant reformers generally went further than Catholic reformers by starkly eradicating sensual elements, for example, drastically reducing the visual impact of church interiors, presumably to focus attention on the words being pronounced there.[93] The Catholic reformation movements also distrusted much of the sensual appeal of visual displays, mystery plays, religious dances, and paraliturgical processions. Their success in holding on to members in the face of vigorous early Protestant appeals, however, may be partly due to carefully controlled use of sensual elements, such as the lavish baroque decoration of Jesuit churches.[94] Much later—as late as the mid–twentieth century in some places—Catholic authorities, too, discouraged sensual religiosity.

In early modern times, nascent elites contested meanings that the religion of the common people promoted. After Lent won the ritual battle, religion came to be identified with the "higher" or more "spiritual" aspects of human existence. Human material concerns and pleasures, human bodies and extreme emotions came to be defined as not proper to religion or religiosity. There may have been only a relatively brief period (perhaps 100 to 150 years) in Europe and North America when religious organizations and elites were sufficiently influential to shape wider societal ideas about "proper" religious comportment and modes of religious expression. In most of northern Europe and North America, church-promoted norms of bodily and emotional constraint, together with emphasis on church-authorized religious belief and knowledge, appear to have influenced individual religion more widely between the 1850s and the 1950s than any time before or since. If that assessment is correct, it means that our sociological forefathers' vantage point for theorizing religion occurred in the middle of a brief historical blip during which religious institutions had unusual cultural influence. In light of these major historical shifts, we need to rethink the usefulness of sociological concepts that privilege religious belief, attitudes, opinions, and knowledge, while ignoring or marginalizing religious practice—especially its bodily and emotional components.

Contested Meanings: Purity and Authenticity of Religious Traditions and Identities

The period of transition between the late medieval and early modern periods was also a time when boundaries between "us" and "them" were created or fortified. Anthropologist Mary Douglas suggests that societies with particular fear of pollution are those obsessed with a sense of danger from people crossing symbolic boundaries.[95] Late medieval society already had many such pollution fears, as exemplified by many myths of Jewish or Moorish desecration of Christian symbols, but the centuries of reformation movements multiplied the contested boundaries between peoples and increased the sense of fear of pollution. Inquisitions and witch hunts were among the more violent outcomes, justifying their violence as necessary to purify the community of dangerous elements. In Spain, for example, Jews who had converted to Christianity (often out of fear of persecution) were particularly suspect; thus the early stages of the Spanish Inquisition were devoted to delineating a boundary between true and fake converts.[96]

Although there had been efforts to denounce heretical teachings since the early centuries of Christianity, earlier disputes over boundaries had been generally confined to teachers and theologians. Along with the shift to emphasizing belief over practice, church authorities during this early modern period of transition turned the focus of heresy examinations to ordinary church members.[97] It was no longer sufficient that Christians simply engage in certain core religious practices; if they also held unorthodox beliefs, they must not communicate them to others.

Historian Carlo Ginzburg analyzed records of sixteenth- and seventeenth-century Inquisition trials of people involved in syncretic agrarian cults in remote parts of what is now northern Italy.[98] The Inquisition was not much concerned with these peasants' theological errors; rather, it was interested mainly in determining whether their practices constituted instances of witchcraft. Ginzburg's study shows clearly that the definitional boundaries of the idea of witchcraft were constructed and expanded specifically in this period of transition. The idea of witchcraft was a project of an intellectual elite of inquisitors. They justified their power to prosecute witchcraft trials by claiming knowledge that uniquely qualified them to identify who fit the very category— witchcraft—they were defining and decrying as a serious problem. The social construction of strong boundaries around true religion (or true religious power) was itself an exercise in power, exercised not only in the courts but also physically on the bodies of those branded as witches or heretics.

Purity concerns mixed with issues of authenticity. In practice, no religion is uninfluenced by its cultural and historical setting. All religions absorb cultural elements (including religious elements) from their surroundings as they develop over time.[99]

European Christian beliefs and practices historically were no less syncretic than those of colonized indigenous peoples of Mexico, but the Inquisition doubted the authenticity of many Mexicans' beliefs and practices.[100] Many

Protestant movements were even more radical in their attempt to divest their religion of all impurities. Interestingly, most of Europe's witchcraft trials occurred in cultural borderlands or culturally diverse regions, such as the Franco-Spanish Basque area or the lower Rhine.[101] Defending symbolic borders of "authentic" religion was, at the same time, a way of defending permeable cultural borders.

The Place of Power in Boundary Contests

Anthropologist Eric Wolff asserts that structural power—the power to determine the terms of discourse—is a particularly effective and invisible form of power.[102] In all of the aforementioned cultural and political contests of meaning, the winners were those who could set the terms of discourse for the others: the courtly mannered elites defining propriety; leaders of religious sects setting the terms for who would be accepted into their membership as religiously qualified; the inquisitors and religious judges defining orthodoxy (correct belief) and orthopraxy (correct practice); the bishops and higher clergy centralizing their control over practices in the hinterlands; regional religiopolitical powers centralizing their control over previously autonomous towns and city-states, and so on.

Those who eventually lost the definitional battles put up considerable resistance and struggle, but the net outcome was that many of their most valued religious practices no longer counted as religion. Powerful social and cultural groups changed the terms of discourse about religion. They had drawn new definitional boundaries.

Conclusion

If we fail to recognize the contested nature of definitional boundaries, we risk adopting an overly institutional—and historically inaccurate—view of religion. That is, we risk entertaining the mistaken notion that religion is a thing, an entity that exists in the real world with its distinguishing features objectively "given" and not subject to historical or cultural change. Sociology needs to historicize not only its debates about secularization[103] but also its use of core concepts defining religion and religiosity.

How can we understand the changing place of religion in society if our very definitional boundaries have resulted from some of the changes we hope to analyze? Such historically and culturally bound conceptual limits prevent us from adequately understanding *non*-European religious expressions—especially popular religion and other indigenous religious expression not made in the image of modern Euro-American religion. What does awareness of historical contests tell us about contemporary contests over the relevant boundaries of religion"? Are there important differences today, compared with early modern times, in the locus of structural power—especially the power to define the terms of discourse about religion? These are all questions scholars might fruitfully examine.

Focusing on individuals' lived religions today, the next chapters examine some of the ways people still practice, as integral parts of their religion, some of the aspects of religion that, in early modern times, were defined out as no longer properly "religious."

3

Popular Religious Expressions Today

U.S. Latinos and Latinas

Let us examine various aspects of individuals' religions-as-lived today, with an eye to noticing precisely those defined-out elements that have become invisible to researchers. What has been called "popular religion" is a good example of how some important parts of people's religious lives remain invisible.

Rethinking "Popular" Religion

Many scholars use the term "popular religion" to refer to "the people's religion," implying a contrast with some *other* religion: religion arising from commoners in contrast to that formed by the elite,[1] nonofficial religion as opposed to official, church-approved religion, or "vernacular" religion distinguished from "standard" religion.[2] What some scholars have called "popular" religion is, clearly, one manifestation of religion that—due to such definitional distinctions—lost social recognition as real religion. If we are to understand individuals' lived religion, however, we must take "the people's religion" (or "popular religion") seriously.

Because the term "popular religion" is badly tainted by pejorative connotations, some scholars have suggested that the concept be discarded altogether. Robert Orsi has argued that concepts like "popular religion" are "deeply and directly implicated in the history of Western racism and colonialism and in three centuries of divisive, bitter internecine Christian conflict."[3] In the long run, I expect that scholars will find the concept so ambiguous and unhelpful that they will abandon it. One purpose of this book is to encourage scholars to consider abandoning the underlying value-laden and ethnocentric distinctions, not just the term. Like Orsi, I focus on lived religion, because it encompasses all the ways individuals address their deepest concerns and attend to their spiritual lives. Thus it is useful to examine what has been called "popular religion" in order to appreciate how people have selected and used elements of popular religious traditions in practicing their religions in their everyday lives.[4]

Once scholars of religion are open to the possibility that individual religiosity animated by those popular religious traditions might be alive and well today, we may begin to notice instances of vibrant popular religiosity more frequently. Those instances are, however, often very complex and confusing, because they are not part of a coherent package—an identifiable "religion"—and not clearly traditional. We should consider the possibility that the people who practice popular religion might be actively creating new and vital popular religious expressions today, in the context of cosmopolitan cities and globalized communication. If so, their lived religions suggest a far more complicated and important phenomenon than sociologists have generally recognized.

Consider, for example, the religious practices of Laura, the Latina described in chapter 1. When she showed us her home altar and talked about what she had chosen to place on it, she described a rich inner life, built on personally selected images and practices, borrowed eclectically from a wide range of cultural resources. She was raised Catholic and considered herself to be Catholic still, although she seldom attended Mass. At the same time, however, she spoke of nurturing her spiritual life, and she gave priority in her busy day to at least an hour of meditation by her *altarcito*. Her home altar held a complex mixture of traditional items (an heirloom cross, pictures of deceased or distant loved ones, candles, flowers, and an amulet) and nontraditional items (amethyst crystals used in healing meditations, oriental incense and a Tibetan prayer bell, a large colorful triptych of Frida Kahlo, and a contemporary, feminist representation of the Virgin of Guadalupe as a young Chicana).

Laura described practices that produced a comfortable blend of elements of her identity. For example, she respected her mother's more traditional Mexican American religious practices, including popular religious practices such as devotions to *la virgincita*, but she identified with them in a transmuted form. When Laura joined her mother in preparing Christmas *tamales*, she experienced cooking as a valued religious practice. At the same time, however, Laura's own religion was very different from her mother's. She described an ongoing struggle, especially during college and graduate school, to understand and respect her parents' values and ways, while coming to her own position, her own identity. She was an avowed feminist, proud of her Mexican heritage and her bilingual fluency, and was closely linked with her extended family.

She is hardly "religious" by official church or standard sociological criteria. Yet Laura's personal religious practices include many elements of Mexican American popular religious expression: home altar, cross, candles, amulets for healing, picture of the Virgin of Guadalupe, holiday ("holyday") food preparation, and celebration of the Day of the Dead. She did not consider herself "religious," but she clearly devoted considerable time and attention to her regular meditation and other meaningful practices. In order to understand the lived religion of people like Laura, we must take such popular religious expressions seriously and try to understand them in their historical and cultural contexts.

Laura's complex religious practices, however, involved something more than replication of her great-grandparents' rural Mexican culture. Her home altar included symbolic elements (of feminism, for example) that were foreign to her predecessors' traditions. Furthermore, Laura attributed no practical effectiveness to amulets (as her great-grandparents probably did) but rather used them as part of a visualization meditation in which she used imagery of her grandmother's limbs becoming pain-free and cured of arthritis. Her daily meditative practice bears more similarities to some Buddhist religious practices than to the petitions for the intercession of saints characteristic of an older Mexican American popular piety.

The more I learned about the eclecticism and religious blending employed by people like Laura—especially this kind of creative combination of elements from diverse ethnic and religious traditions—the more I wondered about ordinary people's religious expressions historically, particularly in Europe before the Long Reformation. This chapter describes U.S. Latino[5] practices derived, in part, from Iberian Catholic popular religion of that late medieval period. Some unexamined Protestant assumptions have slipped into sociological thought, leading many scholars to exclude predominantly Catholic practices as not "real" religion.[6] So when we think of popular religion, even scholars of religion stereotypically imagine it as like the Latin American practices that have been defined out of our conceptual boundaries.

How Do People Use Cultural Traditions?

Rather than treat popular religion mainly as a nonofficial belief system, it is important to focus on how people actually use popular religious elements in their own religious practices and ways of acting in everyday life. Popular religion is not made up of articulated beliefs comparable to the official creeds or theological beliefs. It lacks any authoritative voice that can establish what is or is not a valid part of the tradition. The tradition is no less than everything that is remembered and celebrated as traditional by anyone to whom some of it is transmitted. People express their relevant beliefs mainly through their own individual and family practices and actions in their day-to-day lives. The early twentieth-century Italian Americans of the Harlem ghetto made a distinction between "religion" and "church"; accordingly, religion was "what really matters" in their lives.[7] Religion, in their usage, included a whole range of beliefs and practices through which the sacred was made present in their everyday lives and by which divine power was brought to bear on their quotidian needs and concerns. Religion might be going on in church, but it might equally be going on in the home or streets.

Today, people's religious practice is often informed by popular religious traditions as well as by church traditions. Indeed, it is likely that many genuinely devout church members do not distinguish among these multiple sources of their religious practices. Rather than treat popular religious elements of people's beliefs and practices as somehow defective, ignorant, or inferior versions of church religiosity, we should take these elements more seriously. And we need to allow for the likelihood that, like Laura, the individuals who use popular religious elements may have creatively adapted, combined, invented, and transformed inherited popular traditions.

"Popular" Religion as "Invisible" Religion

Twentieth- and twenty-first century concepts of religion—both among scholars and in the broader cultures of Europe and the Americas—defined at least five key features of late medieval religious beliefs and practices as not religion. Yet these features can be found in many people's popular religious expressions today:

- *The sacred and the profane.* What is people's sense of the place of the sacred relative to the profane world of everyday life? Do people today experience the realm of the sacred as penetrating that of the profane? Do they experience divine power and other manifestations of the sacred as part of everyday space and time?
- *Tapping divine power.* Experiencing the sacred within the profane realm, do people have a heightened sense of access to divine power, as well as a concern about awesome or fearsome aspects of that power?
- *Ambivalence of popular tradition.* Are popular rituals today part of an informal system of social control, ritually degrading (and sometimes,

physically hurting) anyone who violates unspoken community norms?[8]
Popular religious practices can promote both positive and negative
social values—encouraging the community to practice both cooperation and mutual support on the one hand and animosity and violence on the other.

- *Addressing material concerns.* How do people's religious practices address
  their material concerns, such as health, prosperity, and security?
- *Spirituality and materiality.* How do people's religious practices involve their bodies and emotions directly in spiritual experiences?
  Does their religion-as-lived link their materiality with their spirituality, with little or no sense of opposition or dualism between the body
  and mind/spirit?

Let us examine these five features as they are found in the religious lives of
many people today—specifically, in the lived religions of U.S. Latinos and
Latinas and of U.S. southern white evangelicals.

Sociologists would readily recognize some of these contemporary practices
as "religious," while many others do not fit standard definitions of religion. In
some cases (e.g. Laura, the feminist Latina) sociologists might fail to notice the
part of a person's religious life that is drawn from popular traditions. In other
cases (e.g. Ron, the evangelical Christian described in chapter 1) sociologists
might count the popular traditional practices as evidence of church-oriented
religiosity. Both would result in misinterpretation. We would understand all
people's lived religion better if we simply allowed that individuals can and do
draw on both popular and official religious traditions, as possible resources for
elements of their personal practice. In order to comprehend what Luckmann
called "invisible religion"(see note 21 of chapter 1), sociologists need to make
visible the parts of people's lived religions that our definitions made invisible.

Popular Religious Practices Today: U.S. Latinas and Latinos

Moving to San Antonio, Texas, opened my eyes to Latina popular religious
expressions, because in Texas they are very vivid and alive. I had just finished
my study of nonmedical healing, investigating a population of middle- and
upper-middle-class suburbanites in northern New Jersey, so I was fascinated by
the highly developed and relatively widespread practice of *curanderismo* (a
Mexican American form of nonmedical healing) in south Texas. I discovered
that the popular saints who aided in healing also had a wide contemporary
following among the middle classes, as well as the working class and the poor.

Some locally revered saints were church-approved (e.g., St. Anthony, St. Jude, and Nuestra Señora de San Juan de los Lagos), while others were folk saints (e.g., Dom Pedrito Jaramillo and Niño Fidencia) and not recognized by the Roman Catholic Church.[9] The place of Latino popular religious expression in this multiethnic and religiously heterogeneous city is complex, however, because people use popular religious elements for a wide range of purposes, not all of which are for their personal religious or spiritual practice. The complexity—as well as the vitality—of Latina popular religious practices makes them an ideal illustration for my analysis.

The Sacred and the Profane: Pilgrimage, Performance, and Promises

Many Latinos engage in concrete religious practices that can enable them to experience a sense of the sacred in the domestic sphere and their neighborhood communities. Today, as in medieval times, much popular religious practice is devoted to getting in touch with sacred power and somehow tapping it for one's needs. Pilgrimages, processions, and performances are among the most important popular religious traditions by which U.S. Latinas gain access to sacred space and divine powers. Because such public practices blur the boundaries between sacred and profane, they also challenge the boundaries between religious and political ritual. For example, a funeral or Day of the Dead procession may simultaneously express dissent against a repressive government or a corrupt police force.[10]

Popular religious performances are sometimes done in the context of processions and pilgrimages.[11] For example, Holy Week processions in many parts of the world enact aspects of Jesus' last week before death. Various Latin American cultural traditions have had Holy Week pageants depicting the crucifixion of Jesus. These performances were based on elaborate medieval Iberian popular religious penitential practices, some of which (such as self-flagellation and dragging heavy crosses through the streets) were bloody and painful.[12] The medieval and early modern performances and penitential religious practices were often the occasion of intense emotional experience and learned spiritual practices such as public weeping.[13] Like their more drastic medieval antecedents, today's popular religious performances can evoke powerful religious experiences and emotions in individuals who are culturally primed for them.

Like pilgrimages, the Holy Week processions and performances are often undertaken in fulfillment of a vow or *promesa* (promise), which itself is part of how ordinary people believe they can tap divine power for their needs. As in medieval religious practices, sometimes a whole community enters into this kind of reciprocal obligation with its patron saint, for example promising to inaugurate a special honoring event if the saint will intercede to end a drought. More common is the personal *promesa*. For example, a woman might promise that, if her child is healed of his serious illness, she will participate in the Holy Week procession each year for the next five years. Or a man might promise that if he can only get a good job, he will cosponsor the performance of the pageant in the following year.[14]

One such popular religious event extant today is the Christmas-season performance of *Los Pastores*, a drama that has been performed in the in backyards and homes of the Mexican barrios of San Antonio, Texas, since 1913.[15] The play and its participants make no distinction between the religious aspects of the celebration (such as prayers at the temporary altar constructed in a carport or yard) and its profane elements (such as the drinking and joking that accompany it).[16] Both the performers and the sponsors explain that they do it all "para el Niño Dios"—"for the Christ-child."[17]

It is precisely because "el Niño Dios" is experienced in the context of the profane—a neighbor's yard, where only last week the neighborhood teenagers were fixing their low-rider cars—that this popular religious drama can speak profoundly to people's lives. The play itself blends elements of the profane— such as bawdy humor provoked by some of the devil's assistants, or comical representations of an old shepherd's lecherousness—with a deeply reverent evocation of the sacred, particularly the experience of being in the presence of the Christ-child.[18]

Anthropologist Richard Flores argues that this entire devotional ritual performance, its fulfillment of *promesas* and its surrounding festivities, especially the meal, constitutes—not merely reflects—bonds of community. The whole event involves a complex process of gifting and reciprocity, based on reciprocal obligations between humans and a divine figure. The performers enact *Los Pastores* in barrio homes as a gift, charging no fees. The reciprocal obligation of the sponsor-recipients of this gift is the physical effort, time, and money necessary to provide the setup of the place of performance, an appropriate home altar for it, and a meal with plenty of food and drink for the people who perform and attend.[19]

Flores reminds us that, particularly for ritual performances, such gifts must be reciprocated to be efficacious.[20] For the people doing this work, it is a labor of gratitude and of reciprocity that creates bonds, not only among the sponsors, performers, and audience but also between the human community and the sacred, manifest as *el Niño Dios*.[21] The entire event consists of popular religious practices that, taken together, accomplish the experience of the sacred within the profane: They make the blessings of *el Niño Dios* evident to the humble twenty-first-century barrio "shepherds," gathered on plastic-webbed lawn chairs around a beautifully decorated altar constructed in a rickety carport.

Tapping Divine Power: Domestic Shrines and Women's Domestic Ritual Practices

To many Latinos, just as the sacred is ubiquitous, so, too, is divine power accessible to ordinary people in their everyday lives. One has only to know how to tap it.

For instance, many women maintain *altarcitos* and shrines in their homes and gardens, using them for prayer or remembrance, often several times a day.[22] In one house I visited some small religious memento was exhibited in every room, including the bathroom, halls, two porches, and front yard. There was, for example, a plastic statue of St. Jude on the washing machine and a refrigerator magnet with a prayer and picture of Santo Niño de Atocha. The woman who arranged them all used them regularly to focus her many everyday prayers and felt that each object brought something of the sacred into its room. She and her daughter showed enormous reverence for their home altar, set up in the corner of L-shaped living-dining room. Although the woman attended church regularly, she said was better able to pray in the sacred space that she had arranged at home.

Constructing the home altar involves considerable creative expression, as each woman chooses objects for her *altar* that may seem disparate and idio-syncratic to the outside observer. She arranges them in meaningful relation-ships to each other, changing her selection and placement of items according to her and her family's needs. For example, a woman whose son's National Guard unit was to be sent to the war zone in Iraq moved his photo, together with a card depicting Nuestra Señora de San Juan de los Lagos (a manifestation of Mary considered especially helpful in providing solace), to the center of her altar.

More important than the symbolic representation of these values, however, are the spiritual practices in which women engage in the context of these home altars and shrines. Touching objects, lighting candles, and gazing on pictures or statues are all routine practices that link their domestic sacred space with the concerns of everyday life. Laura, for example, used a *milagro* amulet-image of a leg, attached to her grandmother's photo on her home *altar*, as part of her personal ritual-healing meditation. For her, this practice was not merely a rep-resentation of her nurturance of her grandmother; rather, it accomplished their ongoing relationship and promoted healing. Such arrangement of images on the home altar constructs associations among the objects selected, synthesizing spiritual values, relationships, and sacralized space.[23]

Often, Mexican American women's popular devotional practices, in the home as well as in church, reflect a sense of a personal connection with the saints, especially the Virgin of Guadalupe. This kind of relationship with an approachable and understanding yet very powerful, sacred figure allows women to feel directly in touch with divine power that can affect their lives in ways that really matter. Practices like evoking the sacral presence of the Virgin at the home altar, garden shrine, or other familiar space are an important part of the experience. Women also regularly converse with Our Lady of Guadalupe to gain comfort, help, relief, and peace. When asked what kinds of things she talked about with Our Lady of Guadalupe, one twenty-four-year old Latina said, "About my day. About my little girl. About my husband. About my family. Mainly just about family, close family and friends." Another woman explained, "She brings me comfort, sometimes because, ever since I had my children I feel she knows what I mean. She knows how I feel and I can talk to her woman to woman, mother to mother."[24]

This kind of ongoing conversation and sense of sacral presence in the kitchen or living room would be invisible to much sociological research. For instance, if an interviewer asked these women "How often do you pray?" they might answer "About once a day," thinking of praying as saying a specific prayer, such as the Rosary. They do not necessarily think of these frequent practices at the home altar or their regular conversations with the Virgin as prayer. Yet clearly these women are engaging in practices for communicating with and trying to tap divine power to touch their everyday lives.[25]

Ambivalence of Popular Tradition: Patriarchal Family Relations

It is also important to avoid romanticizing popular religious practice and faith. The web of family- and community-based expectations that produces and reproduces popular traditions has negative features as well. Religious traditions—both official and popular—are inherently ambivalent. The same cultural resources can be used for domination, inequality, and violence as well as cooperation, harmony, and mutual respect. The same traditions can inspire authoritarian oppression, war, and abusive personal relationships as well as liberation, peace, and genuine caring relationships. Historically, popular religious movements have spurred religious intolerance, racist violence, and misogyny, as much as (indeed, often more than) official religious institutions in the same society. In popular religion, no authoritative voice exists that can establish what is the correct version of a popular tradition. As a result, the same popular tradition can serve to promote widely varying, even opposing social values.[26]

In the United States today, some of the most harmful community-based expectations that are promoted informally through Mexican American popular religiosity are related to women's roles. Traditional popular practices were based on a patriarchal family structure, in which the male head of the household made important decisions for all other members of the family. Thus, for example, the community traditionally expected a father to pay for an elaborate *quinceañera* (literally, "fifteenth birthday," a coming-of-age celebration) for each daughter to promote her marriageability. This celebration, as well as other ritual parts of the courtship and marriage process, served as a major socioeconomic link between his extended family and certain other community families. All the guests were expected to reciprocate with expensive parties for their daughters. And the daughters were obliged to allow their fathers to control the selection of their male company and, eventually, marriage partner. Today, in the context of the larger U.S. society's confusing and changing family norms, many Mexican Americans feel the tensions between on the one hand patriarchal privileges and financially burdensome traditional expectations and on the other hand the younger generation's demands for greater self-determination in marriage and career, as well as financial support for them to pursue educational, rather than marriage, opportunities.

Both popular religious traditions and official Catholic beliefs and practices historically have supported patriarchal family and community structures of authority.[27] Mexican American women have been particularly vulnerable to abuse, exploitation, and physical violence at the hands of men exercising this culturally sanctioned privilege and power.

Popular religious practices are, however, ambivalent or multivalent. They have no single, fixed meaning or value but can be evoked for dissent and liberation, as well as to support the status quo privilege of those in power. For example, some Mexican American women ask the Virgin of Guadalupe to help them endure the suffering caused by their alcoholic and abusive husbands, while other women find her a source of empowerment to remove themselves and their children from the violent home. Some young mothers contemplate an image of a delicate, fair-skinned Virgin demurely beaming on the Christ-child; others relate to an image of the Virgin as a strong, energetic, brown-skinned young woman who has the strength to assert herself. Thus, while Mexican American popular religious tradition has legitimated male dominance and even violence toward women, some women use the same tradition as a source of not only comfort and hope but, indeed, empowerment and strength to change women's situation—in the family, in the Mexican American community, and in the larger society.[28]

Addressing Material Concerns: Milagros!

Milagros means "miracles," and these are one of the expected outcomes of popular religious practices. People regularly call on sacred power to protect them, to provide for their well-being and health, to reverse their bad fortunes and defend them from adversaries. In Mexican American popular religious expressions, the word *milagros* also refers to small objects—typically (roughly 2 centimeters tall) metal depictions of parts of the body or of whole bodies of men, women, children, or valuable farm animals. A common usage is to attach the image of that which needs healing or help on or near an image representing a source of divine help, for example, a statue of a saint identified with that kind of miracle. Other popular rituals often accompany this action, such as saying specific prayers and lighting votive candles.

In many respects, these two meanings of the word *milagros* should be understood together. In contrast to much official religion, popular religious practices address people's material concerns and use material objects (including the human body itself) to channel divine power to where it is needed in people's everyday lives. Both meanings of the word *milagro* refer to an aspect of religion that, according to classical social theorist Max Weber, modern ways of thinking and acting have largely displaced, resulting in the "disenchantment of the world."[29] During the Long Reformation, both Catholic and Protestant reformers attempted to purify religion and refocus its rituals away from the (presumably baser) material concerns and toward spiritual concerns. Thus, the religious practices people had previously used to address their own and their community's everyday material concerns were defined as marginal and inferior at best or as completely out of bounds, sinful, and punishable at worst.

How, then, do people deal with these material concerns? The world is still a fearsome place. People's families still need real help to have enough food, decent shelter, good health, and safety from dangers. Their bodies still experience pain, hunger, deformity, childbirth and miscarriages, aging and death. Popular religious expressions that blur the sacred-profane dichotomy tend also to blur the spiritual-material dichotomy. From that perspective, it makes sense for people to try to bring those very real material concerns to the attention of their god and to bring divine power to bear on important material conditions of their lives.

Educated elites tend to think that the popular religious perspective is incompatible with rational, scientific ways of thinking. For instance, they assume that no one who understands that diseases are caused by germs and viruses could believe that religious rituals produce healing of those diseases. By contrast, educated Mexican Americans who consult a *curandera* or seek healing through prayer may see no such incompatibility. They are likely to use the assistance of both modern medicine and sacred power (as mediated by a saint, a *curandera*, a prayer group, or a holy shrine). Why? Because they work. In these people's experience, both the medical and the religious approaches are effective some of the time, while neither approach always produces the desired results. Furthermore, both approaches make sense in that they give people ways of thinking about causes of illness or pain. Both medical and religious approaches offer an important kind of effectiveness (especially in the face of fearsome material concerns like serious illness)—simply helping people understand their situation.[30]

Like the medieval villagers who stopped performing devotions for saints whose requested intercession was not effective, today Mexican Americans who use popular religious practices have a pragmatic approach. One woman in her thirties, a second-generation Mexican American, suggested that I seek St. Jude's help in selling my house: "Simply, try it. Praying to St. Jude can't hurt. And he's often helped me, so it's worth a try. But if it doesn't work, try something else." The example she gave of how the saint helped her illustrated that prayer should be used in addition to exerting oneself to accomplish one's goal: It took her three tries to get her high school equivalency diploma. Each time she had taken preparation classes, but only on the third try had she made a special trip to the shrine in town, lit candles, said specific prayers, and made *promesas*. One of these *promesas* was to tell others of St. Jude's effectiveness, so she was fulfilling her promise, in part, by advising me to seek his help. Her detailed instructions illustrate another feature common in popular religious practice: Success requires praying correctly. One must use the correct way to tap divine power.

Spirituality and Materiality

Mexican American popular practices employ people's bodies and bodily senses, postures, and gestures to evoke spiritual meanings and experiences. The home altars, performances, and popular rituals are rich with visual imagery, vibrant colors and lights, scents, sounds, and sensations. There is no dualistic distinction between aspects that are "purely" spiritual and those that are "merely" material.[31] For example, when a family hosts a performance of *Los Pastores*, the preparation of the *altar* is not considered "more spiritual" than the preparation of the meal. Rather, the material (especially the bodily) aspects of popular religious practice are important parts of how the larger religious experience is produced.

Because of their many connections between people's spirituality and their bodies and emotions, popular religious traditions address women's lives and concerns more amply than most official religious traditions do. For example, popular religious practices valorize women's roles as the growers, preparers, and servers of food. Ana María Díaz-Stevens, reflecting on her mother's Puerto Rican popular religious practices, notes the importance in women's spirituality of the home as a sacred-yet-profane site:

> it is precisely in the home before a make-shift altar where this trans-
> formation most often takes place. It is there, in the kitchen, where
> the women of the household and other women from the extended
> family and community, often gather and, over a cup of *café con leche*,
> reminisce about the past, give each other counsel and consolation,
> discuss the events of the community, and plan for family and com-
> munity celebrations which most often are also religious celebrations.[32]

Other popular religious practices address women's concerns about reproduction, for example fertility, pregnancy, childbirth, and maternity. Thus, women are frequently respected religious specialists in Latino popular traditional practices: *rezadoras* (prayer-leaders) for such events as domestic novenas; *curanderas* (healers) for physical, emotional, and spiritual illnesses; *parteras* (midwives) with responsibility for the spiritual, as well as physical, care of the mother and her newborn.[33] When official religions redefined the practice of religion to exclude or devalue involvement of people's bodies and emotions, treating them as distracting or even polluting, then women—considered more contaminated by and trapped in their bodies than men—lost recognition for their religious practices.

We can better comprehend some of the uses of material objects in Mexican American popular religious practices if we try to think about these practices without assuming a dualistic separation between the realm of human bodies and other material objects on the one hand and the spiritual realm on the other. People use objects and their own bodies in popular religious practices that celebrate and remember the sacred-within-the-profane. For instance, one widespread practice is the creation and maintenance of small roadside shrines at the site of lethal car accidents. In many parts of the United States, such shrines are made by Anglos, as well as Latinos, but the practice of making *descansos* (which means literally "resting places") to commemorate such tragic deaths is particularly elaborate in Mexican American communities. The material objects of the shrine include the site itself, crosses and rocks to mark the site of the deaths, often pictures of the deceased, their names, the dates of their deaths, other religious figures, rosaries, candles, flowers, and other objects associated with the lost loved ones. Family and friends engage in ongoing practices at these *descansos*, as at a home altar only less frequently, refreshing the flowers and candles, adding seasonal mementos, and saying prayers. Often, strangers who pass by the shrine also add a prayer, "Que descansen en paz" (may they rest in peace).

The blending of the material and the spiritual is also evident in the practices surrounding the Day of the Dead. In San Antonio, the Mexican American popular celebration of El Día de los Muertos (Day of the Dead, or All Souls' Day, as it was known in the liturgical calendar) was revived in the 1970s, with the encouragement of a Mexican American theologian who was then rector of the cathedral.[34] This popular religious event now occurs with episcopal approval in San Fernando Cathedral's cemetery, as well as in markets, shops, schools, and homes throughout the community. Home and workplace altars called *ofrendas* (because they are offered as a gift in memory of a person or group) serve to commemorate the dead of a family, association, or work group, with photos and memorabilia, along with holiday bread and sugar decorations in the shape of skulls, as well as objects or foods the honored persons valued. Other popular practices include cleaning and decorating family members' graves. Family members sometimes lay out a celebratory feast for the commemorated dead— their favorite foods, drinks, and smokes, assembled at the grave or home *ofrenda*, with other decorations, to make the honored ones feel welcome. On the night of the feast, the family keeps vigil with its dead, conversing, remembering, reconciling, and updating them on what has happened to their family and friends since the last visit. For this night, the dead are surrounded by the people and things they loved in life.[35]

This popular religious celebration is not merely kept alive but appears to be growing in both scope and appeal to diverse people, including university students and professionals, as well as Protestants and persons of non-Latino ethnic backgrounds, in part because it is better than other available options at supporting families dealing with death—remembering, grieving, and connecting with loved ones who have passed. For example, a Mexican American librarian at my university told me she was reading a book on El Día de los Muertos because she wanted to begin to celebrate it in her home, even though they were Protestant and her pastor would be upset if he knew. She thought it would be good for her children to have a way to think about death and their dead grandparents and aunt that was more wholesome and joyous than Anglo Protestant traditions allowed.

In San Antonio's Southtown art galleries, Anglo and Latino artists alike prepare elaborate exhibition altars for the Day of the Dead. This practice, which

FIGURE 3.I. This South Texas roadside shrine, or *descanso* (resting place), is a popular religious way of honoring the spirits of several young persons who died in a car accident at that site, now treated with the same reverence as the *campo santo* (holy ground, cemetery). Courtesy Jim Spickard, used by permission of Toroverde Press.

obviously began as an aesthetic and commercial practice far more than a "religious," "spiritual," or even "ethnic" practice, has evolved into an ongoing tradition with some genuine spiritual appeal.[36] In the 1990s, many artists used their *altares* as something of a parallel to the AIDS quilt, commemorating the members of their community who had died of AIDS. Interestingly, gallery visitors often responded to these *ofrendas* with considerable reverence and respect, while some artists themselves developed "spiritual" practices at the altars to remember their dead.

Another practice in San Antonio, built on the popular religious practice of festive processions for the Day of the Dead, drew participants from many different ethnic and religious groups to make a political statement about people who had died as a result of injustice. Processions protested, for example, unjust deaths caused by repressive regimes' human rights abuses in Latin America. These contemporary practices surrounding the Day of the Dead offer just a glimpse of the creative and expressive uses of popular religious elements in ways that are linked with traditions but are something more than a reenactment of traditional practices. They also illustrate why it would be a mistake to interpret the vitality of these contemporary popular religious practices as relating to only Mexican American ethnic identity, or popular Catholicism, or popular psychology.

These examples illustrate how popular religious expression can adapt and seamlessly incorporate seemingly strange blends of cultural building blocks. If the Day of the Dead were merely a faithful replication of eighteenth- and nineteenth-century Mexican traditions, then today's altars could not offer the dead their favorite Texas barbeque, Big Red soft drinks, U.S. army insignia, or TV remote controls, and the living could not use their Day of the Dead altars to come to terms with the effects of AIDS, the war in Iraq, and urban street violence. Such creative and emotionally expressive adaptations of popular religious traditions like the Day of the Dead sustain their vitality and relevance.

Beyond "Popular Religion": Memory, Creativity, and Imagination

It would be a mistake to try to comprehend these expressions of "popular religion"—Mexican American traditional practices—as a unitary phenomenon. While popular religious traditions have some historical coherence, individuals draw on them selectively and creatively. A traditional religious practice may be especially appealing because it is familiar and culturally comfortable. Traditions may be remembered differently by those who use them, however, such that historically different regions, social classes, and other sectors of society selectively remember different practices as a common tradition. Even less than organized religions' traditions, popular religious traditions are hardly fixed or deterministic. People can create new popular practices, adapt old ones, and ignore those traditions that are not meaningful or useful in their lives.

These examples of contemporary U.S. Latina popular religious practices suggest that we need to rethink our conceptions of how individuals relate to their cultural traditions and religious worldviews. Since Max Weber's foundational essays on modes of social action, sociologists have considered traditional action to be the habitual and overdetermined replication of received patterns of behavior. But each of these examples suggests that people can, individually or collectively, select and creatively adapt even highly traditional practices. In all these examples—even the most commercialized—ordinary people creatively selected elements from their personal and family histories, their (often multiple) ethnic and religious heritages, and their larger cultural and historical context to assemble a meaningful ritual practice.

To go further, beyond simply recognizing popular practices and expressions as "religion," we must learn more about how people use popular religious practices in their everyday lives. Do some consciously select and blend elements (like Laura), while others perceive their practices to be entirely handed down from their elders and merely replicated? How are popular traditions remembered and transmitted, and what aspects of those social processes of transmission and memory affect how some popular traditions change, develop, or endure, while others become static, irrelevant, or forgotten? Is the transmission of elements of popular religious traditions qualitatively different from that of church-oriented, official-religious traditions or ethnic or national traditions? When popular religious expressions are transformed, what related social forces help us to understand or explain the sources of such creativity and change? Does it make any difference if people are generally operating in social contexts that are characterized by considerable travel across cultural borders, by mass media portraying persons of widely varying cultural backgrounds, and by increasingly common interethnic and interreligious friendships, including marriage and family relationships?

Furthermore, we need to learn more about how people decide which practices to use and when. For instance, if a baby is sick, which cultural resources do people employ, combine, use in private, use serially, and so on? Do both the parents pray? Separately or together? Privately, at home, at a shrine, or at a chapel? Do they go to Mass to pray for the sick baby or use a nonliturgical setting for prayer? Which saints' help do they seek—popular saints, as well as church-approved ones? Do they take the child to a sacred place or pilgrimage site? Do the parents seek the help of a *curandera*, a faith-healing evangelist, or some other religious source of help? Do they take the child to a medical doctor or hospital? Do they ask family and friends to pray, have a votive Mass said on behalf of the child, or make *promesas* for future devotions in return for healing? Which of these and other practices do they choose for this child and this illness episode? When do they select and combine healing practices? Do they use certain practices first, and then try others? If the illness is serious, do they try all the healing practices simultaneously? Just as with the need for healing, people often have informal "rules of thumb" for determining when they need a certain type of religious help and not another.

Do elements of people's popular traditions help them with difficult aspects of contemporary life? For instance, popular religious traditions inform many people today that there is no clear boundary between the sacred and the profane. In their experience, churches and other religious organizations have no monopoly on the sacred. Rather, they find the sacred manifest within their profane landscapes, including cityscapes. A few years ago in San Antonio, many people were inspired by the discovery of an image of the head of Jesus in the pattern of a tree's bark—resembling, according to some viewers, the image from a 1940s painting familiar to most Americans. Yes, it was an ordinary tree on an ordinary residential street, but it was also special and revelatory of the divine.

Much of the landscape nowadays, however, is not natural. Popular religious practices sometimes must be adapted to fit the humanly built landscape. Two members of a Latina women's group told, with considerable self-deprecating humor, the story of a time when they burned some traditional herbs and incense at a ritual celebration in a hotel seminar room, only to trigger the sprinkler system and fire alarms. They have subsequently adapted the ritual for such public buildings, using water for purification instead of smoke and an amethyst crystal—even less traditional—in place of copal incense.[37] The humanly built landscape offers, at the same time, new opportunities for manifestation of the sacred, such as people's perception of an image of the Virgin in the glass of a skyscraper.[38]

Unlike medieval villagers, most Americans do not share their ancestors' physical landscapes. Only a few Native American peoples live close to the sacred sites of their religious traditions. And even those Americans who work in agriculture do not enjoy the agrarian rhythms of seasonal changes that can be ritually celebrated as sacred time within the profane time of farmwork. The image of the devout peasant pausing during spring plowing to pray as the Angelus rings hardly describes the work rhythm of today's migrant farmworkers, after-hours janitorial workers, telemarketers, or construction day laborers! The structure of work and time as well as the arrangement of space and the built landscape, do not support the exact replication of popular religious traditional practices. As an economically disadvantaged minority group, most Latino workers lack the power to change their working conditions. It would, however, be worthwhile to gather much more data exploring whether and how people use their popular religious traditions to reframe (and perhaps renew) their quotidian arrangements of work and time, natural and built landscapes, as well as personal and public time, in the context of a high-tech, economically and socially constrained society.

Popular religious expression still serves as a medium for expressing dissent from the larger society or resistance to an oppressive power, and popular culture can still express counterculture. In medieval times, popular religious rituals often involved mockery or subversion of the powerful.[39] In the modern era—especially in the context of colonialism—popular religious celebrations could be used to express resistance to oppressive power, with which official religious organizations were characteristically allied.[40] In some popular religious rituals, the official order is temporarily inverted or mocked; in some popular religious celebrations, wealth is (somewhat) redistributed; and in some, nonpowerful persons can temporarily refuse to cooperate with the work or other social demands of their bosses, husbands, village rulers, and so on.[41]

This function of popular religious expression deserves further research, because it can help us understand how tradition can be a product of considerable creativity and subjective expression, rather than merely habit and passive replication. The use of popular religious practices for dissent and resistance also sheds some light on social activists' religious lives. For example, Mexican American popular religious practices figured prominently in César Chávez's organization and mobilization of the United Farm Workers union movement. These uses of popular religious tradition appear to have been not just instrumental tactics for motivating followers but also inextricably interwoven with the vision of nonviolent activism for social justice that was at the core of Chávez's personal spiritual practices.[42]

Are there identifiable religious practices that promote religious—including popular religious—dissent and activism for social change? Consider, for example, people like Peter (the social activist described in chapter 1), who thought of his considerable efforts for peace and social justice as being at the core of his religion. From his descriptions of his interactions with others and his self-reflective choices about time, work, and family, we get some inkling that his personal religious life was qualitatively different from that of individuals who are not committed to activism for peace and justice. Are there patterns of individual religious belief and practice that are peculiar to or markedly stronger among persons for whom social activism and dissent from the prevailing political-social regime is core to their religion? When social dissenters draw on elements of some popular religious tradition(s) for their own personal religious belief and practice, do they relate to their traditional practices differently than do people who do not dissent from but rather embrace the prevailing political-social regime? Sociologists have paid some attention to these religious movements for social change and dissent, but we have only begun to examine the activists' religious lives.[43]

When I began research for this book, I thought that educated people like Laura were vastly different from "the people" who practiced popular religion. In 1996, a few years into the project, I described her and others I had interviewed as engaging in bricolage,[44] the practice of eclectically choosing the elements of their religious belief and practice, loosely mortaring them together.[45] But it remains an empirical question whether the eclecticism of much contemporary religion-as-lived is, indeed, so very different from people's practices in other times and cultural settings.

The main reason this historical question is important for sociologists is that we have tended to view popular religious practices—especially those of peasants, uneducated immigrants, and premodern times—as highly tradition-bound, passively replicated and transmitted, and not at all autonomously chosen. But what if traditional actions, such as popular religious practice, are informed *also* by individual and/or collective eclecticism and bricolage?

My impression, now, is that the long period of boundary contestation, described in the preceding chapter, resulted only in the more precise articulation and promulgation of official, church-defined traditions (that varied in content, of course, widely among the resulting church groups). The Long Reformation did not, however, prevent individuals, families, guilds, fraternal groups, villages, and other collectivities from continuing to select, to combine creatively, and to adapt practices from popular traditions as well as their church's official tradition. It did not preclude people's amalgamation of religious practices from several popular traditions, especially in the face of grave disruptions to their lives caused by colonization, slavery, frontier living, exile, urbanization, and globalization. Perhaps sociology of religion has underestimated the degree of active creativity exercised by persons whose actions are based on tradition.

A richer appreciation of popular religious expressions shows us one of the ways people continue to address important religious concerns through beliefs and practices that were no longer accepted as properly religious by powerful religious institutions in their society. The creative and adaptive quality of many people's popular religious expressions has prevented some of those traditions from becoming mere vestiges of rural, old-country, old-fashioned folkways.

Thus, today, elements from popular religious traditions are among the important resources from which people construct their lived religions. Many people—including educated, thoroughly acculturated, middle-class persons in modern cities—draw on popular traditions for their own lived religions. In order to understand the place of religion and spirituality in people's lives today, we must be open to all the ways this may happen.

A few years ago, I gave a short talk about local religious healing practices to my classmates in an advanced Spanish course at the San Antonio branch of the Universidad Nacional Autónoma de México. Among Mexican Americans all over the United States, probably the most popular healing folk saint is Don Pedrito Jaramillo, who lived and is buried perhaps ninety minutes' drive south of San Antonio. I showed my classmates pictures of the shrine and the hundreds of notes, letters, pictures, *milagros,* and other mementos of thanks or petition affixed there. I read several of the notes (most in Spanish) that were attached: "Thanks for your help in getting my truck driver's license" (a photocopy was attached). "Today is my baby's first birthday. Without your prayers, she wouldn't be alive for this photo" (photograph and *milagro* were attached). "For help to protect me from jail." "A thousand thanks for getting our eviction stopped, but we still need help to keep our home. Please, pray for us."

One classmate snickered softly as I read these. Later, during our break, another classmate—a quiet, college-educated homemaker and mother of two—asked her "What was so funny about those notes to Don Pedrito?" She replied that she thought it was childish and quaint for anyone to think that some saint was responsible for obtaining a truck drivers' license or an apartment. The other woman said:

I know it's hard for you, being from your [well-known wealthy neighborhood] background. But try to imagine how you'd feel if you were a poor guy from a scruffy little south Texas town, unable to get work without some kind of credentials like that license, but completely unable to understand how the system works. Even after you'd done everything humanly possible to prepare for that test, wouldn't you want the saint's help if you thought it just might make the difference?

After a pause, she added:

My Mama used to take my little brother to that same shrine, because he was so sickly and small. If she were alive to see him today, she'd make another trip down to add her note of personal thanks, because he's a fine, big man now. So, even though I didn't understand then why she kept on asking Don Pedrito for his help and blessings, now I wouldn't ever laugh.[46]

Likewise, we scholarly researchers of religion should not be dismissive of people's religious expressions of their very real material concerns. By over-emphasizing official religious belief, teachings, and organizational member-ship, sociologists and other researchers have simply failed to notice that many people engage, outside or alongside those religious organizations, in valued spiritual practices that address their material concerns and deeply felt emo-tional needs. Popular religious practices are clearly one important way people have, historically as well as today, sought to express those important concerns and address those important needs. I suggest, however, that popular religious traditions, such as those of Mexican Americans, are now only a small portion of the many cultural resources from which individuals of any ethnic or national background can draw.

In order to understand individuals' lived religions, we need to make visible all of the aspects of their religious lives that have been made invisible by the social construction of religion in Western societies. Then, we can begin to see the complex and creative ways many people practice their religion. We must also, however, go well beyond the concept of popular religion in order to com-prehend the many cultural resources—including religious resources put forward by official religious leaders and traditions—that people today may selectively draw on, remember, celebrate, transform, distill, amalgamate, and share.

4

Popular Religions in Practice Today

Southern White Evangelicals

When we take popular religious expressions seriously, we begin to realize the complexity of each individual's religion-as-practiced. Many people use not only official religious traditions but also popular traditions and other unapproved sources of religious beliefs and practices—in combinations or separately, overlapping in layers, serially or simultaneously, hybridized and sometimes completely transformed. It is not only the uneducated, the poor, the immigrants, or socially marginal persons who engage in such combinations of popular religious practices. Indeed, many popular religious elements are now embedded in the routine religious practices and beliefs of many educated, socially stable, economically well-off churchgoers. The fact is that such religious eclecticism and combination typifies nearly every sector of the religious population. It is even true for southern white evangelicals—whom the media and scholars typically imagine as the most committed of churchgoers and most conservative in their "old-time" religious traditions. Their use of popular religious elements, along with official church practices, shows many similarities with the popular religious practices of U.S. Latinos.

Contemporary southern white evangelicals' religious practices derive, in part, from popular religious traditions that developed among early American Protestants. It is far more difficult for scholars to comprehend the extent of popular religiosity among Protestants, because—especially in the United States—many religious organizations (i.e., those recognized as churches) have deeply embedded popular religious traditions. Sociologist Stephen Sharot, using the conceptual distinction of elite-versus-popular religion, argues that "religious organizations have churched America by popularizing religion."[1] The historical successes of many Protestant churches in the United States—especially the considerable growth of church membership in the nineteenth century—were, in large part, due to the amalgamation of popular religious practices and church religious practices. If popular religiosity is coextensive with church religiosity among many American Protestants, that is another good reason to rethink our scholarly definitional boundaries.

Protestant Popular Religious Traditions in the American South

Although moving to San Antonio occasioned my first experiences with most Mexican American popular religious beliefs and practices, many of the Protestant popular religious expressions I encountered there already seemed familiar. My own upbringing on a farm in southern Indiana included a strange combination of mainline Protestant (especially Presbyterian) and Philadelphia-style Quaker influences, in the context of the then vigorous ecumenical movement. My father's family was from old Kentucky and North Carolina rural stock, and he had been raised in southern evangelical churches that had become established in Indiana and other midwestern areas after nineteenth century migrations to better farmlands. However, while attending Purdue University in the 1940s, my father had decided to "become more open-minded." As children, when we visited our father's folks, we would attend church with them. When I asked Dad what denomination that was, he said "It's the Christian church." So I was further confused—were not all the denominations we knew of Christian? Most summer weekends throughout my elementary school years, when we were at our fishing camp at Kentucky Lake, Dad and we older kids also attended Sunday school at a tiny local Baptist church, where I got lots of praise for having memorized many Bible verses but never won the Sunday school prize for reciting the most.

In the small city near our farm, my mother's parents were leaders in the most staid, socially elite Presbyterian congregation, where my parents and all of us children (except the baby) sang in the choirs and attended Sunday school, at least through grade school. I was in seventh grade when my father introduced me to an unprogrammed Friends Meeting (i.e., Meeting was not directed by an order of worship or a leader, but was largely silent meditation). Dad and I attended Meeting (usually in addition to Presbyterian activities) through most of my high school years. In addition, my parents were adult advisers to the city's interdenominational youth group of the Council of Churches. My best friends and I were active in that group, visiting each others' churches, studying the Bible (using *The Interpreters' Bible,* anathema to biblical literalists), and discussing some fairly sophisticated Protestant works of theology (e.g. Bonhoeffer's *Life Together*).

I have often quipped that my career as a sociologist of religion probably began when I was thirteen and was sent to a Quaker boarding school in the hills of eastern Tennessee. My parents were completely unaware of the existence of "shouting Quakers"—an extant Appalachian throwback to the Second Great Awakening of the early nineteenth century—so it came as quite a surprise when I told them of my experiences of required attendance at week-long, nightly camp meetings sponsored by the two little churches in town. There I first witnessed enthusiastic religious expression, for example the elderly lady on the bench beside me who fell to the ground as she was "slain by the Holy Ghost," and the fiery visiting preacher who laid on hands for healing. I walked the elderly lady home after the service, because she was stiff from lying on the ground, and her sister, who never went to the camp meetings, invited me in for cookies and milk. I must have expressed so much concern about the elderly lady that her sister reassured me that it happened every year and that being "slain" was the highlight of her religious activity. Years later, when I was studying Catholic pentecostalism, I remembered that event and realized that the lively New Jersey charismatic Catholic prayer meetings I was then observing were downright sedate in comparison.

The decades that have passed since my early experiences have been a period of considerable diversification among those with roots in the southern white evangelical tradition. While there are probably many people today who are not unlike the poorly educated rural and small-town churchgoers who first introduced me to their southern evangelical religious traditions, the southern white evangelicals I have met in San Antonio include many who are more like Loralee.[2]

Loralee

A family physician, now in her forties and unmarried, Loralee came to San Antonio from a small town in rural northeast Texas to attend medical school. She subsequently decided to stay here and join a "Christian" family practice medical group.[3] She now regularly attends the largest megachurch in the area, a nondenominational evangelical congregation whose pastor has earned some national notoriety for his antigay and anti-Muslim rhetoric. Her office décor and waiting room reading matter subtly reflect her religious beliefs and practices. Her home is also decorated to express religious meanings; for example, the breakfast nook has a picture of Jesus with a caption from an old hymn: "His eyes are on the sparrow, so I know he watches me." More important, her home is the site of domestic religious practices: for example, each morning she reads the Bible verse and devotional message of the day in *Our Daily Bread,* a publication produced by radio evangelists who do not represent any official religious group. Loralee's car also displays bumper stickers and other symbols marking her religious identity, and she is an avid consumer of "Christian" merchandise from local shops and online sources.

She does not hesitate to tell her patients about how she looks forward to the "second coming" (of Christ) in her lifetime, and she promotes abstinence-only sex education for the teenagers in her practice. Because she struggles to keep her weight under control, Loralee has tried numerous "Christian" diet plans and exercise programs. She learned of most of her everyday religious practices from books bought at a "Christian" bookstore. She credits her current pastor's preaching for most of what she knows about the Bible, and remembers only negative things about her childhood years in a Southern Baptist Sunday school. She tithes 10 percent of her six-figure income to her church, glad that it goes toward the extensive media budget, while not at all upset that the pastor opposes using church funds to help the poor. In her private practice, Loralee adjusts her fees to help underinsured persons who have been regular patients but can no longer afford her full fees-for-service; however, she refuses to accept any new uninsured patients or poor persons insured by Medicaid or the State's Children's Health Insurance Program (S-CHIP).

Loralee is a good example of someone whom most standard sociological measures would "count" as very religious. Yet her beliefs and practices have been drawn from diverse sources, including southern evangelical popular traditions and contemporary popular religious media and preaching.

Even more so than the Mexican American popular tradition, Protestant popular religion in the American South has long been mingled with the practices of recognized church groups, as well as with religious programing in the mass media. Indeed, sociologist Stephen Sharot describes this U.S. historical development as "the popularization of church religion."[4] Sharot made encyclopedic comparisons of world religions' popular and elite expressions, focusing his distinctions between popular and elite religion on the nature of religious leadership and the structural differences (e.g. hierarchy) between religious elites and religious "commoners" in each world religion. In this assessment, he points out that there were important structural differences between on the one hand the American churches that had educated clergy and hierarchical elites and on the other those that spread in rural and frontier areas due to the popular appeal of circuit or revival preachers with little education about or concern for correct church teachings or interpretation of scriptures.[5]

When religious groups, organizations, or their spokespersons themselves are forces for spreading elements of popular religiosity, it becomes virtually impossible to delineate the boundaries of official religions, regardless of the denomination with which they self-identify. As a result, elements of popular religious expression inform many southern white evangelicals' lived religion as thoroughly and seamlessly as they do the lived religion of many Mexican Americans. Perhaps our views of popular religious traditions have been tinged by a latent Protestant bias, noticing Catholic—but not Protestant—instances of eclectic borrowing and blending, as well as practices based on popular cultural traditions.[6]

What Does "Evangelical" Mean, if It Includes Popular Cultural Traditions?

One way sociologists have identified evangelicals among the various strands of Protestant religiosity is by establishing which denominational groups affirm key beliefs that are important criteria for discriminating evangelicals from other Protestant groups. According to this strategy, then, individuals who self-identify with one of those denominational groups in response to survey questions are considered to be "evangelicals." This research strategy has been confounded, however, by the enormous within-group diversity of denominations and by the apparent growth of congregations that are like "evangelical" denominations in many ways but adamantly proclaim themselves to be "nondenominational." Likewise, other terms that have been used to refer to different strands of Protestant religiosity (e.g., "mainline," "fundamentalist," "pentecostal," "liberal," and "conservative") are not easy to apply to individuals simply on the basis of their religious affiliation.

Furthermore, even when there is considerable consonance between what a denomination or church organization supposedly "stands for" and what an individual member believes, too much focus on characteristic beliefs is likely to prevent us from noticing the diversity of religious practices of those who assent to the same beliefs. In order to notice the invisible religious elements that inform individuals' religion-as-practiced, it is better to start with a broad, inclusive category that emphasizes commonalities among members of diverse denominations and nondenominational churches that draw on similar religious traditions.

For the purposes of this chapter, I will adapt James Davison Hunter's strategy of using the term "evangelical" for persons who fit certain criteria of religious belief and practice, but recognizing that there are diverse denominational traditions under that umbrella. Unlike Hunter, however, I use this concept of "evangelical" to describe the outlines of the larger evangelical tradition, rather than trying to categorize individuals who fall within these definitional boundaries. Hunter defines an evangelical as

> a Protestant who attests to the inerrancy of Scripture and the divinity of Christ and either (1) believes that Jesus Christ is the only hope for salvation or (2) has had a religious experience—that is, a particularly powerful religious insight or awakening that is still important in his everyday life, that involved a conversion to Jesus Christ as his personal savior or (3) both.[7]

Evangelicals' specific beliefs about scripture are less important, for the purposes of understanding their lived religion, than their Bible-focused practices. Similarly, while evangelicals' beliefs about Jesus might help us understand why an individual engages in certain practices, they do not tell us enough about how, in practice, that individual lives that religion. For the purposes of comprehending evangelical popular religious tradition, I believe the most useful component of Hunter's definition is the experiential aspect—not only the conversion or "born again" experience but also the expectation of certain specific kinds of ongoing experiences of the divine in one's own life. To understand this kind of lived religion, we need a much better understanding of the practices by means of which people realize those experiences.

Under this umbrella concept of evangelicalism, Hunter recognizes several clusters of historical traditions: the Baptist, Holiness-Pentecostal, Reformed-Confessional, and Anabaptist traditions. Rather than think of these traditions as definitive of boundaries separating different types of Protestants, it is more useful to think of these traditions as cultural resources that individuals may draw on in developing their personal religious beliefs and practices. We should focus less on the historical divisions among the denominations that contribute to these traditions and more on how individuals select, interpret, and use evangelical traditions (including popular traditions) in their actual religion-as-lived.

Some Sources of Popular Protestant Traditions among Southern Whites

In the first half of the eighteenth century, after a significant religious revival occurred, mainly in the northern colonies, several Protestant denominations—primarily Methodists, Baptists, and Presbyterians—actively sought to convert southerners, especially nonelite ones (e.g., small farmers). Subsequently, in the nineteenth century, came another period of widespread religious fervor that began in New England and spread rapidly on the then frontier in eastern Kentucky and western North Carolina.

It is useful for sociologists to remember that most of these conversions were not away from some other religious group. Rather, most white converts on the frontier were previously unchurched people of a general Protestant background who already held some of the popular religious beliefs being preached. Even after these periods of religious revival, however, southerners generally were not much involved in church or official religiosity. Many were even antagonistic to religious organizations. Indeed, the (imprecise) statistics available for the antebellum South suggest that churches of all denominations, despite considerable evangelistic success, had attracted only a small minority— about 20 percent of the populace by 1860—into membership.[8]

Historically, Methodists, Baptists, and Presbyterians had differed on specific doctrinal grounds. In the frontier revival years, however, they shared a generalized southern Protestant evangelical culture and emphasis on experiential conversion.[9] That southern evangelical culture incorporated, from those early revivals on, many popular religious elements. Often those popular religious beliefs and practices differed greatly from the teachings and practices of the parent denominations that were sponsoring the revivals.

Since the 1960s or earlier, much of the significance of denominational distinctions has faded, and many persons who identify with evangelical tradition do not identify with a church, much less a denomination. Many of them have had little or no religious education in any denominational tradition, so they know few of the criteria that Baptists or Presbyterians, for example, would use to evaluate specific beliefs and practices.[10] Thus, they are relatively open to the popular religious elements that are proffered through the mass media and commercial marketing, as well as by various entrepreneurial preachers and informal advice networks.

These evangelical popular traditions are also inextricably intertwined with cultural features of the South, before and in the aftermath of the Civil War. What sociologist Nancy Ammerman said of the Southern Baptists in that period applies to other southern evangelical churches:

> The evangelical revivals of the previous generations had achieved their greatest success in just the time that Southerners were establishing a regional identity. As a result, revivalist religion and pious Christian living became as much a part of Southern-ness as the South's "peculiar institution" of slavery. Southerners were thoroughly evangelical and Baptists were thoroughly Southern; culture and religion were inextricably linked.[11]

Furthermore, evangelical tradition is rooted in an expectation of strong emotional and physical manifestations of people's religious experiences. Even though today's middle-class Southern Baptist and Methodist gatherings are far tamer than those of two or more centuries ago, many southerners—church members and the unchurched alike—are familiar with the popular religious tradition of emotionally and physically experiencing divine power.

Southern evangelical Protestantism took much of its distinctive culture from rural religious revivals in the eighteenth and nineteenth centuries. Evangelists developed a social setting, the camp meeting, to preach religion to the "plain folk" of remote farmsteads and mountain settlements on the colonial states' frontiers. These intense, days-long revivals produced many conversions, marked by extreme physical agitation (jerking, falling, dancing, barking), emotional catharsis (often with such physical manifestations as crying, laughing, singing, shouting), and ecstatic spiritual practices (visions, prophecies).[12] The centrality of these intense religious experiences is evidenced by the fact that camp meeting preachers sometimes lost control of the service because the people transferred their attention from the preaching to enthusiastic prayer.[13]

Historically, when intense religious experience has been taken as evidence of the authenticity of a practice—for example, "laying on of hands" or being "born again"—then it has been likely to threaten official religious authority. In these revivals, church-established boundaries became contested, as did official leaders' authority to control them. Uneducated revival preachers' seemingly spontaneous exhortations and camp meeting congregations' intense emotionality were clearly not subject to the evaluation and approval of any authoritative religious body.[14] Even the Methodist church, which was overtly populist and not averse to revival preaching among the working class and uneducated poor, expected congregations and ministers to be responsible to bishops and wider, authoritative church decision-making bodies.

On the American frontier, however, Methodist preachers were virtually unregulated, and new converts could become fully independent circuit preachers after a relatively short apprenticeship as "exhorters" at camp meetings. Baptist preachers, likewise, were neither trained nor regulated by any authoritative denominational body. Often they were fellow farmers, no more literate or educated than their audiences. This characteristic was consonant with Baptists' historical emphasis on individual and congregational autonomy, as well as on their belief that all ordinary laypersons are capable of interpreting scripture, and thus no less qualified than a trained minister to preach. Historian Nathan Hatch reminds us that audiences granted preaching authority in evangelical revivals "to those claimants whose person, language, and deportment best resonated with the interests of common people."[15]

As a result, most southern Protestant churches were based on popular religiosity from their foundation.[16] Official religious beliefs and practices—for example, agreed-on standards for membership, training for ministers, Sunday school curricula, and decisions about correct positions on moral or social issues—developed much later. Since this popular religious tradition historically overlapped with southern church religiosity, ordinary people's lived religions could continue to draw comfortably from the popular traditions, long after their churches and ministers discouraged those practices.

In the revival period, without any effective denominational oversight and control, uneducated preachers often promoted unorthodox amalgams of folk remedies and tales and revelations from their dreams, together with idiosyncratic religious practices and interpretations of scripture. For example, one particularly successful preacher, author, and showman in the early nineteenth century, Lorenzo Dow, was so successful in drawing crowds of prospective converts that the Methodist authorities dared not suppress his preaching. He was a dramatic performer, encouraging enthusiastic and emotional displays (like the "jerking exercise") from his audiences.[17] Melded into his exhortations for sinners to repent, Dow encouraged his audience to believe that he had the power to heal illnesses (he sold patent medicines on the side), raise the devil, and find lost or stolen objects. He also taught that people could find supernatural revelations in dreams, and he alluded to his own visions to support some of his dramatic (and irregular) statements.[18]

Clearly, part of the appeal of Dow's preaching was that it incorporated elements of popular belief and practice that his audience already shared. Popular prejudices, superstitions, and values were, likewise, readily incorporated into the popular religiosity of southern evangelicals, recruited by camp meeting preachers and circuit-riding ministers on the frontier. Thus, even though they gradually became settled in organized churches, southern evangelicals were highly diverse. Some became strict and authoritarian, while others emphasized individuals' conscience as the arbiter. Some subsequently incorporated elements from later religious movements, especially fundamentalism and pentecostalism into their personal beliefs and practices, while others eschewed the rigidity of biblical fundamentalism and the emotionalism of pentecostal religiosity.

Evangelical traditions in America have had flexible boundaries, resistant to some church leaders' efforts to establish an authoritative conservative Protestant orthodoxy. Especially because of their emphasis on religious experience, evangelicals have often been open to diverse cultural influences (including mass media and other popular religious influences), resulting in widely varying patterns by which individuals practice their religion in everyday life.

The recent development of many evangelical nondenominational, generic Christian churches in the South (and elsewhere) further illustrates how popular religiosity becomes blended with church religiosity. Like early nineteenth-century camp meeting preachers, the entrepreneurial founders of these churches avoid denominational oversight or control. Historical bases for denominational divisions have become meaningless to many potential church members, yet many have no way of evaluating the validity of scriptural interpretations or theology in any preacher's message. Thus, like Lorenzo Dow, nondenominational preachers can promote popular religious beliefs and practices that their audiences already accept.

Blended with cultural elements of familiar patterns of religiosity, beliefs and practices that are promoted by popular media and popular preachers thus become indistinguishable from "church" religious beliefs and practices. Rather than interpret membership in such churches as conversion, we would better understand the attraction of many new members as finding a comfortable niche with a congregation of people whose attitudes, values, and lifestyles they already generally share. Similarly, we may need to adjust our notions of religious commitment in light of the eclecticism and blending of popular evangelical practices into church religiosity.[19]

An excellent example of such popular religious combination and borrowing is the nondenominational Lakewood Church of Houston, one of the largest megachurches in the United States today, attended by some thirty thousand persons each week. Its senior pastor, Joel Osteen, inherited the church from his father, who, with no educational qualifications or ministerial training, had founded the church in an abandoned feed store. Although his father was influenced in his preaching by his own Baptist upbringing and later Pentecostal experiences, Joel Osteen (whose only training for the ministry was in helping his father) delivers a more neutral theological message, with little emphasis on salvation or moral condemnation of evil. Rather, preaching a gospel of prosperity, self-help, and encouragement, Osteen has built the church into a huge operation in a former professional basketball arena with sixteen thousand seats, after a $92 million renovation. His book, *Your Best Life Now: 7 Steps to Living at Your Full Potential*, has sold more than 1.5 million copies, making him a millionaire, a feature many followers consider positive and inspiring. His church services offer polished and entertaining musical productions and Osteen's upbeat self-help messages, together with affirmation of people's desires to be successful and prosperous.

We cannot assume that Lakewood's religion-as-preached is replicated in its individual members' religion-as-practiced.[20] Lakewood is, however an example of how thoroughly popular religious elements can be blended into the institutional form of a congregation. That kind of hybridity means that survey measures of individuals' religious belonging and commitment (such as religious self-identification, frequency of attendance, or frequency of prayer) tell us little or nothing about most individual members' actual religious beliefs and practices. With no authoritative oversight, nondenominational preachers like Osteen can promote popular religious practices and popular media messages that their followers already hold, meshing with—rather than challenging— their existing values and attitudes.[21]

Many of those who have incorporated popular religious elements into the everyday practice of their religion are unaware of the sources of these beliefs and practices. They may be completely unconscious of whether or not these practices are consistent with their denomination's official stance—or their congregation may have eschewed denominational norms altogether. Nevertheless, popular religious elements are widely available in southern culture, such that popular Protestant traditions and practices seem far less unusual than the popular Catholic practices of Mexican Americans.

The Sacred and the Profane: Dualistic Practices and Apocalyptic Time

Where do evangelicals find divine power and how do they gain access to it? Many southern evangelicals would answer that divine power is accessible everywhere, but you have to pray right to tap it. Theirs is a world that requires their effort and vigilance in order to assert the sacred in the everyday world of work, leisure, and domestic life.

The sacred is not *simply there*, like the medieval sacred overlay on the landscape. Rather, evangelicals today find it continually necessary to make the connection between the sacred and the secular, in the face of a larger society that does not share the same assumptions about religion. In order to make the sacred present and accessible within the everyday, many evangelicals exert considerable effort to sacralize mundane space and time. By routinely engaging in popular religious practices, such as marking their shops, offices, and business advertisements with religious symbols, they both claim identity as, say, a "Christian business" and assert the relevance of their personal religion to the profane sphere.

The southern evangelical cultural world is hardly "disenchanted." It is full of supernatural powers that are believed to affect everyday life, even if one is not aware of their presence. The angel fad of the 1990s was particularly popular among southern evangelicals, even though angels have no place in most Protestant churches' theology. For many southern women, decorating their homes with images of angels was a sweet way of reminding people of divine protection and presence in daily life. Loralee, the family physician described earlier in this chapter, decorated her office waiting room with chintzy country furniture, a braided rug, a few houseplants, the requisite magazine rack (with only wholesome "family" publications), and no fewer than eighteen angel decorations—porcelain figurines, wooden plaques, framed prints, and plush dolls. A folksy style of country living is linked nostalgically with appreciation for the virtues of "that ole time religion" and the "little brown church in the vale," even though the doctor and the folks who sit in her waiting room may live in large modern houses in suburban housing developments, drive expensive recent-model SUVs and ride-on lawnmowers, and own multiple computers, TVs, VCRs, DVDs, cell phones, and other technological gadgets.

Like the Mexican American women discussed earlier, many southern evangelical women use popular religious objects to connect domestic space with the divine and/or to use their home décor to make a religious statement to visitors.[22] Clothing, pictures and posters, jewelry, coffee mugs, and bumper stickers also serve to convey both a message about religion and the religious identity-claims of the user. At home or in their cars, these women can listen to generic Christian radio stations, CDs, and TV shows; they can buy "Christian" cookbooks and practice "Christian" diet plans.[23] Particularly for the religious socialization of their children, many women buy "Christian" merchandise so as to envelope their family in a good religious atmosphere.[24] In short, individuals may choose widely differing ways of linking sacred and profane in their homes and everyday lives.

More important, they may also use their religious possessions and sacralized space in widely varying ways. For example, a decorative religious placard at the front door could be used as an identity marker to visitors and, simultaneously, a memento of the friends who gifted it as a housewarming present. A family Bible set out on a stand in the living room could be used as a protective symbol, as a memento of previous generations who kept that Bible, or even as an instrumental object for divining the answer to a question.[25]

Although we can readily gather information about what objects are commercially marketed to evangelicals, we need to understand how people use them in their own religious (or nonreligious) practices. For instance, historian Leigh Schmidt suggests paying more attention to the giving and receiving of gift-objects, as a religious practice. He states:

> Thinking of American religious life as a gift economy accentuates the
> small habits of faith, the tactility of memory, the vows of obedience,

the promises of reward, the desperate deals struck with God, the performative gestures of acknowledgment, as well as the hierarchies of conferral and submission.... Gifts then, as with other religious practices, are supple and hybrid, positioned on the overlapping borders of self-interest and self-denial, festive play and strategic purpose, spirit and materiality, public and private, sacred and secular.[26]

Not all the supernatural powers southern evangelicals believe to affect their lives are benign, however. Many believe that diabolical powers are also active, causing illnesses, sinful behavior, and possibly even possession by evil spirits. So protective and counteractive practices are necessary every day. Some evangelicals describe this daily struggle against diabolical powers as "spiritual warfare."[27] Accordingly, Satan is ubiquitous, literally embedded in dangerous everyday activities. Marie Griffith, in her study of a nondenominational pentecostalist movement, Women's Aglow, describes such dangers: "Such forces are believed to seep into one's life and home even without one's knowing it, as when one woman recounted discovering a book she had purchased second-hand was tainted by witchcraft because of the sins of its previous owner."[28]

Prayer was the foremost practice the Aglow members used as an active "weapon" (their term) against satanic power. Protective practices, for which mothers assumed primary responsibility, involved both purging their homes and their children's lives of diabolical influences and surrounding them with Christian influences. For example, one evangelical neighbor urged me not to allow my son to play "Dungeons and Dragons," a fantasy game, because the game itself would invite many devils to enter his mind and control him, even against his will. Fantasy books (such as the Harry Potter series) are, likewise, forbidden, lest Satan enter readers' minds unbidden as they imagine the fantasy world of the story.[29] Offering generic Christian games, books, and music CDs is, thus, a religious practice that serves to protect children from diabolical powers as they play.

Certain places and times, as well as certain amusements and other activities, are deemed especially dangerous. For example, many southern evangelicals oppose allowing children to participate in Halloween activities, not merely because they are upset that Halloween is linked to pre-Christian practices but also, more important, because they believe that the devil uses the event itself to gain control of vulnerable children.[30]

Thus, not only do many evangelicals invoke divine power in their everyday lives but also they engage in specific religious practices to "rebuke Satan" and counteract diabolical power. Some evangelicals treat the Bible as a power-imbued object to be used for protection. And some believe it is necessary to exorcise diabolical powers from a physical location that previous occupants may have spiritually contaminated. For example, a dentist who advertised that his was a "Christian dental practice" feared his new office suite might be spiritually infested if the gynecologist who previously rented it had ever facilitated abortions. So before the movers arrived, he prayed aloud in each room of his new office, commanding in Jesus' name that Satan depart.[31]

Popular religious practices, for example the instrumental use of particular words, enable individuals to call on divine power in everyday settings.[32] Ron described just such use of powerful words: His main everyday practice was to say "in Jesus' name," both to ward off temptation and to make requests of God. His belief in the power of those specific words was so strong that he would often repeat them later, just in case he forgot to say them the first time. He also gave frequent testimonies about the successes of praying that way, and hearing others' testimonies confirmed his belief in the real power of those words. Ron's practice of testifying about the power of that particular prayer form resembles the Mexican American woman's *promesas* to St. Jude, because implicit in the prayer's effectiveness in the future is the obligation to tell others about its past successes.

In evangelical popular traditions, not only is space sacralized but time, too, is full of sacred significance. Widespread among southern evangelicals is the millenarian notion that the end of the world is near and an apocalyptic endtime is at hand. For those evangelicals who believe the end-time is near, mundane time takes on a transformed meaning. Although this idea has come and gone among Christians many times over the centuries and was expressed among some popular religious movements in medieval and early Modern times, the articulation and elaboration of belief in the rapture is relatively recent. Introduced by nineteenth-century fundamentalist preachers, the idea of the rapture is based on popular religious interpretations of verses of the apocalyptic book of Revelations. These interpretations suggest that the truly saved will be taken up to heaven before the final battle (Armageddon) and thus spared the horrors of the end of the world.[33]

Although writers and preachers have promoted the idea of the rapture for more than a century, this belief appears to have become more widespread in recent years. This is no doubt nurtured by evangelicals' consumption of popular religious mass media, such as Hal Lindsay's *The Late Great Planet Earth*. More recently, the "Left Behind" series (1996 on) of adventure novels depicts, with considerable gore and brutality, the triumphal destruction of all the people whom fundamentalist readers consider to be their religious, ethnic, and moral opposition. Some believers are even willing to engage in actions, for example financially supporting Middle-Eastern extremists, to hasten Armageddon, which they hope will usher in the Second Coming of Christ.[34] Clearly, such popular cultural images of an approaching end-time have influenced some believers' sense of the meaning of time.

It is difficult to say what this belief means in evangelicals' religious practice. How does expectation of the imminent end of the world affect the everyday spiritual practices, work, and relationships of those who hold it? Do such believers behave differently (for example, in what they tell their children about the future) from other evangelicals who do not share belief in the rapture?[35] Does the belief raise any fears or anxieties that they and their loved ones might be left behind and damned? If not, what beliefs and practices account for their certainty (compared to their Calvinist or Puritan forebears' fear and uncertainty)[36] that they will be saved and their opposition will be damned? For example, according to one study, some people use the "Left Behind" novels to form personal checklists to be sure they avoid the mistakes of those who, in the novel, thought they were saved but were subsequently left behind. Other readers use the novels' depictions of the enemies to monitor current events for signs that the end-time has begun.[37] Belief in the rapture illustrates how popular religious practices have produced, for some evangelicals, a reenchantment of time.

Tapping Divine Power: "He Walks with Me and He Talks with Me"

Like the popular religious practices of the medieval peasant, those of today's evangelicals treat divine power as accessible to ordinary believers who know how to pray for it. They are based on a notion of the sacred as regularly erupting within profane, everyday life, producing miracles, prophecy, and other evidence of divine intervention in the course of mundane events. The main difference between the southern evangelical popular traditions and the Mexican American popular traditions discussed earlier is in the ways one taps that power and channels it where it is needed.[38]

While many Mexican American popular devotional practices are based on a personal relationship with the saints (especially the Virgin of Guadalupe), many southern evangelical popular religious practices are based on a very similar intimate connection with Jesus. If one were to substitute "Jesus" for "Our Lady" in some of the stories from chapter 3, those narratives would be remarkably like the ones evangelicals tell.[39] For example, at an all-women's prayer meeting I visited, one woman witnessed that talking to Jesus keeps her going through her day. She said that she often felt trapped alone at home with two preschoolers, especially because her husband spends long hours at work and they had moved so often that she never had time to develop close friends in the neighborhood. But, she testified, she could always share her troubles and burdens with Jesus—asking him for guidance, comfort, and help—because he truly understood her and cared about her and her family. Like the young Latina mother (described in chapter 3) who regularly conversed "woman to woman, mother to mother" with Our Lady of Guadalupe, many southern evangelicals believe that Jesus understands them and really listens when they share their personal troubles and concerns.

Many evangelical popular religious practices are based on a sense of a personal relationship with a powerful divine figure who is able miraculously to touch one's life. Many prayers resemble an intimate personal conversation, sometimes with the expectation of hearing (literally or figuratively) Jesus' responses to the prayer. And in order to continue to enjoy the benefits, one must ask for divine help properly and, after receiving it, one must meet certain obligations—as with the Mexican American *promesas*. For instance, during our study of nonmedical healing, one woman told my research assistant that she had asked Jesus to heal her of her daily migraine headaches, and he had healed her so quickly that she had not had time to get her doctor's prescription filled. But then, less than two weeks later, the headaches came back, as bad as ever. She explained that her healing was real, but only temporary, because she had not given thanks enough, or testified publicly to the fact of the healing.[40]

This sense of being able to tap divine power—the feeling that they have received the ability to do things they could not do on their own power—is an important part of many evangelicals' sense of personal empowerment.[41]

Addressing Material Concerns: "Oh, That You Would Bless Me Indeed, and Enlarge My Territory"

Another feature of medieval religiosity that has been defined out as not properly religion is the practice of engaging in religious rituals for instrumental purposes, such as obtaining material success. Early modern Catholic and Protestant churches systematically tried to discourage or eliminate such ritual practices as impure, superstitious, or sinful. Nevertheless, various popular religious traditions retain the use of religious practices for addressing material concerns.

A good example of this is the practice of the Prayer of Jabez, which is based on a few verses of Old Testament scripture. After the recent publication of a best-selling book by that name, many people began to use the prayer daily. The purpose of the practice is to be blessed by God with prosperity, social success, and material well-being and to be protected from harm and temptations.[42]

People say the Prayer of Jabez in order to obtain desired material ends: a job or a promotion, wealth and financial windfalls, a mortgage to buy a new home or business, and so on. Some also testify that saying the prayer brought them success in finding a nicer boyfriend or an attractive fiancée. Others justify their private enjoyment of business profits by their act of having said the prayer and thus having received divine blessings in return. The book tells them that it is okay to pray for wealth and material success. What is more, it is okay to enjoy having a successful lifestyle and spending such wealth, which are divine blessings that true believers receive. In San Antonio, the prayer is sufficiently a part of local evangelical popular culture that some businesses have evoked it in their names, their logos, or other advertising, alongside other marketing cues to attract customers who make a point of patronizing self-identified Christian businesses.

Even churches that might decry quasi-magical uses of Bible verses, however, have promoted the Prayer of Jabez as a way of being a better Christian. People engage in this practice either alongside church-oriented religious practices or completely apart from any church involvement. Like other popular religious practices, the key criterion believers use for continuing this prayer is pragmatic: Does it work? Does it produce at least some of the desired results?

While some uses of the Prayer of Jabez may promote crass materialism, we should never denigrate people's real material concerns: enough money to pay the rent; success in getting a business loan in order to open a store; help in getting a home or health insurance claim paid; an end to drought that threatens their town's water supply; a chance for a decent job. When everyday material concerns matter so much, it is understandable that people would want to know how to "pray right" if it would help.

Often the formula for "praying right" involves a test or proof of faith. Some evangelical preachers link successful prayer for prosperity with giving money— presumably to their own ministry, rather than to charity. For example, one preacher who is head of a megachurch with seating for five thousand precedes the collection of offerings by telling the audience to hold their money high and repeat after him: "Give and it shall be given." He tells his listeners, including the television audience, "When you give, it qualifies you to receive God's abundance" and "If you're not prospering, it's because you're not giving."[43]

Popular religious practices also address healing and protection of health, worries about fertility and safe childbirth, fears of hunger or homelessness, concerns about job security or unemployment, and more. Because such concerns are so important to individual believers, popular religious practices have historically addressed people's material concerns, often despite official religious leaders' denunciations. For example, in early stages of the Long Reformation,

European farmers (even if they were Protestant) wanted the weather bells rung, according to Catholic popular religious tradition, because they felt they could not risk losing their crops.[44] Protestant farmers in colonial America likewise engaged in considerable amounts of what their ministers decried as "superstitious" and "magical" practices relating to the weather and propitious dates for planting.[45] Today, too, people use popular religious practices for any help they can get for their material well-being, in the face of their unpredictable and sometimes overwhelming socioeconomic situations.

Better educated and more aware of the larger world than their early American forebears, southern evangelicals are likely to use their popular religious practices in addition to getting medical help for healing or fertility problems. They may use both a technical and a religious explanation for some problem. And they still use the same criterion earlier generations used to evaluate each religious practice: "Does it work?"

For instance, one young man gave the following ardent testimony[46] at the Wednesday prayer meeting of his church. On his job, he had to spend hours each day using a computer that froze up inexplicably, costing him extra hours of work to reboot and get back to his place in his work. So, earlier that week, he had tried praying over the uncooperative device, laying hands on it and saying a prayer for its "healing." Miraculously, it became unfrozen and did not freeze up any more that day. He encouraged everyone to pray with faith in order to experience God's power in their lives.

His testimony prompted the next—a woman described a similar experience of struggling to balance her checkbook that had become hopelessly "messed up." Laying hands on it and asking God's power to "heal" the checkbook miraculously solved the entire problem.

From the murmurs in the room, I could tell that I was not the only audience member who could have used similar miracles for the seemingly intractable problems of computers and checkbooks!

Material objects are important, not only as the desired result of prayers but also as channels for divine power. The Bible itself is one such object to which some believers attribute divine power. Colleen McDannell notes that Protestant denominations generally disapprove of the practice of using random phrases of the Bible for divination or prognostication, but historically, in many people's everyday religious practice, there is no distinction made between the approved inspirational uses of the Bible and the unapproved instrumental or practical uses. People may value the Bible equally for edification or inspiration, for divination based on a random text, for swearing informal oaths, for picking children's names, for pressing and keeping family mementos, and as an element of décor for the living room.[47] One such practice, described favorably to me by several evangelicals (but decried by others), involves looking for what they considered to be the God-given answer to a specific question by opening the Bible to a randomly selected page and finding some clue in the words on that page that provides the divine response.[48]

Material objects are a significant part of how evangelical popular religious practices elide the worlds of the sacred and the profane. Parts of the human body can also be used as channels, as exemplified by the practice of the laying on of hands. For example, one women's prayer group regularly laid hands collectively on a person seeking prayer, with concentric circles of members around the women who were leading the prayer. The visual image of their hands as conduits of God's power was vivid: Each woman in the outer circles held one hand raised up ("to heaven") and one hand on the shoulder or back of the prayer leader, who held both hands (one on the head and one on the back) of the woman seeking prayer. Using similar imagery, various media evangelists have offered to send members of their audience a "prayer cloth," imbued, through the evangelists' hands and prayers, with divine healing power. Some televangelists encourage people to touch the screens of their television sets to receive the power of laying on of hands that was being channeled through the television signals.[49]

Material objects may hold—literally and metaphorically—important meanings for those who use them in their religious practices. For example, a woman who had attended a program on the Prayer of Jabez at her nondenominational church wore a prayer box pendant on her necklace. Inside the box she kept a piece of rice paper inscribed with the prayer, as both a reminder of its promises and as an ongoing prayer. She chose a similar prayer box as a graduation gift for her daughter.[50] Material objects like this one become part of meaningful practices (such as gifting and wearing the object), relationships (the gift relationship between mother and daughter), and experiences (including the sheer physical experience of feeling the object/prayer "close to my heart").

Many evangelicals also engage in the popular religious use of material objects by collecting and gifting Precious Moments statues and other decorative objects with religious themes. Manufactured since the 1960s, these porcelain figures of angelic children have become top-selling collectibles. In addition, the producers have built a Precious Moments Chapel in the Ozark Mountains region of Missouri, attracting some 500,000–750,000 visitors each year. The figurine designer has decorated the chapel with murals of his wide-eyed children set in biblical scenes. He said the chapel was inspired by his visit to the Sistine Chapel, and he painted the ceiling with Precious Moments angels on floating clouds evoking some of Michelangelo's subjects. The chapel

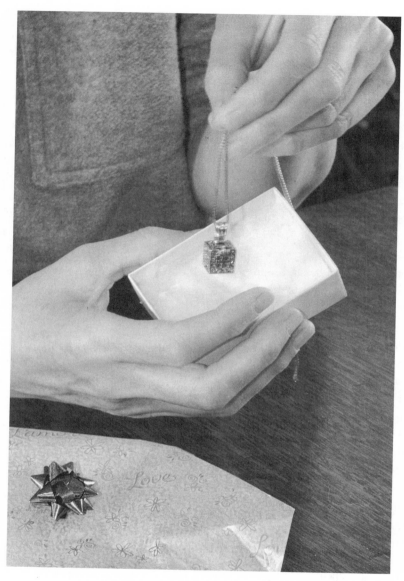

FIGURE 4.1. Material objects, such as this prayer box necklace, are part of evangelicals' popular religious practices: gifting an object to another, remembering the giver and the occasion for the gift, remembering and repeating a special prayer or Bible verse, as well as wearing and feeling the object itself. Courtesy Jim Spickard, used by permission of Toroverde Press.

itself is used for individual religious practices—very like the pilgrimage sites of Mexican American popular religiosity—and visitors attest to receiving divine aid during their visit.[51] The figurines are more central, however, as an expression of popular religiosity.

How do people use these popular religious elements? Two key uses seem to be to celebrate memories and to evoke and deal with powerful emotions. All of the Precious Moments figures represent popular religious sentiments, so purchasers can use theirs as mementos that inspire them, while decorating their homes with valuable collectibles. For example, one collector who possessed nine hundred of them explained, "I'm a Christian, and there's something there for every little moment, a little testimony for every little piece on the shelf."[52]

A common use is for gifting, in which a gift offers its recipient simultaneously the object itself, the important message the object conveys, and—as anthropologists remind us—the reciprocal relationship between gift-giver and -receiver that gifting typically entails. For example, one woman gave her husband a figurine called "My Love Will Never Let You Go" when he was in a rehabilitation program for his alcoholism. Later, when her husband died, her friend gave her the figurine "This Too Shall Pass." In memory of her husband, she positioned the two pieces together—much like the Latinas' arranging of elements of their *altarcitos*—to represent to herself both the pain and spiritual reconciliation she had experienced.[53] Such spatial arrangement of objects is an important usage of popular religious elements in lived religion. Physically juxtaposing objects that carry significant meanings is a domestic ritual that both reflects and performs the connections between those meanings.

It is likely that church spokespersons for most evangelical denominations—especially those that espouse certain historical evangelical themes—would disavow the overall interpretation of scriptures that these figurines and the chapel represent. All the figures are childish and cute; biblical stories are divested of suffering (even the lions to which little Daniel is thrown are smiling and cute); painted words preach a comforting message.[54] At the same time, the chapel and the many figurines obviously help to meet many people's spiritual needs, especially regarding the loss of a loved one and other sources of suffering. Popular religious practices such as these offer alternative resources for dealing with pain, suffering, and loss when the larger society and people's official religions do not offer such effective comfort or hope.

In the conclusion to her extensive study of "material Christianity" in American history, Colleen McDannell argues against excluding popular religious uses of material objects from our understanding of people's religiosity. She states:

When we look carefully at the interaction between people and religious artifacts, architecture and environments, we see that the practice of Christianity is a subtle mixture of traditional beliefs and
personal improvisations. . . . By expanding our understanding of religion to *include those activities that have been ignored as superficial
or condemned as superstitious,* we see that American Christianity has
a distinct material dimension.[55]

Sociologists and other scholars of religion should heed her advice. Too much of
our work has treated the Catholic Latina who rarely attends Mass but sets out
food and drink by her deceased husband's grave for El Día de los Muertos as
engaging in mere "folk religion," while the Southern Baptist churchgoer's
tearful prayers before her domestic shrine with expensive angelic statuary beside her deceased husband's photo are categorized as real "religiosity." On the
contrary, the two forms of popular religious expression are equally, if differently, religious.

Ambivalence of Popular Tradition: "Let Us Break Bread Together"

Popular religious traditions are more likely than official ones to absorb popular
cultural values and practices that promote prejudice, violence, and interpersonal abusiveness. All religious traditions are inherently ambivalent, promoting both conflict and cohesion, violence and peace, friendship and enmity.[56]
But popular religious traditions lack the brakes that official religious authorities
can apply to the inflaming and the expression of violence and to discrimination
toward ethnic, racial, and religious outsiders. When popular values and prejudices become embedded in church religiosity, however, as in the case of many
southern white evangelicals, church authority is particularly unlikely to be used
to confront or change such values and prejudices. Even within the evangelical
popular religious tradition, however, there are ambivalent dynamics, evidenced
clearly in how southern whites treat blacks.

The 1984 film *Places of the Heart* depicts the 1930s culture of small-town
Texas, with all its heartwarming goodness and its ugliest prejudices—about
women's "place," about people with handicaps, and especially about African
Americans. The film ends with an evocative scene of (imagined) transformation and reconciliation in which the town's inhabitants, black and white, living
and dead, receive Communion together in the cozy little community church.
The viewer realizes that the scene is a hope, rather than the real ending of the
story, only when a local Klan leader and the lawman who was accidentally killed

in an opening scene are shown breaking bread with the exiled black protagonist and others who would surely never have been welcome in that white community church. This scene, imaginary as it is, represents the ambivalence of interracial Communion in the southern evangelical popular tradition. That is, the popular tradition includes both: strands of egalitarian religious experience, mutual respect, and racial harmony, as well as the better-known strands of violence, oppression, and racial intolerance.[57]

Southern evangelical popular religiosity had, at its very inception, an ethos of equality and intense sense of togetherness that seemed to surmount, for a while, such distinctions as social class or hierarchy.[58] The early camp meetings and other revivalist gatherings were characteristically populist and generally more egalitarian than any denomination's regular church gatherings in that era. In the early years—before the abolition of slavery and long before the society granted women's equal legal and political rights—camp meetings incorporated not only children and women, as well as men, of diverse social classes[59] but also different racial groups.[60] During these years, the involvement of African American worshipers, slave and free, produced a reciprocal sharing of cultural elements. Indeed, many of the vibrant ways of praying and singing in the southern popular religious tradition resulted from the synthesis of African worship patterns with diverse Euro-American patterns.[61] For example, the tradition of enthusiastic worship of self-identified "shouting Methodists" was clearly a hybrid of the African and Euro-American practices.[62] The vitality of this synthesis of African and Euro-American religious practices reminds us of the historical importance of evangelical popular religiosity in the development of the many southern Protestant denominations, both black and white, that grew out of those early revival years before evangelical congregations became completely segregated by race.[63] After slavery ended, the southern black churches were separated from the white evangelical denominations, but both continued separately to practice much of their blended evangelical popular religious heritage.[64]

The southern white evangelical popular religious tradition, however, has also long embedded racist oppression—including slavery, segregation, discrimination, and violent suppression—of blacks and other racial, ethnic, and religious minorities. Long before the Civil War, slavery was a major issue among evangelicals, causing serious conflicts between these southern churches and their denominational counterparts in the North. For example, Baptists historically had been strongly against slavery and were identified with ordinary "plain folks" like small farmers rather than wealthy plantation owners. Nevertheless, in the early nineteenth century, their small-farmer members in Kentucky and Tennessee typically each owned a few slaves. Abolishing slavery was deeply threatening to such farmers' livelihood, and the popular cultural values of their local congregations supported their owning slaves. So, although abolition had many ardent spokespersons among Baptist leaders at higher levels, it was not surprising that most congregations of southern Baptists broke with their northern counterparts to form new denominations that considered owning slaves morally acceptable.[65] Similar splits occurred among Methodists and Presbyterians.

In the twentieth century, white evangelicals had the potential to draw on their popular Protestant revival traditions to promote a renewal of egalitarian togetherness with black evangelicals, since they shared the same experiential religious heritage. And a few tried to do so. One long-lived effort was Koinonia Farm, founded in 1942 in rural Georgia during the height of segregationism by Clarence Jordan, a white Southern Baptist minister. The members of this racially integrated Christian community practiced egalitarian ideals in both their daily lives together on the farm and their efforts for social justice in the wider society. They internally accomplished many of their goals of reconciliation and fellowship across social boundaries of race and social class, surviving many threats of violence from segregationist neighbors. Much later, Koinonia evolved into a social justice movement that became Habitat for Humanity.[66]

More recently, the nationwide evangelical movement known as the Promise Keepers has held large men's rallies that have tried to produce a sense of brotherhood, with hugs and other gestures of reconciliation among participants of various races and ethnic groups.[67] Especially when such practices are replicated on a regular basis and combined with other intense religious practices, such as weekly "sharing" at a men's prayer group, they have the potential to produce real connections around evangelical practices that participants hold in common. Deep southern cultural values and attitudes, however, make it more normal and comfortable for evangelicals' interactions to be racially separate, and much southern popular Protestantism continues to affirm racial intolerance, discrimination, and separatism.

Specific practices create and maintain clear boundaries between the in-group and the racial (or ethnic, gender, or religious) Other. Historically, one way popular religious rituals have promoted intolerance has been the boundary-procession. A procession is a public ritual involving collective movement from one place to another as a way of marking a place (or series of places) as an important commemorative representation of the group, community, or society. In late medieval Europe, one such elaborate procession was to "beat the bounds," by which a parish/village community was literally and figuratively inscribed. Historian Marc Forster observes that processions were so clearly about communal boundary maintenance that early modern Protestant clergy, in particular, attempted to eliminate or discourage them, because

Protestants generally emphasized individual religiosity during the Long Reformation. Despite clergy and elite attempts to eliminate this kind of ritual for communal boundary maintenance, Protestant popular religiosity continued to support territorial processions, even in modern times.[68]

One example in the United States is the procession of robed Ku Klux Klan members to or around some public space to proclaim their communal defense of territory against blacks, Catholics, or other minority groups.[69] For example, in the 1920s and 1930s, the Klan carried out regular processions, with large numbers of members dressed in full regalia, in San Antonio's plaza beside what Edward Linenthal terms the "sacred ground" of the Alamo. (This activity has continued to the present, albeit with much less ceremony and much smaller numbers.) The Klan has been and continues to be, even today, very much an expression of popular religious sentiment.[70] Although such rituals reflect and reproduce considerable violence toward the out-groups at whom they are directed, we should not dismiss as ineffective these rituals' potential to create in participants an emotional and bodily experience of belonging to the collectivity whose boundaries are ritually demarcated.

Spirituality and Materiality: Body and Emotion in Popular Religiosity

Southern evangelical popular religious traditions are similar to Latino popular religious traditions also in the connections they make between people's material lives and spiritual lives. As the previous examples of prayers for prosperity and healing show, one feature both popular traditions have in common is that they address people's material needs. Another is that both involve people's use of material objects that they imbue with religious meaning. Historian Colleen McDannell points out how such meaningful religious objects, for example arranged in a domestic shrine, serve both to locate the sacred within the profane realm of everyday life and to stir people's memories. She emphasizes that memory is an active and constructive process:

> Rather than being a storehouse from which images and feelings
> can be retrieved at will, it is an imaginative reconstruction of pieces
> of the past.... Since the past is changed through remembering, we
> cannot truly remember it. Instead we look to spaces, gestures, im-
> ages, and objects to embody memory.[71]

Part of the reason that religions, Christian and non-Christian alike, have such a material dimension is that people's material bodies are intimately involved in religious practices and spiritual experiences.[72] Southern evangelical traditions include many religious practices that link bodies and emotions in producing religious experiences. These include prayer postures (such as hands upraised overhead), singing, crying, and shouting, among other practices.

A further interesting practice resembling Latino embodied religious practices is many evangelicals' (relatively recent) use of such performances as Passion plays and Nativity pageants to evoke intense emotions in performers and audience alike. For example, the three largest evangelical churches in San Antonio produce elaborate dramatic spectacles at Easter and/or Christmas, staging them to maximize audiences' emotional involvement through music and special effects. Although less immediate as a bodily experience than live performances and audience participation, watching seemingly realistic cinematic performances is a more familiar (to middle-class Americans, at least) way for viewers to be aroused to intense emotions laden with religious meanings. Mel Gibson's 2004 film *The Passion of the Christ*, depicting the crucifixion of Jesus in bloody detail, attracted large numbers of evangelical Protestants, as well as those Catholics who identified with the older popular Catholic devotional tradition of Passion plays, based on the "spectacle of suffering."[73]

Evangelicals hold certain kinds of religious experience as particularly important. The centrality of their essential conversion-and-commitment experiences (being "born again") is clearly evident. But equally important are the religious experiences they desire in ordinary prayer and in worship services. An example is the following account of one man's intense religious experience.[74] His faith had been deeply shaken when his thirteen-year-old son had died of congenital heart disease, despite all the prayers for his healing and the enormous sacrifices of his parents to care for him through heart surgeries, illnesses, and frailty, over his short lifetime. For months after the child's death, the father experienced little joy or sense of connection when he prayed or attended church. After more than seven months, the first spring-like day happened to be a Sunday, and he attended church with his wife and daughters, as he always had, both before and after his son's death. As usual, the service began with much singing, in which he participated without much enthusiasm. But after about forty minutes of singing, many emotions began to wash over him (grief, pleasure of happy memories, bitter disappointment, longing). Continuing to sing, though crying, he did not really pay attention to the words, but he "knew with conviction" that he was "back" in his "close relationship with the Lord." And he experienced being "at peace" over the loss of his son.

Many evangelicals also particularly value prayer that is experienced as direct communication with God. Anthropologist Tanya Luhrmann described the following conversation with one of several evangelical informants who had powerful experiences of hearing God speak to them.

> A woman explained to me how that worked. "It's kind of like someone was talking to me. That's how real it is. I get responses." How do you know? I ask. "God speaks to me," she replied. . . . I ask You can hear him with your ears, outside your head? "No," she responded. "For some people God speaks with a distinct voice, so you'd turn around because you think the person's right there. For me it hasn't happened like that. Well, I mean kinda, there has been kind of that sense, but not like you'd turn your head because someone was there." . . . She explained that she didn't hear the voice like it really was another voice, but it was more than a passing thought. It was clearly, she felt, not her thought. . . . "It makes you want to say . . . where did that come from? . . . Part of it is that it feels like a revelation. You feel like 'wow,' you know it feels good."[75]

Hearing is not the only sensory religious experience people describe. Taste, touch, smell, and other physical senses are evoked. One woman told interviewer Brenda Brasher about her religious experiences:

> It's a connection, a oneness with the Lord. I feel it physiologically. I feel the hair on my arms go up. I feel the hair on my back go up. I feel my heart racing. A peace that is supernatural happens deep inside of me. Sometimes it is in my heart. Sometimes it feels deeper, right in the pit of my stomach. I have felt it even deeper than that. I think the Lord allows me to feel how he feels. It is like a compassion.[76]

Such intense experiential spirituality is central to many evangelicals' lived religion.[77] Their Bible reading and private prayer practices promote not only the value of the experiences but the experience themselves. Their small prayer-group interactions support experiential spirituality, while helping members "discern" (their term) whether the experiences that they subsequently have are "truly from God." Their church community's worship services often encourage intense, emotional religious experiences. And people draw on popular religious resources to enhance their religious experiences.

The connection of bodies and emotions to individual religious experience is clearly one feature of many (perhaps all) popular religious traditions. Indeed, it is a central feature of evangelical popular tradition. If we want to understand how people live religion while drawing on evangelical traditions, we have to find better ways for comprehending the interconnectedness of their concrete practices, involving bodies and emotions, for producing valued religious experiences.

We need much more ethnographic research on religious experience. All the religious practices described in this book have some experiential component, many of which are profound and compelling. It is likely that religious experience (even a fleeting or ambiguous one) is more important for individual religious conviction than is religious belief.[78] Historically and crossculturally, religions have often involved intense experiences such as ecstasy, catharsis, and possession. Many religious groups and movements among Western religions (including several in modern Europe and the Americas) have promoted ecstatic religious experiences.[79]

Thus far, only a few scholars have given serious research attention to religious experience. Many of the anthropological studies that address religious experience have focused somewhat narrowly on extraordinary experiences, broadly grouped together as "altered states of consciousness," which include mystical experiences, trance states, spirit possession, shamanic healing, and drug-induced states.[80] Most sociologists, however, have either ignored religious experience or presumed it to be a purely psychological phenomenon and thus outside their purview.[81] Some sociologists argue that religious experience is totally subjective and thus not amenable to sociological methods of analysis; at best, social scientists could get narratives about people's experiences.[82] I agree with sociologist Jim Spickard's assessment that on the contrary, religious experience is located not only in an individual's mind or emotions, nor only in an individual's neurophysical body, but in a complex intersection of the social and the subjective. Spickard points out: "Members [of meditative religions, like Zen Buddhism] learn not only to interpret their experiences, but also to have them. They learn to focus their attention in patterned ways, to generate new experiences of self and world."[83] Furthermore, he explains, religious rituals structure their participants' attention, leading them to experience themselves and their world as transformed.[84] Such rituals are amenable to phenomenological analysis, because they result in participants sharing a time-bound experience.[85]

Perhaps even more important for understanding contemporary religious practices are all the less dramatic moments of religious experience that may occur almost routinely, rather than extraordinarily. Many of the interviewees described in this book reported frequent everyday religious experiences. For example, several women (only a few of whom were churchgoers) described having regular, but not predictable, moments of religious experience while praying or meditating in the midst of dishwashing. Other respondents depicted their gardening, dancing, singing, or rocking the baby as the occasions for brief, but profound, religious experiences. If, in individuals' religious practices, the boundaries between sacred and profane are blurred, then there is considerable potential for experiencing the sacred while engaging in seemingly mundane activities like walking, gardening, washing dishes, or serving food in a soup kitchen.[86] We cannot really comprehend individuals' religious lives if we try to ignore the intense religious experiences many people value and seek.

Popular Traditions and Religion-as-Lived

Evangelical religiosity is highly variable from one individual to another, even in matters of salient beliefs and practices.[87] Protestant popular religious practices account for some of this diversity among southern white evangelicals (including among active and highly committed members of the same church). It is useful to consider the complex and varied ways that southern white evangelicals today may be drawing, without necessarily realizing it, on various popular beliefs and practices many of which are embedded in Southern cultural traditions. These persons may be using elements of their churches' traditions in ways that those who are purported authoritative guardians of those traditions have not intended or foreseen. But the nature of tradition has become extremely ambiguous, especially in nondenominational or proprietary congregations, which have no collective authority outside the congregation that could correct the beliefs and practices of the leaders and members. When popular religion is thoroughly embedded in institutions (e.g., Christian churches or Buddhist temples), the actual religion of individual members is likely to be all the more complex.

Sociologist Stephen Sharot has argued that the spread of new popular religious expressions in recent decades is qualitatively different from earlier patterns that were based on local communities. Today's popular religious beliefs, practices, and expressions are proffered by a "loosely structured network of groups, amorphous organizations, and businesses."[88] What that means for the individual's religion is that popular religious options are even further cut loose from institutional direction. As this chapter has illustrated, an individual's religion could include an elaborate combination of, say, a denominational tradition (e.g., Methodist—itself already an amalgam of popular and official religious elements), the preaching of a nondenominational church leader and the particular congregational practices of a nondenominational church, beliefs and practices learned from television or radio evangelists, practices related to objects sold at Christian gift shops, and more. Accordingly, official religions have even less control over the religious commodities (including popular religious commodities) on the market. At the same time, popular religion has become far less unified or socially supported by geographic communities than it once was. Interestingly, Sharot suggests that mass-marketed popular religious resources for individual bricolages among both evangelical Christians and adherents of alternative or so-called New Age healing movements share remarkably similar features: their decentralization and lack of institutionalization.[89]

Nevertheless, this development does not explain much about the actual practices people choose or the social contexts in which they use them. "Commodification" is an apt term for the selling of porcelain figurines, but it does not describe the social relationships in which those figurines are given as valued gifts, nor the personal religious practices of arranging them meaningfully in a home display. Marketing may be responsible for bringing an inspirational book to a person's attention, but it cannot account for his or her selection of one practice the book promotes and decision to ignore the rest. A person may listen each week to a favorite televangelist, but her interaction with other women in a religious weight-watchers' club may be far more important as a source of beliefs and practices for her personal religion. Such elements of individuals' lived religions have remained invisible to sociologists, despite their acknowledgment of a marketplace of popular religious options alongside the official ones.

5

Spirituality and Materiality

Why Bodies Matter

Many of us were brought up thinking that the spiritual realm is completely apart from the mundane material realm—perhaps even opposed to it. Western societies, in recent centuries, have tended to frame spirituality and materiality as dichotomous, in tidy binary opposition. Accordingly, those individuals who wanted to enhance their spirituality would have to overcome the burden of their materiality, deny their material urges and concerns, and transcend the limitations (perhaps also the pollution) of the material body.

I argue, to the contrary, that spirituality fully involves people's material bodies, not just their minds or spirits. The key connection here is not ideas about the body, or simply moral control of the body and its impulses. Rather, spirituality is closely linked with material human bodies—and not just bodies in the abstract. I mean real bodies—arthritic bodies, athletic bodies, pregnant bodies, malnourished bodies, healthy bodies, and suffering bodies. I mean human bodies that labor and rest, bodies that create and destroy, bodies that nurse babies and bodies that torture the bodies of others, bodies that eat, drink, fart, and sweat. With real material bodies, people also touch, hear, see, and taste their material worlds.

So why do these real bodies matter? What do they have to do with spirituality or religious concerns? As the preceding chapters show, we need to focus on religion as practiced and experienced by ordinary people in the context of their everyday lives. Religion, in this broad sociological sense, consists of how people make sense of their world—the stories out of which they live. Lived religion includes the myriad individual ways people put these stories into practice.

Sometimes, an individual's lived religion is closely linked with the teachings and practices of an official religion, such as a Christian denomination; that individual uses his or her group's stories and rituals to shape and interpret individual experience. There is no necessary connection with official religion, however. Many individuals—including active members of those religious groups—choose to believe and practice elements selected from multiple religious or cultural packages. Furthermore, people often use their religion-prescribed practices in ways completely unforeseen by the official religion. We must remember that humans are creative agents, not merely oversocialized automatons.

I am using the term "spirituality" to describe *the everyday ways ordinary people attend to their spiritual lives*. Some people describe themselves as deeply spiritual, and some devote considerable energy and discipline to their spiritual development. Others consider themselves not very spiritual or religious, or not interested in having a spiritual life. Some find spiritual development and support as committed members of a congregation; others see no connection between their spiritual lives and any organized religious group. Some consciously choose practices to enhance their spirituality; others notice their spiritual practices only retrospectively or when asked to think consciously of them (for instance, in response to a sociologist-interviewer).

Lived religion is *constituted by the practices* people use to remember, share, enact, adapt, create, and combine the stories out of which they live. And it comes into being through the often-mundane practices people use to transform these meaningful interpretations into everyday action.[1] Human bodies matter, because those practices—even interior ones, such as contemplation—involve people's bodies, as well as their minds and spirits.[2]

Spirituality and Embodied Practice

If our conception of religion is too narrow, then we fail to comprehend how central people's material bodies are in the very practice and experience of religion. All religions engage individuals through concrete practices that involve bodies as well as minds and spirits. It is easy for us to recognize those bodily practices when we think of, for example, Native American religious experience.[3] In that cultural context, intense bodily involvement in such practices as drumming, dancing, vision quests, smoking, feasting, sweating, and chanting is completely consistent with a high level of spiritual development.

In other contemporary cultures, including those of Europe and the Americas, religious practices and experiences are similarly linked with people's bodies. For instance, think about how you would arrange your physical environment if you wanted to reach a deeply spiritual state of being. Where do you imagine you would be? In a corner of a peaceful garden? In your own room? In an empty chapel? In a processional throng? What postures and gestures would you find conducive to religious experience? Kneeling? Standing? Sitting on a chair? Lying prostrate? Sitting in a lotus position? Eyes closed or open? Head bowed or upright? Hands clapping? Folded on your lap? Uplifted? Holding the hands of others? Arms swaying? Body rocking? Body twirling? Breath slow and drawn out? Breath rhythmic, in time with a drumbeat or music? What physical connection to others do you imagine? Does a human touch promote your spiritual depth or does it get in the way? Do you need to be alone or in a group? And so on.

My point is that like Native Americans, most Euro-Americans also experience certain body practices—postures, movements, and ways of focusing the attention—as more conducive to spiritual experiences than others. Certain visual images, sounds, and smells heighten our spiritual focus and evoke meaningful religious experiences. Also, concrete body practices, such as a deeply felt embrace, promote our sense of connection with our spiritual community (i.e., the others with whom we share collective memories and experiences). Our sense of connection—our identification with family, community, and others—is based on a myriad of remembering practices, involving our bodies and emotions as well as our thoughts.[4]

Where is memory located? In Western ways of thinking, we tend to identify the memory as an operation solely of the brain. But biological and anthropological evidence suggests that memory resides in the whole body, for example, in nerve connections and in the cells of the immune system.[5] That means that memory can be closely connected with our senses and bodily states, including experiences of which we are not even conscious. For instance, traveling in Norway a few years ago, I smelled fresh-baked brown bread, and it kindled a memory of a wonderful loaf I had bought thirty years earlier in Monnickendam, Holland. The olfactory memory was so vivid that, unbidden, it instantly awoke dozens of related memories—sights, sounds, and tastes of my first experiences in Europe.

Anthropologist Pierre Bourdieu[6] suggests that all our senses—not just our physical senses but also our social senses—are involved in remembering practices and embodying practices.[7] Thus, our bodies have embedded in them certain learned senses (such as a sense of justice, sense of good taste, moral sense, sense of disgust, and common sense). For instance, our sense of disgust is learned; it is clearly not the same in all cultures, and babies have not yet acquired it. Yet, once learned, that sense causes us to react to a disgusting scene viscerally, for example needing to vomit if we witness gruesome torture. Each culture imbues the body with a myriad meanings that serve as both maps and repertoires for individual experience and expression. This meaning, however, is not merely a cognitive or symbolic overlay. Rather, through ritual practice, social meanings become physically embodied—much in the way practice makes the music of an étude, become part of the "ways of the hand."[8] If we accept Bourdieu's thesis about embodiment and social practices, then we can understand how senses—not only moral senses but also religious ones—can be acquired and embedded in our bodily experience.

Sociologist Danièle Hervieu-Léger has described religion as a chain of memory by which people are linked with the traditions of their faith community. Most people think of the transmission of such memory as a cognitive process, with children learning about the community's religious beliefs, scripture, and norms. But Hervieu-Léger reminds us that there are other important components, such as emotion, that are transmitted as part of that memory.[9] I suggest that religious or spiritual practices are ways individuals engage their socialized senses in the activation of embodied memory. Bodies matter very much, both in the individual's spiritual life and in the development of a community—a community of memory.[10] Later in this and other chapters, I develop some examples to show why bodies matter for both individual and collective spirituality.

Religious ritual is like a chain of such embodied practices, each link having the potential to activate deep emotions and a sense of social connectedness, as well as spiritual meanings. The practices for engaging in ritual are embodied—embedded in the participant's mind-body as a unity. Body practices can make body metaphor a physical, mental, and emotional reality. For example, in most East Asian Mahayana Buddhism, enlightenment involves the entire body/mind complex: "We become the buddha through our bodies," according to Kukai (774–835 CE), founder of Shingon Buddhism. Kukai emphasized the use of specific spiritual practices to accomplish mental, verbal, and bodily intimacy with the Buddha. Mental intimacy is established by various practices of meditation. Verbal intimacy occurs through the discipline of the mantras, which are not mere representations of ideas (much less prayer-like words and phrases) but, when they are sounded, involve literally bodily harmonization with the vibrations or resonances they produce. Behavioral intimacy occurs through body practices—disciplined bodily postures, especially hand gestures, that not only represent and express the meaning of enlightenment but physically mimic gestures of the Buddha that embody the Buddha's own enlightenment. Accordingly, through these practices, enlightenment becomes

FIGURE 5.1. Embodied practice is central to this writer/musician's spiritual life. Each workday begins with a centering exercise at this simple altar (one of several in his home), where he lights a candle, meditates, and writes what flows from his meditation. Courtesy Jim Spickard, used by permission of Toroverde Press.

a practical reality—not merely a metaphysical theory; the practitioner embodies Buddhahood.[11]

Each link in the ritual chain of practices thus has the potential to evoke social senses related to other links. Through embodied practices, we confirm the reality—not just the symbolic idea—of the ritual act. In this sense, ritual produces a real effect, sometimes privately for the individual practicing it and sometimes for a whole social group engaged in ritual practice.[12] When people describe ritual as "dead" or "lifeless" or "meaningless," they typically refer to ritual practices that have been severed from people's emotions, social ties, and spiritual experiences so that they merely "go through the motions" of a ritual practice. But an utterly *dis*embodied religious belief may be equally lifeless, because it is likely to be relevant only in the believer's thoughts.

Perhaps it is a modern conceit to think that our religious practices are more civilized because they are less linked with our human bodies than premodern practices were.[13] But any religion that speaks only to the cognitive aspect of adherents' experience (i.e., limited to their beliefs and thoughts) cannot address their emotional needs, their everyday experiences, or their whole persons.

Human embodiment, the quality of having and being intimately identified with our human bodies, is a defining part of our humanity. All religions address embodiment in some way, as they speak to human concerns about bodily health, suffering, birth, and death. In theory, Christian religions should be particularly aware of human embodiment because of their central idea of Christ's incarnation and, thus, Christ's humanity. But because of several different historical developments, many Christian groups today are uncomfortable with any emphasis on human embodiment, especially with religious practices that call attention to the material body or treat it as anything but profane.

Human material concerns—such as bodily sickness and pain, childbearing and fertility, and the need for adequate food, shelter, and protection from adversity—are still important to people. Engaging in ritual or practical actions to address those material concerns is, likewise, part of many people's religious practice. I would argue that for many (perhaps most) individuals today, everyday ritual practices that link their spiritual lives with their mundane material lives continue to contribute to their lived religions, albeit in different ways from those of the late medieval and early modern eras.

Ritual Practice: Bodily Grounding of Religion

Because people thought in bodily images (rather than trying to repress them as many nineteenth- and twentieth-century sensibilities were socialized to do), medieval spirituality actively used images of the divine body.[14] The era's mystical spirituality was based on considerable physicality (even though it attempted to transcend the material world).[15] Medieval ritual practice was particularly rich in visual sensations, and hearing, smelling, touching, and tasting were also used to promote everyday religious experience. Physically sensing the smell of burning beeswax candles, the sound of a church bell, the touch of a fingered cross could create a desired religious experience. Performing religiously meaningful postures, gestures, and ritual acts could also produce— physically as well as spiritually—a religious sense of awe and worshipfulness. Bodily sensations produce a confirmation that what one is experiencing is real, not just imaginary. Especially in such an intensely visual cultural setting as medieval society, visual sensations made spiritual experiences vividly real.[16] Sight was linked with insight.

Let me illustrate this characterization of embodied religious practice with my own experience a few years ago. I need to preface this story by mentioning that I am a practicing Quaker. Although they value mystical experience at least as much as medieval Catholicism did, Quakers nowadays do not promote many body practices—mainly just the use of silence for "practicing the presence" of the divine. So the intensely physical, sensual practices of medieval Christians were a little hard for me to fathom, until I experienced a few occasions for physically imagining them.

I was living in Salzburg, Austria, during a sabbatical leave, and was immersed in reading historians' analyses of late medieval religious practices. It was a bitterly cold March night when I walked across the high hills overlooking the old city of Salzburg to the tenth-century Benedictine abbey to hear an American quartet of women singing the medieval chants of Hildegard of Bingen (CE 1098–1179). Even wearing wool socks and slacks, winter boots, and a down coat, I never got warm inside the church. The sanctuary was dark, the wooden seats hard, and the stone walls stark. As the singing began, the only sounds were the rise and fall of the chant and an occasional creak of a pew as someone shifted weight. I tried to imagine the nuns of Hildegard's time praying the early morning canonical hours in such an abbey. Their voices would not have been so beautiful or studied as these performers,' but their minds, bodies, and spirits were probably more focused on the ritual act. Their spirituality would have literally incorporated the sensations they were experiencing, including the numb cold of their fingers, the soaring sounds of the chants, punctuated by deep church bells tolling the hours, the smells of the beeswax candles that dimly lit the choir, and the captivating visual image of a brilliant medieval altar triptych, the only brightly lit object in the cavernous church. As the luminous altar painting riveted my attention, I recalled depictions of medieval religious sensibilities I had read earlier that very week: sight linked with insight; sensual experience linked with spiritual reality; emotions evoked, expressed, and ritually transformed. Although there is no way for an ethnographer today to comprehend adequately the religious experiences of persons living centuries ago, it is methodologically important that we take them seriously and try to understand them on their own terms, rather than in terms of our own cultural assumptions. That night, becoming acutely aware of how my own senses, emotions, and attention were thoroughly enmeshed in a moving experience, even without the intention of religious activity, I began to grasp how such embodied practices as those of the nuns in that abbey, centuries earlier, could engage an entire mind-body-self in a meaning-filled, deeply felt spiritual experience.

Medieval religious practice also involved bodily performance and dramatic enactment. People participated not only by watching public religious displays (e.g., processions) but also by engaging themselves in enactments of religious meanings. Mystery plays, Passion plays, dramatic enactments of biblical or other religious stories, dances and musical performances, and ritual spectacles (such as the penitential processions of Holy Week) were significant parts of lay religiosity.

These regular performances involved participants and spectators in the ritual action through their bodily engagement, making divine power tangibly present. People encountered religious meaning less as thought and more as sensed, or as spiritually experienced, in their bodies and emotions, as well as spirits.

What would sociologists of religion notice or understand differently if we were to reexamine contemporary religious expressions with an eye to religious practice—not just belief? What would we see if we looked for ordinary, mundane ritual practices and other everyday lived religious experiences, rather than indicators of official religiosity? Specifically, how might we comprehend embodied practices in today's patterns of spirituality? Here, I draw three different examples of how contemporary patterns of spirituality involve embodied practices to produce both individual and communal spiritual experience.

Embodied Practice and Contested Boundaries: Food and Eating

Food—obtaining it, preparing it, serving it, and eating it—is one important material aspect of religious practice that was redefined (as not properly religious) during the Long Reformation. According to subsequent boundaries delimiting what would be considered religion, official religions allowed only spiritual food in their truncated ritual practices. For Catholics and some Protestants, spiritual food meant Communion elements, while for other Protestants, the only true spiritual food was sacred scripture.[17] Other food and eating, even that done in the company of the congregation, was denigrated as merely profane or became outright forbidden as licentious. In the "Battle of Carnival versus Lent," according to historian Peter Burke, Carnival's feasts became suspect as occasions for sinful excess (e.g., gluttony), while Lent's austere meals were transformed into mere sustenance.[18] Wakes and weddings—previously occasions of considerable community feasting and entertainment, often in the church building itself—were reduced to private and more moderate, sober, and decorous practices.[19] The few religious meanings of food that were retained were treated as symbols and metaphors.

Because spiritual food was symbolic of important boundaries (i.e., dividing the pure from the impure, a religious community from outsiders, and so on), its meaning was contested.[20] In the nineteenth and twentieth centuries, for example, American Protestant churches had considerable internal disagreement about the proper Communion foods and the appropriate vessels for serving them. One issue for many Protestant groups was whether to substitute grape juice for wine, in keeping with their support of the temperance movement. The other issue was whether to abandon the common cup and serve the wine or grape juice in separate glasses. As early as the 1880s, entrepreneurs marketed trays with slots for tiny Communion cups, to cater to class-conscious laypeople's fears of contamination. By the end of the twentieth century, technology allowed them to market the ultimate mass-produced Communion elements, advertised as "sanitary": an individual prepackaged sip of grape juice in one compartment and a morsel of bread in another, conveniently wrapped in disposable plastic.[21] Thus, even the foods defined as "spiritual" were surrounded with mundane concerns, tinged with social class and racial biases. And the foods defined as "mundane" were separate.

After the Long Reformation, the ritual practices surrounding mundane food—obtaining, preparing, serving, and eating it—no longer counted as religious practices. Thus, when the churches effectively changed the definition of religion, they simultaneously eliminated or greatly truncated most of the ways people previously had involved their bodies in religious practices and experiences. Food and eating retained only minor vestigial significance as metaphors for spiritual nourishment. Indeed, if anything, it was abstaining from eating that was valued spiritually, especially by women ascetics. The material world, with which human bodies were identified, came to be distinguished dramatically from the spiritual realm.

Defined out of official religious practice, festive eating continued to be a part of popular religious expression, for example among ethnic communities celebrating the feast days of their particular old-country patron saints.[22] Unfortunately, sociologists who have viewed popular religious practices as merely vestigial of peasant folkways have failed to observe that many fully acculturated, well-educated, economically comfortable modern persons have likewise found the preparation and eating of special foods and celebration of meaningful feasts to be highly spiritual practices.

Many persons interviewed in my researches described spiritual practices that valorized mundane domestic materiality, such as the processes of growing, cooking, and eating food. For example, two couples who incorporated Buddhist meditative practices into their Christian spirituality described their cooking and eating as "mindful," and as "being fully present."[23] Others described gardening, especially organic gardening, as a spiritual practice.[24] Late modern capitalist societies promote the commodification of time and time-saving practices, such as buying processed foods to heat and serve or consuming fast food.[25] It takes considerable effort to buck this tide. Think about, for example, how much of their everyday routines most adult Americans would have to change in order simply to eat their meals as a mindful practice!

And what about the body experience of preparing food? Can you imagine cooking as a religious practice? My husband and I became aware of what difference mindful food preparation can make when we visited Tassajara Zen Center (a remote retreat in the mountains near Carmel, California).[26] Without electricity and labor-saving appliances, the Buddhist monks made from scratch the hearty soups, hot fresh breads, and tangy salads served to guests, and all the picking, cooking, and serving were an integral to their spirituality. One long-time cook at Tassajara wrote:

> Though recipes abound, for soups and salads,
> breads and entrees, for getting enlightened
> and perfecting the moment, still
> the unique flavor of Reality
> appears in each breath, each bite,
> each step, unbounded and undirected.[27]

Eating and cooking are thus spiritual practices that become paths to enlightenment, a realization of Buddhist be-here-nowness. The spiritual practice is largely a matter of attention, staying mindful of the work of chopping, stirring, kneading rather than getting lost in dreams and emotions; remaining composed in the midst of the business of cooking. Accordingly, cooking is simultaneously a spiritual and material activity.[28] The practice of mindfulness also transforms the serving and eating process at Tassajara. Those who were serving the food related to those who were eating with a mutual respect and sense of honor that is conspicuously lacking not only in commercial restaurants but also in most homes. Those who were eating the food were drawn into the meditative atmosphere. The room was full of quiet conversations, laughter, and smiles, but it would have seemed a sacrilege to bolt the food down and race out or to consume it while raucously recounting bad jokes.

When we allow that food preparation and eating can be highly meaningful spiritual practices, we can have a different appreciation of women's religious roles. The same process of boundary creation during the Long Reformation also effectively marginalized much of women's religious contribution, especially their domestic religious practices. Many people, particularly influential leaders of religious organizations, came to view women's spiritual practices as at best unimportant and at worst downright dangerous. Accordingly, people also came to view women's domestic practices, such as the preparation of the special foods for the Day of the Dead and the feeding of participants at a neighborhood performance of Los Pastores (described in chapter 3), as "merely" cooking. I argue, to the contrary, that these women's popular religiosity reflects a mingling of sacred and profane in their own homes, gardens, and daily life. Food preparation and eating are, for many people, important spiritual practices.

We should not lose sight of the fact that some important everyday practices still take place in the home, in the realm of domestic materiality. For example, one of my colleague-friends considers herself a "spiritual but not religious" Jew-Buddhist-Wiccan. In practice, that means that she does not try to observe many traditional Jewish religious practices at home or synagogue, but she draws on meaningful parts of her Jewish upbringing for her personal spiritual life. Because Jewish religious practices for women were traditionally also mainly domestic practices, my friend found herself "sifting through" those practices to see if any still connected with her inner life. One she rediscovered almost by accident. She had been merrily describing her pathetic attempts, early in her marriage, to keep a kosher kitchen at Passover. Her self-deprecating, humorous stories had our small gathering of women friends in gales of laughter. But when she shifted to describing the (woman's) domestic ritual of lighting a candle for the blessing of the Sabbath loaf of bread, her tone changed dramatically. As she talked, she held her hands and directed her eyes exactly as in the classic prayer gesture, her expression genuinely devout. She, too, noticed that she felt different about that practice, and she exclaimed, "It's *in* my body! That whole blessing—my body remembers it."[29]

That exclamation illustrates what Paul Connerton calls "incorporating practices": ways memories come to be embedded in a person's bodily experience.[30] My friend's lived religion includes that Sabbath blessing somewhat regularly now, but not just in order to fulfill her religious tradition's role expectations for women. Rather, she has adapted it and made it part of her own spirituality.

Similarly, we would better understand women's roles in African American churches if we allowed that the preparation, serving, and eating of church suppers may be as much a religious practice as singing in the choir or preaching. Members consider preparing a church supper not just service but ministry.[31] Anthropologist Peter Goldsmith noted the centrality of food as religious expression in a black Pentecostal church on the Georgia coast. He emphasized that not only did the experience of eating together produce a sense of community but also, indeed, the work of preparing food was an important form of religious production and self-definition.[32]

Often, women's religious practice of food preparation and serving is a form of gifting that builds community interrelatedness and reciprocity. As part of her ethnographic research, Wendy Cadge participated in frequent food-preparation sessions with other women at a Thai Buddhist temple near Philadelphia. She describes their cooking, as well as subsequent giving of food (as alms) to the monks, as a central religious practice, not only for the women themselves but also for the monks and other members, who participated in a communal relationship around that receiving and eating of food.[33] In order to understand women's lived religion fully, we need to appreciate their ritual practices centered on the so-called private, domestic, familial sphere, where their roles are likely to be more active and expressive. These private sphere rituals are at least as important as participation in the public, organizational sphere, where women's ritual roles have traditionally been more passive or nonexistent.

Challenging the Western philosophical tradition that valorizes "knowing work" while denigrating "hand work" or practical work, philosopher Lisa Heldke argues that growing, cooking, and eating food should be understood as forms of "bodily knowledge."[34] She explains:

> The knowing involved in making a cake is "contained" not simply
> "in my head" but in my hands, my wrists, my eyes and nose as well.
> The phrase "bodily knowledge" is not a metaphor. It is an acknowl-
> edgment of the fact that I *know* things literally with my body, that I, "as"
> my hands, know when the bread dough is sufficiently kneaded.

Heldke suggests that growing and preparing food are thoughtful practices that both use and generate emotional and erotic energy—not merely as incidentals but as vital parts of the process.[35] Although persons who engage in such embodied practices do not necessarily understood them as spiritual, their potential to involve integrally a person's knowing body, knowing mind, sensations, memory, emotions, and spirit is evident.

Courtney Bender's ethnography about kitchen volunteers at God's Love We Deliver, a nonprofit, nonreligious organization providing home-cooked meals for people with AIDS, illustrates how varied are people's spiritual practices in relationship to cooking and giving food. One volunteer explained: "There's something real basic about feeding hungry people. . . . I think there's something spiritual that happens when you feed somebody. I think that's so basic, and because it's so basic it's so intimate, even though I don't know who it's going to."[36] Describing her experience of cooking in this context, the same volunteer said, "This is the experience we can have of God. . . . I think work *is* prayer, essentially."[37]

She was describing another embodied practice to which I turn next: when work is a spiritual practice. First, however, I want to highlight what Bender noted about this woman's practice of cooking as a specifically spiritual practice. Unlike the Zen monks at Tassajara, this volunteer did not view all the cooking she did as a spiritual practice; her paid work as a caterer involved frequent days of hectic food preparation, which she clearly distinguished from her weekly commitment to cook at God's Love We Deliver. Bender points out that what enabled her to experience her volunteer cooking as prayer was her "simple intention to make it so." In forming that intention, she brought to it her wish to "do something" for others, her memories of her previous experiences of family and community, and her experience of connection to religious traditions and their practices.[38] This observation is important for our understanding of lived religion, because it shows how individual choice—the decision to distinguish certain practices from other, ordinary, practices—is nonetheless situated in the context of family and communal relationships. Individually chosen practices also exist in the context of memories and traditions that link the individual with those social influences, but not in a deterministic or fixed way.

Ora et Labora: When Work Is a Spiritual Practice

"Pray and Work" was the motto St. Benedict proposed in the sixth century for monks living according to his rule. In principle, the monastic community was continually doing both simultaneously: praying as they worked in the fields, kitchens, and scriptoria, yet working as they prayed together in choir eight times each day and night, as well as in silent meditation and individual prayer.[39] Luther promoted a somewhat different valorization of work in his reformation movement, when he encouraged all Christians, not only the religious virtuosi, to heed divine calling—literally, vocation—to their particular work. All these religious ideals notwithstanding, few people (then or now) appear to experience their work as a central spiritual practice. This discrepancy tells us as much about the nature of most people's work lives as about their spiritual lives and religion-as-practiced. For most people, work occurs in the profane world and is experienced as very separate from their religious or spiritual lives.

Yet there are many exceptions to that generalization. It is worthwhile to consider how and why some people's spiritual lives are closely integrated with their work lives, as exemplified by Peter's work with homeless families and Margaret's joyful toil in her garden. We might ask why it seems so exceptional that the artists interviewed by sociologist Robert Wuthnow described a close interrelationship of their spiritual practice and their work as artists. For example, a potter explained:

> I began to feel a connection between meditation and throwing on the wheel. When you're on the wheel ... it gets to the point of being a meditation-like state, where your perceptions are changing. You begin to see things in a different light, things that are lying dormant at other times.[40]

A dancer observed, "My practice [Buddhist meditation and chanting] is not separate from my life; it's all integrated. My choreography, my performance is all a reflection of my practice."[41] And a sculptor who carved *santos* (statues of saints) and *retablos* (devotional plaques) described her wood-carving work as prayer, inseparable from her spiritual life.[42]

One characteristic these artists share with many of my respondents is the sense of connection of body, mind, and spirit, both in their work and in their spiritual practices. Margaret, who called her daily work in the garden her "worship service," described deeply spiritual connections she made when physically touching the earth (which is why, whenever possible, she gardens without gloves). Other senses were involved in her meditative practice, too, especially smell and sight—the smell of the air after a summer shower, the sight of a butterfly hovering over a flower, the sounds of frogs chirping from a nearby pond, the feel of the dirt-covered skins of newly dug potatoes, and the many shades of green. The quality of her garden work made her spiritual practice richer, while her spiritual practice made her garden work more than a chore, more than just work.

Like Margaret, most people in advanced technological societies have to make a conscious decision to seek only certain kinds of jobs in certain kinds of places in order to accomplish this kind of close integration of their work life and spiritual life. For example, it would be difficult, if not impossible, for a person working as a telemarketer to be able to engage in any personal thought, meditation, creativity, or prayer, while making computer-scripted and computer–paced telephone sales pitches. In contrast to the medieval monastic scriptorium, today's script copying is likely to be performed by a harried keyboard typist with carpal tunnel syndrome linking her body and her work in tension and pain—hardly conducive to reflective attention to anything. For example, one data entry clerk said:

> My fingers are moving all the time, my eyes are staring into a machine.... It's impossible to talk or even to turn around and look at someone else. My job is basically to copy numbers and letters all day, but most of the time I'm not even aware of them. It's like my hands and my eyes are alive and my mind and my body are dead.[43]

Although there might be superficial similarities between such work and that of the potter and gardener described earlier, a person working on a pottery assembly line and a migrant farmworker picking lettuces behind a mechanized pacer lack the autonomy over their space and time to engage simultaneously in any deep spiritual practice. Furthermore, unlike Margaret, the exploited farmworker cannot experience the fruits of his or her labor as a gift to those who will use them.[44]

Considering these differences in the engagement, connection, and attention of the worker, is it any surprise that we sense a difference in their products? The food prepared meditatively by the Buddhist monks is qualitatively different from the food prepared mechanically by workers controlled by "McDonaldized" work processes.[45] Likewise, the artist's pottery—even the "spoiled" pieces—is qualitatively different from that of the assembly line. And vegetables that are produced joyfully, meditatively, and organically (in both the literal and figurative senses of the word) may be qualitatively different from those produced mechanically and harvested by exploited workers.

This connection between spirituality and work—particularly artistic work—is recognizable in Shaker craft work. The Shakers were an eighteenth-century millenarian movement who lived a communal life of ascetic simplicity, celibacy, and hard work. Their spiritual practices, such as singing and dancing—which, interestingly, they called "laboring"—involved, in every detail, their bodies as well as their emotions, minds, and spirits.[46] Shakers believed that they were already living after the return of the Messiah, so they put into practice their sense that they were living in the heavenly next world.

Their work, therefore, was done to bring about a correspondence between their mundane world and the heavenly one it dimly resembled. Belden Lane points out:

> Shakers thus looked upon the material thing, fashioned by assiduous manual labor, as serving a dual purpose. By fulfilling most simply and perfectly its function in this world—whether it be a straight-backed chair, a patterned quilt, or a well-pruned fruit tree, it also became emblematic of the simplicity and perfection of that world to which this one dimly corresponds. Things could, in themselves, carry one more deeply into the multi-dimensional reality made present by the second coming of Christ.[47]

Shakers viewed their attentive work—especially the creation of beautiful and useful things for mundane uses in their heaven-like community—as worship and as imitative of divine creation. Thomas Merton suggested that "the peculiar grace of a Shaker chair is due to the fact that it was made by someone capable of believing that an angel might come and sit on it."[48] Interestingly, Merton, a twentieth-century contemplative monk, recognized important resonances between his Trappist (Benedictine) spiritual practices and those of the Shakers, who had all but died out by the early part of his century. He reportedly applied to his abbot to try to practice Shaker spirituality as preparation for writing a book about them. He wrote: "My part would not be precisely a study of their religion, if by that is to be understood their doctrines, but of their spirit and I might say, their mysticism, in practice, as evidenced by their life and their craftsmanship."[49] In other words, Merton knew that to grasp the Shakers' lived religion, he had to understand experientially their spiritual practices of work.

Making Music Together: Spiritual Practice and Intersubjectivity

The phenomenologist Alfred Schutz used "making music together" as a metaphor for the ways people relate deeply with each other, sharing subjective experiences.[50] Although this metaphor could apply equally to a jazz combo and a religious choir, it gives us a clue about how an embodied spiritual practice (especially singing) can literally produce religious experience and sense of community.

I described earlier a group of musicians (the Anonymous Four) singing a cappella medieval chants written by Hildegard of Bingen. These hymns require considerable vocal interdependence, even though there is no harmony line, because each part is lyrically interwoven such that each singer must come in at the right moment. But there is no conductor, no obvious beat or percussion instrument setting a tempo to coordinate the interdependence. It was fascinating to watch how the singers communicated nonverbally to accomplish this coordination. I noticed how the intonation of a chant was rotated among the four, with the use of rocking and bowing to each other as cues for timing. A clear norm was that no one singer should seem to stand out, either by her volume or virtuosity or badge of leadership. How much more must this interdependence have been a spiritual value in medieval cloisters!

Perhaps because of my own experience of choral singing, I could easily imagine how such singing together could become a moving spiritual experience that literally effected community. And my childhood experiences of my family of seven heartily singing together in the car, around the campfire, and beside my grandmother's piano are deeply embedded—and profoundly embodied—memories of how singing together both reflects and produces unity and harmony. The physical sensations of producing song—sensations of resonance in one's head, of breathing deeply to sustain long notes, of hearing one's own voice meld in harmony with others'—are all deeply sensual yet potentially also spiritual experiences.

The uses of time in making music together also produce an experiential sense of togetherness—perhaps even intersubjective experience. *Intersubjectivity* refers to the apprehension of another's subjective experience, for example emotion, that is not mediated by conscious thought—in which the other or the other's experience is the object of thought. Schutz was interested in how the structure of individuals' "lifeworlds," which are socially shaped and thus shared, made possible such intense social experiences.[51] If we combine Schutz's insights about the complex ways people can transcend everyday boundaries between self and other with Merleau-Ponty's emphasis on the immediate connection between a person's body and consciousness,[52] we get clues about how religious experience can be deeply subjective yet shared experience.[53]

To sing together, we must adjust our timing to fit with others.' Often this means bodily timing, as with our breathing or rhythmic motions like toe tapping or rocking. Breathing is the epitome of an embodied practice.[54] Although all living persons must breathe and do so autonomically, our social, psychological, and religious practices can profoundly affect our breathing patterns. *Pranayama* yoga, for instance, is a physical/spiritual discipline that uses control of the breath to effect other changes in the mind-body-spirit, as a whole. Practitioners hold that one practice of *pranayama*, involving regular rhythmic, slow breathing through alternate nostrils, literally accomplishes physical, emotional, spiritual, and social balance.

Communal religious settings can produce a resonance of several individuals' experiences and thus an even deeper sense of sharing "inner time."[55] A good example of such intersubjective experience is the Navajo chant for healing that lasts for several days and nights, through which participants attune their individual experiences toward the culturally valued sense of harmony between the individual, social group, and environment.[56] Thus, such intense intersubjective experience and shared time can accomplish the needed harmony that constitutes healing.

In Western cultures, the very notion of singing in harmony is, likewise, highly social. If a group is to produce what we have learned culturally to hear as harmonious, individual members cannot wildly improvise or deviate from the group's designated chord. Indeed, some groups interpret the accomplishment of musical harmony as a divine blessing of their group's social and spiritual harmony. For example, several Catholic charismatic prayer groups that I observed especially valued what they called "singing in tongues" for the sense of harmony that emerged. For them, the actual words (i.e., glossolalia) receded in importance (except that participants generally believed that the unintelligible "words" in this kind of singing were God-given). Thus, when "singing in tongues" occurs during a prayer meeting, the prayer group collectively attends only to the resulting harmonious chord.[57]

A dramatically different spiritual use of making music together is the U.S. revival of Sacred Harp (or "shape note") hymn singing.

For this music, unlike most choral singing, a director is not really necessary once singers have learned their parts (facilitated by the simple shape notes and predictable rhythms). People typically sing every song at the top of their lungs, regardless of the beauty of their voices or the accuracy of their pitch. Singing at the top of one's voice, sometimes for three or four hours at a time, is a profoundly embodied practice, affecting breathing, hearing, consciousness, and sense of connectedness with other participants. Interestingly, the revival of Sacred Harp singing appears to be taking place outside church organizations per se, even though it is clearly still a religious expression. Singers at a day-long "sing" may come from a wide range of Christian denominational backgrounds and thus experience a kind of temporary community.[58] My impression, however, is that they are bound together by the practice of Sacred Harp singing far more than by any beliefs held in common. Indeed, several participants have told me that before they could enjoy the singing of these early American hymns, they had to overcome their personal theological objections to the religious ideas the words expressed.

The temporary community of a Sacred Harp sing, although real, is far looser than the community expressed by an Appalachian congregation of Primitive Baptists singing together. Consonant with their extreme form of congregational polity, each Primitive Baptist congregation expresses its unique identity, tradition, and narrowly localistic sense of community in its very practice of singing together.[59] Congregational singing, which often lasts an hour before the official beginning of each worship service, is a central ritual practice in these churches. Each congregation has developed its unique way of singing hymns, and members feel at home only with their own local community's song style. One traditional style that highlights the communal quality of the practice of singing together is "lining out," which involves the song leaders' calling out the words of the next line of a song as the congregation is singing the last words of the previous line. For those who identify with it, the practice creates an experiential sense of spiritually elevated community. One church elder whose congregation kept this tradition explained:

> Now when a song is sung with great movement [of the spirit] ... it will be lined in the same way.... When a song is really sung together, and I'm saying now all of the people in unity and putting forth their voices, being magnified together ... it really causes the man who's [lining] it to be as magnified as the people are in singing. And you'll find a difference.[60]

A completely different communal singing was the Gospel Hour, a two-hour gospel hymn service and sing-along that was held on a weekly basis at an Atlanta gay bar in the 1990s. The performing trio, the Gospel Girls, included two gay men in drag (wearing sequined gowns, wigs, and makeup); many of the mostly gay audience sang together enthusiastically. Many (perhaps most) participants in the Gospel Hour experienced genuine religious feeling and community. One participant said, "My friends and I call it 'coming to services.' " The simultaneous ritual performance of evangelical Christian gospel hymns and of high drag serves to assert an alternative Christian message for gay worshipers and to symbolically erase gender boundaries exaggerated by the dominant society.[61] Singing gospel hymns together both expressed and partially resolved the dissonance experienced by gays whose religious memory is based on southern evangelical tradition.

Each of these kinds of spiritual making music together reflects and reproduces a different kind of spiritual experience. Such experiences clearly involve the body integrally. Embodied practices, such as singing, tap emotions and memories. Collective embodied practices, such as singing or dancing together, can produce an experiential sense of community and connectedness. These three examples of arenas in which embodied practices link materiality and spirituality are hardly exhaustive. Other vocalizations, other motions and postures, other ways of involving the body, mind, and spirit all figure into the religious and spiritual experiences of many individuals and groups.[62] Without the full involvement of the material body, religion is likely to be relegated to the realm of cognition (i.e., beliefs, opinions, theological ideas). Embodied practices, including mundane and seemingly unexceptional activities like singing and preparing a meal, link individuals' materiality as humans and their spirituality.

Marching in Formation: Reflections on a Darker Image

Embodied practices were clearly part of the lived religions of many people described in this chapter, such as the dancers and potters interviewed by Robert Wuthnow. When I had finished reading Robert Wuthnow's book *Creative Spirituality: The Way of the Artist*,[63] I thought, "What interesting people! I would love to talk with some of them." And I envied Bob's research grants that allowed him to spend a whole year meeting artists of all kinds and interviewing them about their spiritual lives. His reports confirmed my own research findings on key questions important for sociological interpretation: Are the personal spiritual practices of persons who do not adhere to the norms for church religiosity necessarily more superficial than that of those who do? Are people who focus on so-called spiritual practices somehow more individualistic and self-centered than those who focus on what they consider "religious" practices? Can we speak of commitment and discipline in reference to spiritualities that are not closely connected with a religious group?

The sculptors, potters, dancers, and musicians Wuthnow interviewed demonstrated high degrees of discipline, commitment, creative expressiveness, and spiritual depth, both in their work lives and their spiritual lives (which many interviewees saw as one and the same). Conveying each person's story with considerable respect, Wuthnow portrays an enormous range of approaches to spiritual development, only a few of which (barely) fit the standard image of church-oriented spiritual practice. Rather, as diverse as their stories are, these artists reflect the kinds of eclecticism and creative adaptations, explorations and struggles, the processes of inner growth and spiritual development and change that many of my own respondents have expressed. Like Wuthnow, I have learned about many spiritual practices not adequately represented in most of the sociological literature on religion and religiosity. Sociologists need to take all kinds of religious and spiritual practices and beliefs into consideration, according them at least as much respect and appreciation as we would the beliefs and practices that fit the dominant model of religion.

But in eschewing the historical boundary-work that has defined religion too narrowly, we have to be careful not to use other implicit boundaries that exclude from our purview the religious and spiritual practices we personally find repulsive. We need to allow for the very real possibility that just as there are creative spiritualities, there may also be destructive spiritualities. Just as some people may seek spiritual practices that bring their lives into a greater sense of harmony, beauty, peace, and compassion, others may engage in practices that develop a purer hatred of the Other and that literally, as well as figuratively, embody violence and aggression.

Consider the image of the following historical event:

With a half moon lighting their path, two thousand Georgians climbed to the treeless plateau on top of Stone Mountain, to witness a dramatic initiation. The Grand Dragon, in his rich green robe, led seven hundred figures, shrouded in white sheets, up the mountainside. Beyond them marched hundreds of other men, initiates with uncovered heads and dark suits. The initiates marched in lock step, single file, each man's arms on the shoulders of the man in front. . . . In the eerie light of the towering flaming cross—three hundred feet tall and two hundred wide—the initiates kneeled and bowed their heads before two white knights, one bearing a cross, the other an American flag. They repeated the oath by which Klansmen were made: "I most solemnly swear that I will forever keep sacredly secret the signs, words, and grip and any and all other matters and knowledge of the klan. . . . I will die rather than divulge same, so help me God." It was May 9, 1946. The ceremonies had been postponed many times, leaders complained, because of the wartime shortage of sheets.[64]

Would not the ritual experience of an initiate or a witness to this impressive event be as affected by these embodied practices as are the experiences of the artists, singers, gardeners, healers, mothers, or other spiritually engaged persons I have described in this chapter? The sheer physicality of the experience—the physical exertion of the climb up the mountainside, the initiates' lockstep march and the physical connection of the arms-to-shoulders postures, the visual images of a huge flaming cross and hundreds of shrouded Klansmen—must have been powerful experientially as well as symbolically. The initiates took on their new identities and identifications with brother Klansmen by ritually embodying key features—the white sheet obscuring their everyday identities, and their new gestures (like the ritual handshake and other occult signs) evoking their new identities as initiates in the Klan.

In this book, I have tried to give some glimpses of how "darker"[65] spiritual practices might well be parts of ordinary people's religious lives. There are darker elements in most official religious traditions, as well as in their relatively unregulated, but parallel, popular religious traditions. History provides plenty of examples of religious beliefs and practices honing people's fears and hatreds, resulting in witch hunts, pogroms, crusades, massacres, and enslavements of peoples. Contemporary spiritualities of hatred and violence can be and have been developed—with a vast repertoire of religious and quasi-religious rituals, because historically rituals have long been associated with power and violence.[66]

What might such practices include? One likely feature is discipline. We tend to recognize discipline, especially self-discipline, as a sign of commitment and seriousness of purpose. People who engage in some religious or spiritual practice with little or no self-discipline seem to be dabbling or, worse, play-acting. For example, when I observed how much energy and discipline my respondents put into their alternative healing practices, I gained considerable respect for their claims that they were engaging in serious spiritual quests. Similarly, Wuthnow was impressed that the spiritual lives of the creative artists he interviewed were structured by remarkable discipline of their bodies/minds/spirits as unitary wholes.

While reading Wuthnow's description of one deeply committed and profoundly expressive dancer, at the same time, I challenged myself to think about how that person's noteworthy discipline differed (except in its positive creative intent) from the comparable military discipline Foucault has described.[67] Foucault emphasized that the primary function of body discipline was the production of "docile bodies." By contrast, the dancer emphasized creative autonomy. I wonder, however, if many people's spiritual or religious disciplines, when followed carefully, are not closer to producing the "docile bodies" of Foucault's dystopic image of modern society. Docile, for following demagogues into crusades against the Other? Docile, for submitting to abusive behavior by someone religiously legitimated as dominant? Docile, for not demanding just wages or safe working conditions? Docile, for marching in time with an authoritarian regime?

The body disciplines that produce a dancer capable of aesthetically pleasing virtuoso performances are not altogether different from those that hone the skills of a military commando capable of efficiently destroying many lives. If they are at all effective, embodied practices are hardly neutral.[68]

In order to understand individuals' religion-as-lived, we must avoid romanticizing certain embodied practices, while ignoring others we may deplore.

Lived Religion Is Embodied

Lived religion consists of the practices people use to remember, share, enact, adapt, and create the stories out of which they live. And lived religion comes into being through the practices people use to turn these stories into everyday action. Ordinary material existence, especially the human body, is the very stuff of these meaningful practices. Human bodies matter, because those practices—even interior ones, such as contemplation—involve people's bodies, as well as their minds and spirits. Here I have used the spiritual practices of preparing and eating food, of working, and of singing together as examples of material embodiment. Material bodies are also linked to spirituality through healing, sexuality and gender, through fertility, childbirth, and nursing, and a myriad other forms of embodied practices.

Our material bodies come to be linked with spirituality through social senses and through the ritual restructuring of our senses of space and time. Bodies matter, because humans are not disembodied spirits. Individuals' religions become lived only through involving individual's bodies, as well as minds, their emotions as well as their cognitions. Spirituality is developed by just such embodied practices.

6

Embodied Practices for Healing and Wholeness

This chapter examines the linkage between people's religious or spiritual practices and their practices for health and well-being. A considerable portion of the beliefs and practices that, after the Long Reformation, were historically defined out—as no longer pertaining to religion—had to do with people's bodies and emotions. When we notice individuals' religious practices, including those made invisible by historical boundary-setting processes, we realize that healing and maintaining health are often prominent parts of their religion-as-practiced.

The idea that religion and health are two utterly separate spheres, to be controlled by separate institutional specialists, is a relatively recent one. Its current form dates back two centuries, at most. Some sociologists use this extreme differentiation of religion and medicine to illustrate the highly rationalized character of modernity.[1] In scientifically advanced Western societies, supposedly, medical responses to illness are based on rational ways of knowing, scientific expertise, and technological control, whereas religious practices for health and healing frequently are considered to be irrational (even superstitious or magical) and ineffective ways of thinking and acting. By the mid–twentieth century, many observers—including some scholars of religion—had come to consider religious and other non-medical practices for health and healing relics of the past, holdovers from old-country, rural folkways, and surely characteristic only of the uneducated and those too poor to afford good medical care.

Interestingly, however, in the last decades of the twentieth century, precisely as modern, scientific biomedicine appeared to have consolidated its knowledge base and institutional control over the whole arena of defining and treating sickness, it became apparent that many people in Europe and the Americas were turning to nonmedical approaches to address some of their health-related needs. When I began my study of the many nonmedical healing approaches used by middle- and upper-middle-class suburbanites, I was not especially interested in religious healing practices, such as those I had already observed among Catholic charismatic groups. Rather, I expected religious approaches to be just one (albeit a prominent one) among many nonmedical approaches to health and healing in the particular demographic region of the study.

What I found, though, was that the vast majority of the persons interviewed considered physical and emotional health, spiritual depth and growth, and sense of well-being to be intertwined in an adamantly holistic linkage of mind, body, and spirit. Most of the nonmedical healing approaches respondents were using regularly had a central focus in the realm of the spirit, however conceived. I could have distinguished the holism of some (for instance, Episcopalian and Jewish) healing approaches as what could be called "religious" and the holism of others (for example, practitioners of *pranayama* yoga, psychic healing, Wiccan rituals, and midwifery for home childbirth) as "nonreligious" only if I had arbitrarily—by definition—excluded those that were not linked with recognized, official religious groups. That realization—that it was only the arbitrary definitional boundaries that made some respondents' practices appear "not religious"—led me from that writing project to this one. This chapter thus does not reiterate many findings from the earlier study but rather focuses on lived religion as a way of comprehending the health and healing practices I observed then, and since.

Although such holistic linkages have never been utterly absent from the religious scene, it is noteworthy that many of these recent religious and quasi-religious movements promoting a mind-body-spirit holism have grown and flourished in societies with highly rationalized, scientific medical institutions. Indeed, this attention to health and spirituality has become widespread in precisely those sectors of American and European societies that conventional wisdom suggested would be most secularized and likely to use only rational-scientific approaches to healing and health maintenance. Today, religious or spiritual practices for health and healing are prominent not only among the poor who cannot afford medical treatments, not only in rural places or among newly urbanized country folk, not only among the immigrants, the women, the uneducated, and other marginalized parts of the larger society. Indeed, many highly educated professionals—including some who work in health professions—use religious or spiritual practices for their own well-being and healing, alongside their selective use of modern medical treatments.[2]

Basically, to understand the relationship between people's health and religion, we must consider broad areas of social life: all the beliefs, practices, and relationships that address people's physical and emotional health and well-being and their religious/spiritual needs and aspirations. These areas were once closely connected in people's everyday lives but by the twentieth century in many societies had become clearly differentiated, as separate institutions, medicine and religion. The process of their differentiation did not just happen accidentally. Rather, in the case of each institution and over many years, concrete historical actors exerted their power and influence to try to control the definitions of important boundaries—especially the definitions that legitimated further control by specialized institutional authorities. These two sets of socially constructed definitional boundaries—medical and religious—share many of the same historical roots. At the societal level, religion and health care are nearly completely separate institutional spheres, but at the level of the individual, they are often seamlessly combined in people's lived religion. Thus, it is no surprise that when we acknowledge previously invisible religious practices as real religion, we may also notice that many healing practices that are not in accordance with the biomedically defined Western model, likewise, are real healing in the experience of the individuals who practice them.

This chapter includes a brief examination of individuals' lived religion as it intersects with their healing practices. That connection between religious practices and healing practices then serves as a springboard for interpreting two important features of healing aspects of individuals' religion-as-lived. The first feature is the holistic emphasis in both religious and healing practices, and this chapter examines particularly the importance of such holism as a basis for some people's critical stance toward two authoritative institutions, religion and medicine. The second feature I examine is the widespread individual and group pattern of eclectic aggregation and creative blending of elements in both areas—religion and healing. Does this represent a genuine form of religious expression or merely a religious façade for extreme individualism and narcissistic self-absorption, as some observers have suggested?

Healing in Practice

The following vignettes describe people whose health and healing practices are important parts of their lived religions.[3] I chose to describe these five, because healing practices are so prominent in their daily lives. Yet in many respects, they are also unexceptional in how they practice their individual religions. The person who engages in alternative, nonmedical healing or health practices could easily be your next-door neighbor or the person sitting beside you in the doctor's waiting room. Religious or spiritual practices for health and healing are largely invisible, though widespread and important, not only in the institutional sphere of religion but also in the institutional sphere of medicine and professional health care.

Marge

Marge is a forty-eight-year old pediatric nurse who works full-time in a large hospital in a well-to-do suburban community. Successful in her career, Marge has the appropriate advanced degrees and experience for high-level administrative positions, but she chose to stay in active nursing on the pediatric ward, because it is where she feels "led to serve." Her husband is a senior partner in a law firm in a nearby city, and the couple has four grown children, the youngest two still in college.

Marge is involved in several groups using alternative healing. She personally utilizes, for her own health and spirituality, some Asian approaches including yoga and meditation. In her healing of others, Marge has used, for about three years, a nonreligious approach to psychic healing called Therapeutic Touch, learned in a series of postgraduate workshops at her school of nursing. She uses her psychic healing methods to "get in touch with" the pain and suffering of the children in her ward; patients do not need to know that she is sending them healing energies as she goes about her routine nursing activities.

Privately, she has been practicing healing for about six years. Her healing practices are highly eclectic, and she tries new "modalities" (her term) as she learns about them, discarding some approaches, keeping others. Her main support group is a psychic healing circle that meets each week in members' homes. When she seeks healing for herself, she usually turns to the members of this group. Together, they explore a wide range of healing practices they call "holistic": they consider mind, body, and spirit a unity.

Marge does healing almost any time, any place, and with anyone— including many people who do not know she is sending them healing energy. Marge described working on healing others even while doing the dishes or in the elevator at work. Sometimes she engaged in healing deliberately and consciously; at other times, she felt, healing was simply a part of her being. She said, "I believe that in every moment of my life I release energy to those around me. I think everybody needs it every moment. . . . I feel that whoever makes connection with me or I make connection with them, I'm using my energy to heal."[4] Marge charges private clients and workshop attendees only nominal amounts, because her professional salary, combined with that of her husband, supports a very comfortable standard of living. She considers her unpaid and paid work as a healer to be offered mainly as a way of meeting others' needs.

Deirdre

Deirdre would not consider herself to be a healer or even to have a part in a healing ministry, but she would say that she believes that the spiritual practices she and her sister use are, indeed, effective in healing. Deirdre is a successful young professional, with a master's degree in social work. When she was in her early thirties and employed in the social service department of a large hospital, she discovered that her youngest sister, who lived with their parents in a distant state, was being sexually molested and probably raped by her own father. The experience of confronting her mother about the sexual abuse was extremely painful for Deirdre, because she discovered that her mother had known all along and had acquiesced in the father's violation of at least three of his five daughters, including Deirdre herself. She insisted on becoming her sister's legal guardian and removed Libby from their home, but it was a long struggle for both sisters to come to terms with the enormity of what had happened to them.

Deirdre accepted the offer of a coworker to help with Libby's recovery, and they began to participate in rituals that the coworker's women's group had created to deal with their own emotional and relationship problems, especially problems with abusive partners and parents. Some of the rituals were consciously invented for an occasion or need. Other rituals were borrowed from Wicca (a feminist neopagan religion to which three women in the group belonged), various feminist psychotherapeutic approaches, and assorted indigenous people's healing practices (which two women in the group studied enthusiastically). Both sisters appreciated especially the group's rituals for safety and protection, and they gradually participated in other rituals that addressed their emotional trauma: rituals of purification and blessing, rituals to release all the participants from the hold of troubled relationships and controlling "hurtful powers," rituals to energize creativity and love, rituals to celebrate their independence and womanhood, rituals to transmute fear and anger, and rituals to generate personal growth and responsibility.

Libby stayed involved in the group for several years until she moved away, but Deirdre attended only occasionally after her first intense twenty months.

She continued to use some of the group's ritual practices, both personally and sometimes professionally, in her subsequent job at a battered women's shelter. As with the women's group rituals, her personal ritual begins with inscribing a safe sacred space in her living room and lighting a special candle (ideally next to some symbol of the season) and ends with a pronouncement of self-acceptance, empowerment, and connection with the nurturing aspect of the universe. Deirdre attributes both her own healing and her ongoing ability to deal with the painful experiences of her clients at the shelter to the "centering" and sense of security she gains from her daily spiritual practices.

Rosalie

Rosalie is very active in the healing ministries of her nondenominational Christian church in an older suburban development, where she and her husband, Bob, live in a modest bilevel near the large appliance store where he works as a manager. Rosalie has not worked outside the home since her first child was born, more than twenty years before our interview. About the time her youngest of three began attending school full-time, Rosalie became increasingly active in her women's prayer circle and discovered that she had some special "God-given gifts" (her term) for healing, especially with other women.

She typically devotes at least one afternoon each week to the women's prayer group, where members pray for each other, their families, and others who ask them for their prayers at a distance. They begin the prayer meeting with prayers of praise to God, and often someone reads a verse of scripture that seems especially meaningful. After fifteen or twenty minutes of fervent prayers, sometimes spoken aloud and sometimes silent, the members of the group share their prayer requests, many of which are about health and healing. Rosalie regularly asked for healing prayer for her mother, who had Parkinson's disease, and for one of her children who was "living too wild and willful." If she or any member of her family was going through an illness—no matter how minor—or going for diagnostic tests, she would bring that up for group prayer as well. Often the group would lay hands on a member who needed special healing help, and they would ask God to use them as "power lines for sending down his healing love." Then, after all members' prayer requests had been heard, sympathy shared, and healing prayers raised, the group turned to another, briefer period of prayers of praise and thanks, before stopping for refreshments.

The religious practice of laying on of hands was a regular part of Rosalie's response to most everyday healing needs, for example her child's earache, her son's fears before a Boy Scout test, her husband's allergies, and her own maladies, including occasional flare-ups of sciatica or having a "blue day." She explained that anyone, even a child, could be used to mediate God's power. She believes that God wants to heal people all the time; so prayer, scripture reading, hymn singing, and laying on of hands are often occasions for God's power to "manifest" in a healing:

> Different kinds of healing scriptures would come. Like, one time I just had this blinding headache when I was driving home at night and the scripture came to me: "If you lay hands on the sick, they will be healed." So I just touched my forehead, gently and lightly, and just said, "In the name of Jesus, I'm healed."[5]

Rosalie expects to need and use continual healing prayer throughout life, "until the final healing which is entry into heaven."

Dolores

A widow in her fifties, Dolores seeks healing for herself and her loved ones through several community resources in her predominantly Latino part of the city. She and her recently deceased husband came to the United States as young people (he from Puerto Rico and she from the Dominican Republic). Her husband made a good living as a postal worker, so they owned their own modest home; now Dolores rents out two rooms to supplement her widow's pension. Childless, she had always helped neighborhood mothers, especially suggesting herbal remedies she learned from her mother, along with prayers and popular religious practices. Dolores maintains, in addition to her personal home altar, a large semipublic outdoor shrine to the Virgin (Mary) and an array of healing saints. Visitors to her home often spend a few moments in prayer or reflection by the shrine, after they leave her front porch. Religious and spiritual practices for health and healing of herself and others are regular and frequent parts of each day for Dolores.

Although she does not consider herself a healer, Dolores is one of the main sources of referral for neighbors, friends, kin and fictive kin,[6] and others, who seek her advice about where to find help for their problems. She has guided many people to particular local *espiritistas,* healers who are in touch with the spirits (in that neighborhood, mainly practitioners of Puerto Rican *espiritismo*), as well as to *curanderas,* curers (in that community, mainly more recent immigrants from Mexico) who use folk medicine, such as herbs, but also pay attention to the saints and the spirits.[7] She also refers neighbors to specific *parteras* (midwives), many of whom also seek assistance from the saints and/or spirits, and to particular local *botánicas,* shops where the herbs, candles, and other substances used in healing are sold.[8] She was proud that she had a good relationship with the "nice young doctors and nurses" at a nearby nonprofit *clínica,* so she could refer people to medical professionals who would not be outraged that their patients wanted to use an *espiritista* or *partera* as well as the clinic's medical treatment. In addition to giving her neighbors and friends her understanding ear, along with a cup of soothing tea, Dolores also gifted these help-seekers with amulets, candles, and cards with pictures and prayers to certain saints whom Dolores considered likely to be most effective in helping with the particular needs they had expressed.

One aspect of Dolores's role in the community cannot be separated from her approach to healing: the care of the dying. Her own mother was the neighbor who helped families with the death of a loved one, and Dolores was very moved by how her mother had cared for her father, aunts, and uncles in their dying days. Dolores was sad that her own husband's death (the result of a car accident) had been in a hospital, miles away, with none of his loved ones surrounding him.

When she described what she did in helping a dying friend or relative, she said it is just like healing: She tries to keep the place "clean," or clear of bad influences, "bad spirits," and then to invite in all the good influences (like the saints) to make the place peaceful, warm, loving, and restful. Dolores explained, "It makes healing either way." In other words, if the practices result in the person recovering health or if the result is letting go and having a peaceful death, either result is healing, in her way of thinking. She tries to use the particular prayers, saints, or *velas* (candles in glass, often decorated with the image of a saint or with a prayer) that were especially meaningful to the dying person or to his or her family. Sometimes she tries to lead the family in prayer and in reconciliation, if there have been conflicts between the dying person and others in the family. But sometimes she just sits for a long time with the dying person and envisions the saints' embrace of them both. And once with a dying child, she held the mother's hand and helped her envision the Virgincita rocking the child to sleep.

Hannah

A vivacious sixty-year-old landscape designer and artist, Hannah attributes her healing and renewed joy in living to the healing services at her former synagogue and the loving support of her husband and close-knit Jewish community—especially the healing rituals of her women's group.[9] Several years earlier, her struggle with breast cancer, together with the debilitating medical treatments that ensued, had made her frightened and depressed. Although she considered her surgeon and chemotherapist to have been extremely competent, Hannah was upset that the entire medical approach to her cancer was too impersonal and technical. She explained:

> They [medical doctors] just treat the physical condition, whatever [it is] . . . but they don't treat the person. It's like they are focused on the diseased tissue, which they might be able to cut out, or [they might] kill the cancer cells and pronounce their treatment "successful," but that wouldn't necessarily mean that the person is well. If you're going to heal, going to make the person really well, you've got to treat the whole person.

Treating the whole person meant, for Hannah, addressing her spiritual, emotional, and relationship needs, not just her breast cancer. Part of that healing was coming to a whole new way of thinking of death and dying, as well as an entirely different way of relating to her present and future. That personal spiritual change dissolved her paralyzing fears and allowed her to enjoy her art work again. She explained that the women's group rituals and focus on everyday spirituality gradually reshaped her core image of how God works in her life. Whereas previously she had thought of God as remote and occasionally active, now she had an immanent sense of God's presence within and around her, as something of a vital force, not only in healing illness, but also in creative expression (including her art and design work), in nature and natural beauty, and in her sense of connection with others.

Because of her emphasis on her identity as an artist, I did not think to ask about her exquisitely arranged, polished walnut fireplace mantel on which were arrayed numerous candles, an arrangement of sand, shells, and starfish, a small brass sculpture, and two pieces of art work that were possibly her own paintings. (I recall one as a somewhat abstract image of a full moon over gentle, rippling waves on a beach and the other as a folksy depiction of eight women holding hands and dancing serenely around a fire.) Not until years later when I learned about the significance of the specific arrangements of Mexican American women's home altars did I wished I had asked Hannah whether her mantel arrangement had any significance in her spiritual practices.

In her everyday life, Hannah used a personal spiritual dance practice she called "dancing my life." Her religious involvement at her synagogue was sporadic, but she put considerable time and energy into her spiritual practices, individual as well as collective. In addition to daily meditation, her most important spiritual practice, done (usually solo) sometimes daily but at least once a week, was an improvised dance in which she identified a theme that had arisen in her life recently or recurringly (for example, themes of "being alone," "flying," and "unfolding"). After meditating briefly on the theme, but without planning her actions, she danced to express that theme. Often, what evolved in the dance was a "complete surprise" to her, but she almost always felt she had expressed, in a satisfyingly integrated way, her deeper feelings about and really important meanings of her life. About once a month, she also danced with two or three of her friends, keeping the theme broad enough that all the participants could relate to it somehow.[10]

It is not coincidental that these five vignettes all depict women. In the course of the research for *Ritual Healing in Suburban America,* many respondents who had sought healing help from others (across vastly different types of healing approaches) said the characteristics of the best healers were their compassion, empathy, and ability really to understand the experience of suffering.[11] Women's ability to empathize made them prominent in healing work in all the types of nonmedical healing we studied. One young man, connected with a self-identified holistic health center, explained:

> A very important part of [healing] is a certain empathetic ability . . . to be able to understand the person you're working with. . . . If you understand the Chinese cosmology of *yin* and *yang,* the *yin* qualities (the so-called feminine qualities of intuitiveness and gentleness) are much more open to that aspect . . . and the only time you find it in men are [those] who understand that they have both a male and female aspect and aren't threatened by that.[12]

Some healers also said that it was their personal experience with suffering that brought them to be able to help others with their healing needs. The experience of suffering is gendered, in part because of how women's bodies are linked to the proximate sources of physical and emotional suffering. For example, our respondents described suffering from a sense of loss produced by such experiences as giving birth to a stillborn baby, undergoing a hysterectomy, and having had a radical mastectomy. Many more respondents described suffering from gender-based social sources of physical and emotional suffering, such as being victims of sexual harassment or serious sex discrimination at work, being trapped by oppressive fathers or husbands, or being victims of domestic violence or rape.[13] Anthropologists Susan Sered and Linda Barnes remind us: "Gender-based oppression represents a form of structural violence that tends to elicit particular attention in contexts of religious healing."[14]

These brief sketches of how five ordinary women regularly used spiritual practices for health and healing for themselves and others suggest that we need to take religious and spiritual approaches to well-being much more seriously than scholars have previously done. Since my early research[15] on nonmedical healing and U.S. religious/spiritual practices for health, many more studies have documented this widespread phenomenon.[16] I have no doubt that most of the people we interviewed had experienced something profound and real, something that was a real healing for them, something that was at least as real a healing as what modern medicine had to offer. They were not using the term "healing" merely as a metaphor to describe something else. We must respect these people's expressions of their experiences and their deep sense that healing worked in their lives. For the purposes of this chapter, I posit that we accept, as sufficient, people's stories of healing in body/mind/spirit.

Health and Healing as Religious Concerns

Why is it so difficult for scholars to allow that religious or spiritual practices might have a real (not just imagined or coincidental) effect on a person's physical and emotional well-being? In order to understand the eruption of so many diverse religious and spiritual approaches to health and healing in modern times, we need better understanding of the historical connections between the institutional sphere of religion and that of Western biomedicine. The point of the historical sketch I will provide here is to note how two institutional spheres, religion and medicine, became separate in parallel processes of contests among powerful interest groups for control of important definitional boundaries. The outcome of their struggles determined what would be accepted, in subsequent centuries, as real religion and real health.

Cultural Connections of Religion and Health

Health and well-being are very much religious or spiritual concerns in many other societies—including many of those with Western religious traditions. For example, the indigenous religions of such peoples as the !Kung of the Kalahari, the Qollahuaya of the Andes, and the Navajo of the southwestern United States all closely connect the spiritual, emotional, social, and physical well-being of individuals, families, tribes, and entire social and ecological environments.[17] Anthropological studies in diverse cultures show that there are no universal criteria for defining health but rather that health functions as a cultural ideal that varies widely over time and from culture to culture. For instance, the ideal of health for a woman in rural Jamaican society emphasizes social interconnectedness and generosity, especially around women's linkage with food. Accordingly, a slim woman would be considered the embodiment of unhealthy, negative qualities like stinginess, barrenness, unsociability, social-emotional-physical dryness, and unwillingness to nurture others.[18]

Religions traditionally have been important sources of cultural ideals, providing images, rituals, and symbols for linking the individual to a larger reality. For example, religions often give special meaning to body symbolism (e.g. blood, milk, hearts, hands, eyes). In most instances, these images, rituals, and symbols simultaneously involve human bodies, emotions, cognitions, and spirits. Thus, expressions of illness can serve as idioms for communicating distress, suffering, and dissent.[19] Many cultures understand the illness of the individual body as an expression of social discord. Likewise, the individual body can serve as a referent for a culture's pattern of individual-to-society relationship. For example, participants in the several days and nights of a Navaho chant (frequently done for healing) can attune their individual experiences, through ritual action, to accomplish the culturally valued sense of harmony between the individual, social group, and environment.[20]

Modern Western societies, for example Sweden, Australia, and the United States, also have notions of health that are cultural ideals that vary in importance from society to society. Western religions historically promoted some aspects of those ideals of health, such as norms of bodily regulation, hygiene, and self-control.[21] Those ideals may still inform, for example, middle-class British or American values that dictate that "to be healthy means to demonstrate to self and others appropriate concern for the virtues of self-control, self-discipline, self-denial, and will power."[22] There is a clear moral expectation that people will try to achieve health, thus defined.

The religious significance of those virtues is not necessarily a part of any individual's attempts to attain those ideals. Marie Griffith's research suggests, however, that contemporary Protestant regimens for sexual and food abstinence may have continued the melding of certain religious ideals with the ideals that serve the secular purposes of the consumer capitalism.[23] Today, the mass media (especially commercial advertising through those media) and related popular culture are more likely to spread cultural ideals of health, because the ideal of health sells goods and services in a consumer culture.[24] Officially promulgated ideals, whether promoted by heads of governmental health agencies or by school curricula, are likely to reflect political agendas (e.g., the deflection of responsibility for health maintenance away from state-sponsored social services and community preventive efforts and onto the individual or immediate family).[25]

Religion and Medicine as Institutional Spheres: Some Historical Background

We need to remember that the definitional boundaries of both spheres—religion and health—are social constructions. The historical sketch that follows uses illustrations mainly from U.S. historical patterns of social construction of religion and of medicine, but similar patterns have occurred in Europe, Canada, Australia, and other places where Western biomedicine and Western forms of Christianity have been dominant.[26]

RELIGION. During the Long Reformation, when the boundaries around what was considered properly religious were redrawn and increasingly controlled, one of the most dramatic shifts was the churches' attempts to control or forbid the many religious practices people used to address their needs for health and healing. Whereas previously laypeople and clergy alike had used religious practices to promote health and healing and to protect themselves and loved ones from illnesses and other dangers, many church leaders now denounced those practices as "magic," "superstition" or "witchcraft."[27]

As I have already discussed, the Long Reformation fundamentally altered the definitional boundaries, such that—especially in Protestant teaching—religion came to pertain to the sphere of the sacred, which was separate and set apart from the sphere of the profane. As social theorists Philip Mellor and Chris Shilling note, human bodies, thus "disenchanted," came to be seen as thoroughly profane.[28] Although healing practices continued (indeed, in many places, flourished) in both Catholic and Protestant popular religious expressions, by the late nineteenth century (i.e., the foundational years of sociology and anthropology as scholarly disciplines), a clear definitional boundary between religion and medicine had been established and was accepted in scholarly discourse.

Elements that were historically defined out as not properly religious often survived as popular religion (discussed in chapters 3 and 4), outside or on the margins of recognized religions. Such popular religious practices typically focused on material concerns such as health, prosperity, and security. For example, popular religiosity in Europe and the Americas often retained the earlier era's view that routine religious practices were instrumental actions for achieving desired material well-being.

We should remember that, in medieval times, such attention to material concerns was not generally considered to be separate from, much less inferior to, purely spiritual concerns. Rituals and other practices people used to attend to spiritual concerns were often, simultaneously, the practices they used to address their material concerns, because the boundaries between sacred and profane realms were permeable and fuzzy. That meant that people could experience manifestations of the sacred as part of the landscape and of mundane daily activities. It also increased ordinary persons' sense of access to divine power, including the power to heal and to protect. Consolidation of ritual power in the hands of official church leaders was thus one of the contested issues in the centuries of the Long Reformation.

Church leaders' efforts to disabuse church members of their trust in the powers of religious and folk healers preceded, by several centuries, the development of modern, rational biomedicine. Well before the Long Reformation, the church attempted to control the exercise of healing power (at least, for healing the upper classes) because the power to heal was believed to come from spiritual sources, either evil or good. The Lateran Council of 1215, which represented the apex of church power in the Middle Ages, forbade physicians to undertake medical treatment without calling in ecclesiastical advice. Healing that took place outside clerical jurisdiction was suspect of having been aided by the devil. The two main groups of healers thus suspect were Jewish doctors and "white witches" (or "good witches," typically women). Jewish (and, in small numbers, Moorish Muslim) physicians in southern Europe had kept their ancient medical lore alive throughout the Middle Ages, while the dominant European medical knowledge was a stagnant form of late Greek medicine (i.e., Galenism). Therefore, the wealthy sought Jewish physicians, to the disgust of Christian clergy, who proclaimed (for example) that "it were better to die with Christ than to be cured by a Jew doctor aided by the devil."[29]

The masses, however, were served by an assortment of folk healers, including white witches—members of the community who used herbs, potions, magic, charms, and pre-Christian (as well as Christian) religious practices to cure disease and ward off evil influences.[30] These healers were subsequently a special target of the Inquisition in several countries. Similarly, witch hunts in Protestant countries (such as England and New England) considered "good" witches to be especially dangerous, because they supposedly used their evil powers for good causes, misleading people to trust them. For healing and protection, the masses also continued to use various popular religious practices that were common lore. Among Catholics, this was mainly in devotions to various saints (some approved but many not approved by church authorities) and the use of materials called "sacramentals," such as blessed candles and blessed water. Although in later modern times, Catholic church officials consolidated considerable control over special healing shrines, such as Lourdes, private devotions to healing saints and individual ritual practices at sites of healing power were still common and widespread even at the height of respect for rational biomedicine in the twentieth century.[31]

Because many Protestant leaders tried, during the Long Reformation, to eliminate the material "stuff" of magic from the churches, worship services, and private religious practices, their lay followers were faced with a more frightening situation in early modern times. That is, they were supposed to resort only to scripture and intense supplication to a remote and fearsome God to address their material needs (such as protection of the crops and the well-being of their family and animals). According to their clergy, in order to demonstrate their trust in God's providence, they should not engage in superstitious practices. The potential disasters that could result from not using the traditional salutary religious practices were grave, however. In response, some early Protestants importuned Catholic neighbors to perform the rituals on behalf of all, and many others continued to combine unapproved magical practices (such as divination) with their approved religious practices (such as reading the Bible).[32] Like their Catholic counterparts, many Protestants continued popular religious practices for healing, as illustrated by the place of faith healing in the camp meetings of U.S. evangelicals.

In addition to Catholic and Protestant popular religious healing, the period between early modernity and high modernity (say, between 1600 and 1950) was marked by many religious movements that addressed health, healing, and bodily well-being. Two early American movements that explicitly connected the realms of the spiritual with the material (i.e., pertaining to matter, like the body or nature) were transcendentalism and Swedenborgianism. Influenced by those movements yet becoming a larger and more influential religious healing movement in the United States was the New Thought movement, which spawned several lasting religious organizations, including Christian Science, the Unity School of Christianity, and the Church of Religious Science. Several observers have identified New Thought and the larger late nineteenth-century metaphysical movement, of which it was a part, as foundations of the late twentieth-century New Age movement.[33] Thus, there were many alternative religious options that did not relinquish the notion that the body and its health were linked with religious practices, but these religious practices existed in the margins.

MEDICINE. The process by which medicine developed into a separate, specialized institutional sphere involved accomplishing recognition as a profession. That recognition was predicated on medicine's development of a distinctive body of knowledge, a corps of specialists with control over this body of knowledge and its application, and public acknowledgment (or legitimation) of the authority of medical specialists.[34] This process of professionalization was essentially a sociopolitical movement to achieve a "monopoly of opportunities in a market of services or labor and, inseparably, monopoly of status and work privileges."[35] Although the roots of this process date from the Enlightenment, biomedicine did not achieve much legitimacy or effective control over the domain of health and healing until the twentieth century. In the United States, the American Medical Association gained political legitimacy and legal monopoly over the practice of medicine before—rather than as a result of—the emergence of the scientific discoveries and the medical practices that made medical doctors' approach to curing appear to be rationally effective.[36]

In the nineteenth century, physicians practiced highly diverse approaches to healing—osteopathy, naturopathy, homeopathy, hydropathy, for instance— each of which was based on different notions of what caused diseases and how sickness could best be treated. The approach called allopathy eventually gained a legal monopoly. It was characterized by heroic measures and invasive treatments, including bloodletting, blistering, purging, and medicating with powerful drugs and poisons like opium and arsenic. The American Medical Association, formed in 1847, represented allopathic doctors as "regular" or orthodox physicians, but allopathy was then actually losing ground to so-called irregular physicians, especially homeopathic doctors, who used far less dangerous treatments and were typically as well trained as the allopathic physicians.[37] By gaining state-sanctioned control over medical education and licensing, the American Medical Association was able to prevent unapproved doctors from practicing medicine, control access to medical education (reducing the numbers of new doctors who would compete for well-paying clients), and close medical schools that had previously recruited such undesirable students as women, blacks, and immigrants.[38] All of this control over the practice of medicine occurred before the profession had much scientific basis for its knowledge, before doctors understood how their own practices were spreading disease and infection (e.g., by not washing hands between performing a surgical amputation and delivering of a baby), and before they could offer medicines, inoculations, or other treatments that were more effective than those of many other kinds of healers.

It was not the successes of rational, scientific biomedicine that produced dominance of "disenchanted" techniques of healing. Indeed, it is likely that at that time, people who used allopathic healers were basing that choice on faith rather than science just as much as those who sought healers who used naturopathy, homeopathy, or faith healing. Thus, we might conclude that the purpose of the early twentieth-century emphasis on medicine's rational and scientific bases was primarily to justify professional dominance. The authorizing process was clearly political—a matter of political influence and power—and certain groups of physicians, such as women (who were disproportionately underrepresented in allopathic medicine, compared to other medical and nonmedical healing approaches) were deauthorized in the process.[39]

The same historical processes that resulted in a radical dichotomy between sacred and profane also produced a denigration of bodily concerns and embodied practice as wholly profane and thus inappropriate for religious attention.[40] Biomedicine claimed control over the health and curing of physical bodies; a separate science claimed aegis over the health and well-being of minds; and religion was relegated to the sphere of the purely spiritual. Interestingly, deviance and its treatment were also differentiated according to this same scheme. Deviance of physical bodies was labeled "sickness" (or disability) and subject to medical control; deviance of the mind or emotions was categorized as "madness" (later "mental illness") and subject to psychiatric control; and deviance of the spirit was considered to be "sin" and subject to religious control.[41]

To a certain extent, many religious groups cooperated in this differentiation, relinquishing all but token religious attention to people's physical and emotional well-being. Many established Christian denominations, for example, criticized those religious groups that preached religious answers to believers' material concerns (such as illness, unemployment, or scarcity of resources for subsistence) as superstitious, less pure forms of spirituality than their own. Recognizing that both religious and medical conceptions are the historical products of social contestation and power struggles enables us to comprehend better why many people seek ways of thinking and acting that reconnect religion with embodied practices such as healing.

Institutional differentiation has produced extensive internal specialization in modern Western medicine, due in large part to the growth of large-scale, bureaucratic settings for the learning and practice of medicine and to the pervasive paradigmatic assumptions of biomedicine itself. One byproduct of the institutional differentiation is that modern medicine focuses on diseases—conceptually linked with discrete pathologies—rather than on sick persons.[42] This differentiated model of medicine limits any religious response to peripheral (albeit valuable) nonhealing roles, such as comforting the dying or helping chronically ill persons to cope with their conditions.

Rationalized biomedicine assumes a mind-body dualism, according to which physical diseases and their causes are presumed to be located strictly within the body.[43] Accordingly, the body can be understood and treated separately from the person inhabiting it. A related biomedical assumption is physical reductionism—the idea that illnesses are, basically, nothing more than disordered bodily functions, such as biochemical or neurophysiological mal-functions. These assumptions exclude social, psychological, spiritual, and be-havioral dimensions of illness. As a result of these assumptions, the medical model views disease as localized in the individual body, almost as a quality of the sick person herself or himself. Another feature of rationalized biomedicine is its strong emphasis on mastery and control over the body, for instance, by means of therapeutic regimens, surgical and pharmaceutical interventions, or technological developments and techniques.[44] Although rationalized biomed-icine has made considerable achievements, in part due to these very charac-teristics, these paradigmatic assumptions have also constricted its ability to meet many of people's health needs. Today's spiritual healing movements among people who are well educated and have access to biomedical treatments may be, in part, an expression of dissatisfaction with the limitations of com-partmentalized, rationalized medicine.

Contemporary Western societies promote particularly high expectations of individual health. Furthermore, American culture—as well as its capitalist economy—promotes the widespread presumption that optimum health is, in principle, achievable. This presumption is based, in part, on a modern Western image of the body and emotions as malleable, controllable, and continually revisable. A corollary belief, actively promoted by health professionals, is that scientific knowledge and technology have expanded the scope of potential con-trol so much that experts are the only appropriate persons to treat all human bodily or emotional experiences. Thus, medical discourse and popular media have redefined, as health issues, many normal human experiences such as pregnancy and childbirth, grief, anxiety, death, anger, eating, exercise, and sex. Accordingly, presumably in the interests of optimum health, not only biolog-ical diseases but indeed all human bodily and emotional experiences have become medicalized.[45]

At the same time, however, Western (and especially American) cultural-political values tend to be highly individualistic. Accordingly, illness is located within the individual alone, and adults are generally held responsible (morally as well as financially) for their own health.[46] By such moral standards, then, one must eat right, exercise, get the right amount of sleep, manage daily stresses correctly, avoid unhealthy environmental conditions and risks, and actively resist unhealthy foods, drink, drugs, sex, feelings, and activities. In a capitalist society, these prescriptions mean that the healthy person is one who consumes correctly—including expending ever-growing amounts of money and effort consuming medical products and services.[47]

As a result of these high expectations surrounding a greatly valued ideal, health has become a salient metaphor for salvation, even for nonreligious

Westerners.[48] In discussing the role of religious ideas in social action, Weber argued that material and ideal interests were primary in impelling people's actions, but that

> very frequently the "world images" that have been created by "ideas" have, like switchmen, determined the tracks along which action has been pushed by the dynamic of interest. "From what" and "for what" one wished to be redeemed and, let us not forget, "could be" redeemed, depended upon one's image of the world.[49]

So, if we were to ask, in the contemporary context, "From what do you most want to be saved/ redeemed/ protected?" many people—religious and nonreligious alike—would be likely to name illness, debilitated old age, pain, or dying.

Lived Religion as Holistic Healing

Lived religion is, for many people, immediately connected with the well-being of their bodies and minds, because they do not experience their spiritual lives as separate from their physical and mental/emotional lives. It makes sense, then, for them to engage in everyday ritual practices, alone or in groups, that address—as a unity—the spiritual, physical, and emotional aspects of their lives, relationships, and selves. Indeed, many people consider problems of personal and social fragmentation, separation, and unwholeness to be at the root of their illnesses and their sense of *dis*-ease. They consider their religious practices not only meaningful but also efficacious, connecting them to a real source of power in their lives. Thus, it makes sense for them to address problems of all aspects of their physical and mental/emotional lives through their religion-as-lived.

If we take seriously the diverse healing practices of people like Marge, Deirdre, Rosalie, Dolores, and Hannah, what can their stories tell us about the lived religions of those who engage in healing, whether seeking health and well-being for themselves or for others? To understand their healing practices—practices that often required considerable effort and commitment—we do not have to agree with their beliefs about what causes illness or their explanations of how nonmedical healing works. We do have to listen to them carefully, however, appreciating that their beliefs, practices, and experiences may operate with a different logic from that of biomedicine yet be completely reasonable. Likewise, we need to allow for the fact that certain aspects of people's beliefs and practices may be at odds with what religious institutions, such as churches and synagogues, represent as religious but nevertheless be a valued part of their religion-as-practiced. For all of these women—each for different reasons—this complex of beliefs and practices we call "healing" really matters in their lives.

At the level of individuals' religion, perhaps the only feature that these women's highly diverse healing beliefs and practices have in common is a strong sense of holism connecting individuals' bodies, emotions, cognitive minds, social relationships, and religious/spiritual experiences and expressions. Their images of the human person involve mind, body, and spirit as a mutually informing whole, not merely as related parts.[50] So comprehensive is this holism that, for many people who participate in holistic healing, their lived religion is identical with the process of healing in all its dimensions. For them, healing becomes an ongoing process throughout life, and the beliefs and practices by which they are engaged in that process are prominent in their lived religion.

In our study of alternative healing approaches, we found that nearly all of our respondents used a language of holism. (The noteworthy exceptions were persons who used only the alternative services of what I call "technique practitioners," those who perform specific alternative techniques in a provider-client relationship modeled on the doctor-patient one, conventional in the United States in recent decades.) By their very nature, however, interviews tended to elicit narratives that emphasized such interrelatedness, regardless of whether such connected themes were truly central in the experience of a given respondent. More telling than the language used in an interview was the way holistic values and imagery shaped these individuals' rituals and routine practices.

Holism in Practice

How, then, is an emphasis on holism manifested in people's everyday actions? One obvious way is symbolically. For example, both Deirdre and Hannah were active in women's groups that used many rituals to locate members' bodies in interconnected space, relative to each other. Several of those rituals involved such symbolism as the circle, weaving, chain, web, and seasons; symbolically, they linked members' mind-body-spirits with each others' mind-body-spirits, with sacralized time and space, and with powerful images of nature and the universe. When apart from others in their group, these women could regularly remind themselves of their interrelationship by engaging in domestic rituals or looking at art work that evoked symbolic imagery of their interconnectedness with each other, nature, the universe, and the sacred.

FIGURE 6.1. Individuals' embodied practices for healing of mind-body-spirit are illustrated by the use of interconnected space—meditating in a circle and practicing
yoga postures (*asanas*) and breathing exercises (*pranayama*)—individually, yet together.
This group includes both persons who have been practicing yoga meditation for only a
few years and some who have practiced for more than 30 years. Courtesy Adelle
Brewer, Synergy Studios, used by permission.

Many of Marge's daily practices involved symbolic postures, gestures,
words, and imagery for cleansing or purifying herself in mind-body-spirit
before trying to deal with others' problems. For example, Marge tried to get to
work early each day in order to spend a few moments meditatively "centering"
herself. If there was time, she prepared a little bowl of lavender water (thus
evoking both her sense of smell and touch) to use in her personal purification
ritual. In her brief meditation, she would identify what needed "cleaning" that
morning; it might be emotional (such as anger toward a difficult coworker),
relational (for instance, a sense of conflict with her mother), physical demands
that might get in the way of the flow of healing energies (like a tension
headache), or spiritual (for example, too great a sense of self-importance for her
recent role in what she considered a nearly miraculous healing of a toddler).
Then, as she sponged the lavender water on her temples, neck, throat, arm,
wrist, and palm, she envisioned washing away the "impurities that could cause

blockages" to the flow of healing energy in her own body and in her healing efforts for others. These simple regular practices literally embodied holism.

Holism also informs people's lived religions through their everyday engagement in the many concrete embodied practices along the lines of those described in chapter 5. For example, Rosalie's use of the laying on of hands for healing was only one of many practices by which she regularly engaged her body, spirit, and mind. She exclaimed that, in her experience, wholeness and holiness were just two ways of thinking about the same thing. So she thought of her Christian healing practices as linked with her Christian mothering practices, which were linked with her Christian cooking practices, as well as Christian practices for feeding her family and her own Christian practices of eating meals and watching her weight, and so on. Because Rosalie believed that Satan was at the root of all sickness and suffering, dragging people into sin and brokenness, she urged specific regular practices to prevent illness and promote healing. She explained:

> I believe that Satan is in control of the dark side of human nature, unless you don't allow him to be in control. . . . [You must protect yourself through] prayer, fellowship with other Christians, Bible reading, speaking out against Satan. You can carry on a conversation if you know he's attacking you. You know he's giving you bad thoughts in your mind that would go against God's way of doing something. You can tell him to get lost, especially quoting Scripture.[51]

By contrast, Hannah (the Jewish artist who used her Jewish and feminist rituals, as well as expressive dance, for healing) explained that the rabbi who had introduced her to Jewish healing practices had emphasized that people are not responsible for their illnesses. That meant that their religious tradition was relevant to healing, not as moral judgment but as a resource to support people in their healing. Her women's group regularly got together for healing rituals that focused on saying and singing blessings adapted from scripture.[52] Hannah insisted that her spiritual practices were "not about preventing death, but about encouraging growth." With her group and in private, Hannah routinely used concrete spiritual practices, including singing and saying prayers of blessing and thanksgiving, dancing and making joyous music, and meditating. She would have agreed with another Jewish woman (who engaged in very similar spiritual practices and holistic healing) who told me that spiritual growth for her meant mindfully "moving myself closer to compassion and connection."[53]

Holistic Healing and Critique of Biomedical Treatment

Many of the respondents in our research project on alternative healing systems had developed strongly negative attitudes toward institutional medicine. One of the criticisms leveled by many respondents, representing many diverse healing approaches, was the medical system's lack of a holistic approach to healing. Even Marge, a highly respected professional nurse who worked in a hospital setting, was critical of the extent to which American medicine does not really address people's health and healing needs. She said that too often a medical group will advertise its services as "holistic" when all they are doing is offering the services of specialists in more diverse treatment specialties (her example was an orthopedic group that included a psychologist and an in-house staff of physical therapists to provide auxiliary services to the orthopedists' patients). She said, "Does that really treat the whole person, or is it more a marketing ploy?" In her opinion, nurses, midwives, mothers (and sometimes also fathers and other family members), and friends made better healers than did doctors, precisely because they were focusing not on curing a disease but on improving the well-being of the whole person. Marge emphasized that real healing required caring.

Hannah's strong criticism of doctors and hospitals was based on her personal experiences with life-threatening cancer and painful treatments, as well as later experiences with holistic alternatives that she came to apply to all areas of her life. She decided, after going through those especially difficult years of treatments, that she had to be much more selective in her use of doctors, medicines, and hospitals. She said that she thinks of herself as something of a contractor of her own health care, so she has changed primary care physicians and encouraged other cancer survivors to find specialists who are more sensitive to the full range of their patients' needs. Nevertheless, she believed that her nonmedical healing practices were proving to be the most important factor in keeping her healthy and enjoying life so fully, and she expected that they would become even more important to her as she faced the inevitable disabilities of old age.

By contrast, Rosalie's criticism was not based on much actual experience with doctors or hospitalization for her family's sicknesses but rather on the strong belief that doctors who treat a sick person's body but ignore the other sources of sickness (spiritual, emotional, etc.) may be working contrary to God's will and thus may cause more harm than good. She, too, was very selective in her uses of doctors and medicines. She frequently encouraged persons who were going to the doctor to pray over the choice of doctor, to "test" the diagnosis and treatment plan with prayer and scripture. In Rosalie's opinion, if those religious tests did not confirm the doctor's treatment plan, then one should not follow it until all better (i.e., "spiritually safe") means were exhausted.

While not rejecting medical explanations of disease causation, our respondents who used spiritual practices for healing generally considered biophysical explanations of the causes of illness insufficient. Some interviewees emphasized multiple causes linked in a web of causation: for example, a complex combination of unhealthy emotional responses, attitudes, lifestyle choices, family discord or breakdown, stressful workplace, economic distress, environmental pollution, and spiritual weakness. Our interviewees often made a distinction between the causes of illness and the meaning of a particular illness episode. For example, one woman who sought psychic healing for her extreme pain said that the cause of the pain was clearly injuries from an auto accident a few years earlier, but the meaning of the current episode of acute pain was somehow connected to some aspect of her life she was not handling well. She said:

> It seems like the universe is trying to get my attention. Once I take
> responsibility for what is triggering that pain, then I can start the
> healing process again. And I will emerge from that process better in
> all parts of my life, not just the site of my injury to my body.[54]

Western biomedicine does not generally address the issue of meaning, because it treats the body and illness as objects, separate from the person who experiences them.[55] By contrast, in many alternative healing approaches, the body and illnesses are assumed to be laden with meaning. Indeed, part of the healing process consists of discovering the meaning of a person's illness episode and then addressing that meaning through embodied practices.

Holistic Healing and the Critique of Institutional Religion's Role

Interestingly, our respondents' holistic healing approaches were also the basis of strong criticism of institutional religion's failure to take its proper place in the entire healing process. Marge asserted that too many people think of religion's role in healing as "like the prayer that someone says after the doctor has already done all he can" for them, just in case the prayer might help tip the balance of fate in their favor. Rosalie said that too many Christians, including some preachers she knew, do not really believe that God really does heal people all the time; without that faith, they fail to engage in healing practices throughout every day.

Deirdre had the bitterest criticism of religion—that it often promotes ill-ness by telling people they have to submit their spirits, minds, and bodies to leaders who use that authority to hurt them.[56] She felt that most religions caused more pain and suffering than they healed. She also reminded us that her women's group was "spiritual, not religious," and that if it had ever become heavy-handed or authoritarian (like religion, in her opinion), she would have left it immediately.

As in the case of their use of physicians and medicines, these women urged selective use of religious authorities and rituals. They valued holis-tic healing practices, which necessarily involve addressing spiritual, as well as bodily, emotional, and social factors. Yet they would reject the authority of any religious leader who promoted a practice that was (according to their sense and experience) hurtful, misguided, or downright sinful. Dolores and Hannah were each loosely connected with a religious organization, yet they cared little about the authority of the particular priests or rabbis who led their congrega-tions. Their lived religion—"what really matters"—was a far bigger and deeper part of their everyday lives than was the religion tied to their church or syna-gogue. One San Antonio woman who was very knowledgeable about medicinal plants, and who ran a *botánica*, drew the following parallel between her use of doctors and her use of priests:

> You need to go to the doctor or the clinic sometimes, like to get tested for diabetes—the doctor can do something you can't do for your-self, so going to the clinic helps you get well. . . . And you need to go to the church sometimes, 'cause only the priest can bless the [host for] Communion, which also helps you.[57]

Evangelical Christians like Rosalie had more difficulty reconciling their beliefs about religious authority with their actual practices for healing. On the one hand, Rosalie really believed that God communicated directly with Christians, through words of scripture or through speaking to them when they are in prayer; on the other hand, she relied on her pastor for interpretation of God's will, and she felt it was Christians' duty to be strictly conservative and obedient to God's law as set forth in the Bible. There had been a few times in her experience in the prayer group when she had felt that God was clearly telling her (or other members) that they should do something other than what their pastor had preached. In these situations, after intense prayer, they would open the Bible to seek confirmation of one direction of action or the other.[58]

Religious beliefs and practices do shape how people understand that for which they seek healing, as well as how their practices address the perceived source(s) of their suffering. For instance, Rosalie described one woman at her church who struggled to break her addiction to cigarette smoking. She had tried what the doctor advised and a smoke-cessation program at work to no avail. Rosalie successfully persuaded her that what really needed healing was her excessive reliance on anything but Jesus—including her reliance on nicotine patches, doctor's prescriptions, comfort food, her smoking buddy at work, and so on.

That a person experiencing problems seeks any religious response or tries particular religious practices is hardly inevitable, however. For example, people's prior religious beliefs might influence whether they would interpret their homosexual practices as sinful and thus the source of their religious and emotional troubles or—to the contrary—whether they would interpret other people's homophobia as the source of their suffering. The former interpretation might lead to their becoming involved with a Twelve Step group that applied spiritual and social practices similar to those of AA to break what they considered to be members' "addiction" to homosexual practices. Subsequently, in interaction with that group, they could learn to self-identify as "ex-gay," and they could practice using a therapeutic language that identified their need for healing as "sexual brokenness."[59] By contrast, interpreting their problems as due to homophobia could lead them to become involved with a gay rights activist group or a religious group that engages in rituals of empowerment and protection from others who would hate and hurt them. Subsequently, in interaction with that group, they could develop greater self-esteem and positive practices for self-protective assertiveness, and they could practice a political or communitarian language that identified their need for healing as the damage done by an inherently abusive patriarchal society.[60]

Interestingly, many healers like Marge and Dolores often do not tell the people they help what their personal understanding of illness causation is. Rather, they ask the persons seeking their help about what their own understanding of the problem is and what healing symbols or powers are most meaningful to them personally. For example, in leading a guided visualization with a person who would soon be undergoing surgery, Marge tried to elicit what imagery that person had of his disease and afflicted organ. Then, using what he told her about his sense of God's healing power, she developed some verbal images of healing power being directed to where it was needed and taught him to meditatively visualize that healing process. In her experience, the person she worked with did not need to believe in the power of healing to experience its benefits, but it helped if the patient participated in some way, perhaps activating some of the body's own self-healing potential. Even when she studied Therapeutic Touch, she said, the students did not have to believe in the power of the healing approach. Rather, as they learned the process, they had convincing experiences of healing power, for example in the considerable warmth in their hands or in physically feeling a disturbance in the patient's body even though their hands were inches above the skin.[61] Thus, both the healers' and the ill persons' beliefs and meanings figured into the process, but often not in the ways we might expect.

Hannah emphasized holism as an integrating theme in all areas of her life, not only for healing but also for her work—which she considered to have changed, as part of her larger healing process, into what she called "integrative" landscape design. Holism also integrated her home atmosphere, domestic rituals, and friendships—especially with other women whose lives she described as being "interwoven" with her own. The strength of her focus on holism was due mainly to the depth of an epiphany she had experienced in her struggle with cancer and depression. Hannah was adamant that her horrible experiences in the aftermath of her medical treatment were largely due to everything that was wrong with the medical profession and hospitals as a result of their being too focused on treating only the diseased part of the body. She felt that part of her healing was to transmute her anger about how she had been treated into creative expression and "positive energy" for caring for others who faced similar health struggles.

For widely differing reasons, these five women had all come to hold holistic images of health and healing that were dramatically different from the ideas that inform the entire biomedical approach. Although their individual lived religions were very diverse and complex, each involved core beliefs and practices that simultaneously addressed bodily, mental, and spiritual well-being. In effect, practicing their religion was the same as practicing healing. So central in their lives were their understandings of how emotions, bodies, social relationships, and spiritual lives are interrelated that holism shaped their key criteria for evaluating and selecting options for health care and religious affiliation. In these women's experience, holistic approaches to health and healing really worked and were effective on many levels, with implications for all areas of their lives. That experience (at least, when it was profound) had subsequently become sufficient to undermine their faith in the authority of major social institutions—medicine and religion—that treat the differentiated parts of people's lives as separate, not whole.[62]

Eclecticism and Creative Blending

There is enormous diversity among individuals in the practices used for both health and religion. Many people today employ eclecticism and autonomy in choosing their individual practices for health and healing. Not only might they choose alternative or nonmedical health practices but also they may exercise autonomy in choosing what professional help to seek and whether or when they comply with doctors' orders. Likewise, many people are eclectically selecting elements of their individual religious belief and practice and combining them in meaningful personal syntheses.

Many individuals do not limit their personal religious beliefs and practices to a particular institutionally prescribed package—even, often, when they are active congregational members. Likewise, many individuals who use medical professionals' services also incorporate many other, sometimes competing, nonmedical healing approaches into their individual practices for health and healing. Some sociologists have suggested that this kind of individual autonomy may represent a completely new pattern of religion.[63] Perhaps, by extension, we should consider whether such autonomy and selective use of various healing approaches may represent a new pattern of health care.

How do people whose lived religion includes holistic healing understand their eclectic and blended practices? People's narratives draw on certain values of their culture or cultural subgroup to frame their stories of their experiences and actions. The words they choose when they tell their stories typically reflect not only their values but also their representation of their motives for the choices they have made—especially when they appear to contravene social expectations. Western societies generally, as well as U.S. society in particular, value conscious, voluntary choice as a pattern of commitment, not only in religion but also in marriage, place of residence, vocation, and so forth. Thus, it is understandable that so many respondents were acutely aware of their multiple options for healing approaches and religious practices.

Remember that our research on alternative healing practices asked about people's choices and combinations of healing beliefs and practices; those (many) who spoke of their religious eclecticism or blending did so because they saw the connection. Most of the interviewees who engaged in holistic healing used a language of personal choice to describe how they came to adopt various specific healing practices; however, they used slightly varying terms of discourse, with important differences in implications about their motives and meanings.

When evangelical Christians like Rosalie referred to "decision" or "choice," they were likely be referring to one big choice—"taking Jesus as my personal savior." That decision, framed as an all-or-nothing choice, greatly narrows the range of subsequent options for choices to be made in the future. But it does not determine the outcome of decisions, or the ways the individual uses the elements chosen. Evangelical Christians may draw on a wide range of cultural resources for their individual religions. As chapter 4 has shown, in addition to the teachings of their denominational or nondenominational churches, many plausible elements may be drawn from popular religious beliefs and practices and the mass media—whether communicated directly, as preached by a televangelist, or indirectly, as alluded to by TV programs like *Touched by an Angel.*

People like Dolores who draw their practices for healing and health from diverse old traditions (not only Roman Catholic but also ethnic traditions—their own and others') are more likely to use the language of continuity and remembering ancient wisdom rather than a language emphasizing individual choice. They may not try to account for their eclecticism, because their cultural traditions already encourage such selection and blending, so it may be taken-for-granted and unproblematic. There is nothing deterministic about those cultural traditions, however (especially in the context of a highly diverse city with people from many different ethnic and religious backgrounds). The eclecticism of a person like Laura (introduced in chapter 1) illustrates how individuals can creatively blend both the old traditions (emphasizing continuity with her Mexican heritage) with newly encountered practices of others (such as the Buddhist aspects of her meditation) and elements of dissent and innovation (e.g., her feminist values).

Other respondents in our study were, like Marge, Deirdre, and Hannah, consciously eclectic in how they chose, combined, and creatively expanded their personal practices for health and healing. Interestingly, though, many of these interviewees' narratives of their experiences did not use terms that emphasized choice, even though they were conscious of having made choices in selecting the elements of their healing practices. The values implicit in the ways they described their eclecticism are revealing. They used languages that highlighted one (or more) of four main themes in their selection and combination of elements: pragmatic experimentation, creativity, journey or process of development, and caring.

Many respondents who were actively engaged in doing healing for others, as well as for themselves, used a language that emphasized pragmatic experimentation. For instance, Marge had attended, over the years, many different workshops to learn many kinds of alternative approaches to healing. She tried a number of them, keeping only a few that "really worked." Over time, Marge said, she had become more selective about which workshops to attend and which alternative healing practices were worth trying. Her main criteria for selection appear (on the basis of stories she told as examples) to have been whether she had personally experienced some sense of the approach's effectiveness and whether she had experienced any sense that the approach might have any negative effects for anyone involved. She especially valued her psychic healing circle as a source of new ideas and practices, because she considered the circle's members highly experienced and judicious.[64]

Less commonly, our respondents described their practices in terms that emphasized creativity, especially the ideal of blending elements of practice together into something essentially new yet more expressive than any of the separate elements. For example, Hannah valued the richness of Jewish tradition but felt that it touched her life more profoundly when reworked with other ritual elements that spoke to her life as a woman, an artist, and a cancer survivor. Hannah's celebrating with such blended ritual elements took place mainly in women's traditional ritual space in the home, for example in creative variations of the Passover seder meal that her women's group held annually. According to some of our respondents, a ritual that was a creative blend of good elements from diverse sources was far richer and thus more effective than a ritual that merely reproduced (no matter how aesthetically) the traditional elements from a single source.[65]

Many of our respondents framed their choices of healing practices in terms of ongoing processes, for example growth, development, and lifelong spiritual journeys. In these narratives, the emphasis was on choices made for a particular stage of a process. Several interviewees talked about previous practices they had engaged in, often with considerable commitment and energy, but no longer used. In contrast to those who, like Rosalie, evaluated options in terms of one comprehensive decision, most of these interviewees described their discarded healing practices as valuable for the stage of their life journey they had been in but no longer a source of growth or healing. For example, Deirdre's coworker (who introduced her to their women's circle) used a language of journey and growth to describe her own involvement in healing (and her hopes for Deirdre and Libby).

Numerous interviewees used a language of caring to describe the basis for the choices of healing practices they had made. For example, Deirdre said she did not find her coworker's talk of journeys personally meaningful. In explaining her involvement with the women's group's rituals and her continued use of several of its healing practices, Deirdre emphasized personal choices about how to care—for her sister Libby, for herself, for her coworker and other group members, for her clients who had suffered similar sexual abuse, and for her mother, whom she viewed as a victim of a form of abuse, too.

In examining these women's eclecticism and blending of elements in their lived religion, I have emphasized the language they have used to frame their stories, because it reveals the personal values underlying their dynamic processes of choosing and blending. If we focused on their many, seemingly disparate practices, we might miss the way their language reflects a basic integrity in their seemingly idiosyncratic choices and combinations.

Their approaches do break with both the biomedical establishment and most official religions in important ways, but their eclecticism—while often somewhat experimental—is not random or frivolous. For instance, many women's spirituality groups, like Deirdre's and Hannah's, reject the hierarchical ideology embedded in the Judeo-Christian tradition, so they frequently appropriate and transform myths and symbols from their own and other traditions into altogether new meanings and images.[66]

While people may have a commitment to holistic approaches to health and healing, they do not necessarily have a commitment to a single set of beliefs and practices, much less a unified or unchanging package of practices or belief system. Indeed, with the exception of some of the most conservative Christians, most of the people interviewed in these studies considered their spiritual-emotional-physical state to be in flux, provisional, and continually developing. We get a similar picture of people's religious lives in the research of anthropologist Jodie Shapiro Davie, who studied a remarkably deep and engaged Presbyterian women's Bible study group. Davie notes:

> I cannot overemphasize the importance of momentariness to the study of the beliefs of the women of the group; my informants are immersed . . . in an attitude that perceives the religious consciousness as constantly in motion, and religious language as approximate. . . . These articulations of faith are not made to endure. They are uttered in the context of a community that exhibits and is built upon a keen awareness of "being in the moment," of a process in action, of temporality.[67]

Indeed, we might conceptualize individuals' talk (like that of the Bible study group Davie studied) about their practices and beliefs in the context of their healing groups as articulating their lived religion in conversation and action.[68]

As the preceding chapters suggest, I am not sure that the eclecticism and bricolage of the people engaged in spiritual or religious healing is all that new as a pattern for lived religion. Only by defining religion so narrowly that we exclude all beliefs and practices that are not centrally part of some institutional package could we dismiss the considerable local and individual variation that characterized people's religion-as-practiced before the Long Reformation. Only by uncritically starting from the definitional separation of religion/sacred from body/profane could we dismiss the many religious options people have long used in their lived religions for preventing and healing illness, helping childbearing bodies and dying bodies, and for addressing people's material needs. Yet the scope of contemporary eclecticism and blending does seem to be somehow different, so it is worthwhile to examine how holistic healing is linked with a pattern of eclecticism and creative blending for individual religious practices.

There are numerous parallels between people's eclectic combinations of health and healing approaches on the one hand and their individual blending of selected yet malleable elements of religious practice and expression on the other. It appears that many of the individuals who are now employing eclectic blending to shape their embodied practices do so out of a critical and questioning relationship to the authority both of religious/cultural traditions and of rational scientific medicine. Informing their sense of what is authoritative, many individuals who engage in healing practices privilege their personal knowledge and experiential evidence over other bases of knowledge. Many others have had experiences that made them doubt the legitimacy of the authority of specific medical or religious authorities. For example, Hannah's health crisis led her to be highly critical of doctors who fail to "treat the whole person," and the contrast between the wisdom of her women's group and the bad advice of one rabbi who failed to understand her needs led her to lose respect for him as her spiritual leader. There appears to be something about adopting a holistic way of thinking about and experiencing their bodies, health, and well-being that encourages people to evaluate critically the judgments of institutional authorities when those judgments fail to take into account something of that holistic approach that seems to comprehend better their lived reality.

This kind of eclecticism and combination of malleable and mutable elements of belief and practice may be one important form of religion in many modern Western societies.[69] Whether that form is fundamentally different from the eclecticism and even idiosyncrasy of medieval Europe's localized religions (as described in chapter 2) or of popular religions in earlier eras up to the present (as described in chapters 3 and 4) is still, in my opinion, an open question that needs more empirical examination and historical comparison to answer. For example, we would need to know whether there are significant shifts in how people relate to the authority of institutions and their spokespersons. How malleable were, for example, popular religious elements of historical eclectic combinations, and how free were individuals to play creatively with these elements in blending their own religious and health practices, in their own local contexts? Are contemporary individuals and groups more free, more able, or more likely to criticize such authorities as clergy and doctors, or more likely to enjoy eclectic and malleable practices in other arenas of life?

It is possible that, if such shifts are real and widespread, they are taking place in multiple institutional spheres—perhaps all institutions in which individual participation-as-lived is relatively independent of institutional functions-as-publicly-represented. We are making a serious mistake if we simply dismiss all such manifestations of religious eclecticism, bricolage, and holistic blending of ritual practices as sheer individualism and ipso facto not really religious.

Reconsidering "Sheilaism"

Robert Bellah and his coresearchers made such eclectic forms of individual religion infamous with their unsympathetic description of "Sheilaism." Their 1985 book *Habits of the Heart* argued that contemporary Americans used primarily a moral language of individualism, which cannot support a unified public order.[70] Their highly critical depictions of several contemporary forms of religiosity in America clearly contrast with their admiration for certain features of the social form of colonial New England Protestantism, which they characterize as "public and unified." They introduce "Sheilaism" with a sense of dismay: "One person we interviewed has actually named her religion (she calls it her 'faith') after herself. This suggests the logical possibility of over 220 million American religions, one for each of us."[71] Sheila was one of several examples Bellah and his colleagues gave of people who would consider themselves "spiritual but not religious."[72]

Sheila Larson, a young nurse, told the interviewer that she believed in God, but had not attended church in a long time. She emphasized: "My faith has carried me a long way."[73] That faith (which, in response to an interview prompt, she called "Sheilaism") was an individually assembled amalgam of beliefs and practices that emphasized caring for one another and being "gentle to yourself." Bellah and his coauthors construed Sheila's individual religion as the epitome of vapid self-absorption and treated it as evidence of how far American religion had digressed from what they considered its traditional public and shared forms.

The fact that "Sheilaism" was the faith of a nurse who had struggled with personal crises connected with matters of health and healing is relevant for our understanding of contemporary individuals' linkages of religion and health. Bellah and his colleagues identify Sheila as someone who had undergone much psychotherapy, but they mention her personal crises not as important mind-body-spirit experiences of illness and healing or dealing with patients' dying but as problems of meaning. It is clear, however, even from the scant description the authors give, that the religious experiences that shaped her faith were not beliefs and were not even about meaning. One was an immediate experience of God's reassurance when she was facing major surgery. The other was an experience of sacral presence when, as a nurse, she was caring for a dying woman whose husband was not able (emotionally? spiritually? physically?) to deal with his wife's condition. The authors treat her narratives of religious experience (perhaps in light of her history of psychotherapy) as purely subjective and bizarre. I doubt that many, if any, of the persons we interviewed in our study of nonmedical healing would have dismissed such stories as unreal, unintelligibly idiosyncratic, or weird, although they would almost certainly have used very different languages for speaking of their own religious experiences.

Because Bellah's team focused their interviews on respondents' beliefs and commitments, expressed in response to very narrowly focused interview prompts, they did not learn much more about the nature of Sheila's religious experiences or her actual spiritual practices (if any).[74] So we will never know whether there may have been more coherence to "Sheilaism" than their book reports. Catherine Albanese observes:

> Forged out of private pain and personal challenge, Sheila Larson's faith made up in individual integrity what it lacked in theological sophistication and expertise. More than that, it was a faith created through combination. In her case, the combining tropes were vague enough not to attract particular attention. Still they were there.[75]

Decrying what they identify as contemporary American trends toward undesirable patterns of individualism and withdrawal into the private sphere, Bellah and his colleagues suggest that, in such "radically individualistic religion" as Sheilaism, "God is simply the self magnified."[76] They are particularly negative about what they call the "therapeutic thinning" of religious belief and practice by individuals' spiritual attention to self-realization.

Contested Definitional Boundaries

Before turning to the issue of individualism and the place of people's concerns for health, healing, and well-being, I would like to consider Bellah's underlying definitional assumptions in light of a social constructionist reading of history, especially that of the Long Reformation. We get a clue about these definitional assumptions in the authors' negative evaluation of individualistic religion by noting a question the authors posed to a clergyman about whether, among his parishioners, "an emphasis on therapeutic self-realization has replaced traditional Christian teaching about sin and redemption."[77] The very posing of this question as one requiring an either/or answer is predicated on narrowly Protestant definitional boundaries, drawn during the Long Reformation. Defining religion in terms of "teachings" and "redemption," this Protestant stance locates the individual, relative to that religion, in terms of personal acceptance of beliefs and moral principles consistent with the religion-as-preached.

There is considerable historical evidence that religion-as-practiced, at the level of the individual, was far from religion-as-preached in the early modern period, when the so-called traditional public and shared form of religion was at its apogee in American colonial life.[78] By defining religion in terms of its public and unified expressions, sociologists and other scholars of religion have been able to treat the enormous diversity in religion-as-practiced in that era as deviant or irrelevant. Thus, Bellah and other interpreters manage to ignore the fact that in most religious groups of that period, women's religious lives were not much involved in that public aspect—not only because they were excluded from leadership and had little public voice but also because their religious lives typically revolved around domestic practices.

Bellah and his coauthors identified the seventeenth-century figure of Anne Hutchinson as the U.S. progenitor of what they call "radically individualistic religion," contrasting her form of religion with the putative "public and unified" quality of colonial-era American religion, represented by the Puritan church against which she dissented. Hutchinson was excommunicated and expelled from the Massachusetts Bay Colony in 1638 for her trenchant theological criticism of most colony leaders, her insistence on the freedom to practice religion as she chose, and her successes as a preacher—not only preaching to women (which was allowed in the private sphere of a woman's home) but also, scandalously, to the many men who wanted to hear her message.[79] All three of these issues are perfect examples of boundaries that were hotly contested during the Long Reformation, as described in chapter 2.

In other words, Hutchinson and other dissenting coreligionists were in the middle of the fray of the Long Reformation. Clearly, to her colony's rulers, her religion was utterly deviant, not only in content but also in authoritative source. Earlier Puritans in England had challenged the Church of England (which had itself challenged the Roman Catholic Church) over control of both doctrinal and ritual power, especially the important power to determine who could be baptized and thus, according to the beliefs of many, have access to salvation. Although adamantly Protestant in that sense, in the 1630s the Puritan church strove to retain the form of religion that existed before the Reformation movements—that is, the form of a unified political-religious structure (or established religion). Anne Hutchinson (and others engaged in what has been called the "antinomian controversy") threatened the religious-political leaders of the Massachusetts Bay Colony mainly because her testimony was ongoing evidence of the established church's inability to control the dissent and to encapsulate the potentially disruptive dynamism of religious reformation within a unified, orderly political-religious structure.[80]

It is ironic that Bellah and his coauthors identify the "public and unified" qualities they so admire in early American Protestantism with the Puritans of the Massachusetts Bay Colony precisely at the historical moment when that or any church's ability to prevent individuals from dissenting or from choosing diverse, unapproved beliefs and practices (yet considering themselves true to their faith) was patently weakening.

Practices for Health, Healing, and Well-Being: Signs of Radical Individualism?

It would be a mistake to make facile generalizations on the basis of the examples I have described in this chapter (as much as to do so on the basis of an interview of Sheila Larson), but my respondents' complex stories do remind us that there exist considerable ranges of people's lived religions—differences in the depth of experience, amount of effort and discipline in practice, and degree of connection or commitment to others. Nevertheless, the kinds of holistic healing practices illustrated in these vignettes of five women suggest a high level of genuine involvement with others, of caring and commitment, of empathy and emotional investment in the well-being of others.

This is surely not abandoning the public sphere and retreating to a religious private sphere, because neither women's healing roles nor their individual religious roles have been traditionally part of that public sphere in the first place. The healing roles and individual religious lives of these five women were nonetheless fully relational, both toward other people and toward the sacred (however understood). Like most of my respondents, according to their holistic perspective, when they are working for the healing of others, at the same time they are promoting their own health and well-being in all aspects. And when they are working for healing social relationships and the well-being of the environment in all its aspects, they are simultaneously promoting their own spiritual development.

There do seem to be some commonalities among many of our respondents who sought holistic healing for themselves and their loved ones. One of these commonalities is that many had personally experienced some kind of serious suffering that affected them as more than merely a physical (or emotional or spiritual) problem. Thus, not only were they open to the possibility that the necessary healing required a holistic approach but also they could become more empathetic with the suffering of others.

Another—closely related—commonality was that the vast majority (especially of those who devoted considerable personal time and energy to holistic healing) were working, paid or unpaid, in helping others. They included highly trained nurses, teachers, counselors, and social workers, but they also included many unpaid care-givers—mothers, hospice volunteers, spouses, and neighbors who were giving of themselves and needing help to prevent their own depletion. These workers, especially the unpaid ones, were typically women. But perhaps the men in those roles (for example, a counselor at a center for young drug addicts and a retired architect who was giving round-the-clock care to his wife, who suffered from advanced dementia) had a more difficult struggle with helping and care-giving roles, because they did not experience much support for a man who took on typically female roles.

SHEILA, CARE-GIVER. Why is it that seeking a personal way of coping with the body-mind-spirit needs of others and of oneself should seem to be "radical individualism"? And why would the eclectic holism of a Marge or Deirdre appear to be not genuinely religious but rather something else (like popular psychotherapy)? One obvious problem with that interpretation is that it accepts uncritically the differentiation of the mental or emotional from the physical or bodily, as well as from the spiritual or religious realms, such that the psychological would not pertain to the religious. Whose interests does such a rigid division of labor and institutional control serve? Clearly, not the interests of the healers and care-givers, whether paid or unpaid! And probably not the interests of sick persons, dependents who need care, and persons who are suffering from needs that specialists cannot meet. By locating medicine and other specialized medical roles in the valued and well-paid public sphere (i.e., business and enterprise) while relegating unpaid or underpaid helping and care-giving roles to the private sphere (especially the isolated home), modern societies have greatly devalued the contributions people like Sheila make to the public good. Then, when the helping and care-giving workers, like Sheila or the counselor of drug addicts, collapse from the burden, how does that society respond? By locating the problem or supposed "sickness" within the individual who is burned out! (Response: she "needs" a prescription for a tranquilizer, or an unpaid leave of absence from the job, or individual psychotherapy.)

"Sheilaism" does appear to have included elements gleaned from the language of popular psychology (which is itself connected with lucrative business interests, such as producers of self-help books, magazines, and courses). That language, per se, does not disqualify Sheila Larson's eclecticism as a faith. It

does, however, give us a clue as to why a care-giver would choose those particular elements (i.e., being gentle with herself and mutual taking-care of others),
in place of her era's gender-role expectation of women—self-abnegation and
self-sacrifice.[81] Rather than choosing elements of a religion that celebrated self-
preoccupation, Sheila seems to have found elements that encouraged her to
extend—to herself, as well as to the people she helped—the same empathy and
care about the feelings and needs of others.[82] It is unlikely she would have
found such elements in the institutional package of many American churches.
Our interviews with many people who were participating, at various levels, in
holistic healing suggest that the eclecticism of "Sheilaism" was an appropriate,
creative, and constructive way (incoherent as hers may have been) for an overwhelmed care-giver to try to change her way-of-being in a restrictive, gendered
work-role by reimagining her relationships with others, herself, and the sacred.

Thus, "Sheilaism" does not really fit even a stereotypical picture of a vapid
religious life, much less a radical, narcissistic individualism. Nonetheless,
some people may use individual choice and pop psychology to justify superficial personal values and everyday practices. The mother of one of my children's preschool playmates seems to have fit that depiction. My conversations
with her first brought several alternative healing approaches to my attention
and stimulated my interest in applying for the National Institute for Mental
Health grant that funded the research for *Ritual Healing in Suburban America*.
As it turned out, very few of the several hundred people actually interviewed in
the study were as ardent, yet fickle, as Doreen appeared to be.

DOREEN, CONSUMER. Raised Catholic, after Vatican II, Doreen began to "cut
loose" (her term) from her rigid Irish-Catholic, working-class upbringing.
College, major, job, husband, place of residence, religious affiliation, even
preschool for the children had all been consciously selected, in part, so as to
distance herself from her parents and everything they had expected of her.
Doreen (as well as her husband) seemed to fit the image of the perennial
seeker, always trying out new alternative therapies. Doreen was the first person
I had met in the United States who routinely consulted a homoeopathist and a
nutritionist; she also sought frequent alternative health services such as co-
lonic irrigation and foot reflexology. She had been through T-groups (a form of
popular psychotherapy) while in college and primal scream therapy and
Rolfing in her late twenties. Although she was fairly constant in pursuing
several of these therapies, the one that became central in her (and her husband's) life for several years was est (Erhard Seminars Training), a group
psychotherapeutic approach that was somewhat notorious for publicly sham-
ing adherents, who paid hefty course fees for that privilege. Even when her

husband was unemployed and money was very tight, they spent part of an inheritance to attend yet more advanced EST seminars.

Before I began my research, the couple split up, and Doreen moved away, so I never had a chance to interview her. But she did stop by for a surprise visit some years later, when she was in her late thirties. She said she had "outgrown" EST, divorced her husband, arranged for her girls to live with their father, and was enjoying the singles' scene. She had a new career as an aerobics instructor at a posh spa, but her new look was due less to physical fitness than cosmetic surgery (she sported a pert nose and a D-cup bosom), hair dyed bright red, a manicure and a pedicure, eye-catching shoes, an expensive wardrobe, and a shiny sports car.

Doreen's self-absorbed pattern of choosing and changing looks and lifestyles, sources of insights and inspiration, careers and partners is not at all unusual among members of the social classes who can financially afford to choose any of those aspects of themselves and their self-presentation, in the context of a media-fed consumer culture. Although her values and practices bear little resemblance to what I have called "lived religion" in this book, the pattern of choosing and changing those aspects of oneself may apply to some people's religious lives as well.

My point in describing that consumerist pattern, as unattractive as it seems, is to remind us that superficial, commodified, and self-centered practices exist—alongside practices that are deeper, altruistic, and selfless—in most groups or organizations that have not utterly withdrawn from the larger society.[83] I cannot help but wonder if they have not coexisted in individuals' religious beliefs and practices, all the while, in Europe and the Americas—including in those early American communities that epitomized, for the authors of *Habits of the Heart,* the "public and unified" face of religion.

Social Factors in Individuals' Health and Healing

Holistic healing, with its practitioners' diverse, eclectic syntheses of elements of belief and practice, is clearly not a form of radical individualism. But how is a person's health, illness, or healing linked to the person's social contexts and the larger society? This chapter gives several clues. If the quality of each individual's social contexts is part of what promotes illness, then changing those social contexts or providing supportive alternative social connections can promote healing, in the broadest sense of the word. It is evident that suffering and healing are often gendered experiences: not only the events/experiences that cause pain and suffering but also the meanings of illness, as well as the practices for producing or enhancing healing, are often different for women compared to men. The connections between work and gender roles (especially for care-givers and persons in the helping professions) explain some sources of sickness and suffering. This chapter has also noted the importance of holism—especially many people's beliefs and practices that emphasize deep interconnectedness among the individual's body, emotions, thinking and feeling, and spiritual existence.

One of the most important themes these findings suggest is the importance of lived religion, such as the dynamic and changing uses individuals make of embodied practices like healing, for our understanding of the relationship of the individual to society. For example, how do social-psychological-spiritual practices such as forgiveness or reconciliation affect the individual's health and well-being? In what ways might a person's lived religion be, literally, sickening and hurtful? How much autonomy do individuals really have to select and combine cultural elements, and do all individuals have it equally or is it a function of social class or degree of modernization in their societies?

7

Gendered Spiritualities

What difference does it make in my religious practice and experience whether I am a man or a woman? What difference does my gender make in how I participate in my religious group(s) or in what religious roles I have in my home and community? Do I, as a woman, relate to my god(s) differently from the way men in my religious group relate to the presumably same god(s)? When I participate in a religious ritual—especially one with considerable body-symbolism—how much of the meaning of that ritual and symbolism is different for me, as a woman, from what it means to others who seem to be participating in the same way in the same ritual, but who are embodied as men? If, in my religion, men's rituals are completely separate from women's, do we all experience the same religion?

Gender profoundly affects people's religion-as-lived, because gender differentiation permeates so many aspects of life in most cultures. There is little causal connection between biological differences and gender expectations of men and women. There exists enormous cultural variation in gender roles, for example, regarding men's involvement in child rearing, cultivating crops, and creating artwork; likewise, cultures vary greatly regarding women's roles in breadwinning, warfare, and healing. Within cultures, there is also considerable variation over time. Thus, what is recognized as traditional in one era may be very different from that of another time period. Gender is based on multiple social-cultural meanings attached to what is socially defined as "male" and "female" (and for some cultures, other gender categories, too).

The religious meanings attached to gendered bodies are likewise socially defined, contested, and changeable. One such meaning, gender hierarchy (specifically patriarchy), has been deeply interwoven into most of the historically dominant, widespread religions, particularly the monotheisms of Judaism, Christianity, and Islam. But the boundaries defining "gender" (as well as the norms defining appropriate behavior for gendered social roles), like those defining "religion," have been historically contested and changing. Thus, periods of rapid change in gender roles and social groups that are particularly affected by those contested norms are likely to evidence religious responses—efforts both to reaffirm older gender prescriptions and definitions and to reimagine, adapt, or change them. For example, historically, immigrant and colonized peoples have had to cope with strains produced by the impossibility of continuing their former ways of life in a new social context. Historian Robert Orsi has documented, with considerable sensitivity, the difficult predicament of generations of immigrant Italian women in the twentieth century. Their devotion to St. Jude was an active spiritual way of dealing with serious role strains, including their culturally prescribed gender and family roles, which were disvalued in the American context.[1]

Because gender differentiation affects so many aspects of people's lives, the social sciences of religion have almost certainly made the mistake of overgeneralizing on the basis of men's religion, religious practices, and patterns of religiosity and perceiving them as universally characteristic of all people's religions.[2] While recognizing that critical caveat, at the same time, we need to be cautious not to make a similar mistake and overgeneralize white Anglo-Saxon Protestant, middle-class women's religion as somehow universally all women's religion, glossing over the real differences in experiences and practices linked with other aspects of people's identities (such as class or race/ethnicity). Furthermore, we must exercise the same caution not to overgeneralize about those other aspects of people's identities, failing to recognize people's commonalities (and indeed, often, sense of solidarity) across lines of race, class, nationality, religion—and gender.

My hunch is that there may be enormous diversity—even in relatively stable traditional societies—in the gendered aspects of people's lived religions. Especially when we focus on people's everyday beliefs and practices (rather than, for example, formal roles in public rituals), we realize the considerable complexity of all the ways people's religion and spirituality are linked with their gender expectations of self and others, their relationships with human and divine others, and their root sense of identity and community. Religion may be genuinely ambivalent, serving both as legitimation for institutionally approved traditional gender roles and gender hierarchies and as a source of gender-role contestation, transformation, and innovation.

As the preceding chapters have shown, many people experience their material bodies (including their socialized senses and culturally formed body norms) as closely linked with their religion-as-lived. Not only popular religious expressions (as described in chapters 3 and 4) but also emerging religious movements offer alternative religious practices that address adherents' mate-rial bodies—especially their health, physical well-being, gender, and sexuality.[3] Many researchers studying the linkage of religion and healing have observed that the experience of suffering is often gendered, as are the practices by which individuals seek healing and health.[4]

Several of the persons described in chapter 6 illustrate the gendering of suffering and healing. Deirdre and her sister Libby sought healing from the scars of sexual abuse by their own father; Dolores ministered, as a *comadre* (godmother), to the sick and dying in her neighborhood; Hannah used her healing practices and community to bring herself through breast cancer, surgery, chemotherapy, and depression. For each of these women, aspects of their gender roles and gendered bodily experiences were central to their suf-fering and their healing.

Historically, as well as today, people have used embodied practices (as described in chapter 5) to shape their self-in-relationship with the divine. Such spiritual relationships both reflect and reproduce parallel human relation-ships, some of which may be highly problematic for the individuals partici-pating in them. For example, how can a man whose father was violently abusive throughout his formative years develop a positive relationship with a god-as-father? How does the woman whose upbringing prepared her only to accept her husband's authority as decisive in all matters then develop the ability to be effective, independent, and maybe even happy, after he has left her or died? Embodied religious practices often socialize people into gendered roles and patterns of relationships. Just as these roles and relationships are, for many, gendered sources of suffering, so, too, many people find alternative embodied practices to be valuable approaches to healing, recovery, and renewal. This chapter focuses on individual and shared spiritual practices that link the gen-dered self with the spiritual self.

Gender in the Stories Out of Which People Live

In my study of alternative, nonmedical healing, I found that surprisingly few adherents were initially drawn into their various healing groups by an active search for healing—or for that matter by an active search for religion or spirituality. Yet many of these respondents (especially the women) told of personal struggles with gender and other identity issues, interwoven with their stories of healing and spiritual development. Even those who appeared to be happy, strong, and successful in many parts of their lives regularly contended with the difficulty of integrating their gender roles with other parts of their identities.

Bernie is a good example of the ambiguities and complexities of gender and spirituality in the stories out of which people live.[5] I chose Bernie's narrative because it exemplifies a religious and spiritual process of renegotiating self- and social identities, around issues of not only gender and sexuality but also race and social class:

Bernie was one of the few African Americans actively involved in a yoga and meditation center. She usually participated in five or more activities each week there, including classes in yoga, vegetarian cooking, and various meditation techniques, as well as frequent sessions for group yoga practice and meditation, and occasional group meals and celebrations. Bernie practiced yoga daily at home, and she had a time and place set aside at work, as well as home, for practicing meditation several times a day. She was involved in a local Unitarian Church and in some of its social activism in the community.

She was the older child of a middle-class couple. (Her mother had worked as a primary school teacher, and her father worked in wholesale merchandising to businesses in the African American community of a southeast U.S. city.) With a middle-class upbringing, Bernie was already somewhat anomalous among her black friends, even before she attended the state university. She subsequently earned her Ph.D. in literature, becoming the first African American to obtain a Ph.D. from that university. At thirty-two, Bernie got her first tenure-track job at a university in New Jersey, at a time when women—much less African American women—were only beginning to gain access to careers in higher education. When I first met her, she was in her early forties, safely tenured and promoted at the university, and the new owner of a modest home in a pleasant suburban town near the yoga center and the university. Her career success and her apparent ease in relating to people of various racial and ethnic backgrounds did not show her years of struggle to find friends and a community where she could "fit in" and "could truly belong."

Bernie described her spiritual life as deep and fulfilling, and she depicted both her church and the meditation center as her "communities." She considered them more important parts of her life than her job (which she loved) and sources of a sense of belonging she had never experienced anywhere else, including with her extended family and her closest college friends. She did not consider herself a religious person, however, and her description of her spiritual evolution did not fit the pattern of a "seeker." She had not found her church and yoga communities while actively looking for religious or spiritual involvement or growth.

As a child, Bernie had attended Baptist Sunday school and vacation Bible school with her sister and cousins, but she had not been to church or "even thought about religion" after early adolescence. To her, the word "religion" connoted moral strictures, enforced by a "bunch of holier-than-thou, judgmental and nosy relatives and neighbors." She was amused when I asked about her religious involvement in her church, because it was not until I posed the question that she thought about the Unitarians as "religious," too. Her sense of "truly belonging" in the Unitarian church was based mainly on feeling close to people who worked toward the same values and social concerns. She animatedly described her involvement in community activism in the company of friends from her church. Interestingly, when she described the other Unitarians working on the same service projects as herself, she emphasized their diversity—in religious background as well as age, sex, sexual preference, and ethnicity. With them, she developed her first close friendships with people very different from herself, including a gay couple and a Chinese American woman. She told of one time when a crew of nine of them were working together on a Habitat for Humanity house and ended the day with a very sweaty group hug. It was then, she said (slapping her forehead) that she had realized

> We were so the same and really equal, not just in the abstract,
> but in how we loved and respected each other. . . . That sense of group
> identity went a long way to heal all the hurts I've known because
> of my race and class and being a woman and—worse—a single
> woman.[6]

Her involvement in that church began about a year after she "got into" yoga and meditation. She first came to the yoga and meditation center to learn yoga for exercise. Recently jilted by a man with whom she had had a fairly long romantic relationship, she was still mourning the loss of her first hope of a marriage partner in fifteen years of adulthood. She had felt "depressed, fat and ugly," as well as under enormous stress (especially since her personal crisis occurred while she was struggling to be a productive scholar in the pretenure probation period). She explained that her crisis was horrible, because it was the first time she had to face the possibility that, as a successful and educated professional black woman, she might never find a good marriage partner, much less start the family she still wanted. Understandably, she dreaded the prospect of trying to "play the dating game" again, especially considering all her "disadvantages" (especially race) in the regional "singles scene."

Gradually, Bernie practiced yoga more and more seriously, both at the yoga center and at home. She began to try out the center's workshops on other practices such as meditation and journaling. She was elated to discover that these practices "worked" for her, relieving stress and giving her insights and hope. She described the visualization exercises during guided meditations as "exhilarating." The imagery evoked in these exercises, including new ways of imagining her body, emotions, and relationships, offered effective ways of changing perceptions and behaviors that troubled her. She felt free to selectively adopt these visualizations, according to what seemed to help at that "stage of growth."

Frequent attendance led to friendships, and she began arranging her schedule so that she and two other women could do yoga and meditation together almost every weeknight. The other women were sympathetic about Bernie's personal problems, and they shared stories of similar struggles: one was newly divorced from an abusive husband of fifteen years, and the other was struggling to balance a demanding career with her personal life. Interestingly, their solidarity around their problems as women was so strong that it was not until they had become good friends that Bernie found out that the others (whom she'd assumed to be "just whites") also had discomforts with their complex racial/ethnic identities.

They expressed their mutual caring through many ordinary women's practices, such as long conversations around the kitchen table, but they also supported each other through practices learned at the center (e.g., giving each other massages or sharing tapes of relaxation music). All three had come to use yoga and meditation as part of their spirituality; however, yoga and meditation had become part of their social and emotional lives as well. Before her involvement in the center, Bernie had no sense of her "need" for healing, but by the time of my interview, she considered herself "healed" of deep problems with her body image and her sense of herself as a woman. She had no new sexual partner, although she still went on occasional "dates." She claimed that she "missed sex but not as much as [she had] expected" she would. Interestingly, Bernie thought that she was "more sexual" now than when she was in a sexual relationship, but in different ways, because her woman's body "feels good" to her for the first time since she was a child.

She felt that she was still working to salve her many old hurts from being an African American in a racist society—especially the pain African American men had caused her as they "put [her] down to make themselves feel better when they'd been put down." She said:

I'm not there yet, but at least nowadays I don't turn all that pain and anger on my own body. I like my body and I like how I feel after practicing [yoga], especially the hard poses that I thought I could never do. And I like how, when I meditate, those feelings or the stresses of work don't seem to matter—they're still there, but they don't overwhelm me any more. So, I'd call that a healing, too.[7]

It would be a mistake for us to interpret Bernie's evolving story as being "about" any one aspect of her life. The story is not just "about" spirituality, or "about" emotional healing, or "about" friendships and social solidarity, or "about" gender or racial identity, and so on. But it is about all of these aspects of living her experiences of being embodied as a tending-toward-heavy, heterosexual, middle-aged, African American woman who has made important life choices about education, career, community, values, and social activism yet who must continually struggle to develop and maintain wholeness and integration among all these parts of who she is and is becoming. If we want to understand people's religions-as-lived, we need to understand all these aspects in their complexity. And as Bernie's story suggests, we should pay particular attention to how gender, sexuality, and emotions are connected to people's spiritual practices and experiences.

Gender and Self-Identity

Gendered spirituality involves an ongoing process of mind-body-spirit practice by which the individual's gender self-identity can be expressed, produced, and transformed. I am using the concept of "gender" broadly, not so much as the tidy dichotomous social roles (masculine or feminine) assigned to most people at birth in accordance with their society's expectations for men and women. Rather, gender seems to include a relatively wide range of options for performing those roles, as well as a wide range of ways of experiencing and expressing gender in social relationships. We need to consider these wider gender options when we interpret people's religious and spiritual practices, in order to assess the hypotheses of social theorists—for example Anthony Giddens—who suggest that late modernity is characterized by relatively malleable expectations for gender identity as part of a larger, ongoing project of working out self-identity.[8]

Religious groups (in the broadest sense of the term) may be social contexts in which people find an audience that affirms the gender roles they perform, perhaps even providing specific religious training to perform those roles well. Gendered spirituality may be a prime example of what sociologist Danièle Hervieu-Léger has identified as a "new work" for religion to accomplish.[9] This chapter explores the connection between individuals' and groups' spiritual practices and how those individuals and groups understand, construct, and perform their gender identities. I suggest that through a gendered spirituality, the individual can interpret and revise his or her biographical narrative: "This is who I am (and how I came to be who I am) as a man" (or woman).

Like ethnic identity and religious identity, gender identity involves a sense of "who I am" that—especially in modern societies—individuals and groups continually negotiate.[10] While the range of options for "doing gender" may be greater now than in earlier times, I wonder if "traditional" gender roles were ever so neatly divided, so arbitrarily fixed, as mid-twentieth-century sensibilities have imagined they were. Many spiritual practices identified in this chapter suggest that gendered spiritualities of earlier eras may have represented a similar diversity of gender options, as well as similar confrontations and negotiations at the margins.

I first noticed the themes of gender and sexuality early in my study of ritual, nonmedical healing.[11] Many of the groups I studied had developed rituals addressed to members' gender-specific physical, emotional, and spiritual needs. Many women spoke of seeking healing in response to troubling reproductive events (e.g., infertility, stillbirth) or for illnesses attributed to their stress and pain from their roles as women, daughters, or wives. For example, one thirty-seven-year-old woman told of the experience for which she sought healing:

> I hurt myself very badly skiing, and I was going through a situation in my life where I felt I could shoulder no more. And it was my shoulder that I tore up. It was very ironic—the fact that it was my left shoulder. The left side is the female side.... I was having a lot of indecision about the female role in my life and I felt "I can't take any more!" It was like, "I can't shoulder any more of this responsibility."[12]

Other respondents described using religious rituals and meditations for healing scars of sexual abuse, spousal abuse, or troubled relationships with parents. For example, several men sought healing for their relationships with their fathers, deceased or living.

Contested Boundaries: Defining and Prescribing "Gender"

Official religions have firmly legitimated Western gender prescriptions, even in modern times. Religious rituals and individual spiritual practices have long served to socialize males and females into what their society considers "gender-appropriate" behaviors and feelings. Historically, many (perhaps all) public rituals (e.g., for marrying couples, initiating knights, purifying new mothers after childbirth, and ordaining priests) have embedded gender roles. Traditional gender prescriptions have been embodied also in individual religious practices, such as Victorian-era domestic piety, which was clearly feminine in both its Protestant and Catholic versions.[13] In many Christian denominations, certain devotions, devotional materials, and inspirational objects have been promoted for gender-specific audiences.[14]

At the same time, however, a gendered spirituality has often been a counterassertion against the mainstream norms. For example, the spirituality of fifteenth-century Beguines, the asceticism and ecstatic dance of eighteenth-century Shakers, and the spiritual practices of twentieth-century Rajneesh devotees have all included gendered religious practices that deviated from some mainstream Western norms. These alternative practices appeared most frequently as nonofficial religious expressions, because (through the historical processes described in chapter 2) official religions came to represent the viewpoints and interests of privileged, dominant, and comparatively educated social classes, as well as males, colonial powers, and dominant ethnic groups.[15] The experiences and interests of subordinate groups generally were relegated to nonofficial religion—expressed in folk healing practices, witchcraft, spirit possession, and unapproved religious movements—religious expressions that were marginalized or actively suppressed. Gendered roles and experiences were at the intersection of these changes in boundaries for acceptable religious practices and practices pertaining to the body. For instance, both official religion and official medicine treated childbearing as utterly profane and midwifery as illegitimate, as well as possibly dangerous, knowledge and practice.[16]

In what historian Norbert Elias has called the "civilizing process," social norms for bodily control and hygiene were created and tightened, for example by defining proper table etiquette, correct bodily comportment (especially in the presence of the opposite sex), and polite ways of dealing with bodily functions. Norms for "civilized" behavior initially applied only to Europe's elites; later they spread among rural gentry and colonial elites, eventually filtering down to the middle and working classes. "Civilized" manners, thus, distanced properly socialized people from animal-like behaviors and appearances.[17] However, even the elites' women were considered more beast-like than their men, because "gentlewomen's" bodies betrayed them by menstruating, childbearing, and lactating. "Civilized" bodies learned senses of shame and repugnance for their own natural functions and features. Indeed, they learned to sense, in Bourdieu's use of the term, social hierarchies of not only gender but also race and class. For instance, high-status white men believed that they were odorless but that women, nonwhites, and lower-class persons had distinctive odors.[18]

Thus, according to Elias, the civilizing process socialized elites, and eventually all but the most marginal members of society, to self-constrain all passions and all emotional expressions (not just the dangerous ones, like rage). "Civilized" people came to use enormous self-control over their bodies and sexual expressions (even the most benign ones, like nursing an infant).[19] And "uncivilized" bodies were isolated, away from public places where they could endanger the "civilized." Sometimes this isolation was temporary (e.g., "treatments" for childbirth, sickness, dying); sometimes it was long lasting (e.g., so-called treatments for insanity or leprosy), and sometimes "uncivilized" bodies (e.g., witches and indigenous peoples of colonized territories) were removed by systematically putting them to death.[20]

Religious groups, too, emphasized propriety, purity, and decorum—especially for women. For example, the Long Reformation resulted in major shifts in norms for behavior in church, as well as during weddings and other festive occasions.[21] Within Christianity, these historical developments resulted in greater dichotomizing of gender roles, because men were identified more with matters of spirit, while women were identified with matters of the body.[22] Interestingly, during the Long Reformation among Catholics and Protestants, women's patterns of piety and spirituality devolved so greatly from men's that people began to consider women "naturally" religious. Based on analysis of England from 1500 to 1720, historian Patricia Crawford concluded, however, that female religiosity was socially produced and varied more by class than by religious affiliation. The era's evolving acceptable patterns of female spirituality and religious expression were socially controlled, but also often successfully contested.[23]

We need to eschew dichotomous thinking about expectations for "male" and "female" in order to understand better women's ritual and spiritual practices as both meaningful and powerful.[24] To include the experiential aspects of religion, we must take seriously the connection between embodiment and spirituality.[25] The historical development of gendered religious practices has been linked to wider social changes. During the Victorian era in the United States, numerous religious practices that were clearly gendered, female or male, came into currency.

Gendered Spiritualities in the Victorian Era

The Victorian period in America was one of dramatic socioeconomic change. The Industrial Revolution, entrepreneurial expansion of scale and scope of economic control, rapid urbanization, and the proletarianization of large segments of the workforce produced profound changes in the nature of work and the role of the family. During this period the sequestered, nuclear family became the dominant middle-class mode, and the world of work became increasingly physically and socially separate from private life, while many middle-class workers experienced considerable bureaucratic constraint and lack of autonomy at work. Some interpreters note that gender roles became far more monolithic and rigid than was the case in the early part of the nineteenth century[26]—so rigidly separate that even the illnesses by which gender-role stresses were expressed were gender appropriate—hysteria for the women and neurasthenia for the men.[27] Interestingly, it was also an era of proliferation of religious and quasi-religious groups offering alternative roles for both men and women.

Several of the "new" religions that emerged in the latter part of the nine-teenth century reinterpreted women's roles, gave women significant leadership positions, and ritually expressed women's needs and experiences. For example, in Spiritualism and the various metaphysical movements (such as Christian Science, Unity, and Religious Science), women were disproportionately represented among the ranks of authoritative leaders, as well as members.[28] These movements' special attention to healing, emotional concerns, relationships with the living and dead, and nonaggressive assertion of power (e.g., using mental powers) made them particularly appealing to women seeking alternative gender identities in a changing society.

Official Christian groups likewise responded to socioeconomic developments with religion-linked gender prescriptions. Many middle-class churches embraced the separation of public and private and actively promoted an ideal of evangelical domesticity that portrayed homes and women as the primary vehicles of redemption. The rhetoric of preaching and the themes of gospel hymns of this period presented the home as the bastion of tranquility in a turbulent world. Women were to be the keepers of these refuges who, through their piety and purity—in opposition to the aggressiveness and competition of the public sphere—would protect and uplift their children and husbands.[29] Women actively embraced and promoted this ideology of domesticity since it elevated their status in the home, even though it circumscribed their range of influence. One result of this institutional differentiation into public (male) and private (female) spheres was the feminization of the churches and nonelite schools.[30] While religion continued to legitimate men's power and status in the public sphere, church-oriented religious practice and experience came to be identified as emotional, nurturing, gentle, and unmanly.

This privatization of religion (and consequently its place in gender-role socialization) is related to the gradual development of the voluntariness of both

religion and gender as sources of identity in contemporary society. All elements of the private sphere—family lifestyle, interpersonal (e.g., father-child)
roles, religious belief and practice, the individual's and family's social circle,
the consumption of the arts, sports, and other "leisure" activities—became less
serious and compelling than the "real" world of work and production. Private
sphere aspects of social life became matters of individual choice, "opinion,"
and taste.

Another feature of privatized (and thereby feminized) Victorian-era religion was that it could not adequately socialize men into what the culture then
defined as "manly." Several religious and quasi-religious movements promoted alternative gendered spiritualities to meet this perceived need of men.
Contemporary outgrowths of these movements include the various fraternal
orders (e.g., Elks), Mormonism, and the Ku Klux Klan. Although the eventual
ideologies of these men's movements differed dramatically, they shared an
emphasis on secret, fraternal initiation that was intended to produce a sense of
transcendence and personal transformation—an experience of conversion to a
new identity that simultaneously was manly, righteous, and upright in the face
of a frightening and awesome God and was bonded with other men in fraternal
solidarity.[31]

Although some of these religious and quasi-religious groups were founded
in earlier periods (indeed, several claimed roots in medieval fraternal societies, such as orders of knights and brotherhoods of crafts or trade guilds), the
multiplication and expansion in the latter part of the nineteenth century was
remarkable. Membership figures for the churches and fraternal organizations
in the second half of the nineteenth century strongly suggest, according to
historian David Hackett, that the middle-class "women were in the churches
and the men were in the lodges."[32] By 1897, more than one in four U.S. adult
males belonged to such organizations as the Odd Fellows, Freemasons,
Knights of Pythias, and Red Men; the proportion among urban males was far
greater, probably more than one in two. Lodges outnumbered churches in most
cities.

Some observers link this widespread attraction to problematic changes in
the American family, in which fathers had become increasingly dominant but
emotionally distant and physically absent, while mothers had become increasingly devoted to child rearing and omnipresent in the home.[33] But while
changes in marriage and family relations, especially patterns in the socialization of the young, are undoubtedly related to shifts in gender roles and identities, they were only one factor in a much larger set of changes.

The fact that both the gendered spiritualities of the Victorian era and
today's men's and women's spirituality movements arose mainly among

middle-class persons suggests that we need also to examine class-linked features of contemporary production and consumption. These movements may be responses to (1) changing patterns of economic production and the place of middle-class workers in the sphere of production, (2) changes in the nature of work itself and changes in the workplace setting, and (3) changes in the modal "self" that is expected or effectively productive in the contemporary work world.

The Victorian-era brotherhoods and many of today's religious and quasi-religious men's movements have in common an emphasis on rituals of initiation;[34] this suggests that we should consider how the issues of dominance, control, and dependency may be linked with the appeal of participation for men. As classical social theorist Georg Simmel noted, secret (or exclusionary) rituals are linked to assertions of status, dominance, autonomy, and boundaries.[35] We might expect organizations engaging in such ritual initiations to be particularly important in periods when those very aspects of members' lives are threatened. A special ritual to separate the in-group (i.e., men) from the out-group (i.e., women) may be more salient when men are experiencing decreased autonomy or control, for example in the workplace.

Historian Mary Ann Clawson interprets Victorian-era fraternalism as part of an ongoing process of class formation in an emerging capitalist social order. By proffering bonds of loyalty ostensibly across class lines—that is, to working-class, middle-class, and some entrepreneurial-class persons—fraternalism held out an ideal of solidarity among white men.[36] Accordingly, boundaries of inclusion and exclusion were redrawn or changed emphasis: The important distinctions became those of gender and race. By end of the nineteenth century, the ideology of most white U.S. brotherhoods held that gender and race differences were inherent—a matter of essence; whereas white men of all classes were basically kin—brothers or fathers and sons. Clawson's analysis of fraternal ritual also suggests why today's gender-focused rituals may point to socioeconomic problems. She argues that these Victorian-era rituals were effective because they both represented and metaphorically resolved contradictions in social life—particularly those brought on by increasing rationalization of the workplace and its rewards structure. Through these rituals, fraternalism also effectively diminished women's claims to a share of authority, power, and influence.[37]

Spiritual and Ritual Practices for the Transformation of Self

How are spiritual practices such as gendered rituals linked with individuals' bodies and very selves? Catherine Bell's work on ritual theory reminds us that ritual practices, such as kneeling, do not merely "symbolize" their meanings, but rather accomplish their messages through the bodily and emotional experiences of those practicing them.[38] Bell's emphasis on the interconnectedness of mind and body in ritual practices and experiences is comparable to the way anthropologists Nancy Scheper-Hughes and Margaret Lock's use the concept of the "mindful body" to describe the deep interrelatedness of body-mind experience in producing illness and healing.[39] For example, a pilgrimage or other spiritual journey involves the body and spirit simultaneously in moving through space, in reaching a special place. The mindful body's journey both represents and accomplishes a spiritual development or change in the individual. Experiencing the journey physically, emotionally, and spiritually at the same time, the individual's mindful body–self (as a whole) is profoundly involved. A pilgrimage thus becomes more than a long and meaningful hike, more than tourism to a symbol-laden place, more than just thinking about or even praying for spiritual growth. The very practice of a journey in mind-body-spirit can thus accomplish transformation.[40]

All religious groups promote (at least for some members) a measure of transformation of self toward a spiritual ideal. Alternative and virtuoso religious groups, however, do so more self-consciously, because they aspire to an ideal they consider higher or better than the one other religions promote or the ideal held up for the masses. Thus, they are particularly likely to encourage some form of what sociologist and social anthropologist Erving Goffman called "mortification of the self," in order to resocialize members' very selves.[41] Goffman reminds us that religious or spiritual "mortification of the self" (e.g., in a monastery) is not utterly different from the dismantling and remaking of the self that is wrought by nonreligious total institutions (e.g., insane asylums, military academies). The process involves concrete practices that strip the individual of vestiges of the "old self," of control over his or her own time and personal space, and of individual choice in a wide range of matters. Mortification of self is accomplished by mind-body practices such as wearing uniform clothing and hairstyles, assuming certain postures and gestures to diminish the old or affirm the new self, and forgoing bodily adornment or the use of mirrors. Religious groups ask adherents to sacrifice not because these things are wrong in themselves but because using them supports the "old self."

Elizabeth Kanter's sociological study of nineteenth-century American communitarian groups (mainly religious or quasi-religious intentional communities) found that most of the relatively successful groups consciously patterned their daily practices in such a way as to transform adherents' core selves.[42] These daily practices addressed every aspect of members' lives and, notably, their bodies. For example, Shakers lived together in celibate communities, believing that the Second Coming of Christ had already occurred and that they had only to put the millennial dream into practice. Their communities had numerous "millennial laws" and other directives specifying such practices as the exact order in which one must dress oneself each morning, the correct posture for sitting during meeting for worship, and even the appropriate way for a Sister to handle the Brethren's clothes when cleaning or sewing them.[43] Because these alternative communitarian societies' ways of life were dramatically different from that of the dominant society, even routine domestic habits and everyday etiquette required unmaking and remaking. For example, radically egalitarian communities had to retrain members who had been habituated since childhood to engage in rituals of deference (such as doffing their hats or bowing) toward their social "betters." Both the ritual life of an intentional community and the training of novice members reveal much about the nature of the embodied self as continuously changing.

Because modern religion often involves groups of people committing to developing "new" selves (no matter how this process is understood—for instance, as "spirituality," "healing," "conversion," etc.), we must revise or refine our conceptualizations of ritual practice that are based on anthropological studies of relatively homogeneous and stable societies.[44] Particularly when a religious group contests the dominant society's meanings of gender, sexuality, and other body-relevant aspects of the self, it must actively promote spiritual practices to reshape its members' bodily experience and expression. The following are just a few historical and contemporary examples of how gendered spiritualities address the making, unmaking, and remaking of adherents' selves through embodied practice.

Spiritual Practices for Dominance

Body postures, gestures, use of space and time serve, simultaneously, to express metaphorically and actually perform political arrangements—power relationships.[45] So when members of political or social elites engage in virtuoso spirituality, their rituals are particularly likely to include specific embodied practices for performing hierarchy and superior status. Secret or exclusionary rituals, as Simmel reminds us, serve to assert status boundaries, dominance, and autonomy.[46] Religious movements promoting exclusive ritual initiations may be especially prevalent in periods when a group's status prerogatives and dominance are threatened.

A medieval Christian pilgrimage illustrates the connection between spiritual practices and, literally, the embodiment of dominance. In the twelfth century, the pilgrimage to St. Patrick's Purgatory, a cave on an island in Ireland's desolate Lough Derg, was transformed into a pilgrimage exclusively for the noble male elite of Europe.[47] Other pilgrimages of the time were typically accessible to all without regard to social class or gender, and their structure generally minimized social distinctions while promoting *communitas*, a temporary experience of intense solidarity with fellow pilgrims.[48] In contrast, the St. Patrick's Purgatory pilgrimage, transformed into a voluntary male initiation rite, became a spiritual practice for inculcating new class-based ideals of masculinity.

The central ritual was a grueling twenty-four-hour vigil in the cave, described by a participant, Knight Owein, as a real (not metaphorical or visionary) journey into the otherworld of heaven and hell. The ordeal offered pilgrims the "opportunity" to undergo the tribulations of Purgatory, followed by ritual "rebirth" if one proved worthy. Dire warnings reminded the pilgrims that many who went before them had "perished in body and soul" because they were not "strong enough to endure the torments."[49] The men prepared for the central ordeal with intense prayer and fasting for fifteen days, making out wills and receiving the sacred rituals for the dead. According to historian Dorothea French, these spiritual practices served to resocialize elite young men into a new, militarized ideal of masculine virtue that was linked to the growing militarization of upper-class society in that era. Young knights developed a militant lay piety, braced for battle by a dramatic religious experience that rendered them heroic in the eyes of others and assured them of their personal salvation.[50]

There is considerable ritual resemblance between such initiations of medieval knights and those in Victorian-era American fraternal lodges that similarly emphasized exclusive, male initiation rituals. In the lodges, initiates ritually died or descended into darkness, confronted a frightening (often masked) judge figure, were given symbolic feats to perform, and were sworn to secrecy about the initiation and group symbolism, and even about seemingly mundane practices of the brotherhood (e.g. secret handshake). Often fraternal orders adopted even the symbolism and rhetoric of knighthood—somehow transposed onto the middle-class American urban scene at the end of the nineteenth century.[51] Endless layers of fraternal initiations asserted status, dominance, and boundaries between members and noninitiates.[52]

Today's masculine-gendered spiritualities have some features of voluntary male initiation, but they are clearly also rituals of transformation of the self. Like the men of Victorian-era fraternal organizations, late twentieth- and early twenty-first-century men are struggling to define masculinity and men's relationships in the face of challenging and changing gender roles of women—especially their own partners. Like the knight initiates, they exclude those over whom they expect to hold dominance (or from whom they fear loss of autonomy) from key rituals.

In the 1990s, for example, a men's spirituality movement arose that based its group rituals on mythopoetic themes (inspired by Robert Bly and other writers) and on diverse, borrowed ideas about male initiation rituals. This and other recent men's spirituality movements appear to have been premised on the sense that although men's statuses and roles might be acceptable or desirable, individual men were not functioning well—indeed, might be emotionally and socially crippled—because of having been inadequately socialized into masculinity. According to some men's movement spokespersons, these problems were caused by unsatisfactory role models (especially fathers) and lack of culturally effective initiation into the male role in modern societies.[53] Thus, the movement offered rituals emphasizing catharsis (especially grieving) over painful products of this earlier socialization process, particularly men's problematic experiences with their fathers. It also used extensive initiation rituals, eclectically borrowed from both contemporary and historical indigenous peoples and from the myths and legends of a wide range of peoples (mainly those now identified as European) as well as from the New Age and "personal growth" movements. Rituals variously emphasized expressing aggression and strength, honoring age and other male sources of status that might be deemphasized in the larger culture, temporarily relaxing some bodily and emotional constraints, and enhancing the sense that initiation was a step to "something more" in men's realization of their gender roles and their masculinity.

Promise Keepers, a U.S. evangelical Christian men's movement, began some years later. It relied heavily on male subcultural appeals, for example, using warfare and team sports as metaphors for Christian commitment. Mass rallies held in sports stadiums included some of the same enthusiasm-building practices as (U.S.) football: cheers (and cheerleaders), loud music, spectacle, and performance of "the wave." The Promise Keepers urged men to accept responsibility for parenting their children, to exercise their authority as head of the family, to become sexually self-disciplined, and to embrace their essential strong, "ruthless" manliness.[54] The group's ideology was based on gender essentialism, identifying authentic manhood as intrinsically aggressive, competitive, and dominating.[55] The movement held that men should exercise their (proper) headship over wives and children, but allowed the possibility of a tender approach to patriarchal control. Simultaneously, it was adamantly about manliness, heterosexuality, and male authority[56]

Like the Victorian-era brotherhoods, Promise Keepers may have appealed particularly to men in the throes of dramatic social and economic change. Earlier forms of hegemonic masculinity may be unsustainable in a socioeconomic system where neither physical strength nor craft skills nor any other gender advantage guarantees a good income. According to one interpreter,

FIGURE 7.1. During a Promise Keepers' gathering in a sports arena, men engage in many embodied practices that promote both a sense of unity and strong masculinity. A United Methodist News Service photo by Daniel R. Gangler, United Methodist Reporter. Photo #77, accompanies UMNS #558 (5 November, 1996), used by permission of UMNS.

their cultural politics redefine masculinity such that it is no longer contingent on the breadwinner role. Promise Keepers remove male authority from social contingency by arguing that all men have power by virtue of a Christ-like maleness, not by their paycheck or physical strength.[57]

By linking their dominance with masculine virtues (e.g. in spiritual warfare) and masculine subculture (especially sports), Promise Keepers' group practices have literally embodied authoritative masculinity.[58]

Spiritual Practices for Submission

Body practices and body symbolism have long been identified with submission to dominance or authority. The supplicant who goes "on bended knee" and the worshiper who bows in prayer not only demonstrate their submission but also subjectively experience a sense of submission. When religions conflate hierarchical human social relations with the individual's position relative to their god(s), then gender, class, age, and other statuses are particularly likely to be expressed in postures, body rituals, and other ways of literally embodying submission.[59] The connection between religious practices and gender roles and sexuality is often complex.

Sociologist Mary Jo Neitz points out that the dominant Western narrative of religious transformation assumes a male perspective. Accordingly, a man— whose pretransformation "old self" enjoyed many privileges—subsequently renounced them, voluntarily submitted to a transforming discipline, and surrendered to his new vision, his "new self," and his new life. She argues that such a path to religious experience is gender specific, because the men in the narrative begin from a position of autonomy from which they can choose submission and renunciation.[60] Without any preexisting autonomy, could women's religious practices of submission or renunciation possibly lead to the same kind of transcendent religious experience?

Male Christian ascetics in the Middle Ages, for example, sought to renounce worldly privileges and possessions. In order to experience God more deeply, they engaged in body practices of submission, such as crossdressing or prostrating themselves at the altar. Female ascetics of the same period could not accomplish by renunciation the same experience as their male counterparts, because they could not give up privileges of dominance that they did not, by virtue of being female, ever have. Some historians suggest that the reason so many medieval women ascetics used abstention from food as an important part of their spirituality was that eating was one of the few "privileges" women had and thus just about all they could renounce.[61] Many ascetic women employed postures and gestures of submission, but these could not have the same effect for transformation to a "new self" as they did for men. For religious women, submissive body practices were only a slightly more exaggerated ritual deference than would have been routinely expected of them by husbands and fathers.

Numerous recent religious and quasi-religious movements also promote spiritual practices to embody submission. The various Twelve Step groups (e.g., AA) are a widespread example, with their emphasis on yielding to a "higher power" in order to overcome alcoholism, addiction, overeating, and so on. Although these movements are not narrowly gender specific, women often do not benefit from the Twelve Step methods because their prior socialization as women has prevented them from having a sense of self-determination from which they could choose submission to a higher power.[62]

Many evangelical and pentecostal Christian groups value submission as a regular religious practice.[63] For example, several Catholic charismatic communities have developed elaborate systems of headship and submission, urging members to submit fully to the authoritative judgment of their "Head." Men as well as women are encouraged to practice submission to a lay or clerical spiritual director. In addition, however, in the home the husband/father is the Head of all household members, and the wife and children are expected to submit to his authority and discipline for the sake of their own spiritual growth. Similarly, the pentecostal Women's Aglow movement expects women to submit to men's authority and spiritual discipline. For example, each member must have her husband's permission to run for office in the organization, and chapters must obtain their male advisers' authoritative guidance for all decisions. In principle, "Headship" means that every member submit to God's will as discerned by his or her Head, but in practice it means that most women's submission is to the authority of a male (e.g., husband, father) who discerns God's will for her. For example, if a woman thought and prayed hard about whether to resume her career after children started school, her sense of God's will on the matter would be subordinate to her husband's sense of God's will.

These evangelical and pentecostal groups encourage specific ritual practices to embody submission. For example, some encourage women to seek their husband's physical blessing (e.g., laying his hand on her bowed head) at the outset of the day's activities. Healing rituals, likewise, emphasize body practices that socialize women toward gender-specific virtues—submission and giving up one's own control of a problematic situation.[64] While both men and women in these evangelical or pentecostal Christian religious movements seek self-transformation through submission, the experience of these practices is dramatically different for women than for men. Given the binary gender norms in these groups, submission to the authority and discipline of one's spiritual Head is clearly a gendered practice and experience.

Practices for Blurring, Transforming, and Subverting Boundaries

What if spirituality and the individual's relationship with the divine are not necessarily hierarchical and thus are not based on dominance and submission? Religious movements that challenge the established hierarchies (in religion, politics, and gender) are especially likely to promote alternative spiritual practices. Some alternative religious movements try to invert hierarchies, but many movements challenge the very social boundaries on which the hierarchical religions are based. Such religious movements are likely to promote gendered spiritualities that challenge both tidy gender dichotomies and tidy hierarchical boundaries.

The medieval Christian mystic Hadewicj, a member of a lay community of devout women called the Beguines, described one such image of spirituality. Hadewicj was an accomplished poet who wrote extensively, in poetry and prose, of divine love and her mystical experiences. Unlike male mystics of the period, however, she described mystical union as mutual (e.g., mutual mirroring of love, mutual penetration) with little or no hierarchical imagery of God and humanity.[65] It is entirely probable that the spirituality of the Beguine laywomen blurred or transformed the cultural boundaries between dichotomous gender roles, dichotomous sexualities, and even the dichotomy between material and spiritual or body and spirit. Elizabeth Petroff writes:

> beguine writers envisioned love as . . . a kind of boundaryless sexuality in which desire and satisfaction cannot be distinguished. This indistinguishability of masculine and feminine, the inherent bisexuality of loving, seems to be another common element in the beguine writers' representations of desire. . . . Body is deeply implicated in their epistemology: knowing is performed not by the soul alone, but by the whole person—body, soul, and heart.[66]

Such blurring of boundaries was clearly a form of dissent in the context of the medieval church's power.[67]

More important, the Beguine writers' extensive blurring of supposedly dichotomous boundaries raises the question of whether sociologists of religion today are too constrained by dichotomous (i.e., male/female) images of gender and sexuality, as well as by dichotomous (i.e., body/mind) images of religion and spirituality. In order to understand religion-as-lived, we need to be open to the very real possibility that we are, mistakenly, starting from assumptions about gender and sexuality that are artifacts of the very historical and cultural processes we intend to analyze. What if we considered a broader conceptualization of sexuality than is prevalent today in Western societies? That prevalent idea of sexuality is far too focused on artificially binary ideas of properly masculine or feminine sexuality, conceived merely in genital and/or erotic terms.[68] This limitation prevents us from appreciating other possible expressions of human sexuality, such as nursing a baby, giving birth, enjoying a caress, or even practicing celibacy (understood as a chosen pattern of expression of, rather than suppression of, sexuality).

Historian Caroline Bynum has traced medieval men's and women's notions of embodiment and gender, as related to their spiritual practices of "imitation of Christ." Never denying the maleness of Jesus, medieval men and women nevertheless associated Christ's humanity with his (incarnate) body— and the body was identified with woman.[69] Thus, according to Bynum,

> they often went so far as to treat Christ's flesh as female, at least
> in certain of its salvific functions, especially its bleeding and
> nurturing. . . . We find that neither medieval gender contrasts nor
> medieval notions of soul and body were as dichotomous as we have
> been led to think by projecting modern contrasts onto them. Thus,
> I would like to argue that we must consider not just the dichotomy
> but also the mixing or fusing of the genders implicit in medieval
> assumptions.[70]

While religious virtuosi of both sexes sought to imitate Christ in their concrete spiritual practices, women imitated Christ bodily more than did men.[71] Bynum notes that

> female *imitatio Christi* mingled the genders in its most profound
> metaphors and its most profound experiences. Women could fuse
> with Christ's body because they *were* in some sense body, yet women
> never forgot the maleness of Christ. . . . Women mystics often simply
> became the flesh of Christ, because their flesh could do what his
> could do: bleed, feed, die and give life to others."[72]

Interestingly, the Long Reformation appears to have coincided with a significant change in the socially constructed notion of how sex and gender were linked. According to Thomas Laqueur, premodern Western thought described human bodies as having one sex and many genders; the differences between males and females were ascribed to degrees of perfection of form rather than to substantive differences. Laqueur notes that by the end of the eighteenth century, writers insisted on a binary system of sex according to which "Not only are the sexes different, but they are different in every conceivable aspect of body and soul, in every physical and moral aspect."[73] In the one-sex model of thought, body fluids such as milk or semen could be used metaphorically and ambiguously for male and female qualities. Thus, for example, an early eighteenth-century Puritan writer could describe himself metaphorically as a baby sucking the nipples of the breast of God.[74]

The shift to a two-sex model of bodily identity, according to Laqueur, was not due to scientific discoveries about human anatomy but was necessitated by the shift in the political order from monarchy, a hierarchical authority legitimated by reference to a divine hierarchy, to the modern era's political order, an authority legitimated by reference to a social contract based on natural rights and equality. Thus, differences in authority came to be justified by nature—essentialized qualities imputed to racialized and sexed bodies. This history of the social construction of the binary idea of the sex of a human body has interesting parallels with historical contests, described in chapter 2, over the boundaries between other binary distinctions, particularly the distinction between the sacred and profane. At stake in both contests were power, authority, and control over and access to culturally valued resources, as well as other privileges.

These historical comparisons suggest why we should not be surprised to find, today, spiritualities that challenge hierarchical notions of relationship with the deity, while refusing to accept tidy, dichotomous notions of gender, sexuality, and the human Other. Religious responses to racism, sexism, and colonial oppression may develop spiritual practices that do not assume dominance and submission as necessary parts of spiritual relationships. For example, in the United States, many women (and indeed some men) within Christian, Jewish, and Buddhist traditions seek to develop spiritualities that allow them ritually to develop and express egalitarian and holistic relationships (with the divine as well as with other humans).

The most obvious examples are emerging spiritual practices of persons who are openly challenging norms of the wider society, particularly the gay, lesbian, bisexual, and transgender communities. Sociologist Mary Jo Neitz suggests that contemporary witchcraft imagines a postpatriarchal heterosexuality that is not based on a "hetero-homo binary."[75] These highly diverse emerging religious movements employ (and often create) spiritual practices that enable people to experience their bodies and emotions in new and transformed ways. These spiritual practices break down the tidy boundaries implicit in norm-laden dichotomies of gender, race, ethnicity, and sexuality, and they open new possibilities for religious experience.[76]

Spiritual practices that embody dominance and submission are linked with social boundaries of power and privilege. Challenges to those boundaries are, likewise, expressed and accomplished by ritual practices transforming the self.

The Significance of Gendered Spiritualities Today

These expressions of what I call "gendered spiritualities" are not merely accidental products in the veritable supermarket of religious and spiritual alternatives but are linked with contemporary identity concerns. I argue that concrete body practices are involved in how gendered selves are socially developed, maintained, and changed, throughout life. If transformations of gender roles and identities are occurring, they are accomplished through embodied practices. For many, but not all, persons who engage in such personal transformations, religious and spiritual practices are paths to embracing new gender roles and literally becoming a new kind of person. These practices, over time, enable the individual to experience the emotions appropriate to the new self and to learn (bodily, as well as cognitively) the postures, gestures, and the very senses appropriate to the transformed self-identity. I also surmise that further empirical study will reveal the ways that similar concrete body practices contribute to all religious experiences and spiritually meaningful emotions.

Religion and spirituality have been connected with gender-linked body practices throughout the ages, but in the twentieth century, the range of options for "doing gender" expanded dramatically. Interestingly, the same period produced a plethora of religious movements that gave attention to body practices relating to health, gender, and sexuality as spiritual concerns.[77] Other movements, such as one promoting childbirth at home rather than in a medical setting, attracted spiritually motivated participants from widely divergent religious traditions (e.g., Orthodox Jews, fundamentalist Protestants, and feminist Wiccans).[78]

At the same time, however, many (perhaps most) persons practicing gendered spiritualities seem to be exploring new patterns of self and self-identity in the context of communities rather than purely in private, as chapter 6 illustrates. Since traditional gender roles and moral constraints can no longer be taken for granted, both those groups that reaffirm gender traditional roles and those that seek alternative or transformed gender roles and opportunities must actively engage in practices that accomplish and sustain their gender identities. Religious movements, especially those employing identity-transforming religious experiences, can thus be prime sites for accomplishing such gender projects throughout individuals' lives.

For many women like Bernie, religious/spiritual communities and embodied practices are important as ways of negotiating new identities and forging new social relationships that have the potential to transcend the boundaries set by sexist, racist, and classist social norms. With both of her communities—the Unitarian social activists and the yoga and meditation practitioners—Bernie experimented with breaking out of her learned ways of being feminine and female, of being embodied as short and tending toward heavyset, of being African American in an ethnically and racially heterogeneous social world, and of being a friend, a daughter, and a parent. (Some months after our conversation about her two "communities," Bernie phoned me to discuss my experience with adoption. She had become actively involved in her Unitarian friends' "parenting circle" for their several children, including the two children a couple of gay members had adopted. So she was considering adopting a child herself and wanted to know, from someone who had both adopted and biological children, how difficult it might be to bond with a child of mixed racial parentage or to give an adopted child an adequate sense of belonging. Bernie's description of her evolving self-identity and communities reminded me of just how dramatic a transformation such alternatives may portend for our society!)

Such embodied practices are important, therefore, as ways of confronting and healing the emotional damage and the social fissures caused by sexism, racism, homophobia, and social class barriers. Like Bernie, many of the people who describe their spiritual experience as one of healing are referring to a sense of wholeness that is no longer fractured by those barriers. Their practices represent a form of dissent and resistance and simultaneously a vision of alternative identities and communities. Gender, sexuality, and gender identity are important themes in many individuals' lived religions, but especially so in circumstances of great cultural diversity and change.

8

Rethinking Religious Identity, Commitment, and Hybridity

When we focus on religion-as-lived, we discover that religion—rather than being a single entity—is made up of diverse, complex, and ever-changing mixtures of beliefs and practices, as well as relationships, experiences, and commitments. Each chapter of this book has provided many instances of how individuals' lived religions are not fixed, unitary, or even particularly coherent.

Rather than conceptualize individuals' religions as little versions of some institutional model, let us rethink the notions we have of the institutional model of religions. Historian Robert Orsi emphasizes that focusing on lived religion highlights religious creativity and lived experience: "The religious person is the one acting on his or her world in the inherited, improvised, found, constructed idioms of his or her religious culture."[1] So in rethinking the institutional model of religions, a good starting point might be a better appreciation of the many and complex ways those religions are the products of considerable human creativity, cultural improvisation, and construction from diverse elements, only some of which were inherited from the same tradition.

Decades ago, as a university student, I was fascinated to encounter considerable informal religious diversity and unfamiliar religious combinations among my professors, one of whom self-identified as a "Zen Presbyterian."[2] The Presbyterian part seemed understandable, since he belonged to a Presbyterian congregation and taught at a Presbyterian college, but what did the Zen part mean? He explained that he had long been a Presbyterian and was happy to be part of the Presbyterian congregation that he and his wife had chosen for their family, but Presbyterian doctrines—especially those that had historically distinguished Presbyterians (and Calvinists generally) from other Protestant groups—were utterly unimportant to him.[3] His own spiritual life included the practice of Zen meditation and poetry writing. (He was a published poet and much of his writing was on religious or spiritual themes.) From his reading of Buddhist, Hindu, and Taoist philosophy and religion, he borrowed ideas and images, but American culture offered few opportunities for him to apprehend the practices through which those religious meanings were experienced and expressed. In the 1950s and 1960s, especially in the American South where he lived, Zen was one of the very few Asian religions that had been translated for Westerners. Were he alive today, he would likely be a Zen Presbyterian who also practiced tai chi, ecospirituality, and labyrinth-walking meditations, intoned Buddhist, Hindu, and Gregorian chants, and demonstrated against U.S. involvement in the war in Iraq.

What assumptions about religion do we make that mistakenly portray this deeply committed individual's religion as utterly anomalous? We seem to have uncritically accepted definitional boundaries that distinguish religious practices of one religious group from another's, viewing them as mutually exclusive. According to those normative criteria, if one is a practicing Presbyterian, then one cannot also practice Zen. Similarly, we assume that people who engage in Hindu chants are, by that very fact, evidently not very committed Christians, even though they may spend even more time singing Christian hymns as well. We also assume that religious affiliation or membership is somehow a master category that determines an entire set of norms for an individual member's entire faith and practice—allowing some practices as "good" or consistent with the organization's religion and condemning others as "bad" or even heretical. We have assumed that individuals have a unitary religion-as-practiced; in order to be a real Presbyterian, the professor would have had to limit his beliefs and practices to those framed by the Presbyterian tradition.

This chapter challenges the Western image of a religion as a unitary, organizationally defined, and relatively stable set of collective beliefs and practices. The hundreds of interviews and observations on which this book is based, together with the burgeoning historical and anthropological literature on religion-as-practiced, have led me to think that extensive religious blending and within-group religious heterogeneity are the norm, rather than the exception. What do we make of such contemporary forms of religious blending? Our scholarly theories about religious socialization, conversion, and religiously plural societies have long depicted religion at the level of the individual in terms of commitment to the relatively coherent beliefs and practices of a single, received faith tradition (as identified through an organized religion such as Catholicism or Judaism). What if this picture of the historical norm is completely mistaken? We cannot make any assertions about contemporary hybridity as a new phenomenon without seriously considering whether scholars' earlier depiction of individual religious belonging was no more than an artifact of their definitional and methodological assumptions.

Furthermore, when we rethink what is religion, we need also to reconsider our conceptions of religious identity and commitment. Perhaps the borders of religious identity and commitment are as contested, shifting, and malleable as the definitional boundaries of religions. When we focus on lived religion, we come to a more useful perspective on people's individual uses of religious and other cultural resources for their self-identities and commitments. And we come to appreciate that other aspects of identity and commitment, including ethnic, gender, and national identities, are equally complex.

Consider, for example, this portion of the narrative of religious identity given by a middle-aged woman, a full-time volunteer worker in a Catholic peace and justice center, who said:

> I think it would be easier to change the color of my eyes or to get a new genetic code than it would be to stop being a Roman Catholic. . . . [but] I really set aside exclusive Roman Catholicism. . . . I remained a religious woman and I have never stopped thinking of myself as a religious woman, ever, not for a moment. But I began to weave in understandings of a variety of different religious and . . . spiritual traditions, and . . . ways of behaving in the world—concrete actions. So the traditions that I looked most closely at were Native [American] traditions, the Jewish tradition (and I—because of intermarrying in my family—have a number of men and women who came out of a Jewish faith tradition) and Zen Buddhism and Tibetan Buddhism.[4]

Clearly, religion is a central part of her self-identity. It is an important motivating force in her personal ways of acting in the world to which she is highly committed, as evidenced by the time and energy she puts into her activism.

She firmly self-identifies as Roman Catholic, but throughout the interview she tells all the reasons she refuses to be the kind of Catholic some members of the hierarchy expect. In her own spiritual practices, she has woven elements of other traditions together with the most salient elements of her Catholic tradition. And she frames this personal bricolage as both firm and changing; it is coherent yet flexible. How can we understand such a pattern of religious identity, with its interwoven strands of diverse elements—not only religious elements but also family, ethnicity, gender, and perhaps also occupation, social class, and so forth? How can we interpret such eclectic choice and creative adaptation? What can we make of a spirituality that is adamantly activist and dissenting, not only from the larger society but also from the authorities who speak in the name of their tradition?

Some scholars have used the term "syncretism" for historical patterns of religious blending or hybridity. Syncretism refers to the mixing of elements of two or more cultures into a combination that is different (at least, from the vantage point of the scholar studying these cultures) from any of the donor cultures. Unfortunately, until relatively recently, few scholars questioned the implicit assumptions and negative biases embedded in their use of the concept.[5] The concept of syncretism is, itself, a byproduct of the boundary-drawing contests described in chapter 2.

Beyond Syncretism: Rethinking Religious Blending

Historian Thomas Tweed tells of an episode observed in the 1990s among Cuban Americans in Florida that illustrates the contemporary contested meanings of religious and ethnic identities. In Miami, the shrine dedicated to Our Lady of Charity, the patron saint of Cuba, has attracted impressive numbers of pilgrims, most of them middle-class white Cubans living in exile in the United States, some for decades. Although the shrine was built and administered under Roman Catholic clerical auspices, its social space is contested, largely by laypersons whose practice of Santería involves parallel rituals to Our Lady of Charity, whom Santería identifies with the Yoruba orisha Ochún. Tweed writes:

> On a warm June day, as the subtropical sun glittered on Biscayne Bay, a middle-aged, lower-class, black woman strode to the water's edge just behind the shrine to Our Lady of Charity. This recently arrived Cuban exile, who dressed in the white of an *iyawó* or Santería initiate, placed a small faded statue of the Virgin on the concrete wall bordering the bay. Ignoring the interior of the shrine where a priest was leading a hundred visitors in saying the Rosary, Mirta faced the sea, raised both arms to the heavens, and began reciting the Rosary aloud. She interspersed the stylized prayers with spontaneous and passionate "sermons" on various topics, as a crowd of twenty-five

gathered around her. When she stopped, about fifty minutes later, visitors pressed in—asking her questions, writing her phone number, and thanking her enthusiastically.[6]

Mirta had intense devotion to the Virgin but never attended formal rituals of the shrine. She explained, "The Virgin, not the Church, helped me to leave Cuba last year."[7] At the same time, however, Mirta identified herself firmly as Catholic.

According to Tweed, the shrine is a site where people (most of them Cuban immigrants) negotiate their religious identities as they struggle over the meaning of shared symbols (especially the Virgin herself), over what it means to be Catholic, and over the church's authority to ban religious practices like Santería.[8] From the point of view of the official religious authorities, in this case Catholic, the contest is between their authoritatively proclaimed authentic religion and what they consider an impure hybrid that was produced by the unauthorized mingling of pagan elements with Christian ritual practice. It is this contest over authority to control the constituent elements of a religion that makes syncretism a theological and political issue. On one level, the story of Mirta at the shrine is about the ongoing contests for legitimacy and authority between a thoroughly hybrid official religion and an equally hybrid popular religion.[9] On the level of the individual, however, there is yet more to this story (to which I will return).

Toward the end of the Long Reformation, theologians gave the term "syncretism" a pejorative connotation: It came to mean the blending of foreign, non-Christian elements with (putatively "pure," "authentic") Christian beliefs and practices. Historians of religion, some two centuries later, tried to reconceptualize syncretism as any intermingling of disparate religions, but most saw the boundaries between those religions as unproblematic. They treated the definitive features separating the religions as given, as qualities essential to the religions themselves, rather than as social constructions.

Anthropology began to use the concept of "syncretism" even more broadly than historians did, after its twentieth-century use by Melville J. Herskovits (who based his approach on his mentor Franz Boas's concept of "culture contact"). According to their interpretation, the world previously consisted of a number of relatively isolated, distinct, and self-contained groups of people, each with its own distinguishable society with its own culture (i.e., its own language, religion, mores, and so on). When these distinct cultures came into contact, due to hunting, trade, exploration, migration, war, and conquest, for instance, there was always potential for borrowing, adapting, and mixing elements of both cultures. Herskovitz applied the concept of syncretism to his studies of

American Negroes' (his term) cultural patterns (for instance, of music, dance, and religion), which he viewed as diverse amalgams of European and African "culture traits."[10]

Anthropologists have moved far from Herskovitz's naïve image of cultures as pure and distinct. Indeed, many anthropologists would agree with Rosalind Shaw and Charles Stewart that syncretism is basically "the process by which cultures constitute themselves at any given point in time."[11] All cultural traditions—including religious traditions—are based on this kind of interpenetration and interaction with external influences. Indeed, such hybridity is part of the dynamism, strength, richness, and appeal of the resulting synthesis. Since "syncretic processes are considered basic, not only to religion and ritual but to 'the predicament of culture' in general," Shaw and Stewart argue that what we should be analyzing is *anti*syncretism.[12] In other words, all cultural groups are fundamentally syncretic, but not all have attitudes or social movements against the syncretism of others. Social scientists should, therefore, ask: Who opposes syncretic religious beliefs and practices, what are their political interests and social locations, and why is the labeling of religious hybridity as inauthentic an issue for certain types of societies in certain historical periods? As chapter 2 has shown, the social construction of contested boundaries is very much a matter of power. Persons whose power, privilege, and status are legitimated by the religious traditions that are socially defined as authentic are likely to feel threatened by any treatment of other practices or traditions as equally authentic. Peter Beyer argues: "Pure [cultural and religious] forms are but previous and legitimated syncretizations and purity is an argument which seeks to protect its self-evidence and thereby disguise the contingency of important social forms such as cultures and religions."[13]

Another reason some people are so threatened by syncretism is that it challenges the privileged status of their own religious positions. To accept that one's own religion has embedded centuries of hybridity is to demystify and humanize it. For example, not long ago, the editorial board of a sociology journal was discussing putting out some special issues that would address historical and crosscultural studies of religious syncretism. One board member protested inclusion of articles about historical hybridity in the genealogies of Catholic and Protestant beliefs and practices. He argued that the journal should not treat "authentic" religions as in any way comparable to "syncretic" religions. His consternation illustrates my point about anti-syncretism well: Many scholars of religion fail to acknowledge that the boundaries separating recognized religions from those religions considered suspect—as syncretic—are themselves political, serving to privilege certain religions—including scholars' own religion or those of their society's dominant classes and ethnic groups.[14]

Religious Hybridity before the Long Reformation

Historians have documented many important instances of how, from their inception, the Christian churches adaptively responded to the cultural meanings and practices of the diverse peoples who had become Christian. Indeed, there was considerable diversity of religious belief and practice in the early church and in the Jewish communities of the first centuries after Jesus' death. In late antiquity, both Christian and Jewish identities were threatened by extensive overlapping and religious blending, such that Christians struggled over the boundary between what they considered to be orthodox Christian belief and practice on the one hand and what was "too Jewish" Christian belief and practice on the other (and therefore considered heretical). Parallel struggles over the boundaries of orthodox identity occurred among Jews: how to identify Jewish beliefs and practices that were "too Christian" (and therefore deviant). In the very contests by which they labeled and identified the heretical Other among them, they brought the purity of orthodox identity (as Jewish or as Christian) into question.[15]

Yet considerable religious hybridity was necessary, especially for any religion existing outside its foundational culture. For instance, people who became Christian in the early churches in various other places (like Antioch, Rome, and Corinth) had preexisting cultural understandings, such as kinship systems, social class structures, languages, gender norms, and everyday cultural practices (such as what they ate or what clothing they wore, and how they provided livings for their families). If they were going to practice Christianity in their everyday lives, it had to be linked with their own culture and not presume that they would somehow be resocialized as Judean in order to practice the religion of the first Christians.

One such syncretic adaptation, among Roman early Christian churches, was the development of the cult of the saints. On the basis of Roman cultural beliefs and practices about the dead and their place in the complex kinship system, many wealthy Christians had begun the practice of reburying the remains (or relics) of martyrs in their family burial plots. They used this private control of relics for sanctifying, as Christian, their burial plots and for familistic rituals (that were also Roman traditional cultural practices) with the relics, such as feasts celebrating the dead. Having one or more martyrs in the family burial plot was also a source of some social prestige and status differentiation. The early Christian bishops responded to people's cultural needs for dealing with death by encouraging the cult of the saints and veneration of their relics, but they restructured the pre-Christian practices. By placing the relics in church shrines and altars, and by transforming these saints into mediators for the whole congregation, the bishops shifted the balance of social power in the community, transcending the narrow kin-based patronage system of Christian communities in late antiquity.[16]

As Christianity spread throughout Europe, the cults of various Christian saints were identified with local holy sites, such as wells, caves, mountains, and stones, in every region. This practice enabled Christianity to absorb and transform pre-Christian, pagan elements of indigenous cultures. For example, the pre-Christian Celtic religion of the British Isles identified specific hilltops, mountains, and springs as sacred sites. Many of these, for instance, literally thousands of holy wells, were then identified with specific, locally venerated Christian saints and continued to serve as sacred sites (for healing, protection, and fertility, for example) as they had in pre-Christian times.[17] Likewise, pre-Christian calendrical rituals, such as those for the winter and summer solstices, were given Christian meanings: the winter solstice (which was celebrated by the Roman sun cult of late antiquity on December 25, according to the pre-Christian Julian calendar) became the date for celebrating Jesus' nativity (i.e., Christmas), and the summer solstice (i.e., Midsummer Night's Eve) became the Feast of St. John, celebrated with bonfires and fire wheels, symbolic of the sun.[18]

Although church authorities established some of these Christian adaptations of pre-Christian rituals, many of them were localized accretions developed by ordinary people. As such, they were seldom systematic or based on formal ideas (much less theology); rather, most of the meaningful popular rituals of medieval Europe were hybrid practices. Commenting on the pervasiveness of such hybridity, historian Stephen Wilson notes, "Peasants were eclectic, taking bits and pieces from here and there and combining them in a whole which only seemed incoherent to interfering reformers."[19]

The example of the Feast of Candlemas shows that often the specific ritual practices of pre-Christian religion could easily evoke Christian meanings as well. Pre-Christian rituals in early spring used metaphors of light (expressed in ritual torch-flames, candles, bonfires, sunlight) and renewed life (expressed in fertility symbols and in rituals commencing spring planting). These metaphors readily made sense in Christian thought and practice, too, so the same feast day could be used by Christians for blessing all the candles to be used ritually for the whole year.[20]

These old European blended elements may already be familiar to most readers, but my emphasis is not on the fact that many Christian practices are hybrids.[21] Rather, the key point is that all religions are necessarily syncretic and continually changing, as people try to make sense of their changing social worlds, including other cultures with which they come in contact. Rethinking their concept of "culture," anthropologists no longer expect to find enduring traditions. Rather they see people as "wrestling with an adventitious present,"[22] calling on various traditions to aid them, and thereby reshaping those very traditions as they are used.

Varieties of Religious Combination

As the preceding chapters have shown, many people nowadays engage in religious or spiritual practices that have been eclectically combined from diverse, often culturally foreign sources. In some ways, today's religious combination appears to resemble some of the cultural syncretism of earlier periods and the hybridities of other cultures. In other respects, there may be important differences. How, then, can we understand various social processes that result in hybridity? And how can we frame the resulting blended religious expressions so that we do not forget that they, too, are continuing to change, adapt, and intermix?

Creolization is a useful metaphor for describing cultural intermixture, for example the historical processes by which elements of various western African religions melded with religious elements brought by Spanish Catholics in various Caribbean settlements to produce such religious syntheses as Santería. The creolization of religion is somewhat like the creolization of language, which produces a new synthesis that has recognizable linguistic features of both (or all) contributing cultures but is itself a real dialect, distinguishable from all the donor dialects.[23]

Like the creolization of language, historically, much of the creolization of religion has occurred under conditions of subjugation, such as slavery, conquest, and colonialism.[24] We might hypothesize that creolization occurring under duress would be qualitatively different from that occurring voluntarily and spontaneously, for example the cultural exchange and intermarriage that sometimes happens when diverse cultural groups live peacefully in close proximity. It is very difficult to test this hypothesis using the historical record, however, because groups remember their histories selectively, and those most oppressed have often left no written record of their own. Too often, what we know of their religions in the early stages of creolization is based on what others (e.g., missionaries, explorers, and slave owners) have recorded. But it would be useful for scholars of ongoing culture contact today to gather systematic data about the very processes of creolization. Perhaps such cultural melding takes different forms under different social/political conditions, because syncretism often expresses a power struggle.[25] The resulting blend may represent accommodation or resistance (or both at once).[26]

One way cultural miscegenation may be different in the twenty-first century, compared to the eighteenth-century colonial period of the Americas or to premodern Europe, is that significant amounts of culture contact now occur long distance. Widespread access to mass entertainment media (e.g. television, radio, CDs), far-flung telecommunications networks (e.g., the internet, telephones, and mobile phones), and the globalized marketing of cultural products (e.g. "American" Cokes, jeans, pop music, films, and McDonald's fast food) certainly promotes the interpenetration of cultures. Much of this global cultural interchange is lopsided, with the cultural elements of powerful, rich peoples displacing or at least competing effectively with those of economically disadvantaged societies.[27]

Often, however, global cultural exchanges are genuinely bi- or multilateral mixtures. A good example of such cultural interpenetration is the current appeal of "world music" in North America and Europe. Furthermore, from vastly different cultures across the globe, musicians are blending cultural elements in creative adaptations. A new synthesis occurs when serious musicians from widely differing cultural traditions make music together, for example the album *Graceland* (made by American singer-composer Paul Simon together with the South African choral group Ladysmith Black Mambazo singing traditional Zulu *isicathamiya* harmonies). Perhaps not overtly political, this cultural synthesis was extraordinary, considering the context of the politically repressive South African apartheid regime at the time (1985–86). At the same time, the resulting cultural syntheses can subsequently act back on the older, contributing cultural traditions.[28] Some readers may object that creative musical blending is more trivial and less central to people's identities than creative religious blending, but I believe that musical syntheses can closely parallel religious ones, because they both involve embodied practices and the potential for the creative expression of intersubjectively shared experiences.

There is evidence that similar crosscultural borrowing, influenced by images from mass media, results in new religious amalgams. For instance, recent new religious movements in Africa borrow many of the trappings of American televangelists' performances. Healing and prophecy are their main practices, using imagery and ritual practices that draw on elements of a pre-Christian African worldview. These new self-identified charismatic churches, typically organized around a single powerful preacher, promote a sense of continuity with two key features of the indigenous worldview: (1) no separation is drawn between the material realm and the realm of the spirit (i.e., spirit is understood to infuse every aspect of life); (2) religious rituals address this-worldly concerns (such as prosperity, fertility, and health). These features of the indigenous worldview meld easily into the Gospel of Prosperity, borrowed from American evangelists.

The preachers in these new religions typically use the Bible as a source of stories to move their audiences, but in none of these stories is Jesus depicted as poor. Indeed, one church hymn says "Jesus is a winner man." Furthermore, the preachers emphasize that those who want their prayers answered should give money (the more money, the more efficacious the prayers). They also proclaim their own wealth, with flashy cars, bodyguards, and conspicuous consumption, as evidence of god's approval of their religiosity.[29] This kind of religious amalgamation of elements from distant cultural sources is increasingly common in the context of globalized economies and communication.

Transnational blending complicates our understanding of who borrows cultural elements from whom. Beginning in the late twentieth century, patterns of immigration—particularly in Europe and North America—changed, due to the frequency and affordability of flights, as well as improved telecommunications contact between the immigrant communities and their communities of origin. Cultural blends thus can take place more readily in both the sending and the receiving communities of persons who migrate.

Immigrants to New England from the Dominican Republic, for example, have carried cultural elements both ways, as they visit their homeland and then return to their homes in the States. According to sociologist Peggy Levitt, these "transnational villagers" have produced creative blends of cultural elements, introducing North American modes of religious participation into religious groups in their country of origin, while enlivening their practice of Catholic devotions in the United States with elements of Dominican popular religious expression.[30] Similarly, Mexican American members of La Luz del Mundo churches (a Pentecostal religious group, hybridized from its inception) regularly return to visit the founder's church in their homeland community in Guadalajara, bringing with them North American beliefs and practices that have been adopted, resulting in changed patterns of women's roles in the church and congregational participation in decision-making.[31]

Bricolage is a social practice by which an individual constructs a creative assembly by eclectically pasting together seemingly disparate, preexisting bits and pieces of meaning and practice.[32] The pieces may appear disparate to the outsider observer, but they are not nonsensical to the person engaging in such creative syntheses, which make sense and are effective in his or her world of meaning and experience. Religious hybridity is often a result of the practice of bricolage, because individuals' blended elements can become culturally shared elements for future individual or group synthesis. We might hypothesize that certain societies and certain historical eras would have social conditions that promote extensive bricolage in all aspects of culture, while other societies and eras would have conditions that reduce the motivation or freedom for individuals to be creative with religious meaning and practice. It may also be that certain cultures begin from values that emphasize collective religious bricolage while others encourage religious bricolage by individuals. Historical and crosscultural comparisons of such religious hybridity would be welcome for expanding our understanding of religious eclecticism and blending. Bricolage is clearly not unique to our time and culture!

The process of creolization thus often includes bricolage, particularly that used by collectivities, such as families or small, close-knit local groups. The concept of bricolage is particularly useful for conceptualizing religious hybridity, because it highlights the degree of agency ordinary people exercise in the construction of their lived religions. The symbols and metaphors may already be part of the donor cultures, but the process of choosing, combining, and assembling the resulting synthesis is, ultimately, a creative process—sometimes consciously so but often more spontaneously creative—that people may engage in as they go about their everyday lives.

Anthropological theorist Claude Lévi-Strauss described bricolage as seemingly inconsistent or idiosyncratic, because to the outsider there is no logic behind the choice of elements and their peculiar combination. But what if, rather than formal, rational logic, such hybridity as occurs in popular religion operates according to "a different logic"?[33] After reviewing the extensive scholarly literature about Latin American popular religions, sociologist Cristián Parker argues: "This symbolical production, of a *bricolage* ('tinkering') type, is rather far removed from the rational, formal, planned, and systematic production of concepts of intellectual thought that employs contents of ideas previously criticized."[34] The way of thinking that characterizes popular religion, according to Parker, accommodates paradox and metaphor.

The idea that the syncretism of popular religion may be based on "another logic" finds support in historian William Taylor's study of hybridity between many diverse indigenous religions and Spanish Catholicism (in both its popular and official versions) in colonial Mexico. Taylor suggests: "Precolonial religion . . . was not so much transformed by Spanish folk beliefs and practices as it was *potentially congruent with them.* . . . Two religions could be practiced together at different levels without explosive tension." One example of congruency, according to Taylor, was that precolonial indigenous people had a "strong sense of the sacred penetrating every aspect of the material world and daily life."[35]

Thus, without much translation or adaptation, they could engage in religious practices introduced from Spanish popular Catholicism, which recognized a similar interpenetration of the sacred and profane. With no problem of inconsistency, then, indigenous Mexican Catholics could continue to engage in culturally important precolonial practices, especially those done for the nourishment, protection, and health of family members, in private household devotions.[36] At the same time, they could participate comfortably in public collective religious practices that were central to both indigenous precolonial religions and to Catholicism. Because the clergy lacked the ability to control closely the indigenous peoples' religious resources, these peoples appear to have been able to creatively adapt diverse elements of Catholic religious practice and put them to local use.[37] This historical example gives us an image of ordinary people—in this case, conquered indigenous groups—exerting their agency in the process of creative yet resistive bricolage.[38]

Another way to think of "another logic" of syncretism is as a form of play—what anthropologist André Droogers calls "the capacity to deal simultaneously and subjunctively with two or more ways of classifying reality."[39] Accordingly, bricolage results from the creative playing with metonyms and metaphors (at different levels of meanings) and the practices by which those meanings are expressed and experienced. Play requires an actor's role (and therefore the actor's agency) in the production of syncretism. The actor who plays with metaphors thus performs in the "creative subjunctive"—that is, acting out of a metaphor as if it meant plural meanings or levels of meanings, all at the same time.[40] Applying this concept to Taylor's description of precolonial indigenous conceptions of the sacred, we can better understand the Christian indigenous Mexican who burns copal in a cave while reciting Christian prayers and takes the ritual very seriously as if it were unitary—fully Christian and fully indigenous—if we interpret his actions as "creative subjunctive play."

This way of thinking about bricolage and syncretism is particularly useful for understanding how some people in a culturally complex modern society may be creatively selecting and adapting cultural traditions for use in their own practice and identities. Anthropologist Ann-Christine Hornborg illustrates how the Mi'kmaq people of eastern Canada have developed rituals of initiation and healing that create a new image of being Mi'kmaq, accomplishing that group identity through embodied practices such as dancing or drumming. Participants are often fully aware that some of the practices are newly created and that some of what they call "traditional ways" are borrowed from other North American indigenous peoples (e.g., the Lakota tribes of the Plains). Yet they take the rituals very seriously, as if they were unitary—wholly Mi'kmaq tradition. What is important is that the created tradition works: Engagement in the rituals, experienced as traditional, accomplishes healing and effects community and individual identity as Mi'kmaq.[41]

In light of such creative uses of tradition, I wonder whether Max Weber's foundational writings on traditional action were seriously mistaken in treating traditional actions as residual, as guided by nothing more than habit or social inertia (in Weber's words, "almost automatic reaction to habitual stimuli").[42] Many studies of premodern religious hybridity (cited herein) show that even so-called traditional peoples engaging in traditional religious practices may have frequently engaged, with relative autonomy, as active agents in individual as well as collective eclecticism and bricolage. Then as now, individuals frequently used traditional elements in ways the traditions' own authoritative guardians did not foresee.[43] Indeed, people often used and tinkered with traditional elements in order to express dissent or dissatisfaction, challenging (implicitly or explicitly) the official guardians' authority to control the tradition itself. This issue of agency in premodern, supposedly "traditional" religious practice is relevant to our reconsideration of individual religious identity in light of today's hybridity, diversity, and contested boundaries.

Many religious groups actively encourage this pattern of borrowing and blending. Indeed, one of the functions of some religious groups is to introduce new cultural elements for members to try, either individually or as part of the group's ritual practices. One example is a lively San Antonio Episcopalian congregation who have offered a range of study groups and mutual support groups promoting spiritual practices from which members could choose. In addition to Bible study groups, the offerings included, among others, several different Twelve Step groups with spiritual practices based on those of AA, a Celtic spirituality group, a contemplative spirituality class, a labyrinth for meditative walking, and a regular contemplative Eucharistic service based on that of the interdenominational Taize community's non-liturgical worship services (in France).[44] Thus, in the same denomination—indeed, the same congregation—there exists enormous diversity and extensive bricolage. And in some respects, the Episcopalians whose main spiritual practices come from a Twelve Step group may have much in common with some members of a local evangelical nondenominational church that also has groups for Twelve Step practices. And Roman Catholics whose spiritual practices are based on Cursillo spirituality may have more in common with these Episcopalians practicing Cursillo spirituality than with their fellow Catholics whose devotions are pre–Vatican II retentions.

Furthermore, even more complex are the blending and borrowing done by interdenominational and interfaith groups that are united by important larger ideals yet value within-group freedom to express their religious faiths and practices. For example, one scholar described the "solidarity community" in Washington, D.C.:

Their religiosity is a splendid bricolage of the radical elements of many traditions (that religious elites such as myself cannot help but

note are doctrinally irreconcilable). Francis of Assisi is blended with
Gandhi's *satyagraha*, Buddhism, Quakerism, songs of the civil rights
movement, the symbols of left-wing Latin American Catholicism,
a sampling of symbols and practices from a variety of world religions
(with particular interest in goddess traditions), all topped off with
a smattering of Bob Dylan. These unruly syntheses, however, ground
profound practical commitments. With them, people craft religiously
and politically committed lifestyles: living in troubled neighbor-
hoods in solidarity with the poor, embracing lives of voluntary pov-
erty, sustaining long-term ministries with the poor and educating the
well-to-do, engaging in civil disobedience and serving time in fed-
eral prison because of it.[45]

Using older notions of syncretism and related hybridity, scholars would have
difficulty interpreting such diversity within official religions, because those
approaches assumed a coherent tradition as the baseline against which syncretic divergence could be plotted. Some scholars have uncritically accepted
the antisyncretist impulse and criticized this kind of within-group religious
diversity and blending, complaining that such practices are not true to the
real tradition. That evaluative stance requires us to question their idea of
tradition.

The Social Construction of Tradition

The definitional boundary-setting period of the Long Reformation was an era
when Western Christian churches attempted to centralize the authority by
which diverse religious beliefs and practices would be judged as acceptable for
Christian faith and practice. It was based on church authorities' claims that
they were the sole legitimate arbiters of the authentic Christian tradition.
Those arbiters therefore denounced syncretism and individual bricolage because they involved unauthorized uses of elements of the authorized tradition.
And authorities treated the kinds of playful hybridity that characterized much
popular religious expression as downright subversive—and indeed, they
sometimes were.[46]

The Long Reformation was very much a contest for control of cultural
traditions—especially those that served as core justifications for the exercise of
power. Both Protestant and Catholic reformers promoted dramatic changes,
using the rhetoric of recalling the churches to their true tradition. But achieving a church-wide sense of a unitary tradition requires that the whole religious

group conveniently forget the power struggles and the various opposing factions' counter-assertions of alternative ways of constructing the religious group's collective memory. Historian Richard Trexler reminds us why scholars need to recognize the political struggles behind the social construction of a group memory. He states: "The historian's willingness to accept at face value a group memory which invariably emphasizes group solidarity amounts to a depoliticisation of social processes going on inside a group and to a deindividuation of the persons involved in this competitive face-to-face behavior towards each other and towards their changing gods."[47] When we remember that all religious traditions are social—and often seriously contested—constructions, then we realize how misleading it is to represent any religious tradition as unitary, unchanging, pure, or authentic.

Tradition and Authority

Today, as in medieval and early modern contests, religious hybridity raises the issue of authority: Who has the authority to articulate a religious group's core tradition?[48] The Long Reformation involved an effort by religious and political leaders to centralize authority. Reformers attempted to wrest authority from laypeople by greatly reducing the local and particularistic religious practices that had allowed nonauthorized laypersons immediate access to the sacred. The contested boundaries between sacred and profane were often at the core of this effort. In Venice, for example, powerful agents (such as bishops and politically powerful families) tried to control authority. According to historian John Martin, previously

> the sacred had been of a spontaneous and accessible character, and
> its relaxed diffusion throughout the city's monasteries, parishes,
> confraternities, guilds, and shrines guaranteed most Venetians a
> feeling of belonging to the greater whole that was republican Venice.
> To a degree that is difficult for us to imagine today, the sacred was
> familiar and literally so.[49]

The powerful tried to suppress all forms of localistic or particularistic access to the sacred (e.g., devotions to the patron saint of silversmiths) because those practices gave considerable authority to laypersons. Thus, according to Martin, in centralizing authority and banning lay devotional practices, the bishops were also affecting Venetians' core ways of belonging in the city.[50] The historical struggles over tradition and authority were very much about people's social identity and solidarity.

Invention and Accretion of Elements of Tradition

What constitutes a cultural tradition is, however, invented—sometimes consciously so.[51] For example, what most of us think of as traditional regional costumes of Europe (such as Scottish kilts and Norwegian *bunaden*) were invented and subsequently promoted as traditional as recently as the early twentieth century.[52] Similarly, as part of the Romantic period's revisioning of the past, Welsh Druidic and Celtic traditions were rediscovered and rehabilitated, and/or consciously invented, in order to celebrate the ancient ancestry of distinctive Welsh culture.[53]

Many religious traditional practices likewise have come into being in relatively recent historical time, so their human sources are fairly obvious. For example, only after Vatican II did Roman Catholics rediscover the traditional practice of receiving Communion while standing rather than kneeling. Interestingly, the change was adopted in an attempt to eliminate the connotation of the kneeling posture—the feudal submission before one's master—which liturgists criticized as a medieval accretion to the sacrament.[54] Nevertheless, some older Catholics who used the traditional posture feel less reverent when they are not doing so. Because they realize that the new practice was instituted relatively recently, neither they nor the people who prefer the new posture would be likely to think of the practice as a god-given tradition.

When the social construction of other elements of religious tradition is more remote in time, the resulting changes are often represented as "the way our religion has always done this." For example, most Christians assume that a church wedding is the way marriage has always been done in their religion. In passing down the story of their tradition, Christians seldom tell the collectively forgotten history in which many early Christians were ambivalent about marriage itself. Some early church leaders thought that celibacy (or even castration) was the ideal for truly committed Christians; for those who could not meet such a difficult ideal, they urged a "chaste" marriage (i.e., without any sexual activity).[55] Until the sixteenth and seventeenth centuries, ordinary people typically wed by private self-marriage—the basis of later common-law marriage—although sometimes couples would go to the church steps to receive the priest's blessing. Indeed, not until the sixteenth century did Christian churches prohibit the practice of concubinage. Church marriage was declared a "sacrament" in the sixteenth century. Later, Protestant reformers denied that marriage was a sacrament yet kept the practice of church weddings.[56] Few Christian churches encourage their members to remember these historical facts about how the Christian tradition of holy marriage developed, because the history makes it only too clear that the traditional norms and practices were the products of human construction.

How does this social constructionist approach to religious tradition help us understand the nature and complexity of religious hybridity? Again, the analogy with the historical development and permutations of languages is useful. It makes little sense to speak of distinct languages in premodern Europe. Rather, there were highly localized dialects—thousands of them, each with much similarity to their neighbors' dialects but also important differences. Cultural contact with other localities led to some intermixing, some borrowing, and some abandoning of former usages, but there was no real need for standardizing all the different dialects.[57] Various periods of consolidation, boundary setting, and centralization came later.

For example, the creation of the French nation-state involved the standardization of the French language by establishing one dialect—that of the political and social elites in the region of Paris—as proper French. Other dialects (such as Occitán and Provençal) became marginalized as substandard (i.e., "impure," "rustic," or "ignorant") variants of proper French, and yet other dialects disappeared altogether.[58] The process by which French was consolidated and standardized as a language was essentially a political one, by which powerful elites successfully controlled the definitional boundaries of what was properly French language. Persons whose original tongue was one of the disapproved dialects had to learn to speak proper French or risk suffering stigma when conversing with others outside their immediate locale. By the twentieth century, however, most people came to assume that the French people naturally speak French as their traditional native language, even though standardized French was anything but "natural" for many French citizens.

Similarly, in premodern Europe, local Christian religions were very much like dialects. There were thousands of them, each with much similarity to their neighbors' Christian beliefs and practices but also with important local differences. For example, the village's patron (and most important) saint varied greatly from one locality to another—so much so that some saints were unknown outside a certain region. The patron saint was the village's special protector and provider, with close ties to that particular piece of the landscape; the village, in turn, owed special devotion to that patron saint. During the Long Reformation, both Catholic and Protestant church leaders tried to consolidate and standardize Christian beliefs and practices by drawing tight boundaries around what would be considered properly "religion" or "Christian." In doing so, they centralized authority—out of the hands of local persons, of laypersons and their religious groups (e.g., confraternities), and of anyone—even clergy—who lacked the delegated authority of the church's central leadership. Those whose local religion did not conform to the authoritatively approved version faced negative sanctions, such as having their parish church or beloved shrine closed. The process was essentially political, and laypeople and lower-echelon clergy often resisted the centralizing process.[59]

Toward the end of the seventeenth century, for instance, the bishop of Grenoble (France) gave each village under his aegis a specific set of instructions for changes it needed to make. He was adamant that they restrict religious celebrations to the saints' days he had approved and that they observe them with decorum. Some villages complied with certain instructions and not with others. Some villages creatively adapted their celebrations to continue to honor their local saints while appearing to cooperate with the bishop.[60] Yet by the beginning of the twentieth century, relatively few of those premodern local religious practices survived in Europe, and their vestigial forms were often greatly changed in significance and importance to local communities.

Thus, some people's traditions were suppressed, while others' were made the official standard for all. At the same time, the new (consolidated) ways of doing things were justified as the authentic tradition, such that subsequent generations either forgot the old ways or practiced them only on the margins.

With the history of the social construction of their traditions forgotten by the mid–twentieth century, Catholics could assume that their church tradition had always celebrated the feast days honoring the consecrated eucharistic host (Corpus Christi) and Mary's innate purity (Immaculate Conception), even though these practices were developed only in the second millennium of their church's history. Similarly, Protestant groups had selective memory of their traditions, as though their faith and practice in 1950 had an unbroken line to their sixteenth and seventeenth century foundations, or perhaps directly to the early Christian church. Even religions whose tradition was invented comparatively recently, such as the Methodists, Mormons, and Adventists, have (in just a few generations) developed the sense that theirs is a unitary and authentic tradition.

New-Old Traditions

The idea of an authentic tradition as the source of one's beliefs and practices is appealing to those who engage in individual bricolage, as well as to those who insist that their church-authorized version is the only true tradition. Marion Bowman studied the varieties of religious practices (both mainstream Christian and alternative spiritualities) used at the end of the twentieth century by townspeople and pilgrims in Glastonbury, England. She found that people used a number of different narratives to explain the meaning of their experiences there. Belief that their practices derived from an ancient tradition was important to both those who consciously engaged in hybrid practices and those who adhered to what they considered pure, church-authorized traditional practices. Diverse received traditions both inspire and constrain further developments, changes, and inventions, some of which may later come to be viewed as continuations of an ancient tradition.

Glastonbury, a very small town, draws people who are making an Anglican or Roman Catholic pilgrimage to local sacred sites that have been pilgrimage destinations for centuries. The town also draws many visitors for Wiccan rituals and goddess conferences, for Orthodox liturgies in the Celtic Orthodox Church, for neo-Druidic courses at the Isle of Avalon Foundation, and many different practices and events tied to various New Age ideas. For example, some pilgrims believe that the earth has energy meridians, like chakras in the body, and that Glastonbury is located at the earth's equivalent of the central heart chakra. Pilgrims and other visitors freely used stories from all of these traditions in their personal hybrid narratives of meaning. In the Bridget Chapel, they might engage in practices that combine devotion to a Celtic Christian saint with appreciation of Bridget[61] as a pagan Celtic goddess; they might attend a workshop on Celtic shamanism and try out a Druidic sweat lodge; or they might participate in an ecumenical Christian service, combining Christian blessings with Beltane rituals for "dressing" (or decorating) a holy-well. Even Glastonbury's Anglican parish church of St. John the Baptist has experienced congregational within-group diversity and hybridity, partly due to many members' experiences of what they call "God's Blessing,"[62] which has recently been incorporated into some parish worship services, blending a pentecostal-style spiritual experience (initially expressed in an American cultural context) with their Anglican liturgical tradition.[63] The open diversity and ecumenical connection of traditions and their many permutations, all together in this one small community, are almost the epitome of contemporary religious hybridity.

Authentic tradition becomes a contested issue, however, when it is linked with the politics and practice of group identity. The locus of group identity has shifted dramatically several times in the centuries since the Long Reformation. As the analogy between local dialects and local religions suggests, medieval group identities were mostly local and particular. In the modern era, group identities became much broader in scope and much more difficult to create and sustain.

Group Identity: Imagined Communities

In his interpretation of the historical roots of nationalism, Benedict Anderson proposes that "all communities larger than primordial villages of face-to-face contact...are imagined."[64] By "imagined," he means how the members of the community think about and create their sense of connectedness, since that tie cannot be understood or (re)produced through face-to-face contact. Note, though, that Anderson's term "imagined" does not mean that such communities are fake or pure fantasy. Rather, it highlights the ongoing conceptual work required to create an image of community, absent face-to-face experiences of group identity. Those "primordial villages" might be able to take their group identity for granted, because their interpersonal contact could produce a pervasive sense that "we are all the same." The word "identity" stems from the concept of sameness; group identity implies some basis for homogeneity.

The development of imagined communities, such as religious, ethnic, and national communities, framed group identity in the context of heterogeneous populations, often spread across a region too large and complex to produce a face-to-face experience of sameness and connectedness. Anderson suggests that religious community was one of the important cultural predecessors of nationalism, as the bond of imagined community. In premodern Europe, for example, many Christians imagined themselves as identified with all other Christians, through loose centripetal ties—by way of bishops and clergy who could use a single sacred language (Latin), giving them access to the common core of sacred texts and rituals.[65] Even though their vernacular practices (such as local, popular religious practices) varied dramatically, premodern Europe's Christians could imagine themselves as a single religious community, called Christendom. This unity was, clearly, an "invented unity," according to cultural historian Gerard Delanty, who emphasizes the political and oppositional quality of this invention: "To imagine Europe involves the privileging of a particular discourse over others. In the Middle Ages this was Christianity against Islam; in the early modern period it was the victory of civilization over nature."[66]

During the Long Reformation, however, conflicts between and within the proliferating religious splinter groups led to increasing emphasis on delineating not only the theological but also the physical boundaries between areas under the aegis of major religious groups. According to Anderson, the process by which "sacred communities integrated by old sacred languages were gradually fragmented, pluralized and territorialized" was linked to a parallel process by which people began to conceptualize states-units as territorial and bounded by politically determined borders (for example, as defined by the 1648 Treaty of Westphalia). Previously, states were defined by their centers—not their borders, which were indefinite. Precisely which ruler was considered sovereign was relatively unimportant to those who lived at the periphery, unless—as was the case in the religious wars of this transitional era—rulers on opposing sides of a battle tried to press them into military service or their village's fields became the embattled "front" (i.e., border).[67]

If the religious principle of defining political boundaries (between a Catholic and a Lutheran principality, for example) became *cuius regit* (i.e., who-ever rules determines the religion of the whole state), that principle made the delineation of borders between principalities an important political act. Such mapping, however, represented a major shift in the concept of a political realm or state. And, according to Anderson, it was a stepping-stone toward the imag-ination of a nation as a source of group identity and solidarity.[68] It also changed the political significance of how religious groups conceived of themselves.

Various (religious, ethnic, and national) imagined communities claim their cultural and historical tradition to be the uniquely authentic story out of which their people collectively live. The notion of an authentic tradition as the basis of one's ethnic or religious group's solidarity is a matter not merely of belief but also of practice. Groups continually engage in authenticating rituals and other concrete practices to strengthen their members' sense of identity and commitment. One fascinating example of how ethnoreligious identity is au-thenticated through practices in ritual gatherings is the elaboration of Scottish heritage celebrations among U.S. southerners. These practices are eclectically drawn from a wide range of historically incongruent elements. One source of authenticating practices is the nineteenth-century romanticized Scots move-ment Highlandism, with its emphasis on a particular model of male warrior-chivalry, together with the symbolism of the Jacobite "Lost Cause"—such as clan tartans and bagpipes. Some of these Highlandist practices (such as be-longing to a clan society of one's Scottish ancestors) are so central to Scottish American ethnic identity that even persons from obviously Lowland Scottish origins form clan societies and wear invented "ancestral" tartans. Public rituals, for example the "Kirkin' of the Tartans," further intertwine the claims of reli-gious and ethnic authenticity, even though historically the mixture of Presby-terian evangelical religiosity and Highlandism was utterly incongruent—the Highlanders actually fought in support of the Crown's efforts to suppress the Lowlander Covenanters (a Presbyterian sect). Authenticating practices enable today's Scots Americans to imagine a shared collective identity based on what they think of as "memories" of a common "ancestral experience."[69]

The claim of authenticity is an important myth for the maintenance of boundaries for the imagined community, because its people typically believe that their sameness is natural. For example, the imagined community of France could claim that French is naturally the authentic language of France; Roman Catholic Christians could base the boundaries of their imagined community on the authenticity of the lineage of popes and bishops, while fundamentalist Christians could claim the authenticity of their translation and interpretation of scripture as the unique basis of their imagined community. In the stories the members of an imagined community tell themselves, especially for the education of their children, they represent the boundaries as natural. Moreover, they represent the boundaries between their imagined community and others outside as though they merely described the people who happen to be born within a natural unity, rather than actively delineating the socially constructed nation, ethnic group, or religious group.[70]

This representation of the solidarity of such a group as a natural bond not only protects the group's legitimating myth's foundations from being questioned but also gives that myth the potential to reify and essentialize group identity. The myth legitimates group identity and solidarity, affirming: This is who we naturally—in our essence—are and always have been. And the myth legitimates oppositional boundaries toward the Other, whose identity is likewise constructed as historically fixed and essential.[71] The idea of a pure and unitary tradition, uninfluenced by any cultural hybridity, is closely connected with this kind of legitimating myth. For example, modern Greek nationalism is based on such essentialism. The rhetoric of Greek nationalist group identity is adamantly against recognizing any non-Greek influences (such as Macedonian or Islamic cultural elements) in the culture's tradition.[72] Similar essentialism was embedded in the racist nationalism that justified Nazi German and, more recently, Serbian campaigns for ethnic cleansing.[73]

If we problematize antisyncretism (rather than syncretism), as Shaw and Stewart[74] suggested, we notice that the antisyncretist impulse is closely linked with the claim of essentialism and the privileging of one's own religion, race, language, or national identity. In principle, any group could develop a tradition as legitimating myth for its identity. By telling itself the story-out-of-which-We-live, the group produces and reproduces itself as a unified collectivity, as Durkheim's concept of collective representation suggests.[75]

Why is it, then, that certain groups' stories have become privileged over others? For example, sociologist Michael Carroll reminds us that U.S. Anglo discourse has long "orientalized" the Southwest, treating its groups of "Others" (such as Navajos, Pueblos, Mexicanos, Hispanos) as exotic.[76] Edward Said's term "orientalism" refers to the ideological discourse by which the West (specifically, Europe) depicted cultures and peoples of the East (specifically, the Middle East) as essentially different—as Other—and as inherently inferior relative to Western ways of thinking and acting.[77] In the modern context, religious group identity is fundamentally political, both for persons identifying with the dominant groups and for those whose group identity is marginalized.

Such group identities are, nevertheless, continually contested. Even the most powerful religious groups cannot completely control the uses of their traditions. When the Cuban immigrant Mirta engaged in Santería practices at the Catholic shrine for Our Lady of Charity, church authority was powerless to prevent the unapproved uses and blending of those traditional elements. Similarly, Protestant church authorities (of any denomination) are unable to prevent nondenominational popular religious practices that, in their opinion, misuse biblical authority or distort their religious tradition. Although some spokespersons for marginalized groups—indigenous peoples, for example—have vehemently protested what they consider the appropriation of elements of their religious traditions, their inability to prevent others from borrowing their cultural elements is not unique to marginalized peoples.[78]

Many scholars of religion have treated the antisyncretic position as somehow normative—for instance, as indicative of higher levels of religious commitment or stricter adherence to a putatively pure religious tradition. Uncritically accepting any group's identity claims leads to failed comprehension of how group identities (whether antisyncretic or highly syncretic) are developed, changed, and maintained in the context of modern and increasingly globalized societies. Ongoing contestations over boundaries and meanings, together with the fact of continuing cultural blending, borrowing, and creativity, mean that people's group identity and traditions are neither fixed nor unproblematic.

Individuals' Religious Belonging and Commitment

In the light of these complexities relating to the many sources of group identity, how shall we understand the nature of individuals' religious identities and commitments?[79] First, at the level of the individual, religion appears to be a multifaceted, often messy or even contradictory amalgam of beliefs and practices that no particular religious group that an individual belongs to necessarily considers acceptable or important. Individuals' lived religion is experienced and expressed in everyday practices—concrete ways of engaging their bodies and emotions in being religious. Religious socialization and ongoing interactions with others may inform, but cannot determine, each individual's personal practices and beliefs.

As we try to grasp such complex patterns of lived religion, we could re-member the example (in chapter 3) of Laura, whose individual religious outlook and everyday practices incorporated elements of Roman Catholicism, along with Mexican American popular Catholicism, feminism, environmentalism, various ethnic cultural practices (such as Mexican American family values), literary and aesthetic imagery, and Buddhist meditative practices, among oth-ers. Laura's lived religion strongly reflected her multifaceted individual iden-tity. Laura experienced those plural elements of her identity sometimes as integrated, sometimes as conflicting and uncomfortably juxtaposed, some-times as the weight of tradition, and sometimes as malleable—open to her creative reshaping as she went through different stages of her life.

Another example of the complexities of religion and individual identity is Thomas Tweed's story of Mirta, the Cuban American woman (described in the first part of this chapter) who was adamant about her dual self-identification as a Catholic and as a devotée of the Afro-Cuban *santa* Ochún, whom Mirta and other devotés revere simultaneously as Our Lady of Charity. Although the story is about religious groups vying over authoritative control of religious resources (such as access to a powerful saint), it is also very much a story of the ongoing cultural hybridity that arises as individuals negotiate meaningful parts of their personal identities. As a recent immigrant, Mirta was not merely practicing her Cuban religious rituals and identities, because it would have been impossible to reproduce them exactly in a foreign culture. Rather, both Mirta and the wor-shipers inside the shrine were mixing valued elements of their native culture with new (to them) elements of ethnic identity in America.

Furthermore, it is clear that individuals are not limited to a single religious option. Their personal religious practices can be informed by many sources, of which a particular religion may be just one—even if an important one—among many cultural resources. Individuals may be committed to several groups, perhaps but not necessarily congruent with each other. Those group identities may influence, but cannot determine, individual members' personal identities. Nor does a deeply religious person necessarily have a single religious identity—like a master or core identity. Rather, from many and often diverse cultural resources, the individual constructs a personal identity amalgam that may blend or draw serially on different elements, foregrounding some elements in one so-cial context and deemphasizing others. Thus, an individual's religious identity may include some sense of connection or continuity with a larger tradition, re-ligious group, family, and other bases of commitment and sense of belonging but is not limited to them. In the very process of living and experiencing their reli-gious identities, individuals creatively adapt and change, expressing their lived religion differently in changing life-stages, relationships, and cultural settings.

Consider the example of Hannah (the Jewish artist described in chapter 6). Hannah's Jewish heritage was very important to her, and she considered herself a committed, practicing Jew. Yet her individual religious identity included, as foremost, how she practiced her lived religion in her routine everyday life. Synagogue rituals and other congregational activities were a small part of that. Her everyday religion was practiced sometimes in her work as an artist and landscape designer, often in the context of her family life at home, frequently in the context of her women's healing group, and regularly in her individual or small group meditative dance. At some times in her life, her commitment to her women's healing group and its activities was more central than her commitment to her synagogue and its services; at other times, her religious commitment was expressed mainly in her artwork and her meditative dance; but she never dropped her identity as also a practicing Jew.

Such a pattern of individual amalgams of religious beliefs and practices, selected from a range of cultural options, is not peculiar to modern societies. By overemphasizing religious organizations and official versions of religion as definitive, sociologists and other scholars of religion may have failed to notice the extent of within-group diversity due to individuals' selection, adaptation, and amalgamation of elements in their lived religions. What does appear to be different, by the twenty-first century, is the enormous range and diversity of cultural options, together with a widespread awareness of those options and individuals' relative freedom to explore them.[80] At the level of the individual, religion is not fixed, unitary, or even necessarily coherent. Rather, each person's religious practices and the stories they use to make sense of their lives are continually adapting, expanding or receding, and ever changing.

Using this more complex sense of people's lived religions, we can seek more nuanced understanding of individuals' ways of religious belonging and commitment. When we no longer assume that individuals' religions can be equated with their religious affiliation or encompassed by their membership in a religious organization, then we realize that we must ask different questions. How can we find a way to think about religious belonging and commitment that enables us to consider the lived religions of such diverse individuals as Bernie (the African American professor described in chapter 7)? Bernie experienced a strong sense of religious community or being "at home" spiritually with several different groups of people—only some of whom were connected with a religious organization—who engaged in similar practices and were committed to the same values as herself. Her Unitarian friends were important as a source of community, not because the group's members were all the same. In fact, Bernie appreciated them for how diverse they were—mixed races, gay couples, unmarried parents, and from a wide range of different religious upbringings—and for how warmly open they were to her difference, as well. People like Bernie are not practicing a privatized religion. Their religious communities are important, but their group-identities do not require individual conformity or within-group sameness.

Rather than purely individualistic selection of elements of religious bricolage, we see many examples of hybridity and consciously chosen religious practices that are clearly expressions of shared values and experiences. For example, *Las Posadas*, a Mexican popular religious tradition at Christmastime, has been transformed into an interfaith and multiethnic protest against U.S. immigration and border enforcement policies. In the Mexican popular tradition, which is also practiced widely in U.S. communities in border states, *Las Posadas* involves a community reenactment of Joseph and Mary being turned away from the inns and, eventually, finding a place in a stable. Its transformed version, called *Posadas sin Fronteras* has been taking place as a simultaneous event on both sides of the border, since the mid-1990s, when the United States drastically changed its immigration policies to the detriment of Mexican and Central American immigrants. *Posadas sin Fronteras* retains many elements of the Mexican popular tradition—procession with *luminarias* to light the way, reenactment, songs and poems in Spanish. At the same time, the event is now much more—an expression of solidarity between Anglos and Latinos, between Protestants and Catholics, between Americans and Mexicans, all united against what they consider an immoral immigration and border militarization policy. Elements of the old popular tradition are celebrated but applied to border injustices (for example, the traditional *luminarias* are each inscribed with the name of a person who died trying to cross the border). Many of the participants appear to be deeply moved by their experience of *Las Posadas* rituals thus adapted, even if none of the traditional or ritual elements were part of their own ethnic or religious tradition.[81]

Such instances of popular religious traditions promoting social dissent and change raise interesting questions about the nature of diversity in public rituals. How do ethnic traditions come to be more widely shared and symbolic of mutual identification across cultural boundaries? Is this something new, in our era of transnational immigration and travel, or has similar diversity contributed to religious and other cultural hybridity for centuries? Are there different patterns of religious practice among individuals whose sense of group solidarity transcends ethnic or religious boundaries compared to individuals who identify only with a single ethnic or religious group?

At the level of the individual, then, everyday religion is often practiced in the public sphere, not just in private. How can we conceptualize public expression of religious commitments to include the everyday religion of people

FIGURE 8.1. *Posadas sin Fronteras,* as celebrated simultaneously on both sides of the border fence separating Tijuana (Mexico) and San Diego, California (United States), adapts Mexican American popular religious practices to express solidarity between Anglos and Latinos, between Protestants and Catholics, between (U.S.) Americans and Mexicans, all united against what they consider an immoral U.S. immigration and border militarization policy. Courtesy Pedro Rios, American Friends Service Committee, San Diego.

like the woman described in the opening of this chapter? Her extensive peace-and-justice activism was at the very core of her religious practice and her intense sense of community with the women with whom she worked and prayed. She self-identified as Catholic and felt strongly that her practice of her Catholic tradition was not only authentic but perhaps closer to the truth of her religion than what her authoritarian bishop prescribed. She was deeply committed, as evidenced by the enormous amount of time and energy she devoted to the everyday practice of Christian activism for peace, human equality, and social justice. And that commitment was nourished by her regular disciplines of communal, as well as individual, prayer and meditation.

Public expression of religious commitment is not only (or even mainly) through participation in formal religious organizations seeking political influence (such as religious organizations seeking to change laws about abortion or capital punishment). Although intense involvement in such organizations is an important instance of how some individuals practice their personal

RETHINKING RELIGIOUS IDENTITY, COMMITMENT, AND HYBRIDITY 213

religions, it is only a particularly noticeable instance. For example, at various stages in their adult lives, Peter (the committed peace-and-justice activist described in chapter 1) and his wife belonged to several such organizations and devoted considerable energy to their projects. They would probably agree, however, that a more important, daily public expression of that commitment came in their ongoing and challenging experiences as parents of adopted racially mixed children. They also expressed their religious commitment publicly in their decision to live in an ethnically mixed and financially struggling working-class community, as well as their commitment to live in voluntary simplicity and to raise their children to reject the consumerism of the larger society.

Individual religious commitment is evidenced less by avowed commitment to and participation in the activities of religious organizations than by the way each person expresses and experiences his or her faith and practice in ordinary places and in everyday moments. To understand modern religious lives, we need to try to grasp the complexity, diversity, and fluidity of real individuals' religion-as-practiced, in the context of their everyday lives. Although studies of religious organizations and movements are still relevant, they cannot capture the quality of people's everyday religious lives. As messy as these lives may be in practice, individuals' lived religions are what really matters to them.

Notes

1. Note that at that time, many Catholics considered these practices "traditional," even though some practices were comparatively new traditions. Chapter 8 critically examines the notion of "tradition" in our interpretation of religious beliefs and practices.

2. In a similar vein, Nancy Ammerman (2006: 227), critiquing the overly simplistic assumptions some prominent sociologists of religion make about religious actors' motivations and orientations, states: "Human action and relationships of all sorts—religious and otherwise—are about a great deal more than maximizing rewards. The relationship between human and divine is sometimes oriented toward meaning, sometimes toward belonging, sometimes toward desired rewards, sometimes toward communion (or relationship), sometimes toward ecstasy, and sometimes toward moral guidance. Attempts to explain religious action that eliminate that human complexity may explain nothing at all."

3. Asad (1993: 29).

4. Orsi (2005: 187–91).

5. Orsi (1985: xvii).

6. These vignettes describe real people, with significant details altered to protect respondents' anonymity; each vignette is very typical of many people I and/or my research assistants interviewed in different parts of the United States in recent decades.

7. The term "Twelve Step program" refers to a set of practices, central to AA, in which the "recovering" person is supposed to go through twelve specific steps along the path to freedom from addiction. Key to the path is

surrender to the "higher power" of God. Early in its history, AA specifically claimed that it was "spiritual" but not "religious." See Kurtz (1996).

8. Historian David Hall (1997) suggested applying the concept of "lived religion" in order better to grasp the complex and changing subjective-yet-shared religious worlds of individuals in the past, for example, a colonial-era Puritan. See also Hall (1989).

9. The term "lived religion" is particularly useful for this book because of its connection with the philosopher Maurice Merleau-Ponty's phenomenological approach to human consciousness as rooted in embodiment. According to Merleau-Ponty, in our lived worlds, our bodies are not perceived as objects but are experienced as part of the perceiving subject. Conceiving of the individual's ongoing religious experience and practice as "lived religion" thus enables us to recognize its connections with human emotions and embodiment. See Merleau-Ponty (1962).

10. For a discussion of this premise and exploration of several outstanding examples, see Orsi (2003).

11. Berger (1967: 45–52).

12. See Ammerman (1996; 2003).

13. Geertz (1973).

14. Orsi (2005: 73–74).

15. Orsi (2005: 73–109).

16. Thich Nhat Hanh (1987).

17. My discussion of other logics underpinning the coherence of various non-official religious expressions is built on the writing of Cristián Parker (1998; 1996).

18. Orsi (1997: 3–7).

19. McGuire (1988).

20. Luckmann (1973).

21. Luckmann (1967).

22. Luckmann (1973) developed this critique with specificity when asked to comment on some Dutch researchers' ambitious proposal that represented the first attempt, to my knowledge, to do an international survey of individuals' religious beliefs and practices that would not be narrowly bound to a specific country's official religion(s)' range of beliefs and practices accepted as "religious." Much later, teams of scholars from various parts of Europe designed and executed several extensive surveys, called the European Values Studies. They encountered similar problems, especially in trying to word the questions in such a way that they meant the same in widely varying cultural contexts. For example, one recent survey asked respondents about their "personal spirituality," but no matter how the authors translated the term, it made no sense to most Eastern Orthodox Christians in Hungary (Miklos Tomka, personal communication). The fact that a questionnaire term makes no sense to some respondents in a population is worth further research, but it cannot be based on the questionnaire or similar databases. My hunch is that because Eastern Christianity did not undergo the same historical boundary-setting struggles that Western Christianity did, its adherents would make different distinctions about what is important in

their individual religious lives and see no point in the distinctions (like "spiritual, not religious" or "religious, not magical") that the heirs of Western Christian definitions might make.

23. I am particularly indebted to David Hall (1989) and Jon Butler (1990) for alerting us to the enormous diversity of religious practice among American Protestants before the mid–nineteenth century. Historians were, likewise, quicker than sociologists to comprehend the creativity and relevance of the popular religious practices of many American immigrants. I have especially appreciated Robert Orsi's (1985; 1996; 2005) and Thomas Tweed's (1996; 1997) nuanced analysis of Italian Americans' and Cuban Americans' religious practices.

CHAPTER 2

1. This problem of basic conceptual assumptions not "fitting" the data is true in the natural sciences, too, as Thomas Kuhn noted in his analysis of how resistant scientists are to paradigm shifts. See Kuhn (1970).

2. For several essays on this reflexiveness in the ethnography of religion, see Spickard et al. (2002).

3. My usage of the term "Protestant" here refers not to specific Protestant beliefs and practices but to an image of "religion" as stripped of "magical" or "superstitious" elements. This concept was promoted especially by many Protestant groups during the Long Reformation, a historical development described further in this chapter.

4. According to James Spickard (2006), scholars' interpretations of the place of religion in modern societies are best understood as stories or narratives, rather than theories, because interpretations that follow a particular story use a common story line. The six main stories that sociological interpretations tell include: secularization, religious reorganization, individualization, supply-side of religious markets, resurgent conservative religion, and globalization.

5. On a social constructionist approach to the sociology of religion, see especially Beckford (2003). For an excellent critical essay about the scholarly quest to distinguish "real" religion from other religion, see Orsi (2005: 177–204).

6. See Muir (1997: 6).

7. Especially useful sources on the Protestant and Catholic Reformation movements include: Forster (1992); Ginzburg (1983); Luria (1989); Martin (1993); Muir (1997); Scribner (1984a; 1984b; 1990).

8. Elias (1978; 1982); Mellor and Shilling (1994).

9. Forster (1992).

10. On the political uses of constructed cultural distinctions, see Anderson (1991); Bauman (1992); Bourdieu (1984); Elias (1978).

11. Stark and Finke (2000: 63–72).

12. Applying such overly institutional criteria, derived from certain patterns of religious practice and characteristic of only a limited region of Europe, also results in some ethnocentric assumptions about religion and religious practices. Indeed, some of those indicators have never been appropriate for the equally old Christian

traditions of eastern Europe (e.g., Romanian or Russian Orthodox) or Jewish traditions in both western and eastern Europe.

13. Asad (1993). Similarly, Peter Beyer's (1998) work shows that scholars have uncritically accepted the concept of "religions" (as in "world religions"), even though it was socially constructed as a political project. In an encyclopedic coverage of nonelite religious practice in both Western and non-Western religions, Steven Sharot (2001) shows clearly that Western definitions of religion simply do not fit Asian religions-as-practiced.

14. Asad (1988; 1993).

15. See Beckford (2003: 71).

16. I use this example because we have a highly readable historical account of peasants' everyday life, beliefs, and practices in such a village in the early 1300s. LeRoy Ladurie (1978).

17. Obelkevich (1979: 5).

18. Following the conventions used by the historians cited in this chapter, the late medieval period here refers roughly to 1300–1500 CE, with considerable regional variability in the timing and degree of various reformation movements' impact. The early modern period began in the 1500s in several parts of Europe but evolved sporadically and unevenly, lasting well into the 1800s (and even later, in some isolated cultural pockets).

19. These brief sketches cannot convey the complexity and nuances of the considerable historical literature on religion during this transitional period, but they suffice to raise important questions about sociology's definitional boundaries.

20. See Christian (1981); Forster (1992).

21. Stark and Finke (2000).

22. Carroll (1996).

23. Christian (1981: 178–80).

24. The Ave Maria was a short Latin prayer (often called "Hail Mary" in English) based on the gospel words of the angel to Mary at the annunciation. Saying this prayer was recommended for all, especially twice a day (early morning and early evening) when they heard the Angelus bell tolling. It was later incorporated into the Rosary, a series of prayers with many Ave Marias and Pater Nosters; to keep track of where they were in the order of these prayers, most people used a string of different sized beads, which itself came to be called the "rosary." The Pater Noster was a longer, difficult Latin prayer (called the "Lord's Prayer" or the "Our Father" in English). Teaching the Pater Noster was a major catechetical effort for priests and parents, because teaching a long and difficult Latin prayer to someone partially literate (at best) required commitment (such that one English curate enjoyed telling a story of how he had tricked a plowman into learning his Pater Noster). Knowing and using the Pater Noster prayer regularly was also an expected part of the common Christian core religious practices (Duffy 1992).

25. Quoted in Ginzburg (1983: 120).

26. Luria (1991: 106–36).

27. Lionel Rothkrug (1979) documents the correlation between the late medieval Bavarian devotions toward Mary as "Queen of Heaven" and the promulgation,

mainly by Franciscan friars, of an imperial image of God, Christendom, and Mary. By contrast, in the culturally similar region of Swabia, a different preaching order, the Dominicans, promoted devotions toward Mary that expressed a piety contrary to the imperial one of Bavaria. By devotions at shrines to Mary's image as the Suffering One and the Sorrowing Mother of the crucified Christ (as in a Pietà), people in the region of Swabia and the Rhineland emphasized Mary's (and, by extension, God's) identification with humanity and human (particularly mothers') tribulations.

28. Wilson (2000: 25–50).

29. Scribner (1984a).

30. Christian (1981: 176).

31. Hayes (2003: Ch.1); Mullett (1987: 46–47).

32. See, for example, Muir (1997: 21).

33. Burke (1978: 109).

34. Hayes (2003).

35. Mullett (1987: 46).

36. Mullett (1987: 46–47); see also Duffy (1992: 95–101, 117).

37. Duffy (1992: 47), emphasis added.

38. Muir (1997: 55–79); Wilson (2000).

39. Scribner (1984b).

40. Scribner (1984b: 51).

41. Muir (1997: 71).

42. St. Bridget, one of the most important popular saints of Ireland, was not canonized as a saint by the Roman church, but her feast day, February 1, has been celebrated as part of the Catholic liturgical calendar, even in modern times. Bridget is depicted with a flame over her head, and her feast day is part of the ritual calendar's celebration of the season of Candlemas (Scribner 1984a). Her connection with candle flame and "light" may be due to her resemblance to female "keepers of the flame," who were key figures in early spring religious rituals in pre-Christian Celtic religion ("Celtic Religion," 1996).

43. Muir (1997: 61–63).

44. Scribner (1984a: 19–22).

45. Muir (1997: 79).

46. See Bourdieu (1977: 114–24).

47. Scribner (1994).

48. Quoted in Scribner (1984b: 73).

49. Scribner (1984a: 25). See also Ashley and Sheingorn (1992).

50. In the early chapters of *The Sociology of Religion*, Weber (1963) clearly includes these premodern European religious conceptions of the location of the sacred as pertaining to "religion." His extensive use of historical and crosscultural examples to tease out conceptually the differentiation of institutionally specialized religious roles and organization is both exemplary and problematic.

Weber's use of dichotomous conceptions may represent the imposition of modern, Western scholarly patterns of thought on religious worldviews with a different "logic," according to Cristián Parker (1994; 1996). Durkheim used the sacred/profane dichotomy as *definitive* of the religious sphere. His assumption that these are mutually exclusive categories may have blinded him to any "elementary forms" (his term) of religion that addressed the sacred within the profane. For instance, Durkheim does not consider women's religious roles, which European observers may have seen as "merely" profane actions (if, indeed, they were even noticeable to outsider males, on whose chronicles Durkheim relied for his anthropological empirical base).

51. Historically, it was primarily Christian theologians, religious leaders, and agents of social control who attempted to make the definitive boundaries between religion and magic utterly dichotomous and exclusive. Scholars of religion have often accepted the distinction, perhaps trying to translate it into terms that might be more valid crossculturally. For example, historian Keith Thomas (1971) treated religion and magic as opposites in his detailed account of the impact of the Long Reformation in England. He depicted Christians before the reformation movements as heavily preoccupied with magic, including magical approaches to church rituals and celebrations. Accordingly, he saw religion prevailing and magic declining in the subsequent developments in England. Increasingly, however, anthropologists of religion and theorists of ritual have argued that it is more useful to see religious/magical orientations and modes of action as being so closely related that attempting tidy distinctions between them only serves to distract us from understanding the importance of what they have in common; see especially Bell (1997: 46–52). Tambiah (1990: 105–10) suggests some other ways of thinking about these orientations to the world; I find especially fruitful for understanding the complexities of individuals' lived religion his analytical distinction between "participation" and "causality" as orientations.

52. Scribner (1993); Wilson (2000); Kaelber (1998).

53. Scribner (1984a).

54. Bourdieu's (1977) concept of "habitus" suggests how senses are *social* and how practices (e.g., ritual) shape the body and emotions in prereflective meanings.

55. See McGuire (1996).

56. Muir (1997: 7). See also Asad (1993).

57. Muir (1997).

58. Muir (1997: 8, 186–212).

59. Muir (1997).

60. Scribner (1984b: 62–68).

61. Vauchez (1993: 88).

62. Scribner (1984a: 18).

63. Christian (1981); Muir (1997: 157); Mullett (1987: 48–49).

64. There was no necessary connection between the saints officially recognized by the church and those to whom local popular devotion was directed. Many popular saints had not lived historically, but that fact was not what mattered in people's veneration. What mattered was whether prayers addressed through that saint worked. If devotions to a saint were effective in meeting people's needs, regardless of whether the story of that saint's life was factual, then they were considered worth

performing. Guinefort, a highly popular saint in what is now France, was a greyhound. According to her legend, she saved the life of her master's baby by killing a snake, but was subsequently killed because he had thought she had tried to harm the child. When he discovered his mistake, he was so full of remorse that he honored his dog with a proper burial and grave marker. Popular sainthood came later, when people discovered that prayers to the faithful greyhound were effective in curing sick babies. Eventually, a substantial cult grew, involving ritual practices to tap the spiritual powers mediated through this saint (Schmitt 1983).

65. Luria (1989: 93–94).

66. During the Long Reformation, Catholic reformers attempted to eliminate devotions to local saints and substitute centralized devotions to church-wide saints, such as various cults of Mary. In place of local popular saints, church authorities promoted new saints and brought the definition of saints firmly under ecclesiastical control in the process of canonization. However, "many new saints had little popular appeal; their cults did not spread widely, and therefore, they had little impact on popular spirituality" (Luria 1991: 110). Mostly the new saints were those who inspired the elites (e.g., Francis de Sales, John of the Cross, Charles Borromeo). The new saints who became popular among nonelite people were those whose "miracles responded directly to the material needs of everyday peasant life" (111).

Many scholars of religion fail to realize that this historical shift away from the people's connection with popular spirituality was a project only of western European reformers, not of all Christian groups of that era. Thus, they cannot understand Eastern Christian (e.g., Eastern Orthodox) practices such as the popular selection of some persons who are eventually recognized as saints, popular practices in pilgrimage, and the importance of embodied practices (e.g., kissing ikons), which have continued, as central, to this day in many parts of the world where the Long Reformation did not occur to rule them out (Kokosalakis 1987; 1995); (Dubisch 1990).

67. Muir (1997: 16).

68. This perspective is still salient in many religions today, including among Christians. Many scholars, however, want to distance themselves from any notion of religion that encompasses such an image of sacred power; perhaps this attitude explains part of the vehemence of some scholars' objections to sociologist Michael Carroll's (1992) book *Madonnas That Maim*. Robert Orsi forthrightly addresses this scholarly ambivalence toward the very idea of a sacred power that can harm as well as help in *Between Heaven and Earth* (2005).

69. Ashley and Sheingorn (1992).

70. Luria (1989: 104).

71. Scribner (1984a: 25).

72. Liturgical prayers were those embedded in the Mass, for example in conjunction with celebration of a saint's day; extraliturgical prayers included popular devotional prayers that were typically transmitted by laypersons, whether or not they were also encouraged by local clergy.

73. Quoted in Duffy (1992: 16).

74. Note that similar valuable role-specific knowledge later got women into serious trouble with both Protestant and Catholic authorities because it made them suspect of witchcraft (Ehrenreich and English 1973).

75. See Wilson (2000: 421–68).

76. Muir (1997: 216–18).

77. Morris (1989: 502).

78. Scribner (1993).

79. The most notorious instance of this is the *Malleus Maleficarum*, a sixteenth-century manual for identifying witches and other humans whose "powers" were believed to come from evil rather than divine sources. Protestant persecutions of witches and others with unapproved powers were based on similar notions of divine power. Noting that learned men who engaged in occult sciences and licit magic were far less endangered by witch hunts than were women or indigenous peoples in the New World, Williams (1995) argues that accusations of witchcraft were, at root, about the exercise of power over a threatening Other. By defining witchcraft, powerful men were "defining dominion." See also Midelfort (1982); Monter (1983).

80. Duffy (1992).

81. Scribner (1993).

82. See Hall (1989); McDannell (1995).

83. This kind of ritual use of "words of power" blurs any distinction between religion and magic (Wilson 2000: 429–32). See also McGuire (1983a).

84. Because Eastern Orthodox churches (in what are now Greece and Russia, for instance) did not experience these historical transformations, they have retained many elements (such as the importance of ordinary laypeople's recognition of a holy personage as a saint) that pertained in Western Christianity before the Long Reformation (Kokosalakis 1987).

85. Luria (1991: 114–17).

86. Orsi (1997).

87. Weber (1958: 105).

88. Scribner (1993: 493).

89. Burke (1978).

90. Burke (1978).

91. Elias (1978).

92. Connolly (1982); Taylor (1995).

93. Muir (1997).

94. Stevens-Arroyo (1998).

95. Douglas (1966).

96. Longhurst (1962).

97. For example, they suspected such seemingly innocuous people as artisan apprentices, literate millers, and anomalous women (Ginzburg 1980; 1983; Martin 1987; Midelfort 1982; Tedeschi 1991).

98. Ginzburg (1983).

99. Shaw and Stewart (1994).

100. Interestingly, for example, some of the earliest ethnographies of New World indigenous peoples were produced to provide the guardians of the official religion (i.e., the Inquisition in Mexico) with a way to distinguish the people's Catholic faith from vestiges of indigenous religiosity (Martin 1994).

101. Monter (1983).

102. Wolff (1990).

103. As suggested in Carroll (1995); Gorski (2000).

CHAPTER 3

1. Sharot's encyclopedic work, comparing world religions, uses the elite/popular distinction. Sharot also separates virtuoso religious elites from priestly religious elites, and he analyzes the accommodations of each religion to the religiosity of the masses, following Weber's distinction in comparing ascetic Protestantism and Judaism with Catholicism and Hinduism, for example. This approach, while valid, results in an overemphasis on ideas and an underemphasis on everyday religious practices; it also results in replicating Weber's misunderstandings about tradition as a basis of social action. See Sharot (2001).

2. This simile with spoken language vernaculars is apt, because the establishment of a "standard," or correct, way of speaking a language is ultimately a political contest, very like the establishment of "standard," or "correct," religion; Benavides (1996); see also, Benavides (2001). On the notion of vernacular religion, see Badone (1990).

3. Orsi (2002: xvi).

4. Enzo Pace (1987: 12–13) argues for a broad conception of popular religion in the context of modern complex processes: "Relatively autonomous forms of production of means of religious communication on the part of social actors—individuals and groups—that take account of subjective needs, of emotional communication, of face to face rapport, as opposed to all the cold forms of functioning of the traditional religious institution."

5. There is difficulty in expressing this concept in gender-neutral terms; the gender-neutral terms used by many sociologists of religion are *Latino/Latina*, sometimes abbreviated as *Latino/a*. Because women figure more prominently than men in much of the research on which this chapter is based, I use the feminine form *Latina* more frequently, but alternate usage of *Latina* and *Latino* when referring generically to persons of either gender.

6. See Butler (1991). Such unexamined assumptions also are buried in the stereotypes of Latino religiosity that fuel ethnocentric antagonisms, such as Huntington's (2004) claims that Latin American immigrants cannot become "real" Americans, due in part to their inability to share American (Protestant) religious culture.

7. Orsi (1985: xvii).

8. Muir (1997: 98–114).

9. As I have researched this book, I have had many more experiences that impressed me with the vitality of popular religious expressions today. For example, the week before I drafted this chapter, I chatted with a man in his thirties who worked at the university library circulation desk. He noticed that I was renewing Robert Orsi's books on popular religiosity and exclaimed, "Cool! St. Jude! He's my favorite!" And, as we talked about why St. Jude was his "favorite," we were joined by his coworker, a middle-aged woman, who chimed in with a story about St. Anthony and why, according to her mother, one should not get impatient with the saint when he seemed not to respond right away. Popular religious saints are significant, not only in the past tense, among middle-class, educated Latinos in this region.

10. On the political significance of medieval processions, see Forster (1992). On Latino and Latin American processions and political dissent (or political solidarity), see Arnold (1985); Goizueta (2002); Howes (1993); Parker G. (1996: 184–186).

11. On European roots of Latin American pilgrimages, see Nolan (1991). See also Garma N. and Shadow (1994); Parker G. (1996); Turner and Turner (1978).

12. This popular Catholic devotional tradition involved participating (by viewing or performing) in what historian Maureen Flynn calls a "spectacle of suffering." The late medieval practice was based on the devotional ideal of identifying bodily and experientially with Jesus' suffering (Flynn 1996). It was supported by the belief that the sense of vision—literally, seeing the spectacle—was both a confirmation of the reality of the holy events and a way of indirectly experiencing it (Flynn 1994). See also Crain (1997); Mitchell (1990). In much of Latin America, this popular devotion was elaborated and mixed with indigenous practices, especially in the nineteenth and early twentieth centuries. See Trexler (2003).

13. Christian (1982).

14. Descriptions of contemporary processions and pilgrimages popular among U.S. Mexican Americans include: Campo (1998); Davalos (2002); Howarth and Gandert (1999).

15. The basic idea of this play, referred to as a *pastorela,* greatly abbreviated, was scripted in English for television and performed in the 1990s by professional actors (e.g., Linda Ronstadt and Cheech Marín), resulting in a polished, but reasonably faithful, sense of the plot. The gist of it is that the presence of the shepherds— ordinary poor people—at the Nativity was so important that the devil's assistants tried to prevent them from reaching Bethlehem by using every temptation and distraction with which ordinary poor people could be lured. Although the play also involves a fight between the angel of good and the angel of evil, the happy ending requires the eventual presence and devotion of the shepherds (represented not only as men but also as women and children).

16. See Flores (2008). Note, too, the similarity with Italian American and Cuban American popular religious festivals, as described in Orsi (1985) and Tweed (1997).

17. Flores (1994).

18. Flores (1994).

19. Flores (1994; 1995).

20. Flores (1994: 176).

21. Flores (1995). Popular religious practices often involve a gift economy more than a market economy, because they are linked with relationships with others—human and divine. See Schmidt (1997); Turner (1987: 457).

22. On domestic shrines and altars, see McDannell (1995: 25–38); Ricciardi (2006); Turner (1999); Tweed (2006: 106–9). The creation of home shrines is a widespread practice in many religions. As McDannell shows with fascinating photographic evidence, historically, American homes—Catholic and Protestant—have had such shrines, albeit with varying usages and religious practices associated with them. An interesting twentieth-century elaboration of domestic shrines among Massachusetts women of Italian and Portuguese descent is documented in the photographs of Dana Salvo (McNiff 1999).

23. Turner (1999). Turner (1987: 456–57) analyzed Sicilian American women's devotional practice (in Texas) of preparing and "giving" an elaborate home altar to San Giuseppi, patron of the family. She argues that—unlike men's gift relationships and gifting practices (which are typically centered on concerns of prestige, ownership, and equitable exchange)—women's gifting on such an occasion should be understood as "a testament to intimacy—a kind of intimacy that is predicated on the values of reproduction."

24. Quoted in Rodriguez (1994: 119–21); see also Nabhan-Warren (2005: 180–96); Peña and Frehill (1998).

25. Unfortunately, we stereotypically imagine popular religiosity as female. Both men and women have used popular religious elements, historically and today. Because women's religious practices were particularly likely to have been marginalized by the historical institutional boundary-setting, women have been disproportionately engaged in popular religious practices in the home. In recent years, studies have shown women to be prominent in a wide range of religious expressions, partly because researchers have noticed and learned about women's religious practices that were previously invisible to other researchers. Another reason women's practices are more evident than men's in this book is that to the extent that I use illustrations from my own previous research (such as on nonmedical healing), they reflect the predominance of women among the persons whom my research assistants and I interviewed.

26. For instance, historically, popular religious tradition in much of Europe promoted virulent anti-Semitism. Some folk saints, for example St. Werner in central Europe, were venerated solely because of myths of their deaths due to arcane Jewish rituals. In consolidating control during the Long Reformation, church authorities (both Catholic and Protestant) proclaimed their right to judge, overrule, and condemn expressions of popular sentiment, including many popular anti-Semitic practices. Muir (1997); Vauchez (1993).

27. Note, too, that the Protestant religious groups that have attracted the most Mexican American members tend also to be those that legitimate patriarchal dominance in contemporary families.

28. Compare Orsi (1996: 78–94). Also see the 1995 documentary *Flowers for Guadalupe/Flores Para Guadalupe: The Virgin of Guadalupe in the Lives of Mexican Women,* produced by Judith Gleason with the collaboration of the Colectivo Feminista

de Xalapa and Elisa Mereghetti, and distributed by Filmmakers' Library. Although it focuses mainly on Mexican locations and practices, it does include parallel practices in the United States.

29. Weber (1958: 105). See also Berger (1967); Merton (1970).

30. Note that similar attitudes were expressed by New Jersey (mainly Anglo) suburbanites who were engaged in a wide range of nonmedical approaches to healing. McGuire (1982). On Mexican American traditions of nonmedical healing that are in use today, see León (2002); Espín (1996); Portilla (2002).

31. See Goizueta (2002).

32. Díaz-Stevens (1994: 26).

33. Díaz-Stevens and Stevens-Arroyo (1998: 71–73).

34. Note that the distinction between church-approved and -unapproved is a changing and sometimes porous boundary. This feature of what has been called popular religion is tied to its capacity to express and mobilize people's dissent from some features of the larger society, as discussed further in this chapter, and elsewhere in this book. McGuire (2007); Rostas and Droogers (1993). See also Beezley et al. (1994); Benavides (1994; 2001); Nepstad (1996); Parker G. (1991).

35. Turner and Jasper (1994); Ardery (2002).

36. Lara Medina has documented the involvement of the arts community in a similar renaissance of Day of the Dead celebrations in southern California. Her interesting report, however, fails to note the complicating factor of commodification of both the religious and aesthetic elements of these celebrations. Medina (2005); Medina and Cadena (2002).

37. Similarly, Haitian practitioners of vodou who live on an upper floor of a city apartment complex must creatively change a ritual that, in an agrarian context, required pouring a liquid offering into the dirt of the house's floor. Brown (1999).

38. Morgan (1998); see also Miles (1985).

39. Muir (1997: 88–97).

40. Parker G. (1998); Rostas and Droogers (1993). See also Benavides (1994; 2001); Maduro (2004).

41. See Lancaster (1988: 27–54).

42. Dalton (2003); Wolfteich (2005).

43. Particularly helpful are the nuanced and complex depictions of volunteers in Bender (2003). Also relevant are practices described in McGuire and Spickard (2003) and Spickard (2005). Some useful insights on religious social-political activists can be gleaned from several essays in Smith (1996a), as well as Maxwell (2002) and Smith (1996b). Also relevant are beliefs and practices of religious women whose dissent is aimed at their religious organizations' as well as the larger society's sexism; see Neitz (1995a); Winter et al. (1994).

44. I discuss in chapter 8 my current thinking about *bricolage* as a descriptor of contemporary religious practices. On *bricolage*, see Lévi-Strauss (1966: 16–33); as creative popular practices, including resistance, see de Certeau (1984).

45. McGuire (1997).

46. This dialogue is not verbatim but is a fairly accurate depiction of the episode.

CHAPTER 4

1. Sharot (2001: 241). Sharot's analysis focuses mainly on the late-twentieth-century promotion of evangelical religiosity in the United States through the mass media, but I think the tradition is much older, dating back to the Great Awakening of the late seventeenth century and to frontier religious practices and preaching in the eighteenth and nineteenth centuries.

2. Identifying details in this description have been greatly altered to protect the anonymity of this person, but the megachurch itself is easily identifiable and is discussed elsewhere in this chapter. Although I have had more previous personal experience with southern evangelical religious expressions than with any of the groups or religious expressions I have studied in my professional research, I have not conducted research explicitly designed to comprehend the religious lives of persons described here. As a result, I have had to rely on anecdotes from personal acquaintances, rather than "representative" evidence, to give a flavor of how educated, middle-class evangelicals use popular religious elements. Recognizing these limitations, I hope this chapter will inspire a spate of good ethnographic research into the lived religion of evangelicals and other churchgoers.

3. I use quotation marks around the designation "Christian" to indicate that these goods and services are marketed as "Christian" in the generic sense, much like a brand name, as Colleen McDannell notes in her analysis of Christian retailing. The designation has come to imply a conservative, nondenominational version of Christian belief and practice. McDannell (1995: 222–69).

4. Sharot (2001: 234–37).

5. See also Lippy (1994); Williams (1980).

6. Luis Murillo, personal communication.

7. Hunter (1983: 141). According to Hunter (65–69), characteristic practices that support evangelical beliefs and experiences include frequent Bible reading especially, but also demonstration of high levels of commitment (e.g., church attendance, tithing, and witnessing to others about one's faith)—however, these are not definitive. I am also following Hunter's model in examining specifically whites' and Protestant versions of these evangelical traditions, but I do so because I argue that southern white evangelicalism's anti-Catholic and antiblack practices are not definitive but are residual of precisely the kind of influence of evangelical popular religion that this chapter addresses.

8. Bruce (1974: 45).

9. Rosenberg (1989: 29–31).

10. See, especially, Roof's data on "Baby Boomer" evangelicals. Roof (2003: 94–96).

11. Ammerman (1990: 35). Other researchers have corroborated Ammerman's depiction of southern religious homogeneity and distinctiveness, even when transplanted to other regions of the United States. Shibley (1996); Woodberry and Smith (1998).

12. Ahlstrom (1972: 429–54); Bruce (1974); Eslinger (1999); Taves (1999).

13. Taves (1999: 103).

14. Although the camp meeting movement may have started with the Presbyterians, their denomination reined in its preachers as the movement grew, requiring that authorized ministers be literate and educated at church-approved institutions. This measure of control reduced their participation in revival movements, so that Baptists and Methodists became predominant among southern Christians. Bruce (1974: 44–60); see also Eslinger (1999: 218–25).

15. Hatch (1989: 134).

16. Historian Jon Butler considers popular religious expression and the creative spiritual syncretism of important antebellum American religious movements (e.g., Mormonism, African American Christianity, and especially Methodism) significant factors in the development of extensive religious diversity in the United States. Butler (1990: 225–56).

17. Hatch (1989: 130–33).

18. Butler (1990: 236–41).

19. From their earliest years, several of the denominational traditions that meshed with popular evangelicalism saw their members routinely mixing the practice of their evangelical piety with participation in other religious groups. For example, early Methodists in England might, in the same week, attend both Anglican church and chapel Methodist services, while also engaging in what both religious groups decried as "magic and superstition." This eclectic blending has led one historian to conclude that Methodism was not a substitute for folk beliefs and practices but rather a translation of them into a "religious idiom" (John Rule, as cited in Wigger 1998: 111).

20. It would be very difficult, but worthwhile, to investigate the religious beliefs and especially practices of individuals who attend nondenominational churches like Lakewood. My hunch is that the range of diverse practices and beliefs is much greater than at denominational churches, or even at nondenominational churches with narrower moral or theological boundaries. Like the evangelical youth studied by Smith and Denton (2005) and like the "seekers" depicted by Roof (1999), members of Lakewood seem to be unlikely to have had much religious training (in any tradition) or much knowledge about Christian scriptures, although they may be acutely aware of moral strictures of other churches that would make them feel guilty. Another hunch is that attenders are more eclectic (than attenders of denominational churches) in their reasons for coming; they are, I would hypothesize, not committed to an entire package of beliefs and practices or even to the congregation, so they may participate only in the aspects of the church that appeal to them. Thus, it would be extremely difficult to get an adequate "sample" of such diverse attenders; beyond the easy-to-identify regulars who volunteer to help with church-sponsored activities, there are thousands who are only occasional attenders, as well as regulars who come for the lively music and uplifting worship service but nothing more, and others who come for healing or emotional support, while yet more are not frequent attenders but form the television audience and read Osteen's publications, and so on. Hopefully, future researchers will find a way to discover such diverse individuals' *actual* religious practices

and experiences, rather than merely assume that the large congregation is a unitary entity.

21. Romano (2005).

22. I emphasize women because the gendered division of labor, with women choosing religious elements of home decoration, applies to both cultures—southern white and Latina. (For comparison with decorative elements of a "Jewish home," see Ochs [1999]). Furthermore, southern white evangelicals have a long cultural history of men resisting the "civilizing" or "domesticating" influences of both home and church. See Ownby (1990).

23. Ammerman (1987); Griffith (2004).

24. McDannell (1995).

25. McDannell (1995).

26. Schmidt (1997: 72). See also Enzo Pace's (2006) application of the gift-economy of religious expression to critique assumptions of rational choice interpretations of the economic bases of people's religious choices.

27. Griffith (1997b: 182–86).

28. Griffith (1997b: 185).

29. This association is the main reason that evangelicals have been active across the United States, and especially in the South, in trying to have the Harry Potter series banned or strictly controlled in school and public libraries. They have also engaged in public book-burnings of these and other books they consider objectionable. According to the American Library Association, in the period 1990–2001, of all the books that people tried to have censored or banned from libraries nationally, the Harry Potter series was the seventh most frequently challenged; www.ala.org/bbooks/.

30. *San Antonio Express News*, "Some see a more sinister side to Halloween: Churches Take a New View," October 31, 2002, p. 7A.

31. This description is based, not on a formal interview but on his description of the event to me and several others at a neighborhood picnic.

32. McGuire (1983b).

33. Williams (1980: 161).

34. Patterson (2002).

35. A story from my father's boyhood is apt here. In the 1920s, his parents very much believed that the end of the world was imminent (especially because of the horrors of World War I and the economic disasters facing small farmers like themselves), and they told their children to prepare for the rapture, in which true Christians would be taken up and spared the agony of the last days, while the rest would be left behind. While in first grade, my father walked a couple of miles home from school one day seeing no one on the way. He found his house empty and silent, unlike every other day, when he came home to his mother, preschool siblings, and often his father, in the house or farmyard. That day, though, everything looked as though his family had disappeared in the midst of their everyday activities. He felt sure that the rapture had come and that all his family, except him, had been taken up to heaven; he was left behind. When he had children of his own, he vowed not to teach them

religious ideas that raised the kind of fear he felt that lonesome evening in the darkening house before his family returned from an unanticipated errand.

36. Hall (1989).

37. Frykholm (2004: 146–49).

38. This similar notion of divine power as available to ordinary believers in the everyday world may be a significant part of why many Latin American Catholics are attracted to charismatic or evangelical movements (within Catholic or Protestant churches). The difference between the two popular religious patterns is not very great, so "conversion" does not involve as big a change as it might seem McGuire (1994: 198). See also Benavides (1994); Freston (1998). In the last fifteen years, a spate of studies have focused on Latin American immigrants in the United States adopting Pentecostalist practices, but there seems to be no recognition of the existence of similar developments among Italian Americans decades earlier. See Parsons (1965; 1969). My hunch is that the earlier immigrants' attraction was based on a similar sense of *congruity* between the popular religious elements of Italian Catholic practices and U.S. Pentecostalist practices.

39. Another parallel in the popular religiosity of some southern whites and some Mexican Americans is the place of folk saints. In chapter 3, I described two early twentieth-century folk saints who are particularly well known among Mexican Americans. There is considerable similarity between these folk saints and southern white folk saints, especially Elvis Presley—not so much in the lives of these men themselves as in the ways later followers attributed special powers and other saint-like characteristics to them and venerated them and their burial places. For example, there are pilgrimages to Graceland, as well as mementos—such as hand fans (like those provided in the pews of many southern churches that lack air-conditioning)—that are decorated with Elvis's face with a saintly gaze. Devotees ask Elvis to intercede in their own relationship problems and describe him as really understanding their troubles; Davidson et al. (1990); King (1993); Marling (1996); McMorris (2002); Wilson (1995).

40. Much of Catholic popular religiosity also considers it an obligation to tell others about a saint's successful intervention; see Orsi (1996).

41. Griffith (1997a; 1997b).

42. This short book, written by an Atlanta evangelist, sold over four million copies in its first months on the market, achieving first place on best-seller lists in the United States in 2001 (Goodstein 2001). The author cites the New King James Version of the Bible verses of I Chronicles 4:10: "And Jabez called on the God of Israel saying, 'Oh, that You would bless me indeed, and enlarge my territory, that Your hand would be with me, and that You would keep me from evil, that I may not cause pain.' So God granted him what he requested." The Prayer of Jabez, as a recent devotional practice, comes from a long popular Protestant tradition that has encouraged believers to use specific religious practices in order to achieve success— prosperity, health, family well-being, and material comforts. See Elzey (1988); Lippy (1994); Schneider and Dornbusch (1958); and Moore (1994).

43. The preacher's own annual compensation in 2001, from the church and the evangelical television station of which he is CEO and primary owner, was over

$1,250,000 (Nazareno 2003). The disparity between his wealth and the relative lack of prosperity of the working-class members of his congregation suggests that this formula for "praying right" may have the effect, intentional or not, of bilking many members of their money.

44. Forster (1992).

45. Hall (1989). See also Lippy (1994: 23–47).

46. The synopses that follow are from my and my research assistant's summaries of five- to ten-minute testimonies collected during our (New Jersey) study of nonmedical healing practices.

47. McDannell (1995: 67–102).

48. Ammerman (1987: 54) describes a concrete example of this practice.

49. Williams (1980).

50. Ketchell (1999; 2002).

51. Quoted in Ketchell (2002: 168).

52. Ketchell (2002).

53. Spicer (2002). The prayer boxes currently sold by James Avery Craftsman (the local jewelry designer cited in Spicer's article) have further popular religious imagery—angels on several surfaces of the box. Consistent with the uses of popular religious practices (such as the Prayer of Jabez) for material wealth and success, these charms cost $75 (in silver) and $450 (in gold), not including the chain.

54. Ketchell (1999; 2002).

55. McDannell (1995: 272); emphasis added.

56. See, for example, Appleby (2000).

57. Popular religions have been historically been more likely than official religions to promote prejudice and violence toward religious or cultural out-groups. For instance, popular rituals to honor St. Werner, venerated in medieval central Europe, were often the occasions for violence toward a community's Jews. The church refused to recognize the child Werner as a saint and tried to discourage the violence, in part because there was reasonable doubt that Werner had ever existed, much less that he had been ritually killed by Jews, as folklore presented the story (Muir 1997: 98–114; Vauchez 1993). In recent decades, in both Europe and the Americas, popular religious movements and aspiring popular religious leaders—including some non-denominational evangelical spokespersons—have likewise often promoted religious, racial, and ethnic intolerance and outright violence, even while official religious spokespersons of most mainstream religious organizations have disavowed their message (Lippy 1994). For example, many people who attend the Passion Play, a popular attraction for evangelical tourists at Eureka Springs, Arkansas, may be unaware that the person who wrote the Passion Play script and created several of the religious tourist attractions (which he called sacred projects) in the town was Gerald L. K. Smith, a blatantly anti-Semitic and antiblack candidate for the U.S. presidency and a leader of the radical Right in the 1930s and 1940s (Sowers 1991).

58. Anthropologist Victor Turner (1969: 132) coined the term *communitas* to describe this kind of intense egalitarian sense of togetherness that is temporarily produced by certain features of rituals. *Communitas* is temporary, however. For

instance, during a week-long camp meeting, the egalitarian sense of togetherness may have been particularly strong during the evening preaching and exhortation sessions when all were participating in a single emotionally powerful shared event, but less strongly experienced the following morning when campers were in family or other small group settings, and nearly completely dissipated for most participants soon after they returned to their home communities and everyday social relations.

59. The transition in these religious movements away from egalitarianism and patterns of religiosity that offended the sensibilities of elite churches began as the frontier became more settled and stable. The Baptists and Methodists in the South gradually changed, as local church meetings (rather than occasional circuit-riding preachers) became the locus of religious activities, and as church members increasingly identified with social class interests of the middle and upper classes. Bruce (1974: 58–60)

As southern evangelicals became settled in local churches, their norms came to emphasize decorum, respectability, and moral self-control (e.g., no drunkenness or carousing). These norms were, however, held mainly by women in the rural South, while men—even if they were church members—avoided church and other social settings dominated by feminized norms. Well into the twentieth century, male sociability and initiation rituals centered on less respectable and controlled settings, such as hunting (Ownby 1990).

60. Eslinger (1999: 213–41).

61. Butler (1990); Hatch (1989: 154–57); Joyner (1995).

62. Taves (1999: 76–117) and other historians note the likely influence of Native Americans as well. See also Hatch (1989: 155–58); Jones (2004).

63. I develop the theme of religious hybridity further in chapter 8, but it is relevant to note here because of its importance in the origins and development of American evangelicalism, especially in the South.

64. Dvorak (1991). Indeed, much of the effectiveness of black religious leaders in the civil rights movement of the twentieth century was due to the consonance of both their rhetoric and style with the popular religious tradition of their southern evangelical black constituencies. See Franklin (1994); Wilmore (1973: 24–52); Spillers (1971).

65. Mathews (1977: 68–80); see also Bruce (1974: 57–58); Rosenberg (1989).

66. K'Meyer (1997).

67. Bartkowski (2004: 112–42).

68. Forster (1992).

69. See Linenthal (1993).

70. Williams (1980: 158).

71. McDannell (1995: 39).

72. Orsi (2005: 74) refers to this process as the "corporalization of the sacred." He explains: "I mean by this the practice of rendering the invisible visible by constituting it as an experience in a body—in one's own body or in someone else's body—so that the experiencing body itself becomes the bearer of presence for oneself and for others."

73. Flynn (1994); Christian (2004). See Morgan (2005: 5).

74. The account that follows is a paraphrase of the one an acquaintance gave me, outside the interview context. I have disguised the details slightly to respect his wishes for confidentiality.

75. Luhrmann (2005: 148).

76. Quoted in Brasher (1998: 97).

77. Schmidt (2000).

78. For illustration of this thesis, see Gilkes (1996); Preston (1988).

79. Garrett (1987); Petroff (1994); Schmidt (2003); Taves (1999); Orsi (2005).

80. Although most anthropological studies are of these experiences in the rituals and practices of other cultures (such as the Bush people of the Kalahari, the Huichol of northern Mexico, and Vodou among the Haitians), several anthropologists have noted that similar altered states of consciousness occur today among, for example, Pentecostalists, snake-handling Appalachian congregations, Sufi mystics, and Christian contemplatives, as well as Buddhist or Hindu meditators, to name a few. Winkelman (1992; 2000); see also Bourguignon (1973); Goodman (1986; 1990; 1992); and Katz (1982).

81. Despite psychologist William James's classical contribution to the study of mystical experiences, relatively few psychologists have studied religious experiences or religious consciousness. The steady work of psychologist Ralph Hood (1985; 2005) and some of his students is a noteworthy exception. See also James (1903); Proudfoot (1985); Spickard (2004).

82. Yamane (2000).

83. Spickard (2004: 174).

84. Spickard (2005).

85. Examples include Spickard's (1991; 2005) own research on Navajo and Catholic Worker rituals and anthropologist Thomas Csordas's (1994; 2005) studies of Catholic charismatic and Navajo healing. Tanya Luhrmann (1989; 2005), another anthropologist, has done similar studies of contemporary witches' experiences of power of the craft and on religious experiences that psychologists have read as "dissociation" (e.g., hearing the voice of God).

86. Religious experiences have intrinsic social components that make them amenable to various qualitative research methods that sociologists and anthropologists use. Several recent sociological and anthropological researchers are applying such methods to address the experiential component of lived religion. For instance, sociologist Courtney Bender (2007) used insightful heuristic interviewing to learn of the spiritual journey of a woman who had an intense religious experience (combining Christian and diverse other religious elements) during guided visualizations to discover her "Reiki guide." Anthropologist Pamela Klassen (2001) used ethnographic methods to study women's home childbirth experiences; despite a wide range of religious backgrounds, many of these women experienced the birth process as a deep spiritual experience.

87. For example, there is some good interview, observational, and survey evidence to show that there is, among evangelicals, considerable complexity in the

patterns of individuals' belief and practice pertaining to gender equality and male "headship" (their term) of marriages and families. See Bartkowski (2004); Gallagher (2003); Gallagher and Smith (1999); Ingersoll (2003); Smith and Lundquist (2000).

88. Sharot (2001: 258).

89. Sharot (2001: 259–62).

CHAPTER 5

1. Orsi (1997).

2. The "lived" body is our vehicle for perceiving and interpreting, for knowing and interacting with our worlds. According to philosopher Maurice Merleau-Ponty (1962), this "lived" body is the basis of our subjective reality, while simultaneously it is the vehicle for perceiving and engaging others. We experience our bodies in terms of "presence"—an immediately lived sensation—locating ourselves in relation to other perceived objects. This experience of embodied presence is both reflexive (as sensation of oneself) and relational (as presence to others). ("Lived body" is not Merleau-Ponty's term but the closest English phrase to both his meaning and the terms of German phenomenologists, especially Husserl, who were exploring similar issues.)

Against Descartes's separation of matters of the mind from material matters, Merleau-Ponty (1962: 37) argues that perception requires unitary body and mind involvement in even the most basic instances of sensing. He emphasizes that the lived body's capacity for self-movement, as a result of perception, is the basis of human agency. He asserts, "Consciousness is in the first place not a matter of 'I think that' but of 'I can.'"

3. Spickard (1991).

4. Connerton (1989).

5. Bill Moyers's 1993 made-for-television series *Healing and the Mind* illustrated some of the biophysical bases for these ideas of mind-body linkages. In these films, Moyers himself struggles to comprehend and find a language to express the notion of a mind-body unity that a cellular biologist is describing to him. Anthropologists Nancy Scheper-Hughes and Margaret Lock (1987) point out that our Western ways of thinking about mind and body are so dualistic that we resort to awkward hyphenated phrases rather than conceiving of a unity such as a mindful body or embodied mind.

6. Bourdieu (1977: 24).

7. Following early Christian thinkers Origen and Gregory of Nyssa, theologian Sarah Coakley (2002) uses the concept "spiritual senses" in a similar parallel to physical senses.

8. Sudnow (1978).

9. Hervieu-Léger (2000).

10. MacIntyre (1984: 194).

11. Kasulis (1993).

12. Bell (1992).

13. Elias (1978).

14. Muir (1997: 149–59). See also Bynum (1995a; 1995b).

15. See especially Bynum (1984). Also Finke (1993); Petroff (1994).

16. Finke (1993); Morgan (1998; 2005); Muir (1997).

17. Regarding food, eating, and late medieval rituals, see Bynum (1991); Muir (1997).

18. Burke (1978).

19. Hayes (2003); Trexler (1984).

20. Douglas (1982: 65).

21. Sack (2000: 9–59).

22. Orsi (1985).

23. McGuire (1988).

24. See McGuire (2007). Several religious and quasi-religious groups have made food growing an important religious practice. The Findhorn community in Scotland is a good example; U.S. examples include some "back to the land" movements in the twentieth century and some communitarian movements in the eighteenth and nineteenth centuries (Gould 1997).

25. Social theorist George Ritzer (1996), a cofounder of the slow food movement (see www.slowfood.com), has criticized the advertising and fast-food industries for this commodification of time involved in food preparation and eating, the extreme rationalization of food preparation (e.g., standardization of each portion and each ingredient to the point that servings of fries are exactly the same in every restaurant of the chain), and the resulting destruction of cultural diversity, enjoyment of cooking, and pleasures of tasting well-prepared food.

26. McGuire and Spickard (1995) included our reflections on that experience.

27. Brown (1985: 2).

28. In McGuire and Spickard (1995), we link this meditative focus of attention with the quality of experience: how one pays attention determines whether a religious or spiritual experience (e.g. during Communion, meditation, or prayer) is transcendent or mundane.

29. The quotation is not entirely verbatim, but the first sentence is. Note the remarkable resemblance of this person's realization to that of a former nun quoted by Robert Orsi (2005: 108). Orsi writes: "She was not 'saying' this prayer, Margaret explained to me. The prayer was 'echoing in my body.' Her childhood prayer was saying her."

30. Connerton (1989).

31. Dodson and Gilkes (1995).

32. Goldsmith (1989). Similar observations apply to women's food preparation and eating in a white Appalachian Primitive Baptist congregation, according to Patterson (1988).

33. Cadge (2005). Interestingly, Cadge contrasts the Thai women's food-gifting as a central spiritual practice with the highly interiorized spiritual practices pursued by members of another Buddhist center, which promoted an Americanized version of Buddhism. The latter's approach also valorized food preparation, emphasizing doing it with mindfulness and awareness. According to Cadge (109), "the practice for

[a person with this Americanized approach] is in her relationship to the act of cooking the food, while for those offering food to the monks at Wat Phila, the practice is primarily in their relationship to those who are eating it."

34. Heldke (1992); note also the parallels between this concept of bodily knowledge in growing and cooking food and the notion of "somatic modes of attention" that anthropologist Thomas Csordas (1993) suggests as a phenomenological understanding of how healing works.

35. The transformative power of such energy is linked directly with cooking and eating in the magical realism of Laura Esquival's novel *Like Water for Chocolate;* the protagonist's emotional and erotic state while cooking a meal is consumed and subsequently experienced by all who eat the meal. A very different emotional energy is embodied in the congregation's eating in *Babette's Feast* (a film based on a short story by Isak Dinesen). The cook's sacrifice, gratitude, and love transform a meal for the members of a dour, ascetic sect into an experience of honest pleasure, communal affection, hope, and joy.

36. Quoted in Bender (2003: 65).

37. Quoted in Bender (2003: 66).

38. Bender (2003: 66–68).

39. Later referred to as the "canonical hours," these specific times for monastic common prayer represented a major shift from the earlier practices of ascetic Christians (such as hermit monks). St. Benedict expected that the monks who lived according to his Rule gather together for common prayer (for example, all praying a psalm specified for that hour of the day). In later centuries, when these prayer hours were officially codified and prescribed for ordinary clergy and others who lived outside monastic settings, "praying the Hours" became a private, rather than community, devotional practice.

40. Quoted in Wuthnow (2001: 114–15).

41. Quoted in Wuthnow (2001: 110).

42. Quoted in Wuthnow (2001: 118–19).

43. Quoted in Back (1981: 41–42).

44. This observation was made by Becky Kane (a gardener who has gifted my family with the fruits of her labor), personal communication.

45. Food prepared by the monks is not ipso facto better (although it is almost certainly better nutritionally) because it is not standardized, as is all that is, in Ritzer's (1996) term, "McDonaldized"—prepared by externally specified, highly rationalized task requirements, so that each component and each step is precisely the same for each item produced. Rather, the monks' loaves today might taste better than yesterday's batch, because today the baker was more mindfully aware of the texture of the dough than he was yesterday, or because today, the assistant who built the fire in the oven paid better attention (literally and spiritually) as he made the coals ready, and so on.

46. Stowe (2004: 64–77).

47. Lane (2001: 168).

48. Quoted in Andrews and Andrews (1966: xiii).

49. Quoted in van Waes (1994); emphasis added.

50. Schutz (1964).

51. Schutz and Luckmann (1989: 109).

52. Merleau-Ponty (1962).

53. Recent efforts to interpret religious experience include those by sociologists, including Courtney Bender (2007), Mary Jo Neitz, and James Spickard (Neitz and Spickard 1990; Spickard 1991; 1992; 2004; 2005), as well as anthropologists, including Thomas Csordas (1994) and Tanya Luhrmann (2005), and historians, including Robert Orsi (2005), Leigh Eric Schmidt (2003), and Ann Taves (1999; 2003).

54. Mauss (1973); see also Crossley (1995; 1997) and Lyon (1997) for more recent applications of Mauss's concept of "techniques of the body."

55. Neitz and Spickard (1990); see Spickard (1991; 2005) on how ritual structures the "co-experiencing" of time and place.

56. Spickard (1991).

57. See McGuire (1982).

58. My description here is based on my own participant-observation of Sacred Harp singing, which I first encountered in the 1990s in Texas. A more recent dissertation (Clawson 2005) is a more thorough study of the tradition and its practice. Months after I finished this chapter, I participated in an octet of professional colleagues (mostly sociologists and anthropologists) singing a Sacred Harp hymn to illustrate key points of R. Stephen Warner's Presidential Address to the 2007 meeting of the Society for the Scientific Study of Religion. Interestingly, most of this religiously diverse group of singers (including four who had been President of the SSSR) experienced a sense of temporary community in the preparation and performance of this music, thus further exemplifying some points of Warner's moving speech.

59. Patterson (1995). See also Sutton (1988).

60. Quoted in Patterson (1995: 53); emphasis added.

61. Gray and Thumma (1997).

62. See McGuire (2007). On dance as embodied practice, see Ness (2004). On dance and other embodied practices in religious experience, see Dox (2005), Taves (1999), Sanders (1996), and Stowe (2004).

63. Wuthnow (2001).

64. Adapted, slightly, from Kertzer (1988: 15).

65. I must acknowledge here that even this careful choice of words has evaluative connotations, because my own religious perspective identifies "the light" with all the attributes of that which is held sacred—truth, goodness, peace, understanding, harmony, and so on.

66. Kertzer (1988); Muir (1997).

67. Foucault (1977).

68. For a more balanced sociological understanding of the entire range of people's personal and group religious or spiritual practices, we need to consider this darker side of some people's religiosity or spirituality. I heartily agree with Robert Orsi's (2005: 177–204) critique of scholars' wishes to distinguish "good" religion from

"bad" religion (or "true" Christianity and "true" Islam from "false" Christianity and "false" Islam).

Religion and religions are inherently ambivalent—or even multivalent. (For good contemporary examples of the ambivalence of religions see Appleby [2000].) And, as many of the instances described in this book show, individuals often engage, sometimes simultaneously, both in practices that advance the constructive features of religion and in practices that promote the destructive aspects. Orsi (2005: 191–92) argues: "It is the challenge of the discipline of religious studies not to stop at the border of human practices done in the name of the gods that we scholars find disturbing, dangerous, or even morally repugnant, but rather to enter into the otherness of religious practices in search of an understanding of their human ground." If people's religion-as-lived includes such practices, we need to understand them, along with the kinder and more constructive religious and spiritual practices we personally find less objectionable.

It is difficult, however, for ethnographers to stay sufficiently neutral and unbiased when trying to understand religiosity or spirituality that revolts or horrifies them. In order to do good ethnographic research, we need to engage our respondents as equals, with respect and understanding, even though we realize that we can never fully share their worlds or lives. (On equality as a methodological ideal, see Spickard [2002].) Nevertheless, it is extremely difficult, if not impossible, to achieve that ideal, because our ethnographic methodology necessarily involves our own subjective (and bodily) involvement.

CHAPTER 6

1. Gordon (1988); McGuire (2002); Turner (1996).

2. McGuire (1988); see also Cant and Sharma (2000), Goldstein (2000), and Eisenberg (1998).

3. All but one of these vignettes describe actual interviewees, with important details altered to protect their anonymity. Because our research on alternative healing systems focused on upper-middle-class communities, I relied on the research of others, particularly anthropologist Vivian Garrison, who was doing parallel research at the time in the working-class and urban poor communities of the same counties of New Jersey. The vignette of Dolores thus is based mainly on Garrison (1977), Harwood (1977), Schensul and Schensul (1982), and Singer and Garcia (1989).

4. As quoted in McGuire (1988: 163).

5. As quoted in McGuire (1988: 63).

6. In many ethnic communities, the tradition of fictive kinship (e.g. the *comadre* or godmother) serves as a valued resource for social and material support; indeed, such neighbors as *comadres* often form important lay referral networks in Puerto Rican communities. See Harwood (1977), Schensul and Schensul (1982), and Garrison (1977).

7. On *curanderismo* in predominantly Mexican American communities, see Espín (1996), León (2002), and Portilla (2002).

8. In principle, men could be healers and *espiritistos*, too, but this vignette represents the common pattern of women recommending women healers and advisers to other women (who may be seeking help on behalf of men and children for whom they care), as part of a community referral network. Note that through community referral networks, people in multiethnic communities, like Los Angeles or Newark, often eclectically use healing approaches of various ethnic groups other than their own, especially if there is some congruence among the approaches. A study by Polk et al. (2005) suggests that a Mexican American in California might go to a *botánica* to obtain herbs for healing and to buy a *vela* (candle) for her home altar; then, while buying a *vela* for devotional prayers through Santo Niño de Atocha (i.e., Holy Child, a popular Mexican manifestation of Christ, considered capable of miraculous healing), might also choose a *vela* for the Seven African Powers (i.e., Afro-Caribbean spirits) because the prayer on it sounds like it might be effective, too. Because of shifts in the immigrant population of the area, many of the *botánicas* in the areas of New Jersey Garrison studied now resemble those in California (described by Polk) in their appeal to a pan-Latino audience.

9. This vignette describes a woman I interviewed (with identifying details altered to protect anonymity), but the details of the Jewish healing movement's contributions to her story are based on more recent research by Susan Sered (2005). Sered documents how women's spirituality groups, organized as celebrations of Rosh Hodesh (New Moon), have creatively blended elements of Jewish thought and biblical narrative with rituals and imagery from other feminist spirituality movements and holistic healing practices, creating an effective communal tie and set of practices that feel comfortably Jewish. It is probable that the woman who told us her experiences with Jewish healing had encountered this movement in its earlier, formative years, because she described her women's group's attention to healing as an unintended development, in response to the fact that so many members had developed serious diseases or were having to cope with the illness or dying of a loved one. She viewed the woman rabbi who introduced healing services in her former synagogue as something of an exception, due to her feminist and experimental approaches to healing, even compared to other rabbis who had more recently begun to promote healing ministries in their synagogues.

10. Elsewhere (McGuire 2007), I have analyzed dancing as an embodied practice, comparable to those I have described in chapter 5.

11. McGuire (1988: 179–80).

12. Quoted from transcript of interview, September 12, 1983.

13. Such social sources of suffering are not peculiar to women. Gender-based suffering occurs for lesbians and gays and for some men as well. Other suffering from structural violence occurs among oppressed minorities, immigrants, and the poor. For example, three of our interviewees had experienced the double difficulty of being blacks in nearly totally white professions and of being professional women in a community where most black men expected their "girlfriends" and wives to be subordinate to them.

14. Barnes and Sered (2005: 19). Sered's (1994: 93) earlier crosscultural research on "women's religions" (i.e., in cultures where women controlled and held important

ritual roles in gendered religious expressions) led her to generalize that "the most conspicuous similarities among women's religions emerge in the realm of suffering and healing." On empathy and the role of healers, see also Hedges and Beckford (2000).

15. McGuire (1982; 1988).

16. See especially the research reported in Barnes and Sered (2005).

17. See Bastien (1987), Csordas (2002), and Katz (1982).

18. Sobo (1994).

19. Scheper-Hughes and Lock (1986; 1987).

20. Spickard (1991).

21. Mellor and Shilling (1997); Turner (1997; 1991). See also Crawford (1984); Lupton (1995).

22. Crawford (1984: 78). See also Litva and Eyles (1994).

23. Griffith (2004: ch. 5 and epilogue).

24. Featherstone (1991).

25. Freund, McGuire, and Podhurst (2003).

26. Portions of this section were previously published in McGuire (1992).

27. Historian Natalie Zemon Davis (1974: 312) reminds us that no tidy borderline exists between religion and magic, particularly in the way ordinary people have practiced them. To understand people's religious life (historically or today), we need to comprehend both elements as part of their religion-as-practiced. Davis proposes that "We [as scholars who aim to comprehend religion as including magic] consider how all of these [beliefs and practices] may provide groups and individuals some sense of the ordering of their world, some explanation for baffling events or injustice, and some notion of who and where they are. We ask what feelings, moods and motives they encourage or try to repress. We look to see what means are offered to move people through the stages of their lives, to prepare for their future, and to cope with suffering or catastrophe. And further, we try to establish the ways in which religious life gives support to the social order . . . and in which it can also criticize, challenge or overturn that order."

28. Mellor and Shilling (1997: chap. 4). This process of "disenchantment" made possible the development of modern medicine and the specialized knowledge of its practitioners in Western societies. When the body had been linked with the realm of the sacred (e.g., through symbolic connection with Christ's Incarnation or through assumptions about the critical role of the bodies of the faithful in the resurrection of the dead), it could not be studied objectively or dissected for the sake of medical science. Freund et al. (2003: 219).

29. Cited in Szasz (1970: 88).

30. See Ehrenreich and English (1973).

31. Colleen McDannell (1995) illustrates this with her analysis of use of Lourdes water and replica Lourdes shrines in America in the nineteenth and twentieth centuries.

32. Forster (1992). For examples of colonial American magical practices, see Hall (1989; 1995).

33. Albanese (2000a), Fuller (2001), Griffith (2004), Heelas (1996).

34. Freidson (1970).
35. Larson (1979: 609).
36. Starr (1982: 88–112).
37. Freidson (1970); Starr (1982).
38. Starr (1982: 112–27).
39. Freidson (1970); Starr (1982).
40. Mellor and Shilling (1997). See especially chap. 2, "Re-formed Bodies," which compares medieval, Protestant modern, and baroque (Catholic) modern bodies, and chap. 4, on how Protestantism "re-formed" bodies as profane. The authors' connection of this process with subsequent Protestant beliefs and practices regarding the body is parallel to Muir's (1997) discussion of the Long Reformation's shift in religious ritual—privileging belief over practice as properly religious.
41. Conrad and Schneider (1980).
42. Kleinman (1988); Gordon (1988).
43. Gordon (1988). See also Kirmayer (1988); Leder (1984).
44. Foucault (1995); Turner (1996).
45. Zola (1983: 261). See also Conrad and Schneider (1980).
46. Crawford (1984); Lupton (1995).
47. Lupton (1995); Featherstone (1991).
48. McGuire (1993); Beckford (1985).
49. Weber (1946: 280).
50. On holistic world images, see also Beckford (1985; 1984) and Hedges and Beckford (2000).
51. Quoted in McGuire (1988: 49).
52. For more detailed description of some Jewish healing groups in the United States, see Sered (2005).
53. Personal correspondence, March 5, 2005.
54. Quoted from transcript of Interview, March 9, 1982.
55. Kleinman (1988).
56. I find myself agreeing with Deirdre's intuitive criterion for evaluating healing approaches. At a professional conference, not long after *Ritual Healing* was published, I was asked whether I personally thought any of the alternative healing approaches I had studied were actually harmful or dangerous to the people who sought help. In responding, I realized that the two "healing" practices that stood out in my memory as probably very harmful were both done in the context of recognizable religious groups (one Catholic charismatic, the other evangelical Protestant) and by recognizably religious leaders, both lay and clerical; neither episode was part of "unofficial" or "alternative" religion. The common feature that, in my opinion, made these "healing" practices so harmful was the leaders' assumption that their divine source of authority (i.e., knowledge of "God's will" for the suffering person) allowed them to force a person to submit to an extremely invasive action (psychologically, physically, and spiritually). Although I personally may find such authoritarian violence reprehensible, I would still recognize these practices as just as "religious" as the religious practices of the healers I admired.

57. Personal communication, November 18, 2002.

58. That confirmation was based not on studying a text in the Bible but something more along the lines of either rereading a passage of scripture (recalled as relevant) to see if it confirmed their sense of what to do or (more often) opening the Bible to a seemingly random (but "God-given") page and searching it for words, as signs of God's will. They believed God would lead them to the "right" word or phrase to help choose their course of action.

59. Erzen (2005).

60. Harris (2005); Foltz (2000); Jacobs (1989; 1990).

61. Ellie Hedges (Hedges and Beckford 2000) observed comparable experiential confirmation of healing power among a group of British nurses who were taking a similar course on "holistic massage" as part of their professional studies.

62. Note that women engaged in the home-birthing movement have a very similar understanding of the significance of their experience, even though they come from very different religious backgrounds (including some very conservative Christian and Jewish groups). Anthropologist Pamela Klassen (2005: 81) observes: "These women's choice of spirituality is a rejection of the authorizing processes that have deemed religion as the realm in which one truly meets God but have abandoned childbirth to superstition or, more recently, medicine."

63. Hammond (1992); Roof and McKinney (1987).

64. Interestingly, it was on the issue of personal responsibility for putative choices made in the past that Marge disagreed strongly with some of the long-term members of her psychic healing group. She objected to their belief that people bring illness, accidents, and other misfortune on themselves by unconsciously choosing those paths. She explained that it was only a theory, completely nontestable, and anyway unnecessary for doing good healing; indeed, in her opinion, it impeded good healing, because others' belief in it reduced their ability to empathize with the person's suffering.

65. This connection between creativity and eclecticism is corroborated in the many stories of women's "ritualizing" described in Northrup (1997).

66. Because women's spirituality groups often accomplish these transformations and combinations without leaving the larger institutional religious organization (as Hannah's experience illustrates), their dissent may be somewhat invisible. One study of this phenomenon calls it "defecting in place" (Winter et al. 1994).

67. Davie (1995: 82–83).

68. Courtney Bender, in her study of volunteers at God's Love We Deliver, examined the complex language of such conversations in more detail. Specifically, she found considerable evidence that the assumed dichotomy between the sacred/religion and the profane/everyday was a simplistic misrepresentation of social reality. Bender (2003: 141) states: "Everyday life is neither a habitual sphere lacking in meaning and thought into which meaning descends nor a sphere that is always given to transformation, value, and symbolic weight.... Daily life's potential for both compels us to reconsider its varied spaces, and it charges us to look carefully once more at these practices as they continue to structure action in our multiple worlds."

69. For a discussion of the contemporary social forms of religion and religions, see Beyer (2003b).

70. Bellah et al. (1985).

71. Bellah et al. (1985: 220–21).

72. To their credit, Bellah and his colleagues acknowledged that there was enormous diversity, from individual to individual, in the actual religions of people in a modern society, and they made an effort to talk with real people about their beliefs and values. Their efforts stand in marked contrast to the work of Rodney Stark (and others), who, at about the same time, was using large-scale survey data to substantiate sweeping generalizations about "religion" (so narrowly defined that individual-level diversity was not only invisible but irrelevant). Stark and Bainbridge (1985; 1987).

73. Bellah et al. (1985: 221).

74. Several critics have appropriately decried the interview methodology used by Bellah and his collaborators (Richard Madsen, William Sullivan, Ann Swidler, and Steven Tipton). The researchers described their methodology as an "active" and "Socratic" interview, designed to press their interviewees to articulate the moral reasoning underlying their personal choices about, for instance, their work and families (Bellah et al. 1985: 304). Critic Jeffrey Stout (1988: 35, 194–96) points out that the Socratic method is a poor (even misleading) tool for learning about people's moral reasoning, because it involves relentlessly pushing respondents to clarify why they assert each reason given until they become confused or try to reframe their personal reasons into terms that fit the philosophical style of the Socratic argument. Used in a research interview, this method becomes a form of intellectual bullying, according to Barnett Pearce (1994: 317), who analyzed these interviews as examples of failed or distorted intercultural communication. For example, in his analysis of the transcript of the interview of the respondent Brian Palmer, Stout notes that Palmer gave a fully satisfactory moral statement but the interviewer did not accept it as an answer, because she (Swidler) was looking only for abstract universal principles as grounds for moral reasoning. See Stout (1988: 195–96). Pearce (1994: 319) concludes that "Swidler bullied Palmer by means of linguistic tyranny. She demanded that he describe his morality in her terms, and then she judged his performance according to her standards."

75. Albanese (2000b: 19).

76. Bellah et al. (1985: 235).

77. Bellah et al. (1985: 242).

78. See especially Hall (1989).

79. Winship (2000).

80. Winship (2000).

81. Linda Woodhead (forthcoming) makes a similar point in her critique of sociologists who dismiss as fuzzy and narcissistic many women's focus on "spirituality" (in contrast with what these sociologists consider "real" religion).

82. This description refers to the vernacular use of the term "narcissism." "Narcissism" is also a psychological pathology label for a serious personality disorder (with several diagnostic criteria that distinguish it from other disorders), but

presumably narcissism in any degree would promote the kind of negative individualism that Bellah (et al.) decries.

83. For this reason, I do not find it helpful to focus, as Clark Roof has, on changes in the "religious-symbolic marketplace." Many of the features Roof (1999: 69–70, 96–109, 305–6) describes as characteristic of the "spiritual marketplace" today have existed all along but were perhaps invisible as religion after the Long Reformation because of definitional blinders. Those features include instrumental uses of religious practices and objects, commodification of religious goods and services, blurred sacred-secular boundaries, blending of symbols and practices, and direct accessibility to the individual. On the past and present commodification, economic exchange, and consumption of religious-symbolic goods and services, see Bowman (1999), Campo (1998), Fairchilds (1997), Heelas (1994), McDannell (1995), Miller (2003), Moore (1994), and Schmidt (1997).

CHAPTER 7

1. Orsi (1996).
2. Jacobs (1991).
3. Research on new religious movements (NRMs) documents this development of new religious practices addressing bodily concerns. See, for example, Barker (1993), Palmer (1994), and Puttick (1997).
4. Sered (2005); see also Csordas (2005); Harris (2005); Klassen (2005); Mitchem (2005).
5. This description portrays a woman I met outside of the context of my research on healing. I have disguised many details to protect her anonymity, but it depicts the key issues of identity construction—gender, race, family, sexuality, education level, and high-status occupation—of the real "Bernie."
6. Personal communication, February 2001.
7. Personal communication, February 2001.
8. Giddens (1991).
9. Hervieu-Léger (1990).
10. Nagel (2003).
11. See McGuire (1988).
12. As quoted in McGuire (1988: 149).
13. See McDannell (1986); Taves (1986). We must remember, however, that the development of this domestic piety was a significant historical change from earlier patterns of gender and religious expectations; such "traditional" norms are not static, in reality, but are social constructions that change, regularly and sometimes extensively, over time.
14. McDannell (1995); Morgan (1998).
15. The interesting exception, in the late medieval and early modern periods, was that upper-class persons in much of Europe considered Jewish and "Moorish" physicians superior to Christian physicians, not because of their religion or ethnicity

per se but because Christian physicians' training was restricted to a stagnant form of Greek medicine that was notoriously ineffective and invasive. Schatzmiller (1995).

16. McGuire (2003). See also, Ehrenreich and English (1973) and Davis-Floyd and Davis (1997).

17. Elias (1978; 1982).

18. Classen (1993). See also Bourdieu (1984).

19. Elias (1982).

20. Elias's notion of self-constraint in the civilizing process is obviously related to Foucault's interpretation of disciplined bodies and the genealogy of prisons and related modes of surveillance and control (Foucault 1995). See also Freund (1982). For a synthesis of how these ideas about social control of the body apply to religious constraints, see Mellor and Shilling (1994) and Turner (1991). On the connection between norms about civilized bodies and the treatment of, as well as resistance by, indigenous peoples of colonized lands, see Comaroff (1985), particularly chapter 7.

21. See Muir (1997).

22. Medieval European ideas about male and female bodies already dichotomized gender roles. For example, they treated the senses as gendered, as well as embodying contrasting cultural values. Men were associated with the visual quality of light (presumably, therefore, rationality) while women were linked with darkness and irrationality. Unlike men, who were associated with heat and action, women were linked with coldness, moistness, and inactivity; this cold moistness was believed to make women prone to putridity and foul odors (Classen 1998: 64–71). Social changes resulting from the Long Reformation served mainly to codify those ideas in prescribed practices for proper male and female behavior and religiosity, thus exaggerating the sense of opposition between male and female gender norms. These changes were accomplished through a set of sometimes extremely violent rituals (e.g., the Inquisition and witch hunts). Muir (1997).

23. Crawford (1993: 73–115).

24. See Fornaro (1985); Sanday (1981).

25. See McGuire (1990).

26. Griffin (1990).

27. Drinka (1984).

28. Bednarowski (1983); Braude (1985).

29. McDannell (1986); Ryan (1983); Sizer (1979); Taves (1986); Welter (1976).

30. Carnes (1989).

31. Carnes (1989: 69–90).

32. Hackett (1991a; 1991b; 1995).

33. Carnes (1989). By locating the central cultural change in the structure of the family, most of these interpretations explicitly or implicitly borrow from psychoanalytic theories, such as Chodorow's, of parent-child relations in socialization. David Hackett (1991b) gives a succinct overview of psychoanalytic interpretations of both Victorian women's and men's gender-role constructions.

34. Indeed, in the growth years of fraternal orders, the creation and enactment of initiation ceremonies into ever-increasing levels of membership was the foremost activity of most lodges (Carnes 1989: 27–30). Several contemporary men's movements use American culture's lack of ritual initiation into "manhood" as a legitimation for their activities; they assume that men psychologically require initiation into their male identities. This idea is precisely parallel to fraternal orders' beliefs about their rituals—many of which were patterned after "primitive" male initiations; they explained ritual initiation into manhood as fulfilling "a 'universal' need among men" (Carnes 1989: 104).

35. Simmel (1906).

36. Interestingly, the parallel fraternal movements among minority males (initially Irish Americans and African Americans) appear to have been initially segregated from the white fraternal movements, less by race than by social class distinctions. For example, particularly in the latter part of the nineteenth century after the end of slavery, white Freemasons developed an ideology that construed race and gender (but not class) as essential qualities of a person, legitimating their discrimination of themselves from those whom they considered innately inferior. By contrast, African American Freemasons (who belonged to separate Prince Hall Masonic lodges—named for the freeman who was first initiated, during colonial times) used their lodges as a mutual help network, but were more inclusive (for example, allowing women to become involved through auxiliaries to the men's lodges earlier and more widely than white Masons did). Also, unlike the white Freemasons, African American males did not choose to be, as the white males generally were, "in the lodges" instead of "in the churches," as was the pattern among white Freemasons. Rather, a substantial proportion of Prince Hall Masons were church leaders and clergy, involved in churches along with their wives. See Hackett (2000).

37. Clawson (1989).

38. Bell (1992; 1997).

39. Scheper-Hughes and Lock (1987). I have applied these authors' concept to describe the mind-body interconnectedness involved in religious experience. McGuire (1996).

40. Confirming evidence of this embodied practice as transformative is in Slavin's (2003) analysis of the pilgrimage to Santiago de Compostela, in Spain.

41. Goffman (1961). Goffman was, of course, borrowing the term "mortification" from the terminology of Catholic asceticism.

42. Kanter (1972).

43. See Andrews (1953).

44. In such limited space, I cannot discuss critiques of these studies in any depth but appreciate especially Thomas Csordas's careful and critical building on Bourdieu's theories. Csordas (1994) accepts Bourdieu's ideas about how a shared habitus enables members' ritual practices (especially such practices as healing) to accomplish—not merely metaphorically—the "sense" of community and the transformation of their selves. He is (correctly, I believe) critical of Bourdieu's (1977; 1990) assumption of homogenized habitus among members of a society or class. This as-

sumption is particularly problematic for understanding groups that address gender and sexuality as contested issues, rather than as given and dichotomous (masculine versus feminine, male versus female) categories of thought and practice.

45. Bourdieu (1990: 71–72) suggests that positions in social space (e.g., hierarchical positions) are linked, through the individual's relationship to his or her own body, "to shape the dispositions constituting social identity (ways of walking, speaking, etc.) and probably also the sexual dispositions themselves." He explains further that "elementary acts of bodily gymnastics . . . most importantly, the specifically sexual, and therefore biologically preconstructed, aspect of this gymnastics (penetrating or being penetrated, being on top or below, etc.) are highly charged with social meanings and values." Thus, the socially informed body experiences—as very real— the political significance of body metaphors for domination and submission, such as "standing up to someone," "looking down on someone," "prostrating at the feet of someone," "getting the upper hand," and "the will to be on top." See also Bourdieu (1977).

46. Simmel (1906). Note, too, that many popular religious rituals (especially those that involve males in fictive brotherhood), in medieval times and more recently, have served to mark similar status boundaries. See Muir (1997: 27–29) on medieval rituals of status passage, such as initiations in youth abbeys and in vassalage.

47. French (1994).

48. See Turner and Turner (1978).

49. Quoted in French (1994: 106).

50. French (1994).

51. Carnes (1989: 69–90).

52. The fraternal lodges' initiations deliberately evoked what I would consider "religious" or "spiritual" experiences (e.g., ritual death and judgment) for male socialization. However, worthwhile comparisons could also be drawn with other contexts for learning embodied practices for "masculinity": the Boy Scouts, the military, college fraternities, sports gyms, hunting trips, and high school football. See Foley (1990); Hantover (1978); Messner (1990); Ownby (1990: 27–32); Sanday (1990).

53. The mythopoetic-inspired men's movement did not spawn as much serious scholarly study as did the Promise Keepers movement, so my discussion of it is based on journalistic reports, personal narratives of informants, and the statements of various movement spokespersons. Apparently balanced descriptions are provided by Adler et al. (1991), Gabriel (1990), and Gelman (1990).

54. See Bartkowski (1999).

55. Donovan (1998).

56. Bartkowski (2004; 2005); Donovan (1998).

57. Donovan (1998: 837–38).

58. Bartkowski (2004; 2005).

59. For good examples from medieval and early modern Europe and the Americas, see Muir (1997: 30–31); Trexler (2002: 430–46).

60. Neitz (1995b).

61. Bynum (1987).

62. Foltz (2000).

63. McGuire (2002: 188–90); Griffith (1997a). See also Brasher (1998: 130–34); Gallagher (2003); McGuire (1982: 194–99); Neitz (1987: 137–45).

64. See Brasher (1998); Griffith (1997b); Ingersoll (2002; 2003).

65. Hadewicj, unlike both male and most female mystics of her time, described an image of both herself and her divine beloved as mutually agentive and mutally receptive. Hood and Hall (1980) suggest that people's sense of their own agency in a relationship, together with their imagery of the divine beloved, makes a significant difference in Western mysticism, because of the obvious parallels with erotic love and the receptivity of a person to being united with another. Their empirical research found that females described both erotic and mystical experiences in terms of re-ceptivity, while males used terms of agency to describe erotic experiences, but not mystical experiences—perhaps because of the difficulty for males of experiencing mystical union with a God imaged as masculine. Jacobs (1992) suggests that female socialization to value connection and attachment over autonomy and separateness may enable women to have mystical experiences as a positive way of expressing "relationality" with divine as well as human others.

66. Petroff (1994: 61).

67. Finke (1993).

68. For critiques of genitalized models of sexuality, see Giddens (1992); Marcuse (1955); Williams (2001).

69. Bynum (1986; 1989; 1991).

70. Bynum (1989: 175–76).

71. The writings of late medieval mystics describe a gendered spirituality in which the mystical experience of divine power is profoundly shaped by human sex-uality, in the broadest sense of the word (Rubin 1991). Some sought spiritual expe-riences (e.g., mystical identification with Mary nursing the infant Jesus) relating to the Christ-child's embodiment (Rublack 1996).

72. Bynum (1989: 187). Bynum argues that the church authorities tolerated and even valued the imagery of embodied spirituality in mystics' visions, because such imagery provided "evidence" against the Cathars' dualistic separation of body and spirit. The Cathars, a popular heretical movement of the period, also represented dissent against the dominant stratification system legitimated by the church. The Cathars preached a radical dualism that identified the physical world as a product of diabolic evil. They believed that sexual difference was instituted by the devil but that both sexes could become "perfects," preach, and administer the sacrament (Lans-ing (1998: 106–25).

73. Laqueur (1990: 4–5).

74. For an analysis of this and other examples of Puritan images of converts' bodies as "feminized," see Dillon (2001).

75. Neitz (2000).

76. In her analysis of gender roles and dominance, Neitz (1994) also distin-guished between the two main witchcraft traditions practiced in the United States. Dianic (named for Diana, the Roman goddess of the hunt) Wiccan practices and

group structures are based on feminist images of women's power and emphasis on the goddess, in contrast to male deities); however, Gardnerian witchcraft (named for Gerald Gardner, who initiated a revival of "the craft" in the middle decades of the twentieth century and organized initiation rituals that he claimed were revivals of early pagan practices). All-female Wiccan groups have developed ritual forms and structural features that encourage empowerment of all initiates and egalitarian relationships within loosely structured groups. By contrast, the Gardnerian groups (characteristically heterosexual and hierarchical, with different levels of initiation) celebrate their secrecy and exclusive access to hidden powers—much like the secret societies described by Simmel (1906).

77. McGuire (1993).

78. Klassen (2001; 2005).

CHAPTER 8

1. Orsi (2003: 173).

2. The diversity formally had to be within a strictly limited set of options, because in those years, the trustees of the college forbade the hiring of non-Christians, Catholics, and probably many unapproved kinds of Protestants (like those they would have labeled "holy rollers") for tenure-track teaching positions.

3. In this attitude, he preceded the baby boomers in finding denominational boundaries to be irrelevant, as reported in Hoge et al. (1994).

4. Quoted in McGuire and Spickard (2003: 143); James V. Spickard conducted and recorded these interviews.

5. Albanese (2000b) suggests that the word "syncretism" is meant to be pejorative, to disavow beliefs and practices so labeled "as corrupt, contaminated, and inferior to high theological traditions."

6. Tweed (1996: 28).

7. Quoted in Tweed (1996: 29).

8. Tweed (1996).

9. Tweed (1996; 1997).

10. See Trexler (2002: 335–73).

11. Stewart (2004: 274); Shaw and Stewart (1994: 26). See also Stewart and Shaw (1994). Some anthropologists question even the analytic concept of "culture," suggesting that it leads to mistaken notions of "cultural difference," ethnicity, and group identity. See Gupta and Ferguson (1992).

12. Shaw and Stewart (1994: 1).

13. Beyer (2005).

14. Maduro (2004). See also Benavides (1995), Maduro (1995; 2002), and Shaw and Stewart (1994).

15. Boyarin and Burrus (2005).

16. Brown (1981).

17. "Celtic Religion" (1996: 154–56). Interestingly, long after Reformation movements' efforts to end or diminish the importance of such sacred sites and

syncretic rituals attached to them, many Protestants, as well as Catholics, continued to venerate them as powerful. For example, well into the nineteenth century, Protestants sought the waters of the holy wells of St. Olav in the western Norway.

18. Muir (1997: 60–72). See also Burke (1978: 180–81) and Wilson (2000).

19. Wilson (2000: 48).

20. Scribner (1984a; 1984b).

21. Albanese (1997) and Lippy (1994: 1–47) give similar examples of cultural borrowing and blending in the history of U.S. religions.

22. James Spickard, personal communication, June 1996. His essays on the implications of this shift in perspectives for ethnographies of religion are trenchant. See Spickard (2002; 2003; 2005; 2007; 2008).

23. Gustavo Benavides (2004: 206) notes that the simile between European Christianity and a language (and, by extension, creole religious practices as like creole variations on dialects) is apt only when we think of a language as "a dialect with an army." See also Benavides (1995; 2001); Hannerz (1987).

24. Likewise, under conditions of violence and force, sacred music is a product of cultural blending. David Stowe (2004: 9) reminds us: "Music has created bridges, to be sure, but bridges often erected in the face of dispersion and death. Sacred music is the scar tissue, fascinating and eerily beautiful, that forms over deep trauma cauterized by spirit and hope." Thus, creolized religious musical expressions (such as the spirituals sung by enslaved Africans in the antebellum American South or the *matachines* dance performed on a community's patron saint's day by Pueblo people in what is now the American Southwest) were very much the byproducts of ruthless subjugation of people. At the same time, such expressions were (and still are) responses to power—sometimes as forms of dissent and often as expressions of community solidarity and hope. See also Gandert (2000); Lamadrid and Gandert (2003).

25. Droogers (1995: 49).

26. Benavides (1994).

27. See Ritzer (2004).

28. For example, a recent music festival in a Gaelic-speaking area on the Isle of Skye (part of the remote Hebrides of Scotland) drew as much as two-thirds of its audience from the islanders rather than visitors like me. One band (cleverly named MacUmba), the star of one evening's show, held the entire packed community hall rapt with its bagpipe-and-drum renditions of Scottish traditional tunes played to a wild Afro-Brazilian beat and accompanied by an overhead computer-orchestrated video of Afro-Brazilian drummers marching in a Brazilian city's Carnival parade. Near me, three generations of a local family were swaying and clapping to the beat. It was the grandmother and her granddaughter who danced and waved their arms most ecstatically, in bodily comportment that was clearly not the norm in their island culture.

29. Gifford (2004).

30. Levitt (1998; 2001). Levitt (2007: 167–68) notes the necessity of broadening our conception of religious life beyond the limitations of the official (Protestant) model. Most of the immigrants she interviewed had religious lives that could not be

adequately understood if church participation in the received tradition were the only aspect one considered. She writes: "They also enact their religious lives in their living rooms and on street corners. The boundary between the secular and the sacred is blurred. Migrants do not always agree on one official canon. Male leaders do not always stand up in front of the sanctuary and tell them what to do. They mix and match elements from different faiths rather than observe strict boundaries between traditions. As a result, migrants are miles ahead of most of us . . . [because they] recognize . . . that *mestizaje* is in the cards that the future holds for all of us." (*Mestizaje* refers to the condition resulting from either miscegenation (interbreeding) or cultural intermixing—or both.)

31. Fortuny Loret de Mola (2002; 1995).

32. Lévi-Strauss (1966: 16–33).

33. This phrase is, in fact, the title of Parker's 1993 book, later published in English translation (Parker G. 1996).

34. Parker G. (1998: 206).

35. Taylor (1996: 49–50), emphasis added. See also Carrasco (1995) for parallel examples of cultural congruence and blending.

36. In addition, it is useful to appreciate this "other logic" in the seemingly inconsistent recent synthesis of elements of Catholic popular religiosity and Protestant Pentecostal popular religiosity, especially in rural indigenous Mexican communities. Leatham (1996).

37. Taylor (1996: 73).

38. Maduro (1995).

39. Droogers (1995: 54).

40. Droogers (1995).

41. Hornborg (2005). Another instance of indigenous community revitalization, healing, and identity-building is the story of how persons of Californio/Chumash (mixed since the time of early Spanish colonies) heritage, together with others from their racially and culturally mixed communities in coastal California, constructed what they considered to be a traditional marine canoe and celebrated its maiden voyage to Santa Cruz island with a traditional feast. They consciously made adaptations to those traditional elements of the seaworthy canoe and feast, inspired by their affinity with other Canoe Nations (such as the Nisqually of Washington State), yet recognizing that the actual traditional ways of doing things in the past were utterly irretrievable. What really mattered was not whether they used recreated traditional tools or modern power tools or whether they celebrated in the (nearly lost) Chumash language or in the English or Spanish of the colonizers. What really mattered was the experience of themselves as a people with some identity as a seafaring First Nation. Cordero reminds us that such cultural hybridity is not only effective but appropriate, as an expression of the local mixed-heritage indigenous community whose options to retain their original traditions had been taken from them in the violence of colonization. It would take a more serious ethnography to discern the long-term impacts of this effort, but Cordero's descriptive story clearly depicts healing, in the sense that I use the term in this book (Cordero 2005).

42. Weber (1978: 26). For a critique of Weber's cultural biases in his theories of traditional action, see Spickard (1998).

43. Cristián Parker (2002) suggests that new syncretisms emerging in modern societies may be like the earlier colonial syncretisms, in that they are based on the already-existing consonance of two or more ways of thinking about or using of religious practices. What is new is the blending of religious-magical elements of ritual practices with images borrowed from technological-scientific practices, such as the use of rays of energy for transmitting healing or for perceiving realities not seen by the naked eye.

44. James Spickard, personal communication. The Taize community, begun more than sixty-five years ago in eastern France, is a lay monastic community that includes Catholic, Protestant, and Orthodox Christians. Its pattern for worship has spread widely, including throughout the U.S. and many parts of Europe. The Taize service for worship typically includes several simple chants, silent prayer, scripture reading, but no sermon or preaching and no priest leading the worship. Founded in Spain more than 55 years ago to train lay pilgrimage leaders, Cursillo (literally, a "little course") was developed as a model for church renewal—initially Catholic, but later it has been promoted within several Protestant denominations (e.g., Episcopalian, Presbyterian, Methodist)—through lay groups reinforcing their members' practice of prayer, study and action in their everyday lives.

45. Miller (2003: 177).

46. Many late medieval popular rituals openly imitated and sometimes mocked church rituals. For instance, one festival event elected a boy "bishop" or "abbot of the fools" to make merry over hierarchical pomp and pronouncements. The rowdy charivari was a mock wedding, and rites initiating young journeymen into crafts guilds imitated church rituals of initiation. Likewise, the entire celebration of Carnival was an "enactment of the 'world turned upside down' "—a period of rituals of reversal: subversion, disorder, and misrule. Burke (1978); Muir (1997: 85–104).

47. Trexler (1984: 259).

48. See Tweed (1996).

49. Martin (1993: 167).

50. Martin (1993).

51. Hobsbawm and Ranger (1983).

52. Trevor-Roper (1983).

53. Morgan (1983).

54. Morris (1989: 304). For a fascinating account of the attempts of twelfth-century theologians to legitimate certain prescribed prayer postures, specifically those that were postures of submission and penitence, see Trexler (2002: 335–73).

55. Bullough (1982); Elliott (1993).

56. Brundage (1982).

57. Anderson (1991).

58. Anderson (1991); Abley (2003: 128–55).

59. Luria (1989); see also Muir (1997: 185–223).

60. Luria (1991: 98).

61. Brigid (or Bride, Bridget), an early Celtic Christian saint (sixth century), was something of a Celtic Minerva (patron of arts, poetry, learning, fine metalwork, and healing). She was identified with the pre-Christian Celtic guardian of the sacred perpetual fire, and her feast day was celebrated on February 1, which coincided with Imbolg, the pagan festival for the beginning of spring. "Celtic Religion" (1996); see also Connolly (1982).

A relevant interaction occurred not long after I read "Celtic Religion" (1996). While hiking in a Texas park, I had a long and enjoyable conversation with two Irish-born nuns who belong to a religious community named for Saint Brigid. I asked them whether they had considered renaming the community, in light of Roman church authorities' concerns that Brigid was not a properly canonized Catholic saint but a mere folk saint. They were, of course, fully aware of the controversy. And they re-plied that her deviant status in the eyes of Rome (i.e., the hierarchy's negative opinion), as well as her pagan "connections," made Brigid all the more endearing to them.

62. Also called the "Toronto Blessing" by many American neo-Pentecostal or charismatic Christians. It is a powerful, immediate experience of blessing by the Holy Spirit, manifested by "gifts of the Spirit," such as hysterical laughter, shaking, speaking in tongues, dancing, being "slain in the Spirit," and often accompanied by a profound sense of inner healing or transformation. For a sociological commentary on this phenomenon, see Poloma (2003).

63. Bowman (2000).

64. Anderson (1991: 6).

65. Anderson (1991: 12–19).

66. Delanty (1995: 31).

67. Anderson (1991: 19).

68. Anderson (1991). This development is also linked with some of the apparent religiousness of nationalism. See Riis (1998).

69. Ray (2003).

70. Anderson (1991: 1–46); see also Hanf (1994). Most sociologists have been surprisingly uncritical of the idea that the boundaries constructed between religions are somehow given or natural properties of those religions and their traditions. Peter Beyer (1998; 2003a) points out that scholars of religion need to rethink their a-historical assumptions how the so-called world religions (as well as denominations and other diverse socially differentiated religions) came to mutually distinguish themselves as religions. Beyer (2006).

71. See Nagel (2003).

72. Stewart (1994: 142).

73. Stewart (1995); see also Delanty (1995: 111–13), and Sikkink and Regnerus (1996).

74. Shaw and Stewart (1994).

75. Durkheim (1965: bk. 3, chap. 4).

76. Carroll (2002: 211–23).

77. Said (1978).

78. We cannot assume that marginalized groups have a unified claim on their own group identities and traditions. Even marginalized groups have internally contested meanings and memories. Consider, for example, the hotly contested traditions surrounding Hopi prophecies (Geertz 1994; 2004). Another set of contested meanings surrounds the syncretic blending of Christian and African elements in slave religion in antebellum America (Joyner (1995) Similarly, Latina feminists may disagree profoundly with other Latinos, especially those who use the ethnic tradition to glorify patriarchal gender and family relations, and with other feminists, especially those Anglo feminists who are blind to the classist and racist assumptions that have historically shaped their women's movement agendas. See Medina (1998: 200; 2005: 207). On the impossibility of ascertaining authority to judge authenticity of elements of Native American spiritualities, see Jenkins (2004).

79. On the nature of religious identities, see Ammerman (2003).

80. Modern Westerners are particularly likely to emphasize their sense of individual agency, considering themselves free to select religious elements for their own faith and practice. And many feel equally free to reject elements of their tradition's teachings (or certain interpretations of that tradition) yet consider themselves to be true to the cornerstone of their tradition. So it is no surprise to find, in modern Western societies, that many persons are engaging in conscious construction of their individual bricolage of religious practices and beliefs. Similar bricolage has been reported in Europe and the United States. See Albanese (1997; 2000b); Dobbelaere et al. (2002); Hervieu-Léger (1998); Pace (1989); Roof (1999); Voyé (2001).

81. Hondagneu-Sotelo et al. (2004).

References

Abley, Mark. 2003. *Spoken Here: Travels among Threatened Languages.*
New York: Houghton Mifflin.

Adler, Jerry, Karen Springen, Daniel Glick, and Jeanne Gordon. 1991.
"Drums, Sweat and Tears." *Newsweek*, June 24, 46–51.

Ahlstrom, Sydney E. 1972. *A Religious History of the American People.* New
Haven, Conn.: Yale University Press.

Albanese, Catherine L. 1997. "Exchanging Selves, Exchanging Souls:
Contact, Combination and American Religious History." In *Retelling
U.S. Religious History*, edited by T. A. Tweed. Berkeley: University of
California Press, 200–206.

———. 2000a. "The Aura of Wellness: Subtle-Energy Healing and New
Age Religion." *Religion and American Culture* 10 (winter): 29–55.

———. 2000b. "The Culture of Religious Combining: Reflections
for the New American Millennium." *Cross Currents* 50 (1–2):
16–22.

Ammerman, Nancy T. 1987. *Bible Believers: Fundamentalists in the Modern
World.* New Brunswick, N.J.: Rutgers University Press.

———. 1990. *Baptist Battles: Social Change and Religious Conflict in the
Southern Baptist Convention.* New Brunswick, N.J.: Rutgers University
Press.

———. 1996. "Organized Religion in a Voluntaristic Society." *Sociology of
Religion* 58 (3): 203–15.

———. 2003. "Religious Identities and Religious Institutions." In Dillon,
Handbook of the Sociology of Religion, 207–24.

———, ed. 2007. *Everyday Religion: Observing Modern Religious Lives.* New
York: Oxford University Press.

Anderson, Benedict. 1991. *Imagined Communities: Reflections on the Origin and Spread of Nationalism*. Rev. and extended ed. London: Verso.

Andrews, Edward Deming. 1953. *The People Called Shakers: A Search for the Perfect Society*. Oxford: Oxford University Press.

————, and Faith Andrews. 1966. *Religion in Wood: A Book of Shaker Furniture*. Bloomington, Ind.: Indiana University Press.

Appleby, R. Scott. 2000. *The Ambivalence of the Sacred: Religion, Violence, and Reconciliation*. Savage, Md.: Rowman and Littlefield.

Ardery, Julie. 2002. "Day of the Dead." *Texas Co-op Power* (newsletter) (November): 1–7. http://texas-ec.org.

Arnold, Pierre. 1985. "Pèlerinages et Processions comme Formes des Pouvoir Symbolique des Classes Subalternes: Deux Cas Péruviens." *Social Compass* 32 (1): 45–56.

Asad, Talal. 1988. "Towards a Genealogy of the Concept of Ritual." In *Vernacular Christianity*, edited by W. James and D. H. Johnson. New York: Lilian Barber Press, 73–87.

————. 1993. *Genealogies of Religion: Discipline and Reasons of Power in Christianity and Islam*. Baltimore: Johns Hopkins University Press.

Ashley, Kathleen, and Pamela Sheingorn. 1992. "An Unsentimental View of Ritual in the Middle Ages or, Sainte Foy Was No Snow White." *Journal of Ritual Studies* 6 (1): 63–85.

Back, Aaron. 1981. *Occupational Stress: The Inside Story*. Oakland, Calif.: Institute for Labor and Mental Health.

Badone, Ellen. 1990. Introduction to Badone, *Religious Orthodoxy and Popular Faith in European Society*, 3–23.

————, ed. 1990. *Religious Orthodoxy and Popular Faith in European Society*. Princeton, N.J.: Princeton University Press.

Barker, Eileen. 1993. "The Paul Hanly Furfey Address—1992: Behold the New Jerusalems! Catch 22s in the Kingdom-Building Endeavors of New Religious Movements." *Sociology of Religion* 54 (4): 337–52.

Barnes, Linda L., and Susan S. Sered, eds. 2005. *Religion and Healing in America*. New York: Oxford University Press.

Bartkowski, John P. 1999. "Godly Masculinities Require Gender and Power." In *Standing on the Promises: The Promise Keepers and the Revival of Manhood*, edited by D. S. Claussen. Cleveland: Pilgrim Press, 121–30.

————. 2004. *The Promise Keepers: Servant, Soldiers, and Godly Men*. New Brunswick, N.J.: Rutgers University Press.

————. 2005. "Faithfully Embodied: Religious Identity and the Body." *DisClosure* 14: 8–37.

Bastien, Joseph. 1987. "Qollahuaya-Andean Body Concepts: A Topographical-Hydrological Model of Physiology." *American Anthropologist* 87: 595–611.

Bauman, Zygmunt. 1992. "Soil, Blood and Identity." *Sociological Review* 40: 675–701.

Beckford, James A. 1984. "Holistic Imagery and Ethics in New Religious and Healing Movements." *Social Compass* 17: 259–72.

———. 1985. "The World Images of New Religious and Healing Movements." In *Sickness and Sectarianism*, edited by R. K. Jones. London: Gower, 72–93.

———. 2003. *Social Theory and Religion.* Cambridge: Cambridge University Press.

Bednarowski, Mary Farrell. 1983. "Women in Occult America." In *The Occult in America: New Historical Perspectives*, edited by H. Kerr and C. L. Crow. Urbana: University of Illinois Press, 177–95.

Beezley, William H., Cheryl English Martin, and William E. French. 1994. "Introduction: Constructing Consent, Inciting Conflict." In *Rituals of Rule, Rituals of Resistance: Public Celebrations and Popular Culture in Mexico*, edited by W. H. Beezley, C. E. Martin, and W. E. French. Wilmington, Del.: Scholarly Resources, xiii–xxxii.

Bell, Catherine. 1992. *Ritual Theory, Ritual Practice.* New York: Oxford University Press.

———. 1997. *Ritual: Perspectives and Dimensions.* New York: Oxford University Press.

Bellah, Robert N., Richard Madsen, William M. Sullivan, Ann Swidler, and Steven M. Tipton. 1985. *Habits of the Heart: Individualism and Commitment in American Life.* Berkeley: University of California Press.

Benavides, Gustavo. 1994. "Resistance and Accommodation in Latin American Popular Religion." In Stevens-Arroyo and Díaz-Stevens, *An Enduring Flame*, 37–67.

———. 1995. "Syncretism and Legitimacy in Latin American Religion." In Stevens-Arroyo and A. I. Pérez y Mena, *Enigmatic Powers*, 19–46.

———. 1996. "Redefining Syncretism." Unpublished paper presented to the conference of the Program for the Analysis of Religion among Latinos, Chicago, 5–7 April.

———. 2001. "Power, Intelligibility and the Boundaries of Religions." *Historical Reflexions: Réflexions Historiques* 27 (3): 481–98.

———. 2004. "Syncretism and Legitimacy in Latin American Religion." In *Syncretism in Religion: A Reader*, edited by A. M. Leopold and J. S. Jensen. New York: Routledge, 194–216.

Bender, Courtney. 2003. *Heaven's Kitchen: Living Religion at God's Love We Deliver.* Chicago: University of Chicago Press.

———. 2007. "Touching the Transcendent: Rethinking Religious Experience in the Sociological Study of Religion." In Ammerman (2007), 201–18.

Berger, Peter L. 1967. *The Sacred Canopy: Elements of a Sociological Theory of Religion.* Garden City, N.Y.: Doubleday.

Beyer, Peter F. 1998. "The Modern Emergence of Religions and a Global System for Religion." *International Sociology* 13 (2): 151–72.

———. 2003a. "Defining Religion in Cross-national Perspective: Identity and Difference in Official Conceptions." In Greil and Bromley, *Defining Religion*, 163–88.

———. 2003b. "Social Forms of Religion and Religions in Contemporary Global Society." In Dillon, *Handbook of the Sociology of Religion*, 45–60.

———. 2005. "Au Croisement de l'Identité et de la Différence: Les Syncrétismes Culturo-Religieux dans le Contexte de la Mondialisation." *Social Compass* 52 (4): 417–29.

————. 2006. *Religion in a Global Society*. London: Routledge.

Bourdieu, Pierre. 1977. *Outline of a Theory of Practice*. London: Cambridge University Press.

————. 1984. *Distinction: A Social Critique of the Judgement of Taste*. Cambridge, Mass.: Harvard University Press.

————. 1990. *The Logic of Practice*. Translated by R. Nice. Stanford, Calif.: Stanford University Press.

Bourguignon, Erika. 1973. *Religion, Altered States of Consciousness, and Social Change*. Columbus: Ohio State University Press.

Bowman, Marion. 1999. "Healing in the Spiritual Marketplace: Consumers, Courses and Credentialism." *Social Compass: International Review of Sociology of Religion* 46 (2): 181–89.

————. 2000. "More of the Same? Christianity, Vernacular Religion and Alternative Spirituality in Glastonbury." In Sutcliffe and Bowman, *Beyond New Age*, 83–104.

Boyarin, Daniel, and Virginia Burrus. 2005. "Hybridity as the Subversion of Orthodoxy? Jews and Christians in Late Antiquity." *Social Compass* 52 (4): 431–41.

Brasher, Brenda. 1998. *Godly Women: Fundamentalism and Female Power*. New Brunswick, N.J.: Rutgers University Press.

Braude, Ann D. 1985. "Spirits Defend the Rights of Women: Spiritualism and Changing Sex Roles in Nineteenth-Century America." In *Women, Religion and Social Change*, edited by Y. Y. Haddad and E. B. Findly. Albany: State University of New York Press, 419–31.

Brown, Edward Espe. 1985. *The Tassajara Recipe Book: Favorites of the Guest Season*. Boston: Shambala.

Brown, Karen McCarthy. 1999. "Staying Grounded in a High-Rise Building: Ecological Dissonance and Ritual Accommodation in Haitian Vodou." In *Gods of the City: Religion and the American Urban Landscape*, edited by R. A. Orsi. Bloomington: Indiana University Press, 79–102.

Brown, Peter. 1981. *The Cult of the Saints: Its Rise and Function in Latin Christianity*. Chicago: University of Chicago Press.

Bruce, Dickson D., Jr. 1974. *And They All Sang Hallelujah: Plain-Folk Camp-Meeting Religion, 1800–1845*. Knoxville: University of Tennessee Press.

Brundage, James A. 1982. "Concubinage and Marriage in Medieval Canon Law." In Bullough and Brundage (1982), 118–28.

Bullough, Vern L. 1982. "Introduction: The Christian Inheritance." In Bullough and Brundage (1982), 1–12.

Bullough, V., and J. Brundage, eds. 1982. *Sexual Practices and the Medieval Church*. Buffalo, N.Y.: Prometheus.

Burke, Peter. 1978. *Popular Culture in Early Modern Europe*. London: Temple Smith.

Butler, Jon. 1990. *Awash in a Sea of Faith: Christianizing the American People*. Cambridge, Mass.: Harvard University Press.

————. 1991. "Historiographical Heresy: Catholicism as a Model for American Religious History." In *Belief in History: Innovative Approaches to European and*

American History, edited by T. Kselman. Notre Dame, Ind.: University of Notre Dame Press, 286–309.

Bynum, Caroline Walker. 1984. "Women Mystics and Eucharistic Devotion in the Thirteenth Century." *Women's Studies* 11: 179–214.

———. 1986. " '...And Woman His Humanity': Female Imagery in the Religious Writing of the Later Middle Ages." In *Gender and Religion: On the Complexity of Symbols*, edited by C. W. Bynum, S. Harrell, and P. Richman. Boston: Beacon Press, 257–88.

———. 1987. *Holy Feast and Holy Fast: The Religious Significance of Food to Medieval Women*. Berkeley: University of California Press.

———. 1989. "The Female Body and Religious Practice in the Later Middle Ages." In *Fragments for a History of the Human Body*, vol. 1, edited by M. Feher. New York: Unzone, 161–219.

———. 1991. *Fragmentation and Redemption: Essays on Gender and the Human Body in Medieval Religion*. New York: Zone Books.

———. 1995a. *The Resurrection of the Body in Western Christianity: 200–1336*. New York: Columbia University Press.

———. 1995b. "Why All the Fuss about the Body? A Medievalist's Perspective." *Critical Inquiry* 22 (autumn): 1–33.

Cadge, Wendy. 2005. *Heartwood: The First Generation of Theravada Buddhism in America*. Chicago: University of Chicago Press.

Campo, Juan Eduardo. 1998. "American Pilgrimage Landscapes." *Annals of the American Academy of Political and Social Science* 558 (July): 40–56.

Cant, Sarah L., and Ursula Sharma. 2000. "Alternative Health Practices and Systems." In *Handbook of Social Studies in Health and Medicine*, edited by G. L. Albrecht, R. Fitzpatrick, and S. C. Scrimshaw. London: Sage, 426–37.

Carnes, Mark C. 1989. *Secret Ritual and Manhood in Victorian America*. New Haven, Conn.: Yale University Press.

Carrasco, David. 1995. "Jaguar Christians in the Contact Zone." In Stevens-Arroyo and Pérez y Mena, *Enigmatic Powers*, 69–79.

Carroll, Michael P. 1992. *Madonnas That Maim: Popular Catholicism in Italy since the Fifteenth Century*. Baltimore: Johns Hopkins University Press.

———. 1995. "Rethinking Popular Catholicism in Pre-famine Ireland." *Journal for the Scientific Study of Religion* 34 (3): 354–65.

———. 1996. "Stark Realities and Androcentric/Eurocentric Bias in the Sociology of Religion." *Sociology of Religion* 57 (3): 225–40.

———. 2002. *The Penitente Brotherhood: Patriarchy and Hispano-Catholicism in New Mexico*. Baltimore: Johns Hopkins University Press.

"Celtic Religion." 1996. In *Encyclopedia of Religion on CD ROM*. New York: Macmilllan Library Reference, 154–56.

Christian, William A., Jr. 1981. *Local Religion in Sixteenth-Century Spain*. Princeton, N.J.: Princeton University Press.

———. 1982. "Provoked Religious Weeping in Early Modern Spain." In *Religious Organization and Religious Experience,* edited by J. Davis. London: Academic Press, 97–114.

———. 2004. "Provoked Religious Weeping in Early Modern Spain." In *Religion and Emotion: Approaches and Interpretation,* edited by J. Corrigan. Oxford: Oxford University Press, 33–50.

Classen, Constance. 1993. *Worlds of Sense: Exploring the Senses in History and across Cultures.* London: Routledge.

———. 1998. *The Color of Angels: Cosmology, Gender and the Aesthetic Imagination.* London: Routledge.

Clawson, Laura R. 2005. "I Belong to This Band, Hallelujah: Faith, Community, and Tradition among Sacred Harp Singers." Ph. D. diss., Princeton University.

Clawson, Mary Ann. 1989. *Constructing Brotherhood: Class, Gender, and Fraternalism.* Princeton, N.J.: Princeton University Press.

Coakley, Sarah. 2002. *Powers and Submissions: Spirituality, Philosophy and Gender.* Oxford: Blackwell.

Comaroff, Jean. 1985. *Body of Power, Spirit of Resistance: The Culture and History of a South African People.* Chicago: University of Chicago Press.

Connerton, Paul. 1989. *How Societies Remember.* Cambridge: Cambridge University Press.

Connolly, Sean J. 1982. *Priests and People in Pre-famine Ireland, 1780–1845.* Dublin: Gill and Macmillan.

Conrad, Peter, and Joseph W. Schneider. 1980. *Deviance and Medicalization: From Badness to Sickness.* St. Louis, Mo.: Mosby.

Cordero, Julianne. 2005. "The Gathering of Traditions: The Reciprocal Alliance of History, Ecology, Health, and Community among the Contemporary Chumash." In Barnes and Sered (2005), 139–57.

Crain, Mary M. 1997. "The Remaking of an Andalusian Pilgrimage Tradition: Debates Regarding Visual (Re)presentation and the Meanings of 'Locality' in a Global Era." In *Culture, Power, Place: Explorations in Critical Anthropology,* edited by A. Gupta and J. Ferguson. Durham, N.C.: Duke University Press, 291–311.

Crawford, Patricia. 1993. *Women and Religion in England, 1500–1720.* London: Routledge.

Crawford, Robert. 1984. "A Cultural Account of Health." In *Issues in the Political Economy of Health Care,* edited by J. McKinlay. New York: Tavistock, 60–103.

Crossley, Nick. 1995. "Body Techniques, Agency and Intercorporeality: On Goffman's Relations in Public." *Sociology* 29 (1): 133–49.

———. 1997. "Corporeality and Communicative Action: Embodying the Renewal of Critical Theory." *Body and Society* 3 (1): 17–46.

Csordas, Thomas J. 1993. "Somatic Modes of Attention." *Cultural Anthropology* 8: 135–56.

———. 1994. *The Sacred Self: A Cultural Phenomenology of Charismatic Healing.* Berkeley: University of California Press.

———. 2002. *Body/Meaning/Healing.* New York: Palgrave Macmillan.

———. 2005. "Gender and Healing in Navajo Society." In Barnes and Sered (2005), 291–304.

Dalton, Frederick John. 2003. *The Moral Vision of César Chávez*. Maryknoll, N.Y.: Orbis Books.

Davalos, Karen Mary. 2002. "'The Real Way of Praying': The Via Crucis, Mexicano Sacred Space, and the Architecture of Domination." In Matovina and Riebe-Estrella, *Horizons of the Sacred*, 41–68.

Davidson, J. W., Alfred Hecht, and Herbert A. Whitney. 1990. "The Pilgrimage to Graceland." In *Pilgrimage in the United States*, edited by G. Rinschede and S. M. Bhardwaj. Berlin: Dietrich Reimer Verlag, 229–52.

Davie, Jodie Shapiro. 1995. *Women in the Presence: Constructing Community and Seeking Spirituality in Mainline Protestantism*. Philadelphia: University of Pennsylvania Press.

Davis, Natalie Zemon. 1974. "Some Tasks and Themes in the Study of Popular Religion." In *The Pursuit of Holiness in Late Medieval and Renaissance Religion*, edited by C. Trinkaus and H. A. Oberman. Leiden: Brill, 307–36.

Davis-Floyd, Robbie, and Elizabeth Davis. 1997. "Intuition as Authoritative Knowledge in Midwifery and Homebirth." In Davis-Floyd and Arvidson, *Intuition: The Inside Story*. London: Routledge, 145–176.

de Certeau, Michel. 1984. *The Practice of Everyday Life*. Vol. 1. Berkeley: University of California Press.

Delanty, Gerard. 1995. *Inventing Europe: Idea, Identity, Reality*. New York: St. Martin's Press.

Díaz-Stevens, Ana María. 1994. "Analyzing Popular Religiosity for Socio-Religious Meaning." In Stevens-Arroyo and Díaz-Stevens, *An Enduring Flame*, 17–36.

Díaz-Stevens, Ana María, and Anthony M. Stevens-Arroyo. 1998. *Recognizing the Latino Resurgence in U.S. Religion: The Emmaus Paradigm*. Boulder, Colo.: Westview Press.

Dillon, Elizabeth Maddock. 2001. "Nursing Fathers and Brides of Christ: The Feminized Body of the Puritan Convert." In *A Centre of Wonders: The Body in Early America*, edited by J. Lindman and M. L. Tarter. Ithaca, N.Y.: Cornell University Press, 128–43.

Dillon, Michele, ed. 2003. *Handbook of the Sociology of Religion*. Cambridge: Cambridge University Press.

Dobbelaere, Karel, Luigi Tomasi, and Liliane Voyé. 2002. "Religious Syncretism." *Research in the Social Scientific Study of Religion* 13, n.s.: 221–43.

Dodson, Jualynne E., and Cheryl Townsend Gilkes. 1995. "'There's Nothing Like Church Food': Food and the U.S. Afro-Christian Tradition: Re-membering Community and Feeding the Embodied S/spirit(s)." *Journal of the American Academy of Religion* 63 (3): 519–38.

Donovan, Brian. 1998. "Political Consequences of Private Authority: Promise Keepers and the Transformation of Hegemonic Masculinity." *Theory and Society* 27: 817–43.

Douglas, Mary. 1966. *Purity and Danger: An Analysis of Concepts of Pollution and Taboo*. New York: Praeger.

————. 1982. *Natural Symbols*. 3rd ed. New York: Pantheon Books.

Dox, Donnalee. 2005. "Spirit from the Body: 'Belly Dance' as a Spiritual Practice." In *Belly Dance: Orientalism, Transnationalism, and Harem Fantasy*, edited by A. Shay and B. Sellers-Young. Costa Mesa, Calif.: Mazda Press, 304–41.

Drinka, George Frederick. 1984. *The Birth of Neurosis: Myth, Malady and the Victorians*. New York: Simon and Schuster.

Droogers, André. 1995. "Syncretism, Power, Play." In *Syncretism and the Commerce of Symbols*, edited by G. Aijmer. Göteborg, Sweden:/Göteborg University, 38–59.

Dubisch, Jill. 1990. "Pilgrimage and Popular Religion at a Greek Holy Shrine." In Badone, *Religious Orthodoxy and Popular Faith in European Society*, 113–39.

Duffy, Eamon. 1992. *The Stripping of the Altars: Traditional Religion in England, c.1400–c.1580*. New Haven, Conn.: Yale University Press.

Durkheim, Émile. [1915] 1965. *The Elementary Forms of the Religious Life*. Translated by J. W. Swain. New York: Free Press.

Dvorak, Katharine L. 1991. *An African-American Exodus: The Segregation of the Southern Churches*. Brooklyn: Carlson.

Ehrenreich, Barbara, and Deirdre English. 1973. *Witches, Midwives, and Nurses: A History of Women Healers*. New York: Feminist Press.

Eisenberg, David M., R. B. Davis, S. L. Ettner, S. Apel, S. Wilkey, and M. Van Rompay. 1998. "Trends in Alternative Medicine Use in the United States, 1990–1997: Results of a Follow-up National Survey." *Journal of the American Medical Association* 280 (18): 1569–75.

Elias, Norbert. 1978. *The Civilizing Process*, vol. 1: *The History of Manners*. Translated by E. Jephcott., New York: Pantheon Books.

————. 1982. *Power and Civility*. Translated by E. Jephcott. *The Civilizing Process*, vol. 2. New York: Pantheon Books.

Elliott, Dyan. 1993. *Spiritual Marriage: Sexual Abstinence in Medieval Wedlock*. Princeton, N.J.: Princeton University Press.

Elzey, Wayne. 1988. "Popular Culture." In *The Encyclopedia of American Religious Experience*, vol. 3, edited by C. H. Lippy and P. W. Williams. New York: Scribner's, 1727–41.

Erzen, Tanya. 2005. "Sexual Healing: Self-Help and Therapeutic Christianity in the Ex-gay Movement." In Barnes and Sered, 265–80.

Eslinger, Ellen. 1999. *Citizens of Zion: The Social Origins of Camp Meeting Revivalism*. Knoxville: University of Tennessee Press.

Espín, Olivia M. 1996. *Latina Healers: Lives of Power and Tradition*. Encino, Calif.: Floricanto Press.

Fairchilds, Cissie. 1997. "Marketing the Counter-Reformation: Religious Objects and Consumerism in Early Modern France." In *Visions and Revisions of Eighteenth-Century France*, edited by C. Adams, J. R. Censer, and L. J. Graham. University Park: Pennsylvania State University Press, 31–52.

Featherstone, Mike. 1991. "Consumer Culture, Postmodernism, and Global Disorder." In *Religion and Global Order*, edited by R. Robertson and W. R. Garrett. New York: Paragon House, 133–59.

Finke, Laurie A. 1993. "Mystical Bodies and the Dialogics of Vision." In *Maps of Flesh and Light: The Religious Experiences of Medieval Women Mystics*, edited by U. Wiethaus. Syracuse, N.Y.: Syracuse University Press, 28–44.

Flores, Richard R. 1994. "Para el Niño Dios: Sociability and Commemorative Sentiment in Popular Religious Practice." In Stevens-Arroyo and Díaz-Stevens, *An Enduring Flame*, 171–90.

———. 1995. *Los Pastores: History and Performance in the Mexican Shepherd's Play of South Texas*. Washington, D.C.: Smithsonian Institution Press.

———. 2008. "Los Pastores and the Gendered Politics of Location." In *Mexican American Religions: Spirituality, Activism and Culture*, edited by G. Espinosa and M. T. Garcia. Durham: Duke University Press, 206–220.

Flynn, Maureen. 1994. "The Spectacle of Suffering in Spanish Streets." In *City and Spectacle in Medieval Europe*, edited by B. Hanawalt and K. Reyerson. Minneapolis: University of Minnesota Press, 153–68.

———. 1996. "The Spiritual Uses of Pain in Spanish Mysticism." *Journal of the American Academy of Religion* 64 (2): 257–78.

Foley, Douglas E. 1990. *Learning Capitalist Culture: Deep in the Heart of Tejas*. Philadelphia: University of Pennsylvania Press.

Foltz, Tanice G. 2000. "Thriving, Not Simply Surviving: Goddess Spirituality and Women's Recovery from Alcoholism." In *Daughters of the Goddess: Studies of Healing, Identity, and Empowerment*, edited by W. Griffin. Walnut Creek, Calif.: AltaMira Press, 119–35.

Fornaro, Robert J. 1985. "Supernatural Power, Sexuality and the Paradigm of 'Women's Space' in Religion and Culture." *Sex Roles* 12 (3/4): 295–302.

Forster, Mark R. 1992. *The Counter-Reformation in the Villages: Religion and Reform in the Bishopric of Speyer, 1560–1720*. Ithaca, N.Y.: Cornell University Press.

Fortuny Loret de Mola, Patricia. 1995. "Origins, Development and Perspectives of La Luz del Mundo Church." *Religon* 25: 147–62.

———. 2002. "The Santa Cena of the Luz del Mundo Church: A Case Study of Contemporary Transnationalism." In *Religion Across Borders: Transnational Immigrant Networks*, edited by H. R. Ebaugh and J. S. Chafetz. Walnut Creek, Calif.: AltaMira Press, 15–50.

Foucault, Michel. [1977] 1980. "Truth and Power." In *Power/Knowledge: Selected Interviews and Other Writings*, edited by C. Gordon. New York: Pantheon Books, 109–33.

———. [1975] 1995. *Discipline and Punish: The Birth of the Prison*. Translated by A. Sheridan. New York: Vintage Books.

Franklin, Robert Michael. 1994. "The Safest Place on Earth: The Culture of Black Congregations." In *American Congregations*, vol. 2, edited by J. Wind and J. Lewis. Chicago: University of Chicago Press, 257–84.

Freidson, Eliot. 1970. *The Profession of Medicine*. New York: Dodd, Mead.

French, Dorothea R. 1994. "Ritual, Gender and Power Strategies: Male Pilgrimage to St. Patrick's Purgatory." *Religion* 24: 103–15.

Freston, Paul. 1998. "Pentecostalism in Latin America: Characteristics and Controversies." *Social Compass* 45 (3): 335–58.

Freund, Peter. 1982. *The Civilized Body: Social Domination, Control and Health.* Philadelphia: Temple University Press.

Freund, Peter, Meredith B. McGuire, and Linda Podhurst. 2003. *Health, Illness, and the Social Body: A Critical Sociology.* Upper Saddle River, N.J.: Prentice-Hall.

Frykholm, Amy Johnson. 2004. *Rapture Culture: Left Behind in Evangelical America.* New York: Oxford University Press.

Fuller, Robert C. 2001. *Spiritual, but Not Religious: Understanding Unchurched America.* New York: Oxford University Press.

Gabriel, Trip. 1990. "Call of the Wildmen." *New York Times Magazine,* October 14, 36–39, 47.

Gallagher, Sally K. 2003. *Evangelical Identity and Gendered Family Life.* New Brunswick, N.J.: Rutgers University Press.

Gallagher, Sally K., and Christian Smith. 1999. "Symbolic Traditionalism and Pragmatic Egalitarianism: Contemporary Evangelicals, Families, and Gender." *Gender and Society* 13 (2): 211–33.

Gandert, Miguel, Ramón Gutierrez, Enrique Lamadrid, Lucy R. Lippard, Chris Wilson, and Helen R. Lucero. 2000. *Nuevo México Profundo: Rituals of an Indo-Hispano Homeland.* Albuquerque: Museum of New Mexico Press.

Garma Navarro, Carlos, and Roberto Shadow, eds. 1994. *Las Peregrinaciones Religiosas: Una Aproximación.* Iztapalapa, Mexico: Universidad Autonoma Metropolitana.

Garrett, Clarke. 1987. *Spirit Possession and Popular Religion: From the Camisards to the Shakers.* Baltimore: Johns Hopkins University Press.

Garrison, Vivian. 1977. "Doctor, Espiritista or Psychiatrist? Health-Seeking Behavior in a Puerto Rican Neighborhood of New York City." *Medical Anthropology* 1: 65–180.

Geertz, Armin W. 1994. *The Invention of Prophecy: Continuity and Meaning in Hopi Indian Religion.* 2nd ed. Los Angeles: University of California Press.

———. 2004. "Worlds in Collusion: On Social Strategies and Misrepresentations as Forces of Syncretism in Euro-American and Native American Affairs." In *Syncretism in Religion: A Reader,* edited by A. M. Leopold and J. S. Jensen. New York: Routledge, 237–54.

Geertz, Clifford. 1973. *The Interpretation of Cultures: Selected Essays.* New York: Basic Books.

Gelman, David. 1990. "Making It All Feel Better." *Newsweek,* November 26, 66–68.

Giddens, Anthony. 1991. *Modernity and Self-Identity: Self and Society in the Late Modern Age.* Stanford, Calif.: Stanford University Press.

———. 1992. *Transformation of Intimacy: Sexuality, Love and Eroticism in Modern Societies.* Stanford, Calif.: Stanford University Press.

Gifford, Paul. 2004. "Persistence and Change in Contemporary African Religion." *Social Compass* 51 (2): 169–76.

Gilkes, Cheryl Townsend. 1996. " 'Go and Tell Mary and Martha': The African American Religious Experience." *Social Compass* 43 (4): 563–82.

Ginzburg, Carlo. 1980. *The Cheese and the Worms: The Cosmos of a Sixteenth-Century Miller*. Translated by J. Tedeschi and A. Tedeschi. New York: Penguin.

———. 1983. *The Night Battles: Witchcraft and Agrarian Cults in the Sixteenth and Seventeenth Centuries*. Translated by J. Tedeschi and A. Tedeschi. Baltimore: Johns Hopkins University Press.

Goffman, Erving. 1961. *Asylums: Essays on the Social Situation of Mental Patients and Other Inmates*. New York: Doubleday.

Goizueta, Roberto S. 2002. "The Symbolic World of Mexican American Religion." In Matovina and Riebe-Estrella, *Horizons of the Sacred*, 119–38.

Goldsmith, Peter. 1989. *When I Rise Cryin' Holy: African-American Denominationalism on the Georgia Coast*. New York: AMS Press.

Goldstein, Michael S. 2000. "The Growing Acceptance of Complementary and Alternative Medicine." In *Handbook of Medical Sociology*, edited by C. E. Bird, P. Conrad, and A. M. Fremont. Upper Saddle River, N.J.: Prentice-Hall, 284–97.

Goodman, Felicitas D. 1986. "Body Posture and the Religious Altered State of Consciousness: An Experimental Investigation." *Journal of Humanistic Psychology* 26 (3): 81–118.

———. 1990. *Where the Spirits Ride the Wind: Trance Journeys and Other Ecstatic Experiences*. Bloomington: Indiana University Press.

———. 1992. *Ecstasy, Ritual, and Alternate Reality: Religion in a Pluralistic World*. Bloomington: Indiana University Press.

Goodstein, Laurie. 2001. "A Book Spreads the Word: Prayer for Prosperity Works." *New York Times*, May 8, A1, A23.

Gordon, Deborah. 1988. "Tenacious Assumptions in Western Medicine." In Lock and Gordon, *Biomedicine Examined*, 19–56.

Gorski, Philip S. 2000. "Historicizing the Secularization Debate: Church, State, and Society in Late Medieval and Early Modern Europe, ca. 1300 to 1700." *American Sociological Review* 65 (February): 138–67.

Gould, Rebecca. 1997. "Getting (Not Too) Close to Nature: Modern Homesteading as Lived Religion in America." In Hall, 217–42.

Gray, Edward R., and Scott L. Thumma. 1997. "The Gospel Hour: Liminality, Identity and Religion in a Gay Bar." In *Contemporary American Religion: An Ethnographic Reader*, edited by P. E. Becker and N. L. Eiesland. Walnut Creek, Calif.: AltaMira, 79–98.

Greil, A. L., and D. Bromley, eds. 2003. *Defining Religion: Investigating the Boundaries between Sacred and Secular*. Religion and the Social Order, vol. 10. Oxford: Elsevier.

Griffin, Clyde. 1990. "Reconstructing Masculinity from the Evangelical Revival to the Waning of Progressivism: A Speculative Synthesis." In *Meanings for Manhood: Constructions of Masculinity in Victorian America*, edited by M. Carnes and C. Griffin. Chicago: University of Chicago Press, 183–204.

Griffith, R. Marie. 1997a. *God's Daughter's: Evangelical Women and the Power of Submission*. Berkeley: University of California Press.

————. 1997b. "Submissive Wives, Wounded Daughters, and Female Soldiers: Prayer and Christian Womanhood in Women's Aglow Fellowship." In Hall, 160–95.

————. 2004. *Born Again Bodies: Flesh and Spirit in American Christianity*. Berkeley: University of California Press.

Gupta, Akhil, and James Ferguson. 1992. "Beyond 'Culture': Space, Identity, and the Politics of Difference." *Cultural Anthropology* 7: 6–22.

Hackett, David G. 2000. "The Prince Hall Masons and the African American Church: The Labors of Grand Master and Bishop James Walker Hood, 1831–1918." *Church History* 69 (4): 770–802.

————. 1991a. "Gender and Social Class in Late Nineteenth-Century American Protestantism." Paper presented at the annual meeting of the American Academy of Religion, Kansas City, 23–26 November.

————. 1991b. "Women and Men in Nineteenth-Century American Religious Culture." Paper presented at the annual meeting of the International Society for the Sociology of Religion, Maynooth, Ireland, 19–23 August.

————. 1995. "Gender and Religion in American Culture, 1870–1930." *Religion and American Culture* 5 (2): 127–57.

Hall, David D. 1989. *Worlds of Wonder, Days of Judgment: Popular Religious Belief in Early New England*. New York: Knopf.

————. 1995. "The Mentality of the Supernatural in Seventeenth-Century New England." In *Religion and American Culture: A Reader*, edited by D. G. Hackett. New York: Routledge, 27–52.

————, ed. 1997. *Lived Religion in America: Toward a History of Practice*. Princeton, N.J.: Princeton University Press.

Hammond, Phillip E. 1992. *The Protestant Presence in Twentieth-Century America*. Albany: State University of New York Press.

Hanf, Theodor. 1994. "The Sacred Marker: Religion, Communalism and Nationalism." *Social Compass* 41 (1): 9–20.

Hannerz, Ulf. 1987. "The World in Creolisation." *Africa* 43: 27–40.

Hantover, Jeffrey P. 1978. "The Boy Scouts and the Validation of Masculinity." *Journal of Social Issues* 34 (1): 184–95.

Harris, Grove. 2005. "Healing in Feminist Wicca." In Barnes and Sered, *Religion and Healing in America*, 253–63.

Harwood, Alan. 1977. *Rx: Spiritist as Needed: A Study of a Puerto Rican Community Mental Health Resource*. New York: Wiley.

Hatch, Nathan O. 1989. *The Democratization of American Christianity*. New Haven, Conn.: Yale University Press.

Hayes, Dawn Marie. 2003. *Body and Sacred Place in Medieval Europe, 1100–1389*. London: Routledge.

Hedges, Ellie, and James A. Beckford. 2000. "Holism, Healing and the New Age." In Sutcliffe and Bowman, *Beyond New Age*, 169–87.

Heelas, Paul. 1994. "The Limits of Consumption and the Post-Modern Religion of the New Age." In *The Authority of the Consumer*, edited by R. Keat, N. Whiteley, and N. Abercrombie. London: Routledge, 102–15.

———. 1996. *The New Age Movement: The Celebration of the Self and the Sacralization of Modernity*. Oxford: Blackwell.

Heldke, Lisa M. 1992. "Foodmaking as a Thoughtful Practice." In *Cooking, Eating, Thinking: Transformative Philosophies of Food*, edited by D. W. Curtin and L. M. Heldke. Bloomington: Indiana University Press, 204–29.

Hervieu-Léger, Danièle. 1990. "Religion and Modernity in the French Context: For a New Approach to Secularization." *Sociological Analysis* 51 (S): 15–25.

———. 1998. "Secularization and Religious Modernity in Western Europe." In *Religion, Mobilization, and Social Action*, edited by A. Shupe and B. Misztal. Westport, Conn.: Praeger, 15–31.

———. 2000. *Religion as a Chain of Memory*. Translated by S. Lee. New Brunswick, N.J.: Rutgers University Press.

Hobsbawm, Eric, and Terence Ranger. 1983. *The Invention of Tradition*. Cambridge: Cambridge University Press.

Hoge, Dean R., Benton Johnson, and Donald A. Luidens. 1994. *Vanishing Boundaries: The Religion of Mainline Protestant Baby Boomers*. Louisville, Ky.: Westminster Press.

Hondagneu-Sotelo, Pierrette, Genelle Gaudinez, Hector Lara, and Billie C. Ortiz. 2004. " 'There's a Spirit That Transcends the Border': Faith, Ritual, and Postnational Protest at the U.S.-Mexico Border." *Sociological Perspectives* 47 (2): 133–59.

Hood, Ralph W., Jr. 1985. "Mysticism." In *The Sacred in a Secular Age*, edited by Phillip E. Hammond. Berkeley: University of California Press, 285–97.

———, ed. 1995. *Handbook of Religious Experience*. Birmingham, Ala.: Religious Education Press.

———. 2005. "Mystical, Spiritual, and Religious Experiences." In *Handbook of the Psychology of Religion and Spirituality*, edited by R. F. Paloutzian and C. L. Park. New York: Guilford Press, 2348–64.

Hood, Ralph W., Jr., and James R. Hall. 1980. "Gender Differences in the Description of Erotic and Mystical Experiences." *Review of Religious Research* 21 (2): 195–207.

Hornborg, Anne-Christine. 2005. "Eloquent Bodies: Rituals in the Context of Alleviating Suffering." *Numen* 52 (3): 357–94.

Howarth, Sam, and Miguel A. Gandert, eds. 1999. *Pilgrimage to Chimayo: Contemporary Portrait of a Living Tradition*. Albuquerque: University of New Mexico Press.

Howes, Marie. 1993. "Priests, People and Power: A North Peruvian Case Study." In Rostas and Droogers (1993), 145–60.

Hunter, James Davidson. 1983. *American Evangelicalism: Conservative Religion and the Quandary of Modernity*. New Brunswick, N.J.: Rutgers University Press.

Huntington, Samuel P. 2004. *Who Are We?: The Challenges to America's National Identity*. New York: Simon and Schuster.

Ingersoll, Julie. 2002. "Against Univocality: Re-reading Ethnographies of Conservative Protestant Women." In Spickard et al. (2002), 162–74.

———. 2003. *Evangelical Christian Women: War Stories in the Gender Battles*. New York: New York University Press.

Jacobs, Janet L. 1989. "The Effects of Ritual Healing on Female Victims of Abuse: A Study of Empowerment and Transformation." *Sociological Analysis* 50 (3): 265–79.

———. 1990. "Women-Centered Healing Rites: A Study of Alienation and Reintegration." In *In Gods We Trust: New Patterns of Religious Pluralism in America*, edited by T. Robbins and D. Anthony. New Brunswick, N.J.: Transaction, 373–83.

———. 1991. "Gender and Power in New Religious Movements." *Religion* 21: 345–56.

———. 1992. "Religious Experience among Women and Men: A Gender Perspective on Mystical Revelation." *Research in the Social Scientific Study of Religion* 4: 261–79.

James, William. [1903] 1961. *The Varieties of Religious Experience*. New York: Modern Library.

Jenkins, Philip. 2004. *Dream Catchers: How Mainstream America Discovered Native Spirituality*. Oxford: Oxford University Press.

Jones, Arthur C. 2004. "Black Spirituals, Physical Sensuality and Sexuality: Notes on a Neglected Field of Inquiry." In *Loving the Body: Black Religious Studies and the Erotic*, edited by A. B. Pinn and D. N. Hopkins. New York: Palgrave, 235–46.

Joyner, Charles. 1995. " 'Believer I Know': The Emergence of African American Christianity." In *Religion and American Culture: A Reader*, edited by D. G. Hackett. New York: Routledge, 185–208.

Kaelber, Lutz. 1998. *Schools of Asceticism: Ideology and Organization in Medieval Religious Communities*. University Park: Pennsylvania State University Press.

Kanter, Rosabeth Moss. 1972. *Commitment and Community: Communes and Utopias in Sociological Perspective*. Cambridge, Mass.: Harvard University Press.

Kasulis, Thomas P. 1993. "The Body—Japanese Style." In *Self as Image in Asian Theory and Practice*, edited by T. P. Kasulis, R. T. Ames and W. Dissanayake. Albany: State University of New York Press.

Katz, Richard. 1982. *Boiling Energy: Community Healing among the Kalahari Kung*. Cambridge, Mass.: Harvard University Press.

Kertzer, David. 1988. *Ritual, Politics, and Power*. New Haven, Conn.: Yale University Press.

Ketchell, Aaron K. 1999. "The Precious Moments Chapel: Suffering, Salvation, and the World's Most Popular Collectible." *The Journal of American Culture* 22 (3): 27–33.

———. 2002. " 'These Hills Will Give You Great Treasure': Ozark Tourism and the Collapse of Sacred and Secular." In *The Invention of Religion: Rethinking Belief in Politics and History*, edited by D. R. Peterson and D. R. Walhof. New Brunswick, N.J.: Rutgers University Press, 156–75.

King, Christine. 1993. "His Truth Goes Marching On: Elvis Presley and the Pilgrimage to Graceland." In *Pilgrimage in Popular Culture*, edited by I. Reader and T. Walter. London: Macmillan, 92–104.

Kirmayer, Lawrence J. 1988. "Mind and Body as Metaphors: Hidden Values in Biomedicine." In Lock and Gordon, *Biomedicine Examined*, 57–94.

Klassen, Pamela E. 2001. *Blessed Events: Religion and Home Birth in America.* Princeton, N.J.: Princeton University Press.

———. 2005. "Procreating Women and Religion: The Politics of Spirituality, Healing, and Childbirth in America." In Barnes and Sered, *Religion and Healing in America,* 71–88.

Kleinman, Arthur. 1988. *The Illness Narratives: Suffering, Healing, and the Human Condition.* New York: Basic Books.

K'Meyer, Tracy Elaine. 1997. *Interracialist Christian Community in the Postwar South: The Story of Koinonia Farm.* Charlottesville: University of Virginia Press.

Kokosalakis, Nikos. 1987. "The Political Significance of Popular Religion in Greece." *Archives des Sciences Sociales des Religions* 64: 37–52.

———. 1995. "Icons and Non-verbal Religion in the Orthodox Tradition." *Social Compass* 42 (4): 433–50.

Kuhn, Thomas S. 1970. *The Structure of Scientific Revolutions,* 2nd enl. ed. Chicago: University of Chicago Press.

Kurtz, Ernest. 1996. "Twelve Step Programs." In *Spirituality and the Secular Quest,* edited by P. Van Ness. New York: Crossroads Herder, 277–302.

Lamadrid, Enrique R., and Miguel A. Gandert. 2003. *Hermanitos Comanchitos: Indo-Hispano Rituals of Captivity and Redemption.* Albuquerque: University of New Mexico Press.

Lancaster, Roger N. 1988. *Thanks to God and the Revolution: Popular Religion and Class Conscious in the New Nicaragua.* New York: Columbia University Press.

Lane, Belden C. 2001. *Landscapes of the Sacred: Geography and Narrative in American Spirituality.* Baltimore: Johns Hopkins University Press.

Lansing, Carol. 1998. *Power and Purity: Cathar Heresy in Medieval Italy.* Oxford: Oxford University Press.

Laqueur, Thomas. 1990. *Making Sex: Body and Gender from the Greeks to Freud.* Cambridge, Mass.: Harvard University Press.

Larson, Magali Sarfatti. 1979. "Professionalism: Rise and Fall." *International Journal of Health Services* 9 (4): 607–27.

Leatham, Miguel C. 1996. "Practical Religion and Peasant Recruitment to Non-Catholic Groups in Latin America." *Religion and the Social Order* 6: 175–90.

Leder, Drew. 1984. "Medicine and Paradigms of Embodiment." *Journal of Medicine and Philosophy* 9: 24–43.

León, Luis D. 2002. " 'Soy una Curandera y Soy una Catolica': The Poetics of a Mexican Healing Tradition." In Matovina and Riebe-Estrella, *Horizons of the Sacred,* 95–118.

Le Roy Ladurie, Emmanuel. 1978. *Montaillou: The Promised Land of Error.* New York: Vintage.

Lévi-Strauss, Claude. 1966. *The Savage Mind.* Chicago: University of Chicago Press.

Levitt, Peggy. 1998. "Local-Level Global Religion: The Case of U.S.-Dominican Migration." *Journal for the Scientific Study of Religion* 37 (1): 74–89.

———. 2001. *The Transnational Villagers.* Berkeley: University of California Press.

———. 2007. *God Needs No Passport: Immigrants and the Changing American Religious Landscape.* New York: New Press.

Linenthal, Edward Tabor. 1993. *Sacred Ground: Americans and Their Battlefields.* Urbana: University of Illinois Press.

Lippy, Charles H. 1994. *Being Religious, American Style: A History of Popular Religiosity in the United States.* Westport, Conn.: Greenwood Press.

Litva, Andrea, and John Eyles. 1994. "Health or Healthy: Why People Are Not Sick in a Southern Ontarian Town." *Social Science and Medicine* 39 (8): 1083–91.

Lock, Margaret, and Deborah Gordon. 1988. *Biomedicine Examined.* Dordrecht: Kluwer.

Longhurst, John E. 1962. *The Age of Torquemada.* Lawrence, Kans.: Coronado.

Luckmann, Thomas. 1967. *The Invisible Religion: The Problem of Religion in Modern Society.* New York: Macmillan.

———. 1973. "Comments on the Laeyendecker et al. Proposal." In *Acts of the CISR.* Lille, France: Conference Internationale de Sociologie Religieuse, 55–68.

Luhrmann, Tanya. 1989. *Persuasions of the Witch's Craft: Ritual Magic and Witchcraft in Present-Day England.* Oxford: Blackwell.

———. 2005. "The Art of Hearing God: Absorption, Dissociation, and Contemporary American Spirituality." *Spiritus* 5 (2): 133–57.

Lupton, Deborah. 1995. *The Imperative of Health.* Thousand Oaks, Calif.: Sage.

Luria, Keith P. 1989. "The Counter-Reformation and Popular Spirituality." In *Christian Spirituality: Post-Reformation and Modern,* edited by L. Dupré and D. E. Saliers. New York: Crossroad, 93–120.

———. 1991. *Territories of Grace: Cultural Change in the Seventeenth-Century Diocese of Grenoble.* Berkeley: University of California Press.

Lyon, Margot L. 1997. "The Material Body, Social Processes and Emotion: 'Techniques of the Body' Revisited." *Body and Society* 3 (1): 83–101.

MacIntyre, Alasdair. 1984. *After Virtue: A Study in Moral Theory.* 2nd ed. Notre Dame, Ind.: University of Notre Dame Press.

Maduro, Otto. 1995. "Directions for a Reassessment of Latina/o Religion." In Stevens-Arroyo and Pérez y Mena, *Enigmatic Powers,* 47–68.

———. 2002. "On the Theoretical Politics of Defining 'Religion.'" *Social Compass* 49 (4): 601–5.

———. 2004. "'Religion' under Imperial Duress: Post-colonial Reflections and Proposals." *Review of Religious Research* 45 (3): 221–34.

Marcuse, Herbert. 1955. *Eros and Civilization: A Philosophical Inquiry into Freud.* Boston: Beacon Press.

Marling, Karal Ann. 1996. *Graceland: Going Home with Elvis.* Cambridge, Mass.: Harvard University Press.

Martin, John. 1987. "Popular Culture and the Shaping of Popular Heresy in Renaissance Venice." In *Inquisition and Society in Early Modern Europe,* edited by S. Haliczer. Totowa, N.J.: Barnes and Noble Books, 115–28.

———. 1993. *Venice's Hidden Enemies: Italian Heretics in a Renaissance City.* Berkeley: University of California Press.

————. 1994. "Theories of Practice: Inquisition and the Discovery of Religion." Unpublished paper presented at Trinity University Humanities Symposium, Trinity University, San Antonio, Texas, 17 November.

Mathews, Donald G. 1977. *Religion in the Old South*. Chicago: University of Chicago Press.

Matovina, Timothy, and Gary Riebe-Estrella, eds. 2002. *Horizons of the Sacred: Mexican Traditions in U.S. Catholicism*. Ithaca, N.Y.: Cornell University Press.

Mauss, Marcel. [1934] 1973. "Techniques of the Body." *Economy and Society* 2: 70–88.

Maxwell, Carol J. C. 2002. *Pro-life Activists in America: Meaning, Motivation, and Direct Action*. Cambridge: Cambridge University Press.

McDannell, Colleen. 1986. *The Christian Home in Victorian America, 1840–1900*. Bloomington: Indiana University Press.

————. 1995. *Material Christianity: Religion and Popular Culture in America*. New Haven, Conn.: Yale University Press.

McGuire, Meredith B. 1982. *Pentecostal Catholics: Power, Charisma, and Order in a Religious Movement*. Philadelphia: Temple University Press.

————. 1983a. "Discovering Religious Power." *Sociological Analysis* 44 (1): 1–10.

————. 1983b. "Words of Power: Personal Empowerment and Healing." *Culture, Medicine and Psychiatry* 7 (3): 221–40.

————. 1988. *Ritual Healing in Suburban America*. New Brunswick, N.J.: Rutgers University Press.

————. 1990. "Religion and the Body: Rematerializing the Human Body in the Social Sciences of Religion." *Journal for the Scientific Study of Religion* 29 (3): 283–96.

————. 1992. *Religion: The Social Context*. 3rd ed. Belmont, Calif.: Wadsworth.

————. 1993. "Health and Spirituality as Contemporary Concerns." *Annals of the American Academy of Political and Social Science* 527 (May): 144–54.

————. 1994. "Linking Theory and Methodology for the Study of Latino Religiosity in the United States Context." In Stevens-Arroyo and Díaz-Stevens, *An Enduring Flame*, 191–203.

————. 1996. "Religion and Healing the Mind/Body/Self." *Social Compass* 43 (1): 101–16.

————. 1997. "Mapping Contemporary American Spirituality: A Sociological Perspective." *Christian Spirituality Bulletin* 5 (1): 1–8.

————. 2002. *Religion: The Social Context*. 5th ed. Belmont, Calif.: Wadsworth.

————. 2003. "Contested Meanings and Definitional Boundaries: Historicizing the Sociology of Religion." In Greil and Bromley, *Defining Religion*, 127–38.

————. 2007. "Embodied Practices: Negotiation and Resistance." In Ammerman 2007, 187–200.

McGuire, Meredith B., and James V. Spickard. 1995. "Feeding Religiosity: Food Preparation and Eating as Religious Practice." Paper presented at the annual meeting of the Society for the Scientific Study of Religion, 27–29 October.

————. 2003. "Narratives of Commitment: Social Activism and Radical Catholic Identity." *Temenos* 37–38: 131–49.

McMorris, Christine. 2002. "Amazing Graceland." *Religion in the News* 5 (3): 15–16, 24.

McNiff, Shaun. 1999. "Celebrations of Memory: Dana Salvo and the Mother of Grace Club." In *Mother of Grace: An Exhibition of Gloucester Photographs by Dana Salvo*, catalog of exhibition, Cape Ann Historical Museum. Gloucester, Mass.: Cultureport. www.cultureport.com/cultureport/artists/salvo/index01.html.

Lara. 1998. "Los Espíritus Siguen Hablando: Chicana Spiritualities." In *Living Chicana Theory*, edited by C. Trujillo. Berkeley: Third Woman Press, 189–213.

———. 2005. "Communing with the Dead: Spiritual and Cultural Healing in Chicano/a Communities." In Barnes and Sered (2005), 205–15.

Medina, Lara, and Gilbert R. Cadena. 2002. "Días de los Muertos: Public Ritual, Community Renewal, and Popular Religion in Los Angeles." In Matovina and Riebe-Estrella, *Horizons of the Sacred*, 69–94.

Mellor, Philip A., and Chris Shilling. 1994. "Reflexive Modernity and the Religious Body." *Religion* 24: 23–42.

———. 1997. *Re-forming the Body: Religion, Community and Modernity*. Thousand Oaks, Calif.: Sage.

Merleau-Ponty, Maurice. 1962. *Phenomenology of Perception*. Translated by C. Smith. London: Routledge and Kegan Paul.

Merton, Robert K. [1938] 1970. *Science, Technology, and Society in Seventeenth-Century England*. New York: Harper.

Messner, Michael. 1990. "Boyhood, Organized Sports, and the Construction of Masculinities." *Journal of Contemporary Ethnography* 18 (4): 416–44.

Midelfort, H. C. Erik. 1982. "Witchcraft, Magic and the Occult." In *Reformation Europe: A Guide to Research*, edited by S. Ozment. St. Louis, Mo.: Center for Reformation Research, 183–209.

Miles, Margaret R. 1985. *Image as Insight: Visual Understanding in Western Christianity and Secular Culture*. Boston: Beacon Press.

Miller, Vincent J. 2003. *Consuming Religion: Christian Faith and Practice in a Consumer Culture*. New York: Continuum.

Mitchell, Timothy. 1990. *Passional Culture: Emotion, Religion and Society in Southern Spain*. Philadelphia: University of Pennsylvania Press.

Mitchem, Stephanie Y. 2005. " 'Jesus Is My Doctor': Healing and Religion in African American Women's Lives." In Barnes and Sered (2005), 281–90.

Monter, William. 1983. *Ritual, Myth, and Magic in Early Modern Europe*. Brighton, England: Harvester.

Moore, R. Laurence. 1994. *Selling God: American Religion in the Marketplace of Culture*. New York: Oxford University Press.

Morgan, David. 1998. *Visual Piety: A History and Theory of Popular Religious Images*. Berkeley: University of California Press.

———. 2005. *The Sacred Gaze: Religious Visual Culture in Theory and Practice*. Berkeley: University of California Press.

Morgan, Prys. 1983. "From a Death to a View: The Hunt for the Welsh Past in the Romantic Period." In Hobsbawm and Ranger (1983), 43–101.

Morris, Colin. 1989. *The Papal Monarchy: The Western Church from 1050 to 1250.* Oxford: Clarendon Press.

Muir, Edward. 1997. *Ritual in Early Modern Europe.* Cambridge: Cambridge University Press.

Mullett, Michael. 1987. *Popular Culture and Popular Protest in Late Medieval and Early Modern Europe.* London: Croom Helm.

Nabhan-Warren, Kristy. 2005. *The Virgin of El Barrio: Marian Apparitions, Catholic Evangelizing and Mexican American Activism.* New York: New York University Press.

Nagel, Joane. 2003. *Race, Ethnicity, and Sexuality: Intimate Intersections, Forbidden Frontiers.* New York: Oxford University Press.

Nazareno, Analisa. 2003. "Million-Dollar Minister." *San Antonio (TX) Express-News,* 6 July, A1, A12.

Neitz, Mary Jo. 1987. *Charisma and Community: A Study of Religious Commitment within the Catholic Charismatic Renewal.* New Brunswick, N.J.: Transaction.

———. 1994. "Quasi-religions and Cultural Movements: Contemporary Witchcraft as a Churchless Religion." *Religion and the Social Order* 4 (12): 127–49.

———. 1995a. "Constructing Women's Rituals: Roman Catholic Women and 'Limina.'" In *Work, Family, and Religion in Contemporary Society,* edited by N. T. Ammerman and W. C. Roof. New York: Routledge, 283–304.

———. 1995b. "Feminist Theory and Religious Experience." In Hood (1995), 520–34.

———. 2000. "Queering the Dragonfest: Changing Sexualities in a Post-patriarchal Religion." *Sociology of Religion* 61 (4): 369–91.

Neitz, Mary Jo, and James V. Spickard. 1990. "Steps toward a Sociology of Religious Experience: The Theories of Mihaly Czikszentmihalyi and Alfred Schutz." *Sociological Analysis* 51 (1): 15–33.

Nepstad, Sharon Erickson. 1996. "Popular Religion, Protest and Revolt: The Emergence of Political Insurgency in the Nicaraguan and Salvadoran Churches of the 1960s–80s." In *Disruptive Religion: The Force of Faith in Social Movement Activism,* edited by C. Smith. New York: Routledge, 105–24.

Ness, Sally Ann. 2004. "Being a Body in a Cultural Way: Understanding the Cultural in the Embodiment of Dance." In *Cultural Bodies: Ethnography and Theory,* edited by H. Thomas and J. Ahmed. Oxford: Blackwell, 123–44.

Nolan, Mary Lee. 1991. "The European Roots of Latin American Pilgrimage." In *Pilgrimage in Latin America,* edited by N. R. Crumrine and A. Morinis. Westport, Conn.: Greenwood Press, 19–49.

Northrup, Lesley A. 1997. *Ritualizing Women: Patterns of Feminine Spirituality.* Cleveland: Pilgrim Press.

Obelkevich, James, ed. 1979. *Religion and the People, 800–1700.* Chapel Hill: University of North Carolina Press.

Ochs, Vanessa L. 1999. "What Makes a Jewish Home Jewish?" Material History of American Religion Project. www.materialreligion.org/journal/jewish.html.

Orsi, Robert Anthony. 1985. *The Madonna of 115th Street: Faith and Community in Italian Harlem 1880–1950.* New Haven, Conn.: Yale University Press.

——. 1996. *Thank You St. Jude: Women's Devotion to the Patron Saint of Hopeless Causes.* New Haven, Conn.: Yale University Press.

——. 1997. "Everyday Miracles: The Study of Lived Religion." In Hall (1997), 3–21.

——. 2002. "Introduction to the Second Edition: Faith and Community in Italian Harlem, 1880–1950." In *The Madonna of 115th Street: Faith and Community in Italian Harlem 1880–1950,* 2nd ed. New Haven, Conn.: Yale University Press, ix–xxxviii.

——. 2003. "Is the Study of Lived Religion Irrelevant to the World We Live In?" *Journal for the Scientific Study of Religion* 42 (2): 169–74.

——. 2005. *Between Heaven and Earth: The Religious Worlds People Make and the Scholars Who Study Them.* Princeton, N.J.: Princeton University Press.

Ownby, Ted. 1990. *Subduing Satan: Religion, Recreation and Manhood in the Rural South, 1865–1920.* Chapel Hill: University of North Carolina Press.

Pace, Enzo. 1987. "New Paradigms of Popular Religion." *Archives de Sciences Sociales des Religions* 64 (1): 7–14.

——. 1989. "Pilgrimage as Spiritual Journey: An Analysis of Pilgrimage Using the Theory of V. Turner and the Resource Mobilization Approach." *Social Compass* 36 (2): 229–44.

——. 2006. "Salvation Goods, the Gift Economy and Charismatic Concern." *Social Compass* 53 (1): 49–64.

Palmer, Susan J. 1994. *Moon Sisters, Krishna Mothers, Rajneesh Lovers: Women's Roles in New Religions.* Syracuse, N.Y.: Syracuse University Press.

Parker G., Cristián. 1991. "Christianity and Popular Movements in the Twentieth Century," In Popular Culture in Chile: Resistance and Survival, edited by K. Aman and C. Parker. Boulder, Colo.: Westview Press.

——. 1994. "La Sociología de la Religión y la Modernidad: Por una Revisión Crítica de las Categorías Durkheimianas desde América Latina." *Revista Mexicana de Sociología* 4: 229–54.

——. 1996. *Popular Religion and Modernization in Latin America: A Different Logic.* Maryknoll, N.Y.: Orbis Books.

——. 1998. "Modern Popular Religion: A Complex Object of Study for Sociology." *International Sociology* 13 (2): 195–212.

——. 2002. "Les Nouvelles Formes de Religion dans la Société Globalisée: Un Défi á l'Interprétation Sociologique." *Social Compass* 49 (2): 167–86.

Parsons, Anne. 1965. "The Pentecostal Immigrants: A Study of an Ethnic Central City Church." *Journal for the Scientific Study of Religion* 4: 183–97.

——. 1969. *Belief, Magic, and Anomie: Essays in Psychosocial Anthropology.* New York: Free Press.

Patterson, Beverly Bush. 1988. "Finding a Home in the Church: Primitive Baptist Women." In *Diversities of Gifts: Field Studies in Southern Religion,* edited by R. W. Tyson, J. L. Peacock, and D. W. Patterson. Urbana: University of Illinois Press, 61–78.

——. 1995. *The Sound of the Dove: Singing in Appalachian Primitive Baptist Churches.* Urbana: Illinois University Press.

Patterson, Margot. 2002. "Will Fundamentalist Christians and Jews Ignite Apocalypse?" *National Catholic Reporter*, October 11, 13–16.

Pearce, W. Barnett. 1994. *Interpersonal Communication: Making Social Worlds*. New York: HarperCollins.

Peña, Milagros, and Lisa M. Frehill. 1998. "Latina Religious Practice: Analyzing Cultural Dimensions in Measures of Religiosity." *Journal for the Scientific Study of Religion* 38 (4): 620–35.

Petroff, Elizabeth Alvida. 1994. *Body and Soul: Essays on Medieval Women and Mysticism*. Oxford: Oxford University Press.

Polk, Patrick A., Michael Owen Jones, Claudia J. Hernández, and Reyna C. Ronelli. 2005. "Miraculous Migrants to the City of Angels: Perceptions of El Santo Niño de Atocha and San Simón as Sources of Help and Healing." In Barnes and Sered (2005), 103–20.

Poloma, Margaret M. 2003. *Main Street Mystics: The Toronto Blessing and Reviving Pentecostalism*. Walnut Creek, Calif.: AltaMira Press.

Portilla, Elizabeth de la. 2002. "San Antonio as a Magical Crossroads: Healing and Spirituality in the Borderlands." Ph.D. diss., University of Michigan.

Preston, David. 1988. *The Social Organization of Zen Practice: Constructing Transcultural Reality*. Cambridge: Cambridge University Press.

Proudfoot, Wayne. 1985. *Religious Experience*. Berkeley: University of California Press.

Puttick, Elizabeth. 1997. *Women in New Religions: In Search of Community, Sexuality, and Spiritual Power*. New York: St. Martin's Press.

Ray, Celeste. 2003. " 'Thigibh!' Means "Y'all Come!" ': Renegotiating Regional Memories through Scottish Heritage Celebrations." In *Southern Heritage on Display: Public Ritual and Ethnic Diversity within Southern Regionalism*, edited by C. Ray. Tuscaloosa: University of Alabama Press, 251–82.

Ricciardi, Gabriella. 2006. "Telling Stories, Building Altars: Mexican American Women's Altars in Oregon." *Oregon Historical Quarterly* 107 (4): 536–53.

Riis, Ole. 1998. "Religion Re-Emerging: The Role of Religion in Legitimating Integration and Power in Modern Societies." *International Sociology* 13 (2): 249–72.

Ritzer, George. 1996. *The McDonaldization of Society*. Thousand Oaks, Calif.: Pine Forge Press.

———. 2004. *The Globalization of Nothing*. Thousand Oaks, Calif.: Pine Forge Press.

Rodriguez, Jeanette. 1994. *Our Lady of Guadalupe: Faith and Empowerment among Mexican-American Women*. Austin: University of Texas Press.

Romano, Lois. 2005. " 'The Smiling Preacher' Builds on Large Following." *Washington Post*, January 30, A1.

Roof, Wade Clark. 1999. *Spiritual Marketplace: Baby Boomers and the Remaking of American Religion*. Princeton, N.J.: Princeton University Press.

———. 2003. "Religion and Spirituality: Toward an Integrated Analysis." In Dillon, *Handbook of the Sociology of Religion*, 137–48.

Roof, Wade Clark, and William McKinney. 1987. *American Mainline Religion: Its Changing Shape and Future*. New Brunswick, N.J.: Rutgers University Press.

Rosenberg, Ellen M. 1989. *The Southern Baptists: A Subculture in Transition.* Knoxville: University of Tennessee Press.

Rostas, Susanna, and André Droogers. 1993. "The Popular Use of Popular Religion in Latin America: Introduction." In *The Popular Use of Popular Religion in Latin America,* edited by S. Rostas. Amsterdam: Centre for Latin American Research and Documentation, 1–16.

Rothkrug, Lionel. 1979. "Popular Religion and Holy Shrines: Their Influence on the Origins of the German Reformation and Their Role in German Cultural Development." In Obelkevich (1979), 20–87.

Rubin, Miri. 1991. *Corpus Christi: The Eucharist in Late Medieval Culture.* Cambridge: Cambridge University Press.

Rublack, Ulinka. 1996. "Female Spirituality and the Infant Jesus in Late Medieval Dominican Convents." In *Popular Religion in Germany and Central Europe, 1400–1800,* edited by R. W. Scribner and T. Johnson. New York: St. Martin's Press, 16–37.

Ryan, Mary P. 1983. *Womanhood in America: From Colonial Times to the Present.* New York: Franklin Watts.

Sack, Daniel. 2000. *Whitebread Protestants: Food and Religion in American Culture.* New York: St. Martin's Press.

Said, Edward W. 1978. *Orientalism.* New York: Pantheon Books.

Sanday, Peggy Reeves. 1981. *Female Power and Male Dominance: On the Origins of Sexual Inequality.* New York: Cambridge University Press.

———. 1990. *Fraternity Gang Rape: Sex, Brotherhood and Privilege on Campus.* New York: New York University Press.

Sanders, Cheryl J. 1996. *Saints in Exile: The Holiness-Pentecostal Experience in African American Religion and Culture.* New York: Oxford University Press.

Schatzmiller, Joseph. 1995. *Jews, Medicine, and Medieval Society.* Berkeley: University of California Press.

Schensul, Stephen L., and Jean J. Schensul. 1982. "Healing Resource Use in a Puerto Rican Community." *Urban Anthropology* 11 (1): 59–79.

Scheper-Hughes, Nancy, and Margaret M. Lock. 1986. "Speaking 'Truth' to Illness: Metaphor, Reification, and a Pedagogy for Patients." *Medical Anthropology Quarterly* 17: 137–40.

———. 1987. "The Mindful Body." *Medical Anthropology Quarterly* 1 (1): 6–41.

Schmidt, Leigh Eric. 1997. "Practices of Exchange: From Market Culture to Gift Economy in the Interpretation of American Religion." In Hall, 69–91.

———. 2000. *Hearing Things: Religion, Illusion, and the American Enlightenment.* Cambridge, Mass.: Harvard University Press.

———. 2003. "The Making of Modern Mysticism." *Journal of the American Academy of Religion* 71: 273–302.

Schmitt, Jean Claude. 1983. *The Holy Greyhound: Guinefort, Healer of Children since the Thirteenth Century.* Cambridge: Cambridge University Press.

Schneider, Louis, and Sanford M. Dornbusch. 1958. *Popular Religion: Inspirational Books in America.* Chicago: University of Chicago Press.

Schutz, Alfred. 1964. "Making Music Together: A Study in Social Relationship." In *Collected Papers II: Studies in Social Theory*, edited by A. Brodersen. The Hague: Martinus Nijhoff, 159–78.

Schutz, Alfred, and Thomas Luckmann. [1983] 1989. *The Structures of the Life-World*. Vol. 2. Translated by R. M. Zaner and D. J. Parent. Evanston, Ill.: Northwestern University Press.

Scribner, Robert W. 1984a. "Cosmic Order and Daily Life: Sacred and Secular in Pre-industrial German Society." In *Religion and Society in Early Modern Europe, 1500–1800*, edited by K. von Greyerz. London: Allen and Unwin, 17–32.

———. 1984b. "Ritual and Popular Religion in Catholic Germany at the Time of the Reformation." *Journal of Ecclesiastical History* 35 (1): 47–77.

———. 1990. "The Reformation Movements in Germany." In *The New Cambridge Modern History*, vol. 2, 2nd ed., edited by G. R. Elton. Cambridge: Cambridge University Press, 69–93.

———. 1993. "The Reformation, Popular Magic, and the 'Disenchantment of the World.'" *Journal of Interdisciplinary History* 23 (3): 475–94.

———. 1994. "Elements of Popular Belief." In *Handbook of European History, 1400–1600: Late Middle Ages, Renaissance, and Reformation*, edited by T. A. Brady Jr., H. A. Oberman, and J. D. Tracy. Leiden: Brill, 231–55.

Sered, Susan S. 1994. *Priestess, Mother, Sacred Sister: Religions Dominated by Women*. New York: Oxford University Press.

———. 2005. "Healing as Resistance: Reflections upon New Forms of American Jewish Healing." In Barnes and Sered (2005), 231–52.

Sharot, Stephen. 2001. *A Comparative Sociology of World Religions: Virtuosos, Priests, and Popular Religion*. New York: New York University Press.

Shaw, Rosalind, and Charles Stewart. 1994. "Introduction: Problematizing Syncretism." In Stewart and Shaw (1994), 1–26.

Shibley, Mark A. 1996. *Resurgent Evangelicalism in the United States: Mapping Cultural Change Since 1970*. Columbia: University of South Carolina Press.

Sikkink, David, and Mark Regnerus. 1996. "For God and the Fatherland: Protestant Symbolic Worlds and the Rise of German National Socialism." In Smith (1996a), 147–66.

Simmel, Georg. 1906. "The Sociology of Secrecy and of Secret Societies." *American Journal of Sociology* 11 (4): 441–98.

Singer, Merrill, and Roberto Garcia. 1989. "Becoming a Puerto Rican Espiritista: Life History of a Female Healer." In *Women as Healers: Cross Cultural Perspectives*, edited by C. S. McClain. New Brunswick, N.J.: Rutgers University Press, 157–85.

Sizer, Sandra. 1979. *Gospel Hymns and Social Religion: The Rhetoric of Nineteenth-Century Revivalism*. Philadelphia: Temple University Press.

Slavin, Sean. 2003. "Walking as Spiritual Practice: The Pilgrimage to Santiago de Compostela." *Body and Society* 9 (3): 1–18.

Smith, Christian S. 1996a. *Disruptive Religion: The Force of Faith in Social-Movement Activism*. New York: Routledge.

————. 1996b. *Resisting Reagan: The U.S. Central American Peace Movement.* Chicago: University of Chicago Press.

Smith, Christian S., and Melinda Lundquist. 2000. "Male Headship and Gender Equality." In *Christian America? What Evangelicals Really Want*, edited by C. Smith. Berkeley: University of California Press, 160–91.

Smith, Christian S., and Melinda Lundquist Denton. 2005. *Soul Searching: The Religious and Spiritual Lives of American Teenagers.* Oxford: Oxford University Press.

Sobo, Eliza J. 1994. "The Sweetness of Fat: Health, Procreation and Sociability in Rural Jamaica." In *Many Mirrors: Body Image and Social Relations*, edited by N. Sault. New Brunswick, N.J.: Rutgers University Press, 132–54.

Sowers, Leslie. 1991. "Passion Play: Founders Politics Shadow Drama." *Houston Chronicle*, 12 October, Religion sec., 1.

Spicer, Emily. 2002. "Prayer Box Stays Close to the Heart." *San Antonio (TX) Express-News*, June 20, San Antonio Life sec., 1F.

Spickard, James V. 1991. "Experiencing Religious Rituals: A Schutzian Analysis of Navajo Ceremonies." *Sociological Analysis* 52 (2): 191–204.

————. 1992. "For a Sociology of Religious Experience." In *A Future for Religion? New Paradigms for Social Analysis*, edited by W. H. Swatos Jr. Newbury Park, Calif.: Sage, 109–28.

————. 1998. "Ethnocentrism, Social Theory and Non-Western Sociologies of Religion: Toward a Confucian Alternative." *International Sociology* 13 (2): 173–94.

————. 2002. "On the Epistemology of Post-colonial Ethnography." In Spickard et al. (2002), 237–52.

————. 2003. "Slow Journalism? Ethnography as a Means of Understanding Religious Social Activism." Project on Religion, Political Economy, and Society, working paper 36. http://www.wcfiareligionproject.org/rsrchpapsum.asp?ID=721.

————. 2004. "Charting the Inward Journey: Applying Blackmore's Model to Meditative Religions." *Archiv Für Religionpsychologie* 26: 157–80.

————. 2005. "Ritual, Symbol, and Experience: Understanding Catholic Worker House Masses." *Sociology of Religion* 66 (4): 337–58.

————. 2006. "What is happening to religion? Six visions of religion's future." *Nordic Journal of Religion and Society* 19 (1): 13–29.

————. 2007. "Micro/Qualitative Approaches to the Sociology of Religion: Phenomenologies, Interviews, Narratives, and Ethnographies." In *Handbook of the Sociology of Religion*, edited by J. A. Beckford and N. J. Demerath. Thousand Oaks, Calif.: Sage, 104–27.

————. 2008. "Ethnography/Religion: Explorations in Field and Classroom." In *Handbook of the Sociology of Religion*, edited by P. Clarke. Oxford: Oxford University Press.

Spickard, James V., J. Shawn Landres, and Meredith B. McGuire, eds. 2002. *Personal Knowledge and Beyond: Reshaping the Ethnography of Religion.* New York: New York University Press.

Spillers, Hortense J. 1971. "Martin Luther King and the Style of the Black Sermon."
    Black Scholar 34 (1): 14–27.
Stark, Rodney, and Roger Finke. 2000. *Acts of Faith: Explaining the Human Side of
    Religion.* Berkeley: University of California Press.
Stark, Rodney, and William Sims Bainbridge. 1985. *The Future of Religion:
    Secularization, Revival and Cult Formation.* Berkeley: University of California
    Press.
———. 1987. *A Theory of Religion.* New York: Lang.
Starr, Paul. 1982. *The Social Transformation of American Medicine.* New York: Basic
    Books.
Stevens-Arroyo, Anthony M. 1998. "The Evolution of Marian Devotionalism within
    Christianity and the Ibero-Mediterranean Polity." *Journal for the Scientific Study of
    Religion* 37 (1): 50–73.
Stevens-Arroyo, Anthony M., and Ana María Díaz-Stevens, eds. 1994. *An Enduring
    Flame: Studies of Latino Popular Religiosity.* New York: Bildner Center for Western
    Hemisphere Studies.
Stevens-Arroyo, Anthony M., and Andrés. I. Pérez y Mena, eds. 1995. *Enigmatic
    Powers: Syncretism with African and Indigenous Peoples' Religions Among Latinos.*
    New York: Bildner Center for Western Hemisphere Studies.
Stewart, Charles. 1994. "Syncretism as a Dimension of Nationalist Discourse in
    Modern Greece." In Stewart and Shaw, 127–44.
———. 1995. "Relocating Syncretism in Social Science Discourse." In *Syncretism and
    the Commerce of Symbols,* edited by G. Aijmer. Göteborg, Sweden: Göteborg
    University Press, 13–37.
———. 2004. "Relocating Syncretism in Social Science Discourse." In *Syncretism in
    Religion: A Reader,* edited by A. M. Leopold and J. S. Jensen. New York:
    Routledge, 264–85.
Stewart, Charles, and Rosalind Shaw. 1994. *Syncretism/Anti-syncretism: The Politics of
    Religious Synthesis.* London: Routledge Press.
Stout, Jeffrey. 1988. *Ethics after Babel: The Languages of Morals and Their Discontents.*
    Boston: Beacon Press.
Stowe, David W. 2004. *How Sweet the Sound: Music in the Spiritual Lives of Americans.*
    Cambridge, Mass.: Harvard University Press.
Sudnow, David. 1978. *Ways of the Hand: The Organization of Improvised Conduct.* New
    York: Harper and Row.
Sutcliffe, Steven J., and Marion Bowman, eds. 2000. *Beyond New Age: Exploring
    Alternative Spirituality.* Edinburgh: Edinburgh University Press.
Sutton, Brett. 1988. "Speech, Chant, and Song: Patterns of Language and Action in
    a Southern Church." In *Diversities of Gifts: Field Studies in Southern Religion,*
    edited by R. W. Tyson, J. L. Peacock, and D. W. Patterson. Urbana: University
    of Illinois Press, 157–76.
Szasz, Thomas S. 1970. *The Manufacture of Madness.* New York: Dell.
Tambiah, Stanley J. 1990. *Magic, Science, Religion and the Scope of Rationality.* Cam-
    bridge: Cambridge University Press.

Taves, Ann. 1986. *The Household of Faith: Roman Catholic Devotions in Mid-nineteenth-century America.*

———. 1999. *Fits, Trances, and Visions: Experiencing Religion and Explaining Experience from Wesley to James.* Princeton, N.J.: Princeton University Press.

———. 2003. "Detachment and Engagement in the Study of 'Lived Experience.'" *Spiritus* 3: 186–208.

Taylor, Lawrence J. 1995. *Occasions of Faith: An Anthropology of Irish Catholics.* Philadelphia: University of Pennsylvania Press.

Taylor, William B. 1996. *Magistrates of the Sacred: Priests and Parishioners in Eighteenth-Century Mexico.* Stanford, Calif.: Stanford University Press.

Tedeschi, John, ed. 1991. *The Prosecution of Heresy: Collected Studies on the Inquisition in Early Modern Italy.* Binghamton, N.Y.: Center for Medieval and Renaissance Studies.

Thich Nhat Hanh. 1987. *Being Peace.* Berkeley: Parallax Press.

Thomas, Keith. 1971. *Religion and the Decline of Magic.* New York: Scribner's.

Trevor-Roper, Hugh. 1983. "The Invention of Tradition: The Highland Tradition of Scotland." In Hobsbawm and Ranger (1983), 15–41.

Trexler, Richard C. 1984. "Reverence and Profanity in the Study of Early Modern Religion." In *Religion and Society in Early Modern Europe, 1500–1800,* edited by K. v. Greyerz. London: Allen and Unwin, 245–69.

———. 2002. *Religion in Social Context in Europe and America, 1200–1700.* Tempe: Arizona Center for Medieval and Renaissance Studies, Arizona State University.

———. 2003. *Reliving Golgotha: The Passion Play of Iztapalapa.* Cambridge, Mass.: Harvard University Press.

Turner, Bryan S. 1991. *Religion and Social Theory: A Materialistic Perspective.* London: Sage.

———. 1996. *The Body and Society: Explorations in Social Theory.* Thousand Oaks, Calif.: Sage.

———. 1997. "The Body in Western Society: Social Theory and Its Perspectives." In *Religion and the Body,* edited by S. Coakley. Cambridge: Cambridge University Press, 15–41.

Turner, Edith. 1987. *Spirit and the Drum: A Memoir of Africa.* Tucson: University of Arizona Press.

Turner, Kay. 1999. *Beautiful Necessity: The Art and Meaning of Women's Altars.* London: Thames and Hudson.

Turner, Kay, and Pat Jasper. 1994. "Day of the Dead: The Tex-Mex Tradition." In *Halloween and Other Festivals of Death and Life,* edited by J. Santino. Knoxville: University of Tennessee Press, 133–151.

Turner, Victor W. 1969. *The Ritual Process.* Chicago: Aldine.

Turner, Victor W., and Edith Turner. 1978. *Image and Pilgrimage in Christian Culture: Anthropological Perspectives.* New York: Columbia University Press.

Tweed, Thomas A. 1996. "Identity and Authority at a Cuban Shrine in Miami: Santería, Catholicism, and Struggles for Religious Identity." *Journal of Hispanic/Latino Theology* 4 (1): 27–48.

————. 1997. *Our Lady of the Exile: Diasporic Religion at a Cuban Catholic Shrine in Miami.* Oxford: Oxford University Press.

————. 2006. *Crossings and Dwellings: A Theory of Religion.* Cambridge, Mass.: Harvard University Press.

Vauchez, André. 1993. *The Laity in the Middle Ages: Religious Beliefs and Devotional Practices.* Translated by M. J. Schneider. Edited by D. E. Bornstein. Notre Dame, Ind.: University of Notre Dame Press.

van Waes, Bernard (Fr.). 1994. "Thomas Merton and the Shakers." *Merton Journal* 1 (1): www.thomasmertonsociety.org/shaker.htm

Voyé, Liliane. 2001. "Contemporary Syncretism in Europe." Paper presented at the Societé Internationale de Sociologie des Religions, Ixtapán de la Sal, México, 27–29 July.

Weber, Max. 1946. *From Max Weber: Essays in Sociology.* Edited and translated by H. H. Gerth and C. W. Mills. New York: Oxford University Press.

————. [1920] 1958. *The Protestant Ethic and the Spirit of Capitalism.* Translated by T. Parsons. New York: Scribner's.

————. [1922] 1963. *The Sociology of Religion.* Translated by E. Fischoff. Boston: Beacon Press.

————. [1922] 1978. *Economy and Society: An Outline of Interpretive Sociology.* Edited by G. Roth and C. Wittich. Berkeley: University of California Press.

Welter, Barbara. 1976. *Dimity Convictions: The American Woman in the Nineteenth Century.* Athens: Ohio University Press.

Wigger, John H. 1998. *Taking Heaven by Storm.* Oxford: Oxford University Press.

Williams, Gerhild Scholz. 1995. *Defining Dominion: The Discourses of Magic and Witchcraft in Early Modern France and Germany.* Ann Arbor: University of Michigan Press.

Williams, Peter W. 1980. *Popular Religion in America: Symbolic Change and the Modernization Process in Historical Perspective.* Englewood Cliffs, N.J.: Prentice-Hall.

Williams, Simon J. 2001. *Emotion and Social Theory: Corporeal Reflections on the (Ir)rational.* London: Sage.

Wilmore, Gayraud S. 1973. *Black Religion and Black Radicalism: An Examination of the Black Experience in Religion.* Garden City, N.Y.: Doubleday.

Wilson, Charles Reagan. 1995. *Judgment and Grace in Dixie: Southern Faiths from Faulkner to Elvis.* Athens: University of Georgia Press.

Wilson, Stephen. 2000. *The Magical Universe: Everyday Ritual and Magic in Pre-modern Europe.* London: Hambledon and London.

Winkelman, Michael. 1992. *Shamans, Priests and Witches: A Cross-cultural Study of Magico-Religious Practitioners.* Anthropological Research Papers no. 44. Tempe: Arizona State University Press.

————. 2000. *Shamanism: The Neural Ecology of Consciousness and Healing.* Westport, Conn.: Bergin and Garvey.

Winship, Michael P. 2000. " 'The Most Glorious Church in the World': The Unity of the Godly in Boston, Massachusetts, in the 1630s." *Journal of British Studies* 39 (1): 71–98.

Winter, Miriam Therese, Adair Lummis, and Allison Stokes. 1994. *Defecting in Place: Women Claiming Responsibility for Their Own Spiritual Lives.* New York: Crossroads.

Wolff, Eric R. 1990. "Facing Power—Old Insights, New Questions." *American Anthropologist* 92: 586–96.

Wolfteich, Claire. 2005. "Devotion and the Struggle for Justice in the Farm Worker Movement: A Practical Theological Approach to Research and Teaching in Spirituality." *Spiritus* 5: 158–75.

Woodberry, Robert D., and Christian S. Smith. 1998. "Fundamentalism et al: Conservative Protestants in America." *Annual Review of Sociology* 24: 25.

Woodhead, Linda. Forthcoming. "Characterising Spirituality: Dead Ends and New Avenues." In *Religions of Modernity: Relocating the Sacred to the Self and the Digital,* edited by S. Aupers and D. Houtman. Leiden: Brill.

Wuthnow, Robert. 2001. *Creative Spirituality: The Way of the Artist.* Berkeley: University of California Press.

Yamane, David. 2000. "Narrative and Religious Experience." *Sociology of Religion* 61 (2): 171–89.

Zola, Irving K. 1983. *Socio-Medical Inquiries: Recollections, Reflections and Reconsideration.* Philadelphia: Temple University Press.

Index

Wilson, Stephen, 192
Winter, Miriam Therese, 242n66
Witch, witch-craft, witch-hunt, 42, 132,
    222n79, 245n22, 248n76
Wolff, Eric R., 43
Woodhead, Linda, 243n81

Words of power
    magical uses, 37, 84–86, 222n83
    name of Jesus, 9, 79–80
    promises, vows, 50–51, 81–82
Work, *see* Spiritual practices
Wuthnow, Robert, 109, 115–118